The One Year® Book of
FAMILY DEVOTIONS

V O L U M E   2

Admit your need -
"For all have sinned and fall short of the glory of God" (Romans 3:23).

Believe in Christ— "Believe in the Lord Jesus, and you will be saved" (Acts 16:31).

The ABC's of Salvation

Commit yourself to Christ— "Yet to all who received Him…He gave the right to become children of God." (John 1:12)

Being truly sorry for your sins, and through the power of Christ forsaking them, go forward to live for Christ. He will give forgiveness, power, victory, purpose, the Holy Spirit and life eternal!

The ONE YEAR BOOK OF *family* DEVOTIONS

VOLUME 2

TYNDALE HOUSE PUBLISHERS, INC.
WHEATON, ILLINOIS

Copyright © 1989, Children's Bible Hour. All rights reserved.

Cover photo copyright © 2000 by David Hanover/Stone. All rights reserved.

Revised and updated in 2000.

Stories written by Katherine Ruth Adams, Brenda Benedict, Judi K. Boogaart, Carol J. Brookman, Daniel A. Burns, V. Louise Cunningham, Brenda Decker, Jorlyn A. Grasser, Jan L. Hansen, Ruth I. Jay, Dean Kelley, Beverly Kenniston, Nance E. Keyes, Phyllis I. Klomparens, Sherry L. Kuyt, Agnes G. Livezey, Deborah S. Marett, Hazel W. Marett, Sara L. Nelson, Mary Rose Pearson, Raelene E. Phillips, Victoria L. Reinhardt, Phyllis Robinson, Deana L. Rogers, Catherine Runyon, Lynn Stamm-Rex, Tom VandenBerg, Charlie VanderMeer, Geri Walcott, Linda M. Weddle, Barbara J. Westberg, and Carolyn E. Yost. Authors' initials appear at the end of each story. All stories are taken from issues of *Keys for Kids*, published bimonthly by the Children's Bible Hour, Box 1, Grand Rapids, Michigan 49501.

The One Year is a registered trademark of Tyndale House Publishers, Inc.

Unless otherwise indicated, all Scripture quotations are taken from the *Holy Bible*, New Living Translation, copyright © 1996. Used by permission of Tyndale House Publishers, Inc., Wheaton, Illinois 60189. All rights reserved.

Scripture quotations marked NIV are taken from the *Holy Bible*, New International Version®. NIV®. Copyright © 1973, 1978, 1984 by International Bible Society. Used by permission of Zondervan Publishing House. All rights reserved.

Scripture quotations marked NKJV are taken from the New King James Version. Copyright © 1979, 1980, 1982 by Thomas Nelson, Inc. Used by permission. All rights reserved.

First printing, September 1989

Library of Congress Catalog Card Number 88-71950

ISBN 0-8423-2510-7, softcover

Printed in the United States of America

04   03   02   01   00
10   9   8   7

CONTENTS

You have in your hands a year's worth of delightful stories, all taken from *Keys for Kids*, a devotional magazine published by the Children's Bible Hour. For years the Children's Bible Hour has made *Keys* available free of charge to any family requesting a copy. Their fine ministry to families has been much appreciated over the years, and Tyndale House was proud to present *The One Year Book of Family Devotions*. So well-received was that book that Tyndale now presents this second volume of the many stories from *Keys for Kids*.

Each day's story provides a contemporary illustration of the day's Scripture reading. Following each story is a "How about You?" section that asks children to apply the story to themselves. Following this is a memory verse, usually taken from the Scripture reading. Many of these memory verses are taken from the New Living Translation, but in some cases another version has been used for the sake of clarity. Each devotion ends with a "key," a two- to five-word summary of the day's lesson.

The stories here are geared toward families with children ages 8 to 14. Children can enjoy reading these stories by themselves, but we hope that you will use them in a daily devotional time for the whole family. Like the many stories in the Bible that teach valuable lessons about life, the stories here will speak not only to children but to adults. They are simple, direct, and concrete, and, like Jesus' parables, they speak to all of us in terms we can understand. Like all good stories, they are made for sharing, so look at them as the basis for family sharing and growth.

This book includes a Scripture index and a topical index. The Scripture index is helpful if you want to locate a story related to a passage that you want to draw your family's attention to. The topical index is here because certain concerns arise spontaneously and unexpectedly in any family—illness, moving, a new baby, for example. We hope you will use the book faithfully every day, but the indexes are here so that you will not just be locked into the daily reading format. Feel free to use any story at any time it relates to a special situation in your family.

RYAN CAME INSIDE after jogging a few miles. His face was covered with sweat. "Wash up, Ryan. Dinner is ready," Dad said.

After supper Ryan announced his plans for the evening—more running and exercises. Dad frowned. "You've been spending more than enough time training for the track meet," he said. "As a matter of fact, Son, you've been neglecting your other responsibilities."

"Yes," added Mother. "I'm concerned about your devotional life. Weren't you going to spend more time in Bible reading this year?"

Ryan looked down at the floor. "There's nothing wrong with wanting to have a strong body, is there?" he asked quietly.

"Not at all," Dad replied. "But a healthy body is only part of a complete person. In the Bible Paul wrote often of running races and training our bodies."

"He did?" Ryan looked up, his eyes wide with interest.

"Yes. He wrote to Timothy that physical exercise is important but that spiritual exercise is the most important," replied Dad. "Just as you work hard to get physically fit and build up your muscles, so you must work at living God's way to build up your Christian life. You need to practice such things as Bible reading and prayer and telling others about Jesus. It takes hard work."

Ryan thought about his dad's words. Then he nodded and smiled. "OK, Dad," he said. "I'll try to balance my chores, devotions, homework, and track."

HOW ABOUT YOU? Is there a special activity that takes too much of your time? Perhaps you play sports, watch TV, or have a pet with which you spend your free time. Maybe you spend a lot of time with your best friend. Whatever you do, be sure you don't neglect your time with God. *L.S.R.*

TO MEMORIZE: Physical exercise has some value, but spiritual exercise is much more important, for it promises a reward in both this life and the next. *1 Timothy 4:8*

GETTING FIT

FROM THE BIBLE:

If you explain this to the brothers and sisters, you will be doing your duty as a worthy servant of Christ Jesus, one who is fed by the message of faith and the true teaching you have followed. Do not waste time arguing over godless ideas and old wives' tales. Spend your time and energy in training yourself for spiritual fitness. Physical exercise has some value, but spiritual exercise is much more important, for it promises a reward in both this life and the next. This is true, and everyone should accept it. We work hard and suffer much in order that people will believe the truth, for our hope is in the living God, who is the Savior of all people, and particularly of those who believe.

Teach these things and insist that everyone learn them. Don't let anyone think less of you because you are young. Be an example to all believers in what you teach, in the way you live, in your love, your faith, and your purity. Until I get there, focus on reading the Scriptures to the church, encouraging the believers, and teaching them. 1 TIMOTHY 4:6-13

Get spiritual exercise

2 January

STILL THE SAME

FROM THE BIBLE:

Forever, O Lord,
your word stands firm in
heaven.
Your faithfulness extends to
every generation,
as enduring as the earth you
created.
Your laws remain true today,
for everything serves your
plans.

PSALM 119:89-91

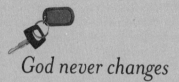

God never changes

DAD JUST WALKED OUT on us. *No reasons, no apologies,* Andy thought. *I wonder why.* His mom tried to help him understand, but he knew she didn't really understand it herself.

One day Mom said, "Our house costs too much, Andy. We're going to move into an apartment. It will be a big change, but we'll get used to it."

Moving was not something Andy had planned on. As long as he could stay in the same neighborhood and go to the same school, he could pretend things were still the same. But now—a new school and all new kids?

Moving day came, and with it all the changes Andy dreaded. The only thing that didn't change was their church, but even there people acted differently.

In Sunday school one day, Mr. Robinson called on Andy to recite the memory verse. "I am the Lord, and I do not change," Andy quoted. "Malachi 3:6."

Mr. Robinson nodded. "Even if the whole world seems upside down, God is always the same," he said. "God loves us and will be with us, just as he was with Abraham in his journeys, with Daniel in the lions' den, and with Jonah in the whale." As Andy listened to Mr. Robinson, he realized that God had been with all of his people throughout the changes they experienced.

Andy breathed a quiet prayer, just between himself and God. "Thank you for staying with Mom and me. I'm glad you're just the same as when Dad was with us. Please help me remember that even though things change, you will never change or go away."

HOW ABOUT YOU? Are you discouraged when changes come? The Bible gives many examples of people who had to learn about God's care during changing times. God promises to care for you in difficult times just as he cared for them. *P.I.K.*

TO MEMORIZE: I am the Lord, and I do not change. *Malachi 3:6*

3 January

TIME TO GET UP!

"**MICHAEL**," Mom called. "I told you to get up a long time ago. Now hurry! We'll soon be leaving for church!" Michael sleepily opened his eyes. It was so hard to get up! He put one foot on the floor, then the other. "Michael, are you hurrying?" Mom called from the hallway.

"Yeah, I'm hurrying," Michael answered, but he didn't hurry at all. He put on his shirt and pants and then flopped down on the bed again. In fact, the next time Mom checked on him, he was fast asleep.

"You're just going to have to get to bed earlier." His mother sighed as she woke him again.

The next day was Michael's birthday. As soon as Michael heard his dad and mom get up, he jumped out of bed, too. He threw his clothes on as fast as he could and then ran downstairs to open his gift.

"Hmmm," Mom said. "It's funny how easy it was for our sleepyhead to get out of bed this morning but not yesterday."

"Today's a special day, Mom!" said Michael, eyeing the big box on the table.

"Sundays are special days, too, Michael," she replied.

"Right," said Dad. "Did you know that people in some countries have to worship Christ in secret because it's against the law? Sometimes we forget that going to church is special."

Michael looked at his birthday present. He knew his parents were right. He decided to take the ribbon from the birthday gift and pin it to his bulletin board. "This will remind me that Sunday is a special day, too," he said.

HOW ABOUT YOU? Do you have trouble getting up for church? Treat Sunday as a special day. Go to bed early on Saturday night so you'll be ready to serve and worship the Lord on Sunday. *L.M.W.*

TO MEMORIZE: This is the day the Lord has made. We will rejoice and be glad in it. *Psalm 118:24*

FROM THE BIBLE:

I was glad when they said to me, "Let us go to the house of the Lord." And now we are standing here inside your gates, O Jerusalem. Jerusalem is a well-built city, knit together as a single unit. All the people of Israel—the Lord's people—make their pilgrimage here. They come to give thanks to the name of the Lord as the law requires. Here stand the thrones where judgment is given, the thrones of the dynasty of David. Pray for the peace of Jerusalem. May all who love this city prosper. O Jerusalem, may there be peace within your walls and prosperity in your palaces. For the sake of my family and friends, I will say, "Peace be with you." For the sake of the house of the Lord our God, I will seek what is best for you, O Jerusalem.
PSALM 122:1-9

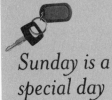

Sunday is a special day

4 January

THE OLD MANSION

FROM THE BIBLE:

When they arrived, Samuel took one look at Eliab and thought, "Surely this is the Lord's anointed!" But the Lord said to Samuel, "Don't judge by his appearance or height, for I have rejected him. The Lord doesn't make decisions the way you do! People judge by outward appearance, but the Lord looks at a person's thoughts and intentions."

Then Jesse told his son Abinadab to step forward and walk in front of Samuel. But Samuel said, "This is not the one the Lord has chosen." Next Jesse summoned Shammah, but Samuel said, "Neither is this the one the Lord has chosen." In the same way all seven of Jesse's sons were presented to Samuel. But Samuel said to Jesse, "The Lord has not chosen any of these." Then Samuel asked, "Are these all the sons you have?"

"There is still the youngest," Jesse replied. "But he's out in the fields watching the sheep."

"Send for him at once," Samuel said. "We will not sit down to eat until he arrives."

So Jesse sent for him. He was ruddy and handsome, with pleasant eyes. And the Lord said, "This is the one; anoint him."

1 SAMUEL 16:6-12

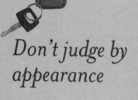

Don't judge by appearance

"I CAN HARDLY wait to see the old mansion!" exclaimed Ashley. She and her parents were on their way to visit Grandma and Grandpa White, who had become caretakers of a large estate. As they drove, Ashley talked about her day at school. "There's a new girl in my class, and her clothes are totally ugly."

Mom answered, "Ashley, you shouldn't judge people by the way they look."

Several hours later Dad pulled into an overgrown driveway. Weeds had taken over the lawn and the flower boxes were empty. "This looks like a dump!" Ashley exclaimed.

But when her grandparents led them in, Ashley could hardly believe her eyes. The hardwood floors gleamed, and a spiral staircase curved from the hallway to the second floor. "This is so nice, but why is the outside so awful?" she asked.

Grandpa smiled. "The old place is being restored, but the firm that was hired for the outside work can't begin till next month. That's why there's such a difference between the inside and the outside."

"Just like the inside and the outside of some people," said Mom as she looked at Ashley. "Like that new girl at school. Didn't you just assume she wasn't worth knowing because of the way she dressed? The heart of a person is much more important than the way that person looks."

Ashley looked around the house and then looked out at the front yard. She hated to admit it, but her mother was right. "Next week I'm going to get to know that new girl," she told her mother.

HOW ABOUT YOU? Have you ever rejected people because of the clothes they wore? Remember, God says it's the inside that counts. Will you be a friend to a classmate who's left out because of the way he or she looks? *L.M.W.*

TO MEMORIZE: Stop judging by mere appearances, and make a right judgment. *John 7:24* (NIV)

IT WAS TIME to measure again. José was eager to see how much he'd grown. For four years now, Dad had marked the new height on his closet door.

"When Aunt Carmen comes home from the mission field," José said, "she'll be surprised by how much I've grown!"

"Four years make quite a difference," his dad agreed.

José remembered the day Aunt Carmen had left for the mission field. He had just asked Jesus to be his Savior. Aunt Carmen had been so pleased. She'd hugged him when they saw her off at the airport. "You'll be practically grown by the time I come home," she had said. "I'll pray you grow to be more like Jesus, too!"

And now Aunt Carmen was due to return. José knew she would notice physical growth. But would she see spiritual growth as well? He decided to ask Dad about it.

Dad smiled. "That's a good question," he said. "Now, let's see—I know that you used to have a terrible temper. Do you think you're controlling it better now?"

"I yelled at Nathan last week," José confessed. "But I apologized later."

Dad nodded. "I'd say that's progress. And what about those boys you've been inviting to Sunday school? I think you've made progress in helping others learn about Jesus. What about Bible knowledge? Do you know more about God than you did when Aunt Carmen left?"

José nodded. "Yeah. I've learned a lot in Sunday school."

"Then Aunt Carmen ought to be pleased—like I am," said Dad.

HOW ABOUT YOU? Have you taken inventory to see if you've grown spiritually? Do you spend time with God, learning from his Word and talking to him? Are you more friendly, kind, and loving than you used to be? *R.I.J.*

TO MEMORIZE: Grow in the special favor and knowledge of our Lord and Savior Jesus Christ. *2 Peter 3:18*

GROWING TWO WAYS

FROM THE BIBLE:

Then the way you live will always honor and please the Lord, and you will continually do good, kind things for others. All the while, you will learn to know God better and better.

We also pray that you will be strengthened with his glorious power so that you will have all the patience and endurance you need. May you be filled with joy, always thanking the Father, who has enabled you to share the inheritance that belongs to God's holy people, who live in the light.
COLOSSIANS 1:10-12

Grow spiritually

6 January

UNLIMITED TREASURE

FROM THE BIBLE:

The law of the Lord is perfect, reviving the soul. The decrees of the Lord are trustworthy, making wise the simple. The commandments of the Lord are right, bringing joy to the heart. The commands of the Lord are clear, giving insight to life. Reverence for the Lord is pure, lasting forever. The laws of the Lord are true; each one is fair. They are more desirable than gold, even the finest gold. They are sweeter than honey, even honey dripping from the comb. They are a warning to those who hear them; there is great reward for those who obey them.
PSALM 19:7-11

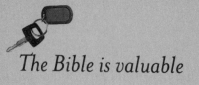

The Bible is valuable

"HI, MOM, what smells so good?" Christa asked as she put her schoolbooks on the kitchen table. "It smells like the backyard when the lilacs are blooming."

Mom smiled. "You're right, Christa. A friend at work gave me a bottle of perfume for my birthday. It's called "Lilacs." Her husband works at the cosmetic company where it's made, so she gets perfume at a discount."

Christa picked up the bottle. "Can I try some?"

"Sure," Mom said.

Every now and then during the next few weeks, Christa would smell lilacs and know that Mom had been using the new perfume.

One day Christa and her mother were at a department store, looking for a new dress for Christa. "Mom, look," said Christa as they passed the perfume counter. "There's a bottle of Lilacs."

"Sure enough!" Mom stopped to look at the display.

"Look at the price!" Christa exclaimed.

"Oh, my! I had no idea it cost that much!" groaned Christa's mother. "Here I've been using it just about every day! If I had known how expensive it was, I would have saved it for special occasions."

Christa smiled. "My Sunday school teacher told us the Bible is like that," she said. "Most people have a Bible, but they don't realize how valuable it is."

"You're so right, Christa," agreed Mom. "The Bible is more valuable than expensive perfume. But the wonderful thing about the Bible is that we can use it every day and we'll never run out of it!"

HOW ABOUT YOU? Do you realize how important the Bible is? Do you realize that it explains how you can have eternal life? Do you know that it gives you guidelines for living your life? Thank the Lord for giving you the Bible. Study it and find the priceless treasures inside. *L.M.W.*

TO MEMORIZE: Your law is more valuable to me than millions in gold and silver! *Psalm 119:72*

GETTING A GOOD REPORT

"MOM, LOOK! I've got an application to work at school sweeping and stuff." Taylor was so excited he couldn't stop talking. This would be his first job. "Who can I give as references?" he asked.

Mom suggested the Ferrintinos, but Taylor looked a little sheepish. "I cut in front of Mrs. Ferrintino at the store the other day," he said. "I pretended I didn't see her, but I think she knew."

Looking disappointed, Mom next suggested Mr. Valdez. Taylor had to explain that Mr. Valdez had caught him teasing a little boy. "I was trying to look tough in front of the other guys," he admitted.

"Taylor," said his mother, "I think you're finding out how important your actions are. Put the application away for now. It's suppertime."

After supper Dad read from Acts 16. "That's interesting," said Mom. "It seems that before Paul took Timothy with him on a missionary journey, he asked for references."

"Yeah," said Taylor, "and I'll bet Timothy was glad that the men gave him a good report. It would be exciting to go on a missionary trip!"

"It sure would," agreed Mom. "Imagine what would have happened if they'd said, 'Tim's a pretty good guy, but we saw him teasing a little kid.' "

Taylor laughed but quickly became serious. "You're right, Mom," he said. "I'm going to watch my behavior from now on."

HOW ABOUT YOU? Would you have a difficult time getting a good reference? Unkind things that you do can affect other people's opinions of you. Ask Jesus to show you things you stop doing that may hurt your testimony to others. *P.R.*

TO MEMORIZE: Don't let anyone think less of you because you are young. Be an example to all believers in what you teach, in the way you live, in your love, your faith, and your purity. *1 Timothy 4:12*

FROM THE BIBLE:

Paul and Silas went first to Derbe and then on to Lystra. There they met Timothy, a young disciple whose mother was a Jewish believer, but whose father was a Greek. Timothy was well thought of by the believers in Lystra and Iconium, so Paul wanted him to join them on their journey. In deference to the Jews of the area, he arranged for Timothy to be circumcised before they left, for everyone knew that his father was a Greek. Then they went from town to town, explaining the decision regarding the commandments that were to be obeyed, as decided by the apostles and elders in Jerusalem. So the churches were strengthened in their faith and grew daily in numbers.
ACTS 16:1-5

All actions are important

8 January

RAGING WAVES

FROM THE BIBLE:

Dearly loved friends, I had been eagerly planning to write to you about the salvation we all share. But now I find that I must write about something else, urging you to defend the truth of the Good News. God gave this unchanging truth once for all time to his holy people. I say this because some godless people have wormed their way in among you. . . .

When these people join you in fellowship meals celebrating the love of the Lord, they are like dangerous reefs that can shipwreck you. They are shameless in the way they care only about themselves. They are like clouds blowing over dry land without giving rain, promising much but producing nothing. They are like trees without fruit at harvesttime. They are not only dead but doubly dead, for they have been pulled out by the roots. . . .

These people are grumblers and complainers, doing whatever evil they feel like. They are loudmouthed braggarts, and they flatter others to get favors in return.

But you, my dear friends, must remember what the apostles of our Lord Jesus Christ told you.
JUDE 1:3-4, 12, 16-17

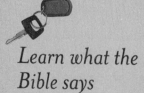

Learn what the Bible says

BRYAN WAS visiting his grandparents in Florida. He liked being outdoors in the sunshine, especially when he thought about the cold and snow at home in Minnesota. The neatest thing about visiting his grandparents was that they lived near the ocean and could walk to the beach from their house.

One evening Bryan and his grandfather were playing catch. It was windy, and they could hear the waves beating against the rocks even though they were a couple of blocks away. "I've never heard the waves sound so loud," Bryan said.

"They do get noisy sometimes," Grandpa agreed. "Would you like to walk down and see them?"

"Sure." After Bryan put his ball and glove away, he and his grandfather walked to the ocean. "Wow! Look at those waves!" Bryan exclaimed. The water was crashing against the shoreline, sending spray high into the air.

"They're fun to watch," agreed Grandpa. "But the people who live in the houses along here are afraid the water will wash away some of the soil from their yards. The waves can be quite destructive. Bryan, did you know that the New Testament letter of Jude talks about waves? It uses waves to describe people who teach false doctrine. Jude says that those who twist and change what is written in the Bible are like wild waves of the sea, destroying the people who believe what they say."

"I'm glad I believe in Jesus," Bryan said. "And I'm glad I go to a church where the truth is preached."

HOW ABOUT YOU? Have you ever watched waves beat against the shore? Remember, wild waves are a picture of false teachers who use words that sound as though they come from the Bible. Learn what God's Word really says so you will not be fooled by "wild waves." *L.M.W.*

TO MEMORIZE: But you, my dear friends, must remember what the apostles of our Lord Jesus Christ told you. *Jude 1:17*

THE WAX FIGURES

KENDRA WAS helping her mother make some wax figurines for the crafts fair. "Keep working on the figurines while the wax is still hot," encouraged Mother. "Remember, it's easier to form them while the wax is soft."

Kendra nodded, but a few minutes later the telephone rang, and she dashed off to answer it. It was Beth, her very best friend from school. As the girls talked, Kendra lost track of time. When she finally hung up the phone, more than fifteen minutes had passed!

Back in the family room, Kendra picked up her figurine. The wax had hardened, and it was almost impossible to form the figure as she wanted. Noticing this, her mother spoke. "That reminds me of something we've talked about before, Kendra—the importance of allowing God to mold you as he wants. When people get older, they often become cold and hard, just as that wax did. Then they're often less interested in learning about God."

Slowly Kendra nodded her head. "You know, Mother, I was thinking of that, too. Beth just told me that her neighbor Mr. Jackson is very old and doesn't feel well. I remember hearing Grandpa tell us how he witnessed to old Mr. Jackson for years and years. I guess he still hasn't accepted the Lord." Kendra paused and looked at the cold, hard wax. "I don't want to be like this. I want to let God mold me now while I'm young(and through my whole life."

FROM THE BIBLE:

Young man, it's wonderful to be young! Enjoy every minute of it. Do everything you want to do; take it all in. But remember that you must give an account to God for everything you do. So banish grief and pain, but remember that youth, with a whole life before it, still faces the threat of meaninglessness.

Don't let the excitement of youth cause you to forget your Creator. Honor him in your youth before you grow old and no longer enjoy living.

ECCLESIASTES 11:9–12:1

Accept Jesus now

HOW ABOUT YOU? Do you have questions about being a Christian? About God? Maybe you think you'll ask your questions later, when you're older. Remember, when you get older, you could lose interest in finding out about God. Learn all you can while you are young. *R.E.P.*

TO MEMORIZE: Don't let the excitement of youth cause you to forget your Creator. Honor him in your youth before you grow old and no longer enjoy living. *Ecclesiastes 12:1*

10 January

NEVER AGAIN

FROM THE BIBLE:

For we are not our own masters when we live or when we die. While we live, we live to please the Lord. And when we die, we go to be with the Lord. So in life and in death, we belong to the Lord. Christ died and rose again for this very purpose, so that he might be Lord of those who are alive and of those who have died.

So why do you condemn another Christian? Why do you look down on another Christian? Remember, each of us will stand personally before the judgment seat of God. For the Scriptures say,

" 'As surely as I live,' says the Lord,
'every knee will bow to me and every tongue will confess allegiance to God.' "

Yes, each of us will have to give a personal account to God.
ROMANS 14:7-12

You're accountable to God

"WE'VE BEEN WATCHING you. Come with us." Cold fear chilled the back of Kyle's neck. The woman who'd spoken signaled a man nearby, who moved to Kyle's side.

Where's Chuck? wondered Kyle. Taking a few candy bars was Chuck's idea, and now he'd disappeared into thin air. Kyle's thoughts raced through his mind as he walked with bent head between the two security guards.

In a small room the woman said sternly, "Open your jacket and put everything on the table." Then Kyle was asked questions about everything: his name, address, school, parents, friends. Had he ever shoplifted before? Was he alone in the store? On and on. Kyle thought it would never end. "OK, Kyle. Call your parents," the lady guard said finally.

"Oh no, please," protested Kyle. "I'll never do—"

"Call them," interrupted the woman.

When Kyle heard his mother's voice on the phone, he tried not to cry while he explained the awful thing that had happened. "I'll be right there," said Mother.

When his mother came, Kyle couldn't look at her. As they drove home, she spoke gently. "Why, Kyle? You knew better." The sadness of her tone made him feel awful. "You've made me very sad today, Son, and you've made it necessary for me to punish you. But I want you to know that you have wronged God, too."

"I know," Kyle said quietly. "Please forgive me. I'll never do it again. I promise."

HOW ABOUT YOU? When you know you've hurt your parents, is it hard to look them in the eye? Just as you are accountable to your parents, you are also accountable to God. Confess those things you've done wrong. Ask God to forgive you and to help you in a way that pleases him. *P.I.K.*

TO MEMORIZE: Yes, each of us will have to give a personal account to God. *Romans 14:12*

PONIES AND COOKIES

ERICA LOVED to entertain her little brothers, Arturo and Justin. "Sit down," she'd say, "and I'll read to you." The active boys would sit quietly as Erica read books to them and showed them the colorful pictures inside.

One day Erica took a book to her mother. "This book says ponies are baby horses. Aren't baby horses called 'foals'?"

Mother nodded. "Ponies are really a type of small horse," she said. "They're smaller than regular horses even when they're grown up. Whoever wrote this book made a mistake. They probably meant to write that ponies are *not* baby horses. I'm glad you're thinking about what you read. Just because something is in a book doesn't mean it's true." Then Mother handed Erica a bowl. "Let's bake some cookies," she said.

They followed the directions carefully, but when they tasted the first batch of cookies, both Erica and her mother frowned. "These don't taste quite right," Erica said.

"I think they have too much salt in them," said Mother. "I wondered about that while we mixed them, but I assumed the cookbook was right."

"I guess cookbooks can be wrong just like kids' books," observed Erica.

"You're right, Erica. You have to be careful with any book written by people," said Mother. "Any time you read, it's a good idea to ask yourself, 'Is this true or false? Good or bad?' There's only one book you don't have to question."

"I know what that is!" Erica said. "The Bible."

Mother smiled. "Right," she agreed.

HOW ABOUT YOU? Do you believe everything you read? Remember, people can make mistakes. The only book you can fully trust is the Bible, because every word in it was inspired by God. *S.L.N.*

TO MEMORIZE: For the word of the Lord holds true, and everything he does is worthy of our trust. *Psalm 33:4*

FROM THE BIBLE:

And by that same mighty power, he has given us all of his rich and wonderful promises. He has promised that you will escape the decadence all around you caused by evil desires and that you will share in his divine nature. . . .

Because of that, we have even greater confidence in the message proclaimed by the prophets. Pay close attention to what they wrote, for their words are like a light shining in a dark place—until the day Christ appears and his brilliant light shines in your hearts. Above all, you must understand that no prophecy in Scripture ever came from the prophets themselves or because they wanted to prophesy. It was the Holy Spirit who moved the prophets to speak from God.

2 PETER 1:4, 19-21

Think about what you read

12 January

SECRET SIN

FROM THE BIBLE:

When you follow the desires of your sinful nature, your lives will produce these evil results: sexual immorality, impure thoughts, eagerness for lustful pleasure, idolatry, participation in demonic activities, hostility, quarreling, jealousy, outbursts of anger, selfish ambition, divisions, the feeling that everyone is wrong except those in your own little group, envy, drunkenness, wild parties, and other kinds of sin. Let me tell you again, as I have before, that anyone living that sort of life will not inherit the Kingdom of God. . . .

Those who belong to Christ Jesus have nailed the passions and desires of their sinful nature to his cross and crucified them there. If we are living now by the Holy Spirit, let us follow the Holy Spirit's leading in every part of our lives.
GALATIANS 5:19-21, 24-25

Don't ever do wrong

"QUICK! Someone's coming," David's friend Brian whispered. David punched the button on the VCR remote control just in time.

Dad came into the family room, picked up the dictionary, and left.

David knew he shouldn't turn the VCR back on. The movie Brian had brought over had violent scenes and bad language.

After supper David's younger sister Carolyn was contentedly sucking her thumb. "What's that in your mouth?" Dad asked. Carolyn quickly took her thumb out of her mouth. Later that evening, David noticed Carolyn lying on the couch, her head buried under a pillow. He sneaked over and pulled the pillow off his sister's head. Carolyn was again sucking away on her thumb!

"Sucking your thumb may damage your teeth whether anyone sees you do it or not," Dad told her gently.

It seemed to David that Dad looked right at him while he spoke. David didn't think Dad knew about the movie, but the damage was done. David couldn't forget the violence he had seen or the bad language he had heard. Besides that, he was aware that God knew all about it.

As David prayed later that night, he confessed what he had done. He also asked God to give him courage to say no to temptation.

The test came a few days later. "My dad has this great R-rated movie," Brian told him. "We can watch it before my folks get home."

"No, thanks," said David.

HOW ABOUT YOU? Do you read magazines, watch movies, or listen to music in secret? If so, is it because you know it's wrong? Even if you hide it from others, doing something wrong will still hurt you. Ask God to help you walk away from temptation. *K.R.A.*

TO MEMORIZE: But if you do what is wrong, you will be paid back for the wrong you have done. For God has no favorites who can get away with evil. *Colossians 3:25*

DON'T HARVEST THE EDGES

TONY LIKED to hang around his father's repair shop and watch as Dad worked. One Saturday Dad was fiddling with a broken toaster. Finally he set the toaster down. "All finished," he said. On a card he wrote, "Labor, one hour—$10.00." Then he cleaned the toaster.

Tony frowned. "Dad, you counted wrong," he said. "I know you worked on that thing for over an hour, besides the time you spent cleaning it." When his father just smiled, Tony continued. "Whenever you round off the amount somebody owes you, I know you always make it lower, not higher. How are you ever going to make money that way?"

"Oh, I'm managing," Dad replied cheerfully. "I believe that if I give my customers good service and don't charge any more than I have to, they'll keep coming back. Besides, the Bible teaches that we shouldn't 'harvest the edges.' "

Tony looked confused. "Huh? I don't get it."

"Well, in Leviticus God told farmers to leave some of their crop behind when they harvested it, so that poor people could take what they needed. I figure that the principle applies to my business, too. It means I shouldn't try to squeeze every nickel I can out of my customers."

"If the farmer did all the work, he should keep all the harvest," objected Tony.

"But it's God who gives us the strength to work, and he blesses our efforts," Dad reminded Tony. "You've got a good head for business, Son, but you need to learn to be more generous. Even if nobody else notices, God will!"

HOW ABOUT YOU? Do you cheat others in little ways—skipping chores when you think Mom won't notice, doing a sloppy job on your schoolwork? Begin making an effort to do a little more than what is required. *S.L.K.*

TO MEMORIZE: Some who are poor pretend to be rich; others who are rich pretend to be poor. *Proverbs 13:7*

FROM THE BIBLE:

"When you harvest your crops, do not harvest the grain along the edges of your fields, and do not pick up what the harvesters drop. It is the same with your grape crop—do not strip every last bunch of grapes from the vines, and do not pick up the grapes that fall to the ground. Leave them for the poor and the foreigners who live among you, for I, the Lord, am your God.

"Do not steal.

"Do not cheat one another.

"Do not lie.

"Do not use my name to swear a falsehood and so profane the name of your God. I am the Lord.

"Do not cheat or rob anyone.

"Always pay your hired workers promptly. . . ."

"When you harvest the crops of your land, do not harvest the grain along the edges of your fields, and do not pick up what the harvesters drop. Leave it for the poor and the foreigners living among you. I, the Lord, am your God."

LEVITICUS 19:9-13; 23:22

Be generous, not greedy

14 January

DOGS OR CATS?

FROM THE BIBLE:

O Lord, what a variety of things you have made! In wisdom you have made them all. The earth is full of your creatures. Here is the ocean, vast and wide, teeming with life of every kind, both great and small. See the ships sailing along, and Leviathan, which you made to play in the sea. Every one of these depends on you to give them their food as they need it. When you supply it, they gather it. You open your hand to feed them, and they are satisfied. But if you turn away from them, they panic. When you take away their breath, they die and turn again to dust. When you send your Spirit, new life is born to replenish all the living of the earth.

May the glory of the Lord last forever! The Lord rejoices in all he has made!

PSALM 104:24-31

Even animals can teach

"WHICH DO you like best, Grandma," asked April, "your dog or your cat?"

Grandma put Ashes, the cat, on her lap, but Ashes jumped right down. "Well, Ashes can be quite aloof. Dusty, on the other hand, always accepts my attention."

"I think I'd rather have a dog like Dusty," April announced.

"Both animals can teach us lessons about God," Grandma continued. She picked up a ball and threw it. "Fetch, Dusty," she said. Dusty chased after the ball, brought it back, and wagged his tail, waiting for the ball to be thrown again. "He wants to do what pleases me."

"And we should want to please God, right?" asked April, as Ashes rubbed against her leg. "What do you learn from your cat, Grandma?"

Suddenly a ball of gray fur landed on Grandma's lap. Grandma stroked the cat's head. "When Ashes does jump on my lap, it's special, because it's her choice to come to me," said Grandma. "Do you remember the robots we saw at the science fair that did whatever they were commanded to do? Would you like a hug from a robot?"

"No," giggled April. "That wouldn't mean much."

"We aren't robots either," said Grandma. "God created us with a free will. He is pleased when we choose to come to him."

"So your dog shows us we should want to please God by doing what he wants," April said. "And your cat shows us that God wants us to willingly give him our love. But which do you like best?"

"I like them both," Grandma said with a smile.

HOW ABOUT YOU? Do you like animals? God often teaches lessons through them. Treat all animals with kindness and watch their behavior. Maybe the Lord will use an animal to teach you an important lesson. *V.L.C.*

TO MEMORIZE: For all the animals of the forest are mine, and I own the cattle on a thousand hills. *Psalm 50:10*

WHEN KENT'S Sunday school teacher suggested that the class go together to watch the space-shuttle launch, Kent was thrilled. The week seemed to pass slowly, but finally Saturday arrived. Early that morning Kent and six other excited boys met Mr. Marshall at church.

"Hope we're early enough to get a good view," exclaimed Kent—and they were! About an hour after they reached their viewing point the big space shuttle was launched. Seeing the bright, fiery light and the smoke trail that followed the lift-off was something Kent would never forget.

Back in the van, Mr. Marshall turned on the radio so they could listen to an announcer review what had taken place. They also heard the people at the space control center talk with the astronauts.

"Well," said Mr. Marshall, "whenever you think of what you saw this morning, I want you to remember that Christians will participate in a 'lift-off' someday."

"Hey, that's right," said Kent. "You mean when Jesus comes, don't you?"

"Exactly," answered Mr. Marshall. "When he returns, he'll take all Christians to live in heaven with him. It will all happen quick as a flash, or as the Bible puts it, 'in the twinkling of an eye.' " He looked at the boys. "I'm glad you all made it to the lift-off today. My prayer is that each of you will also be ready for that wonderful event when Jesus comes again."

HOW ABOUT YOU? When Jesus returns in the clouds, those who have confessed their sins and asked for God's forgiveness will rise to be with him. Are you one who has done that? If not, talk to a trusted friend or adult to find out more. R.I.J.

TO MEMORIZE: When everything is ready, I will come and get you, so that you will always be with me where I am. *John 14:3*

THE BIG EVENT

FROM THE BIBLE:

"Don't be troubled. You trust God, now trust in me. There are many rooms in my Father's home, and I am going to prepare a place for you. If this were not so, I would tell you plainly. When everything is ready, I will come and get you, so that you will always be with me where I am. And you know where I am going and how to get there."

"No, we don't know, Lord," Thomas said. *"We haven't any idea where you are going, so how can we know the way?"*

Jesus told him, "I am the way, the truth, and the life. No one can come to the Father except through me."

JOHN 14:1-6

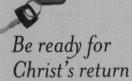

Be ready for Christ's return

16 January

I REMEMBER

FROM THE BIBLE:

"You have said, 'What's the use of serving God? What have we gained by obeying his commands or by trying to show the Lord Almighty that we are sorry for our sins? From now on we will say, "Blessed are the arrogant." For those who do evil get rich, and those who dare God to punish them go free of harm.' "

Then those who feared the Lord spoke with each other, and the Lord listened to what they said. In his presence, a scroll of remembrance was written to record the names of those who feared him and loved to think about him. "They will be my people," says the Lord Almighty. "On the day when I act, they will be my own special treasure. I will spare them as a father spares an obedient and dutiful child. Then you will again see the difference between the righteous and the wicked, between those who serve God and those who do not."

MALACHI 3:14-18

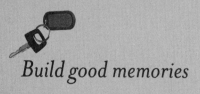

Build good memories

TONY ORTEGA'S grandfather had just died. He felt nervous about attending the service. "Remember the wonderful things Grandpa taught you," his mother said. "And keep in mind that it is only his body in the casket. He is with the Lord in heaven."

Tony nodded. He knew that everyone will die someday until the time when Jesus comes back. And he knew that when Christians die, they go to be with Jesus.

"Death is not to be feared if we are part of God's family," his mother added. "Of course, we'll miss Grandpa, and that makes us feel sad. But we can be happy for him. And until we join him, we can be thankful for the wonderful memories we have."

Tony's father asked, "Tony, what do you remember most about your grandfather?"

Tony thought for a minute. "I remember how kind he was to me, how he helped other people, and how he prayed for me."

"Your grandfather would be pleased to know he was remembered for those things," said Dad with a smile. "We should all live in a way that leaves good memories."

HOW ABOUT YOU? When God calls you to heaven someday, what memories will you leave behind? More important, what will be written in God's "scroll of remembrance"? Will it be recorded that you were honest, kind, helpful, and loving? That you prayed for others and served the Lord? Live so that you'll be happy to have God and others remember your deeds. *R.I.J.*

TO MEMORIZE: Then those who feared the Lord spoke with each other, and the Lord listened to what they said. In his presence, a scroll of remembrance was written to record the names of those who feared him and loved to think about him. *Malachi 3:16*

IT WAS Saturday morning, and Juanita was hurrying to her Girl Scout leader's home to make sandwiches for a sale. When she arrived, Mrs. Powers greeted her hurriedly. "Hello, Juanita," she said smiling. "I'm glad you're early. I need to pick up one of the girls. Please let the others in."

After Mrs. Powers left, Juanita started making the sandwiches. She opened a long roll and piled it with ham, salami, and cheese. Then she popped the sandwich in a plastic sandwich bag. *This is fun!* she thought.

When the other girls began to arrive, they were surprised at Juanita's progress. Even Mrs. Powers praised her when she returned, but then her expression changed. "Juanita," she said, "you should have washed your hands before you started working."

Juanita blushed as she looked at her filthy hands. "I'm sorry; I'll go wash them right now," she stammered.

"I think you should," agreed Mrs. Powers. "But we'll also have to throw away the sandwiches you made."

As Juanita went to wash her hands, she remembered a verse about washing hands to serve the Lord. She thought about how she had goofed off in Sunday school and had argued with her mother about which pew to sit in during church. Then she had sung a solo in church. *I guess that was like trying to serve God with unwashed hands,* thought Juanita. *Before I try to do anything for Jesus, I'm going to make sure I "wash" myself on the inside first!*

HOW ABOUT YOU? Do you serve the Lord by singing in the choir, helping out in children's church, or working in the nursery? That's good, but you also need to "wash your hands" regularly by confessing your sins so you can live close to God. *S.L.K.*

TO MEMORIZE: Draw close to God, and God will draw close to you. Wash your hands, you sinners; purify your hearts, you hypocrites. *James 4:8*

UNWASHED HANDS

FROM THE BIBLE:

*Who may climb the mountain
     of the Lord?
  Who may stand in his holy
     place?
Only those whose hands and
     hearts are pure,
  who do not worship idols
  and never tell lies.
They will receive the
     Lordblessing
  and have right standing with
     God their savior.*
PSALM 24:3-5

*Serve God with
clean hands*

18 January

TRUE OR FALSE

FROM THE BIBLE:

Turn away from evil and do good. Work hard at living in peace with others.

The eyes of the Lord watch over those who do right; his ears are open to their cries for help. But the Lord turns his face against those who do evil; he will erase their memory from the earth.

The Lord hears his people when they call to him for help. He rescues them from all their troubles. The Lord is close to the brokenhearted; he rescues those who are crushed in spirit.

PSALM 34:14-18

Be truly sorry for sin

"**THE ANSWER** is no, Jason. That's final!" Mother was firm. As Jason bolted out of the room, a swear word exploded from his lips. "Jason! Come back here this minute!" Mother ordered. "Did you say what I think you said?" Jason gritted his teeth and stared at the floor. Mother sighed deeply. "Son, what's wrong?"

"Mother, I didn't mean to," Jason pleaded. "It just slipped out. I'm really sorry. All the guys at school say those words, and they stick in my mind. I promise I'll never do it again. I'm sorry!"

"I believe you are," she said. "We'll forget it this time."

Later that evening loud, angry words burst from Jason's room. "How many times have I told you to stay out of my stuff?" he roared.

As Mother started down the hall, she heard Sarah cry, "But, Jason, I just wanted to borrow a pencil. I didn't mean to break your model. I'm sorry."

"That's what you said when you lost my watch. You're not really sorry! You're just sorry you got caught." Jason didn't see his mother come into the room as he picked up the broken model, cursing softly.

"Jason!" At the sound of Mother's voice, Jason jumped and dropped the model. "Jason," she said. "Sarah isn't the only one whose apology may be fake. Didn't you tell me earlier you were sorry you said a bad word?" Jason nodded slowly. Mother continued. "True repentance is more than saying 'I'm sorry.' It's being sorry enough for what you have done to stop doing it."

HOW ABOUT YOU? Do you ever say "I'm sorry" simply to keep out of trouble? False repentance might fool others for a while, but it never fools God. *B.J.W.*

TO MEMORIZE: "Therefore, I will judge each of you, O people of Israel, according to your actions, says the Sovereign Lord. Turn from your sins! Don't let them destroy you!" *Ezekiel 18:30*

CELESTE WAS in a bad mood. "I don't see why I have to sing at the nursing home Friday night," she said.

"When you joined the choir," said Mother, "you knew it would cost you some free time."

"What free time?" grumbled Celeste. "Church takes up most of Sunday. Then there's prayer meeting Wednesday night and choir practice Saturday mornings."

Celeste turned to her little sister, Tammy, who had come into the room holding a small box. "Is that your present for Grandma's birthday?"

"Yes—want to see it?" Tammy smiled and lifted the lid off the box.

"Oh, a pretty scarf," Celeste said. "Take off the price tag before you wrap it."

Tammy shook her head. "I want Grandma to know it cost a lot!"

"Don't do that, silly," Celeste scolded. "It will seem like you're bragging."

Mother nodded. "Celeste is right," she said. "The important thing is not the price of your gift but the fact that you love Grandma."

As Tammy left the room, Celeste laughed. "If Tammy only knew how much Grandma has spent on gifts for her, she wouldn't think what she paid for that scarf was such a big deal." She glanced at her mother. "Why are you looking at me like that?"

"Maybe you leave your 'price tag' showing, too," replied Mother. "You were talking about how much you're doing for God and how much it costs you. Perhaps you need to remember how much God has done for you and what it cost him."

HOW ABOUT YOU? Do you think you've made a lot of sacrifices for God? Remember, God gave you everything you have. If you truly love him, serve him willingly and cheerfully. Don't brag or complain. *S.L.K.*

TO MEMORIZE: Each man should give what he has decided in his heart to give, not reluctantly or under compulsion, for God loves a cheerful giver. *2 Corinthians 9:7* (NIV)

PRICE TAGS & PRESENTS

FROM THE BIBLE:

"Take care! Don't do your good deeds publicly, to be admired, because then you will lose the reward from your Father in heaven. When you give a gift to someone in need, don't shout about it as the hypocrites do— blowing trumpets in the synagogues and streets to call attention to their acts of charity! I assure you, they have received all the reward they will ever get. But when you give to someone, don't tell your left hand what your right hand is doing. Give your gifts in secret, and your Father, who knows all secrets, will reward you.

"And now about prayer. When you pray, don't be like the hypocrites who love to pray publicly on street corners and in the synagogues where everyone can see them. I assure you, that is all the reward they will ever get. But when you pray, go away by yourself, shut the door behind you, and pray to your Father secretly. Then your Father, who knows all secrets, will reward you."

MATTHEW 6:1-6

Serve God cheerfully

20 January

GET OUT OF THE DUMP

FROM THE BIBLE:

But the day of the Lord will come as unexpectedly as a thief. Then the heavens will pass away with a terrible noise, and everything in them will disappear in fire, and the earth and everything on it will be exposed to judgment.

Since everything around us is going to melt away, what holy, godly lives you should be living! You should look forward to that day and hurry it along—the day when God will set the heavens on fire and the elements will melt away in the flames. But we are looking forward to the new heavens and new earth he has promised, a world where everyone is right with God.

And so, dear friends, while you are waiting for these things to happen, make every effort to live a pure and blameless life. And be at peace with God.

2 PETER 3:10-14

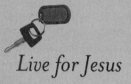

Live for Jesus

STEVE AND his family lived in an area where there was no trash pickup, so each week he and his dad put the garbage cans in their truck and took them to the county dump. One afternoon, as he and his dad were unloading the truck, Steve noticed some mice among the trash.

"I can see why a mouse would love to nest in that trash," Dad said. "There's always plenty of food and lots of papers for building materials. But some men are going to burn all this trash. The mice will lose their homes and everything in them."

As Steve and his dad drove away, Steve couldn't resist one last look at the mice, who were scampering about as though they had nothing to worry about.

When they arrived home, Steve went to his bedroom to change his clothes. As he opened the closet door, a bunch of his belongings fell out. "This place is a dump," he muttered. As he glanced around the room, he saw his posters, video games, and comic books. He saw his baseball mitt, soccer ball, and model spaceships. He saw his books and his Boy Scout manual. *Hmmm,* thought Steve. *I'd hate to be like those mice, spending all my life on things that won't last. Maybe it's time to get out of the dump and start spending more time on things that really matter!* Steve took his Bible from the dresser drawer and placed it beside his bed.

HOW ABOUT YOU? Are you so wrapped up in your own plans, projects, and activities that you have little time for God? Now is a good time to concentrate on doing things that help you become more like Jesus. Remember, this life is only temporary. Only the things we do for Jesus will last forever." *S.L.K.*

TO MEMORIZE: Since everything around us is going to melt away, what holy, godly lives you should be living! *2 Peter 3:11*

"**MOM, MAY** we buy this cereal today?" Stephanie asked, giggling at her mother's raised eyebrow. "Just kidding, Mom," she said. "I know this one has a ton of sugar." She replaced it with a different kind. Then, with a grin, she parroted Mom's often repeated words, "You are what you eat." Mom smiled.

When they arrived home, Stephanie flipped on the radio and began humming the melody of a popular rock song. But Mom turned off the radio. "The words of that song encourage a life that isn't pleasing to God," she said.

"But it has a nice tune," Stephanie protested.

"Listening to that kind of music is like eating food that isn't good for us. Our minds 'eat up' the words whether we pay attention to them or not," Mom said.

As Stephanie helped her mom put away the groceries, she thought about how she often listened to the radio at Cheri's house. She and Cheri were usually doing something else while they listened, but she could still sing all the words to the songs they heard.

"We are what we think about," said Mom. "We need to fill our minds with thoughts that are pleasing to God so we'll grow spiritually."

Stephanie put the box of cereal she had chosen in the cupboard. "From now on I'll choose music like I choose cereal," she decided.

HOW ABOUT YOU? Do you listen to certain kinds of music or do anything else that encourages an unchristian way of life? What you hear or look at gets into your mind whether you are aware of it or not. God is pleased when you focus on things that help you grow spiritually. *K.R.A.*

TO MEMORIZE: Then the Spirit of the Lord came upon me, and he told me to say, "This is what the Lord says to the people of Israel: . . . I know every thought that comes into your minds." *Ezekiel 11:5*

FOOD FOR THOUGHT

FROM THE BIBLE:

O Lord, you have examined my heart and know everything about me. You know when I sit down or stand up. You know my every thought when far away. You chart the path ahead of me and tell me where to stop and rest. Every moment you know where I am. You know what I am going to say even before I say it, Lord. You both precede and follow me. You place your hand of blessing on my head. . . .

Search me, O God, and know my heart; test me and know my thoughts. Point out anything in me that offends you, and lead me along the path of everlasting life.
PSALM 139:1-5, 23-24

Feed your mind good thoughts

22 January

ALL BY MYSELF

FROM THE BIBLE:

"[King Nebuchadnezzar] was taking a walk on the flat roof of the royal palace in Babylon. As he looked out across the city, he said, 'Just look at this great city of Babylon! I, by my own mighty power, have built this beautiful city as my royal residence and as an expression of my royal splendor.'

"While he was still speaking these words, a voice called down from heaven, 'O King Nebuchadnezzar, this message is for you! You are no longer ruler of this kingdom. You will be driven from human society. You will live in the fields with the wild animals, and you will eat grass like a cow. Seven periods of time will pass while you live this way, until you learn that the Most High rules over the kingdoms of the world and gives them to anyone he chooses.'

"That very same hour the prophecy was fulfilled, and Nebuchadnezzar was driven from human society. He ate grass like a cow, and he was drenched with the dew of heaven. He lived this way until his hair was as long as eagles' feathers and his nails were like birds' claws."

DANIEL 4:28-33

Don't be proud

"**LOOK AT** that cool tree house!"

Sitting on the carpeted floor of his new hideout, Mario heard the voices float up from the street.

"Yeah. That's Mario Patino's. His dad is a carpenter, so Mario had all the tools and materials he needed. He claims he built it all by himself, but I don't believe him." Mario recognized Dylan's voice.

Mario glared angrily at the backs of the two boys disappearing down the street. "Did so build it!" he said under his breath.

When his grandparents came the following week, Mario proudly showed Grandpa Patino his work.

"You did a good job," approved Grandpa. "Isn't it nice to have a carpenter dad to give you the knowledge, materials, and tools?"

Mario frowned. Dylan had said the same thing. "But I built it!" Mario insisted. "I built it all by myself!"

Grandpa grinned. "There are very few things we can do alone."

"You drive a truck by yourself," Mario argued.

"I do and I don't," Grandpa replied. "The company I work for supplies the job and the truck. God gives me the strength and knowledge to drive it. And the government builds the highways I drive on."

Mario grinned. "All right, Grandpa, you win. Dad taught me how to build things. He loaned me his tools, God gave me the strength, and together we built this tree house."

HOW ABOUT YOU? Do you sometimes get proud of your work and forget to be thankful to those who help you? Don't make the same mistake King Nebuchadnezzar did. Give thanks to God for helping you. *B.J.W.*

TO MEMORIZE: Now I, Nebuchadnezzar, praise and glorify and honor the King of heaven. All his acts are just and true, and he is able to humble those who are proud. *Daniel 4:37*

A SURE GUIDE

THE JOHNSONS—Heather, Brad, Mother, and Dad—had spent the past few days with Grandpa and Grandma. Mother had driven the family car while Dad drove a truck they'd borrowed so they could take along some items to store in the grandparents' attic.

The family treasured the long talks, funny jokes, and delicious food. It was hard to say good-bye, because it would be four years before the Johnsons would come back from Peru, where they were going as missionaries. As they prepared to go home, fog settled in. "Oh, dear," moaned Mother. "John, how will I ever see the way home?"

"The fog lights on this truck will pierce through the mist, so I'll lead the way," said Dad. "Just follow me and keep your eyes on my taillights."

Mother nervously gripped the steering wheel, but as the children prayed and sang, she gradually relaxed. When they safely reached home, they all thanked God.

"As I was driving, I couldn't help but think that God was using this fog to prepare us for Peru," said Dad. "Because we're going to an unfamiliar country, the future seems 'foggy' to us. The people, customs, and language are relatively unknown to us, so we don't know exactly what's ahead. But God knows all about it. He'll take care of us."

"That's right," agreed Mother. "I had your taillights to guide me, and we all have the Lord to guide us as we go to Peru. We can trust him."

FROM THE BIBLE:

The Lord rewarded me for doing right, because of the innocence of my hands in his sight.

To the faithful you show yourself faithful; to those with integrity you show integrity. To the pure you show yourself pure, but to the wicked you show yourself hostile. You rescue those who are humble, but you humiliate the proud. Lord, you have brought light to my life; my God, you light up my darkness. In your strength I can crush an army; with my God I can scale any wall.

As for God, his way is perfect. All the Lord promises prove true. He is a shield for all who look to him for protection. For who is God except the Lord? Who but our God is a solid rock? God arms me with strength; he has made my way safe. He makes me as surefooted as a deer, leading me safely along the mountain heights.

PSALM 18:24-33

Jesus will guide you

HOW ABOUT YOU? Do you worry about a different school, an unfamiliar town, a new family or stepparent, or a new challenge? God knows your fear and your future. Read his Word for instruction and encouragement. Then ask God to guide you—he will!
J.L.H.

TO MEMORIZE: For that is what God is like. He is our God forever and ever, and he will be our guide until we die. *Psalm 48:14*

24 January

PART OF THE TEAM

FROM THE BIBLE:

And so, dear brothers and sisters, I plead with you to give your bodies to God. Let them be a living and holy sacrifice—the kind he will accept. When you think of what he has done for you, is this too much to ask? Don't copy the behavior and customs of this world, but let God transform you into a new person by changing the way you think. Then you will know what God wants you to do, and you will know how good and pleasing and perfect his will really is.

As God's messenger, I give each of you this warning: Be honest in your estimate of yourselves, measuring your value by how much faith God has given you. Just as our bodies have many parts and each part has a special function, so it is with Christ's body. We are all parts of his one body, and each of us has different work to do. And since we are all one body in Christ, we belong to each other, and each of us needs all the others.

ROMANS 12:1-5

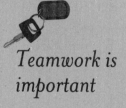

Teamwork is important

"I'M TIRED of Bible club," complained Megan as she came into the kitchen. "I didn't feel like playing during game time today, but my leader said I had to, so I did. Then the other kids on my team got mad at me because they said I wasn't trying hard enough. Let *them* try hard if they like it so well. I didn't feel like it."

"Well," said Dad, "you can't blame them for being unhappy with you. You were part of the team, and a team can't work well unless all the members participate enthusiastically. Besides, there may have been new kids there—perhaps even some non-Christian kids who were wondering what being a Christian is all about—and your grouchy attitude is what they saw."

"Oh, Dad! They didn't need me," grumbled Megan as she went to her room. A moment later her dad heard her shout, "Jason, stop it! Give that to me!"

"What's going on?" asked Dad as he hurried down the hall.

"Jason broke my alarm clock," Megan answered, pointing to her little brother.

Dad examined the clock. "Well," he said, "it looks OK, except for the hour hand. But you don't need that."

"Dad!" protested Megan. "No one can tell time without the hour hand!"

"Oh," Dad said with a grin. "You mean all the parts are important?"

"Of course." Megan looked at her dad. "I know what you're saying. A clock can't work unless all the parts are working, and a team can't work without all the members playing."

Dad tugged Megan's ponytail. "Right!" he said.

HOW ABOUT YOU? Do you play on a team? Do you help the team win, or do you complain that things are unfair or that you don't like what the leader asks you to do? Be a willing participant with a good attitude. *L.M.W.*

TO MEMORIZE: A kingdom at war with itself will collapse. *Mark 3:24*

"**JANICE,**" said Mom one Saturday afternoon, "I'm going down to the estate sale at the end of the block. Do you want to come?"

"Sure," Janice replied eagerly. "Is it like a garage sale?"

"In a way," her mother answered. "But in this case, the lady who lived in the house died. And her relatives are having the sale to dispose of all the things she's collected over the years."

The two walked down the block to a large brick house where a number of people were milling about, examining furniture, dishes, and other objects. After looking it all over, Mom paid for some glassware she had selected, and they walked out.

Janice was unusually quiet on the way home. "You know, Mom," she said finally, "I'd sure hate to think that someday people might be going through my things and even taking some of them home."

"I know what you mean," agreed Mom, "and that makes me think of something else." She looked at her daughter seriously. "It's not only our worldly possessions that will be exposed when we die. The Bible says that someday the records in heaven will be opened, and all of our thoughts and actions will be exposed. We won't be able to keep any secrets as we stand before God."

"That makes me want to live as good a life as I can for God," said Janice.

"Yes," her mother said, nodding. "I feel that way, too."

HOW ABOUT YOU? Do you ever wonder what it will be like to meet God someday? That day is going to come, and many of the things that seem important now will be meaningless then. Have you prepared for your eternal future? Be sure you know Jesus Christ as your Savior. If you haven't yet done so, talk to a trusted friend or adult. *S.L.K.*

TO MEMORIZE: It is destined that each person dies only once and after that comes judgment. *Hebrews 9:27*

NO MORE SECRETS

FROM THE BIBLE:

Meanwhile, the crowds grew until thousands were milling about and crushing each other. Jesus turned first to his disciples and warned them, "Beware of the yeast of the Pharisees— beware of their hypocrisy. The time is coming when everything will be revealed; all that is secret will be made public. Whatever you have said in the dark will be heard in the light, and what you have whispered behind closed doors will be shouted from the housetops for all to hear!

"Dear friends, don't be afraid of those who want to kill you. They can only kill the body; they cannot do any more to you. But I'll tell you whom to fear. Fear God, who has the power to kill people and then throw them into hell."

LUKE 12:1-5

No more secrets

26 January

WORLD OF WARS

FROM THE BIBLE:

Jesus told them, "Don't let anyone mislead you. For many will come in my name, saying, 'I am the Messiah.' They will lead many astray. And wars will break out near and far, but don't panic. Yes, these things must come, but the end won't follow immediately. The nations and kingdoms will proclaim war against each other, and there will be famines and earthquakes in many parts of the world. But all this will be only the beginning of the horrors to come.

"Then you will be arrested, persecuted, and killed. You will be hated all over the world because of your allegiance to me. And many will turn away from me and betray and hate each other. And many false prophets will appear and will lead many people astray. Sin will be rampant everywhere, and the love of many will grow cold. But those who endure to the end will be saved. And the Good News about the Kingdom will be preached throughout the whole world, so that all nations will hear it; and then, finally, the end will come."
MATTHEW 24:4-14

God gives peace

"**BOY,** have I got a hard assignment tonight," Stephen announced as he and his brother and sister began to do their homework. "I have to memorize a bunch of dates about the Civil War."

"And *I'm* learning about the battles of the Revolutionary War," said John.

"All I have to do is go through the newspaper and cut out articles for our current events project," Jolene told her brothers. "That doesn't sound too hard compared to what you guys have to do."

"Just make sure you don't cut any of the comics," said Stephen, grinning.

The three children worked quietly for a while, then Jolene sighed. "Almost all the articles in this paper are about troubles and wars in one place or another."

"I wonder why," said Stephen. "I thought people are supposed to be making the world a better place."

"That's true," agreed Mom, who had just walked into the room, "but as Christians, we shouldn't be surprised. The Bible says there will always be wars and rumors of war. Politicians talk about peace, but their desire for power often gets in the way. God is left out of the picture."

"It's scary," Jolene said. "It makes me glad I'm a Christian."

Mom smiled and said, "As Christians, we can have peace of mind no matter what happens."

HOW ABOUT YOU? Do you ever wonder why the world is not getting better? Do you wonder why there are so many wars? Because the world's leaders are human, they have difficulty getting along with each other. They often refuse to follow God's way. Isn't it good to know that in spite of the chaos in the world around you, you can put your trust in God and have peace? *L.M.W.*

TO MEMORIZE: Don't worry about anything; instead, pray about everything. Tell God what you need, and thank him for all he has done. If you do this, you will experience God's peace. *Philippians 4:6-7*

IT WAS lunch time, and Karen watched as her little brother Kyle sat stubbornly shaking his head, refusing to eat the strained peas Mother was offering.

"Maybe you should give him applesauce," suggested Karen. "He likes that."

"Yes, he can have some," responded Mother. "But he also has to learn to eat other foods that he needs." Mother took Kyle out of his chair and set him on the floor. "We'll try feeding him again in a few minutes."

A short time later, Karen heard a rustling noise coming from behind the kitchen door. There was Kyle, rummaging in the trash bag. "Oh, Mother!" said Karen.

Mother rushed to the rescue, but Kyle cried when she took a banana peel out of his mouth.

"Wasn't that silly, Mother?" asked Karen, turning on the TV to see what was on. "Kyle sure doesn't know what's good for him, does he?"

"No," Mother replied, "he doesn't." She paused, then added, "Very often Christians don't, either. We pay no attention to the gifts God provides for us to help us be joyful and grow to be like him. Instead we try to fill our needs with things from this world that aren't important or necessary or even good for us. Those things are 'garbage' compared with the things of the Lord. They are 'peelings,' not 'peas.'"

Karen agreed with her mother, turning off the TV. "I think I'll go do my Sunday school lesson."

HOW ABOUT YOU? Do you have a need in your life? A need for fellowship? For spiritual growth? For emotional fulfillment? For a sense of achievement? The things of this world will never satisfy those needs. Let God do it. Whatever your need, give God the chance to satisfy it. *S.L.K.*

TO MEMORIZE: And this same God who takes care of me will supply all your needs from his glorious riches, which have been given to us in Christ Jesus. *Philippians 4:19*

PEAS OR PEELINGS

FROM THE BIBLE:

The Lord is my shepherd;
I have everything I need.
He lets me rest in green
meadows;
he leads me beside peaceful
streams.
He renews my strength.
He guides me along right paths,
bringing honor to his name.

Even when I walk
through the dark valley
of death,
I will not be afraid,
for you are close beside me.
Your rod and your staff
protect and comfort me.
PSALM 23:1-4

God meets needs

28 January

STOP THAT NOISE!

If I could speak in any language in heaven or on earth but didn't love others, I would only be making meaningless noise like a loud gong or a clanging cymbal. If I had the gift of prophecy, and if I knew all the mysteries of the future and knew everything about everything, but didn't love others, what good would I be? And if I had the gift of faith so that I could speak to a mountain and make it move, without love I would be no good to anybody. If I gave everything I have to the poor and even sacrificed my body, I could boast about it; but if I didn't love others, I would be of no value whatsoever.

1 CORINTHIANS 13:1-3

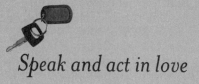

Speak and act in love

"BYE, MARCIE. See you tomorrow," said Jill. As soon as Marcie had gone, Jill mumbled, "I can't stand that girl!"

"Why, Jill!" exclaimed her mother. "Didn't you tell me you've been witnessing to Marcie?"

"I'm *trying*," retorted Jill. A horrible clanging noise started coming from her brother's room. "What's that noise?" she asked.

Mother laughed. "Pete borrowed Grandpa's antique dinner gong for his science project about sound."

Jill groaned. Although she liked most of the brass antiques Grandpa collected, the gong was ugly. Now Pete would probably be banging it all evening!

Pete banged the gong right outside Jill's door while she was doing her homework. "Mom!" Jill shouted. "Make him stop!"

Instead of saying anything to Pete, Mother came into Jill's room and sat down. "I don't like that noise any better than you do," she said, "but when I thought of our conversation about Marcie this afternoon, I decided to let Pete clang it a little. I thought it might teach you something." She handed Jill an open Bible. "Here, read the first verse of 1 Corinthians 13."

"I understand," Jill said, after reading the verse. "Saying that I want Marcie to know the Lord and then treating her the way I do is like the sound of that brass gong Pete is clanging. It's just a bunch of noise without any value."

HOW ABOUT YOU? Do you pretend to like someone while you're really thinking mean thoughts? If there's someone who really bothers you, ask the Lord to help you sincerely care about that boy or girl so that you can show him or her God's love. *L.M.W.*

TO MEMORIZE: If I could speak in any language in heaven or on earth but didn't love others, I would only be making meaningless noise like a loud gong or a clanging cymbal. *1 Corinthians 13:1*

THE BINOCULARS

JEREMY eagerly tore the wrapping paper off the birthday present his parents had given him. "Binoculars! Thanks!" he exclaimed, quickly pulling them out of the box. He turned them over and over in his hands. "Can we go to the state forest preserve? It has some good lookout points where I could try these out."

"Sounds great!" agreed Dad. "Let's go!"

Before long, Jeremy and his dad stood together on one of the park's lookout points and took turns looking through the binoculars. As Jeremy took a turn, he silently watched something for a moment. "Look, Dad!" he said in a whisper. "I see a doe and twin fawns." Dad took the binoculars and soon located the animals. He watched them for a minute. "Aren't they great?" whispered Jeremy.

Dad laughed and handed the binoculars back. "Yes, they are," he said out loud. "But you don't need to whisper."

Jeremy looked again. "Just think, those animals have no idea we're watching them," he said in awe. "We can see every move they make, but they're so far away that they don't even know we exist!"

"That is amazing," agreed Dad. "It reminds me that we're being watched, too."

"We are? Who's watching us?" Jeremy asked.

"God is. He sees the mistakes we make, and he sees the good things we do," explained Dad.

"I knew that, but I never thought about it quite that way," said Jeremy. "I think I'll be more careful of what I do, knowing that God is always watching."

HOW ABOUT YOU? Are you aware that God sees you 24 hours a day? Remembering that God's presence is always with you can help you make better decisions. Next time you wonder if it's worth the effort to do what's right, remember, God is watching! *V.L.R.*

TO MEMORIZE: For the Lord sees clearly what a man does, examining every path he takes. *Proverbs 5:21*

FROM THE BIBLE:

"He sees everything I do and every step I take.

"Have I lied to anyone or deceived anyone? Let God judge me on the scales of justice, for he knows my integrity."

*The Lord looks down from heaven
and sees the whole human race.
From his throne he observes
all who live on the earth.
He made their hearts,
so he understands everything they do.*

JOB 31:4-6; PSALM 33:13-15

God is watching

30 January

FALSE LABELS

FROM THE BIBLE:

Everyone who believes that Jesus is the Christ is a child of God. And everyone who loves the Father loves his children, too. . . .

Since we believe human testimony, surely we can believe the testimony that comes from God. And God has testified about his Son. All who believe in the Son of God know that this is true. Those who don't believe this are actually calling God a liar because they don't believe what God has testified about his Son.

And this is what God has testified: He has given us eternal life, and this life is in his Son. So whoever has God's Son has life; whoever does not have his Son does not have life.

I write this to you who believe in the Son of God, so that you may know you have eternal life.
1 JOHN 5:1, 9-13

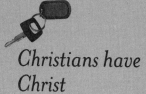

Christians have Christ

BARB'S SUNDAY school class was having a slumber party at the Gordons' cottage. "Sleep well, girls," said Mrs. Gordon, the teacher.

A sleepy looking bunch of girls assembled in the dining room the next morning. Their eyes opened wide, however, as they surveyed the table. "Pickles? For breakfast?" Rhonda spoke for them all.

"Of course not," replied Mrs. Gordon. "Right after devotions we'll have bacon and eggs, cereal, and toast. And I want you all to try my strawberry jam!" She held up a huge jar for all to see.

"Jam?" exclaimed Barb. "That's a jar of pickles!"

"The label says 'Strawberry Jam,'" Mrs. Gordon insisted.

Beth spoke up. "But there are pickles in the jar!"

"You're right, of course." Mrs. Gordon looked at each of the girls and said, "I hope you aren't like this 'jam'—wearing a false label. Most of you wear the label 'Christian.' However, just as a jar of strawberry jam must have jam inside, a Christian must have Christ."

Mrs. Gordon picked up her Bible. "Turn with me to 1 John 5," she said. After they finished reading, Mrs. Gordon spoke again. "This passage tells us that if we don't have Jesus Christ, we don't have life. We can look inside this jar and see what's there. We can't look inside one another, but God can. Does he see Christ in you?"

HOW ABOUT YOU? To be a Christian, you must admit that you are a sinner and believe in Jesus Christ, the Son of God, as your Savior and Lord. Believe that he died for you, that he rose again, and that he will forgive your sins. Ask him to lead you and to give you eternal life. He will! *H.W.M.*

TO MEMORIZE: So whoever has God's Son has life; whoever does not have his Son does not have life. *1 John 5:12*

CHECKUP TIME

MARIA GOT into the car and slammed the door. "Why can't I take care of Carlos at home? Why do I have to baby-sit in a waiting room?"

"I've explained that we're going to Grandma's house after we visit Aunt Kathleen at the hospital," said her mother. It would take too long to go back home for you."

Maria pouted as her father drove to the hospital. In the waiting room, she rummaged through the magazines on a table and then picked up one she knew her parents would never allow her to read at home.

"Read a story out loud to me," Carlos begged.

She handed him a kids' magazine. "Here, you look at the pictures."

Maria was so engrossed in her reading that she jumped when her Dad said, "Time to go, Maria."

Maria hastily slipped her magazine under the stack on the table. "How was Aunt Kathleen?" Maria asked quickly.

"She's going to be fine. Because she went to the doctor when she had the first warning symptom, they found what was wrong early."

Maria let out a big sigh. "Oh, that's good."

"It's important to heed early warnings," Mother said. "I see some danger signals in your life, Maria." Based on your attitude and your reading material, I'd say you need a spiritual checkup."

Father put his arm around Maria. "Heeding a physical warning symptom may have saved Aunt Kathleen's life on this earth. Heeding the warnings your mother and I give you could save your life forever."

FROM THE BIBLE:

Here is a sample of John's preaching to the crowds that came for baptism: "You brood of snakes! Who warned you to flee God's coming judgment? Prove by the way you live that you have really turned from your sins and turned to God. Don't just say, 'We're safe—we're the descendants of Abraham.' That proves nothing. God can change these stones here into children of Abraham. Even now the ax of God's judgment is poised, ready to sever your roots. Yes, every tree that does not produce good fruit will be chopped down and thrown into the fire." LUKE 3:7-9

Heed early warnings

HOW ABOUT YOU? Have you been warned about your attitude or actions lately? Did you resent it? It could be a blessing in disguise. An early warning could save you from trouble later. *B.J.W.*

TO MEMORIZE: They heard the warning but wouldn't listen, so the responsibility is theirs. If they had listened to the warning, they could have saved their lives. *Ezekiel 33:5*

1 February

TO GRANDMA, WITH LOVE

FROM THE BIBLE:

Meanwhile, Jesus was in Bethany at the home of Simon, a man who had leprosy. During supper, a woman came in with a beautiful jar of expensive perfume. She broke the seal and poured the perfume over his head. Some of those at the table were indignant. "Why was this expensive perfume wasted?" they asked. "She could have sold it for a small fortune and given the money to the poor!" And they scolded her harshly.

But Jesus replied, "Leave her alone. Why berate her for doing such a good thing to me? You will always have the poor among you, and you can help them whenever you want to. But I will not be here with you much longer. She has done what she could and has anointed my body for burial ahead of time. I assure you, wherever the Good News is preached throughout the world, this woman's deed will be talked about in her memory."

MARK 14:3-9

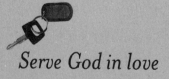

Serve God in love

JUAN worked busily on a picture for his grandmother, who was coming for a visit soon. He finished drawing a house, then worked on trees. Juan enjoyed art, and his teacher had told him he had a talent for it. Nearby Juan's younger sister, Angelica, also worked on a picture. She held hers up. "Looks like scribbling to me," Juan scoffed.

When Grandma arrived, Juan gave her his drawing. "This is good work, Juan," Grandma exclaimed. When Angelica held out her picture, Grandma praised her work, too. But she noticed Juan's scowl.

Later, when Juan and Grandma were alone, she asked him about it. "Why did you scowl when I praised Angelica for her picture?"

"It was just scribbling," replied Juan.

"But I saw the love that went into it," Grandma explained. "I saw that Angelica had worked just as hard to please me as you had."

Juan still looked a little doubtful, but he nodded slowly. "I guess that means you'd love me just as much if I couldn't draw well," he said. Then he added with a grin, "And that's good."

"That's right," agreed Grandma. "Shall I tell you something else that's good? God is pleased by the things we do for him out of love. We may think some of our actions, or deeds, aren't important, but they're special to God because he notices the love you put into them. Giving a helping hand, a friendly smile, or an encouraging word is just as important to God as any other job."

HOW ABOUT YOU? Do you ever feel that what you have done for God may be more important than what someone else has done? Or perhaps you feel your actions are less important. God sees the love in your deeds, no matter what they are. *C.E.Y.*

TO MEMORIZE: She has done what she could and has anointed my body for burial ahead of time. *Mark 14:8*

"**BE QUIET,** Daisy," murmured Ellen sleepily as she burrowed deeper into her bed. The barking continued, but Ellen ignored it. Suddenly, a furry pooch landed on the bed beside her, barking furiously. Ellen pushed the dog away. "Quiet!" she commanded again.

Daisy ran down the hall toward Ellen's parents' room. Then *thump!* She was back again, pouncing on Ellen and barking loudly. Ellen sat up, very annoyed. "Lie down and be still!" she said. Instead, the dog ran out the door, barking and looking to see if Ellen was following.

Ellen sniffed the air. What was that smell? It was smoke! She leaped from her bed and ran into the hall, where her parents were just coming from their room. Soon they were all out in the yard, waiting for the fire trucks.

The next morning Ellen read about the fire in the newspaper. "Dog Saves Home and Family," the headline read. She hugged Daisy. "Sorry I got mad at you," she apologized. "I'm glad you kept trying to wake me up."

Mother looked over at Ellen. "Sometimes it's good to be awakened, isn't it?" she said thoughtfully. "That will be a good thing for you to keep in mind when you see your friend Alicia again."

"Alicia?" asked Ellen. "What do you mean?"

"Yesterday you said you weren't going to try to witness to Alicia anymore because it seems to annoy her. In a way she's saying, 'Let me sleep.' But she needs to wake up to her need for Jesus," explained Mother. "Daisy loved you enough to keep after you even when you didn't like it. So don't give up on Alicia."

HOW ABOUT YOU? Are you afraid to witness to your friends because they might be annoyed or angry? Don't give up witnessing to them. *H.W.M.*

TO MEMORIZE: Don't be afraid of suffering for the Lord. Work at bringing others to Christ. Complete the ministry God has given you. *2 Timothy 4:5*

LET ME SLEEP

FROM THE BIBLE:

At the end of the seven days, the Lord gave me a message. He said, "Son of man, I have appointed you as a watchman for Israel. Whenever you receive a message from me, pass it on to the people immediately. If I warn the wicked, saying, 'You are under the penalty of death,' but you fail to deliver the warning, they will die in their sins. And I will hold you responsible, demanding your blood for theirs. If you warn them and they keep on sinning and refuse to repent, they will die in their sins. But you will have saved your life because you did what you were told to do. If good people turn bad and don't listen to my warning, they will die. If you did not warn them of the consequences, then they will die in their sins. Their previous good deeds won't help them, and I will hold you responsible, demanding your blood for theirs. But if you warn them and they repent, they will live, and you will have saved your own life, too."
EZEKIEL 3:16-21

Keep witnessing

3 February

A FINE-FREE DAY

FROM THE BIBLE:

Now you are free from sin, your old master, and you have become slaves to your new master, righteousness.

I speak this way, using the illustration of slaves and masters, because it is easy to understand. Before, you let yourselves be slaves of impurity and lawlessness. Now you must choose to be slaves of righteousness so that you will become holy.

In those days, when you were slaves of sin, you weren't concerned with doing what was right. And what was the result? It was not good, since now you are ashamed of the things you used to do, things that end in eternal doom. But now you are free from the power of sin and have become slaves of God. Now you do those things that lead to holiness and result in eternal life. For the wages of sin is death, but the free gift of God is eternal life through Christ Jesus our Lord.

ROMANS 6:18-23

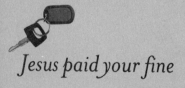

Jesus paid your fine

"**OH BOY!** This is my lucky day," Steve shouted. "Listen to this, Mom." From the newspaper he read, "Wednesday has been declared Fine-Free Day at the local library. All overdue books may be returned without paying a fine."

Mom smiled. "The librarian will be sorry when she sees you coming!"

Soon Steve was on his way to return his overdue books. As he pedaled toward the library, Mr. Burns staggered out of his house. *Drunk again!* Steve thought.

"Hi ya, Steve," Mr. Burns slurred. "Where ya goin'?"

"To the library to return overdue books." Steve stopped his bike. "Today is Fine-Free Day."

"Sure wish they'd have Fine-Free Day at city hall." Mr. Burns's blurry eyes stared at the boy. "Hey, yer a Christian. Ya suppose God has a Fine-Free Day?"

Steve blinked, then replied, "Sure he does, Mr. Burns. Today is Fine-Free Day with God, too. Jesus paid our fine at Calvary. If you'll turn your life over to him, he'll forgive you!"

Mr. Burns shook his head. "Ya only have a few sins. I've got a pack of 'em."

Steve pointed at his backpack, crammed with books. "It makes no difference to the librarian if I have one overdue book or ten. I don't have to pay a fine today. And it makes no difference to God if I have a few sins or a whole pack."

"Ya really think so, son?" Mr. Burns asked. "I'll have to think that over."

HOW ABOUT YOU? Are you carrying sins for which you need to repent? Whether they're a "few little sins" or a "lot of big ones;" they must be paid for. To find out more, talk to a trusted Christian friend or adult. *B.J.W.*

TO MEMORIZE: For God says, "At just the right time, I heard you. On the day of salvation, I helped you." Indeed, God is ready to help you right now. Today is the day of salvation. *2 Corinthians 6:2*

"I FEEL TERRIBLE," Jason complained. "My nose is stuffy and my throat is sore."

"I know," his mother sympathized. "Here's some juice for you. Just stay on the couch. In a few days your cold will be better."

A short time later Jason called his mother. "I still feel terrible," he said.

Mother brought a wet cloth for Jason's forehead, fixed his pillow, and tucked his cover around him. "Now you just rest," she said.

But Jason didn't feel like resting. He kept on moaning, sighing, and whining until finally Mother said, "Jason, I've done all I can for you. I know you're uncomfortable and that it's not fun to be sick. But you must learn not to complain. The Bible tells us to be patient in trouble."

"What kind of trouble?" asked Jason.

"Any circumstance that makes you miserable or unhappy," said Mother. "That could mean not feeling well or being mistreated or other things that aren't pleasant."

"But I hate being sick. How can I be patient about that?" Jason argued.

"Complaining won't help you or anyone else. In fact, it will make you and those around you feel worse. If you learn to be cheerful and uncomplaining even when you're not feeling well, you bring glory to God," explained Mother, as she poured more juice in Jason's glass. "Follow Jesus' example. He didn't complain when he suffered."

"Well, I never knew the Bible said anything about how to act when I have a cold," said Jason. "From now on I'll try to be more patient."

HOW ABOUT YOU? When you're sick, do you complain constantly about your aches and pains? You should let your parents or teacher know if you're not feeling well, but once you're getting help, there's no need to keep on complaining. Instead, ask Jesus for patience. *C.E.Y.*

TO MEMORIZE: Be glad for all God is planning for you. Be patient in trouble, and always be prayerful. *Romans 12:12*

ACHES AND PAINS

FROM THE BIBLE:

Therefore, since we have been made right in God's sight by faith, we have peace with God because of what Jesus Christ our Lord has done for us. Because of our faith, Christ has brought us into this place of highest privilege where we now stand, and we confidently and joyfully look forward to sharing God's glory.

We can rejoice, too, when we run into problems and trials, for we know that they are good for us—they help us learn to endure. And endurance develops strength of character in us, and character strengthens our confident expectation of salvation. And this expectation will not disappoint us. For we know how dearly God loves us, because he has given us the Holy Spirit to fill our hearts with his love.

ROMANS 5:1-5

Be patient in trouble

5 February

FAMILY FEUD

FROM THE BIBLE:

"I say, love your enemies. Do good to those who hate you. Pray for the happiness of those who curse you. Pray for those who hurt you. If someone slaps you on one cheek, turn the other cheek. If someone demands your coat, offer your shirt also. Give what you have to anyone who asks you for it; and when things are taken away from you, don't try to get them back. Do for others as you would like them to do for you.

"Do you think you deserve credit merely for loving those who love you? Even the sinners do that! And if you do good only to those who do good to you, is that so wonderful? Even sinners do that much! . . .

"Love your enemies! Do good to them! Lend to them! And don't be concerned that they might not repay. Then your reward from heaven will be very great, and you will truly be acting as children of the Most High, for he is kind to the unthankful and to those who are wicked. You must be compassionate, just as your Father is compassionate."

LUKE 6:27-36

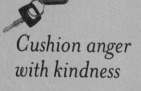

Cushion anger with kindness

DING, DONG! The doorbell had been ringing for some time, but Jane and her family were yelling at each other and hadn't heard it. Jane finally noticed her friend Kerri tapping on the living room window.

Embarrassed, she went outside and closed the door. "I'm sorry, Kerri," she said. "I forgot you were coming over. I was tied up in a family discussion." She paused when she saw Kerri looking at her. "Well, actually, it was a fight."

"Yes, I heard," said Kerri softly.

Jane sighed. "I don't know why we can't get along," she said. "We say we're Christians, but we don't act like it. I don't want to argue with my family. And I don't think they like the fighting either. But what can I do about it?"

Just then Jane and Kerri heard the squeal of brakes and a crash. They rushed down the sidewalk and saw that a car had banged into a truck. The drivers got out to look at the damage. "I'm sorry I ran into you," said the driver of the car.

The truck driver said, "I don't see any damage to my truck. My bumper cushioned the impact."

As Jane and Kerri walked back toward Jane's house, Kerri said, "That accident made me think of something. The truck driver's bumper was like a cushion, so no damage was done. Maybe you need to be like a cushion when your family is grumpy. The Bible says, 'A gentle answer turns away wrath.' So if you answer softly and kindly it may stop the family feuds."

HOW ABOUT YOU? When someone is angry with you, do you reply sharply? Or do you keep your temper and try to answer quietly and patiently? The way you respond to anger can make a difference in your life. *S.L.K.*

TO MEMORIZE: A gentle answer turns away wrath, but harsh words stir up anger. *Proverbs 15:1*

HONEST ERNESTO

"**ONE HUNDRED,** two hundred, three, four, five," counted the man as he placed green bills on the table in front of Ernesto's father. Then Ernesto watched as the man drove off with the family's older car.

"Dad, why did you let that man have our car for only five hundred dollars?"

Ernesto's father smiled. "The money was just a down payment."

"Oh, I see." Ernesto nodded. "But, what if he decides not to buy the car?"

"Then he'll lose the down payment," replied Dad. "He wouldn't give me the money unless he intended to buy the car. It's like his guarantee.

"And we have the Holy Spirit as God's 'guarantee' to Christians. The Holy Spirit lives inside us as proof that God has purchased us and will someday give us everything he promised."

"That's great, Dad," said Ernesto. "Hey, what if you try to get the car back?"

"That wouldn't be honest," Dad replied. "When I accepted the down payment, I gave up my right to own the car. In a similar way, Jesus purchased us with his blood. We now belong to him, but we're not always honest with him, are we?"

"What do you mean?" Ernesto asked.

"Even though we've given ourselves to Jesus, we sometimes try to take our lives back and have our own way. God won't go back on his promise to give us eternal life. So we need to be honest and keep our commitment to him, too."

HOW ABOUT YOU? Have you given your life to Jesus Christ? If so, the Bible says that God has given you his Holy Spirit as a "down payment" until you receive the rest of his wonderful blessings in heaven. *S.L.K.*

TO MEMORIZE: The Spirit is God's guarantee that he will give us everything he promised and that he has purchased us to be his own people. This is just one more reason for us to praise our glorious God. *Ephesians 1:14*

FROM THE BIBLE:

And this is his plan: At the right time he will bring everything together under the authority of Christ—everything in heaven and on earth. Furthermore, because of Christ, we have received an inheritance from God, for he chose us from the beginning, and all things happen just as he decided long ago. God's purpose was that we who were the first to trust in Christ should praise our glorious God. And now you also have heard the truth, the Good News that God saves you. And when you believed in Christ, he identified you as his own by giving you the Holy Spirit, whom he promised long ago. The Spirit is God's guarantee that he will give us everything he promised and that he has purchased us to be his own people. This is just one more reason for us to praise our glorious God.
EPHESIANS 1:10-14

Be honest with God

7 February

THE BROKEN THUMB

FROM THE BIBLE:

The human body has many parts, but the many parts make up only one body. So it is with the body of Christ. . . .

Yes, the body has many different parts, not just one part. If the foot says, "I am not a part of the body because I am not a hand," that does not make it any less a part of the body. . . . Suppose the whole body were an eye—then how would you hear? Or if your whole body were just one big ear, how could you smell anything?

But God made our bodies with many parts, and he has put each part just where he wants it. What a strange thing a body would be if it had only one part! Yes, there are many parts, but only one body. The eye can never say to the hand, "I don't need you." The head can't say to the feet, "I don't need you."

In fact, some of the parts that seem weakest and least important are really the most necessary.

1 CORINTHIANS 12:12-22

Do your part

SHELLY WAS the youth group secretary, but she had broken her thumb. "Could you take notes for me this afternoon?" Shelly asked Shawn as the student leaders met one Sunday.

"Sure," said Shawn.

As ideas were discussed, Doug, their president, offered a suggestion. "How about planning a summer missions trip and giving everyone something to do—you know, get everyone involved?"

"Sounds like a good idea," said their leader, Mr. Craig. "As a matter of fact, for the next few weeks we'll be studying the church, which the Bible often refers to as 'the body' of Christ."

"What about kids who can't do anything?" asked Shelly. "Let's face it, there are some kids who don't seem to have anything to offer."

"Shelly," replied Mr. Craig, "how important is your thumb?"

"My thumb?" asked Shelly. "Well, last week I might have said I could live without it. But now that it's broken, I see how much I really need it. What does that have to do with our missions trip?"

"Jesus says that's how it is with his body, the church," explained Mr. Craig. "Each member is important for the total body to function properly."

"Oh, I see what you mean," said Shelly. She looked at her thumb. "I guess we can find something for everybody to do," she said with a grin.

HOW ABOUT YOU? Each Christian is an important member of the body of Christ, the church. Can you show concern for others? Make visitors feel welcome? Give your time, talents, or money? Organize things? Make a card to encourage someone? Do your part. *D.L.R.*

TO MEMORIZE: Now all of you together are Christ's body, and each one of you is a separate and necessary part of it. *1 Corinthians 12:27*

8 February

KEVIN AND JESSICA were having a great time on a week-long visit to their grandparents' home. The ground was covered with snow, and they would stay outside for hours, building snow forts and walking on the ice-covered lake. Then they would come in and sip hot chocolate in front of the fire.

One afternoon they persuaded Grandpa to go for a walk with them. They took off down the road, laughing and talking and occasionally throwing a snowball at each other. Suddenly Grandpa whispered, "Hey, kids! Don't move. Look over there!" Kevin and Jessica looked where Grandpa was pointing. A huge bird sat on the branch of a tree. "It's an eagle," whispered Grandpa. Suddenly, with a powerful flap of its wings, the eagle took off over the treetops.

"Wow!" Kevin said. "That's one strong bird!"

"You're right," agreed Grandpa. "You can be strong like that, too," he added.

"How?" Kevin asked.

"Those who wait on the Lord shall renew their strength. They shall mount up with wings as eagles," replied Grandpa. "That's in Isaiah 40."

"I've heard that verse, Grandpa," said Jessica. "But I never thought about what it meant before."

"It's a picture," said Grandpa, "a magnificent picture of the strength we have when we put our trust in the Lord."

HOW ABOUT YOU? Do you have problems at school? Do you live in a tough home situation? Is it hard for you to make friends? Trust Jesus to help you. He doesn't promise to take problems away, but he does promise to give you the strength needed to handle them. The next time you see a picture of an eagle, think of God's promise. *L.M.W.*

TO MEMORIZE: I can do everything with the help of Christ who gives me the strength I need. *Philippians 4:13*

WHAT A BIRD!

FROM THE BIBLE:

*O Lord, you are my rock of
   safety.
  Please help me; don't refuse
   to answer me.
For if you are silent,
  I might as well give up and die.
Listen to my prayer for mercy
  as I cry out to you for help,
  as I lift my hands toward your
   holy sanctuary.*

*Don't drag me away with the
   wicked—
  with those who do evil—
those who speak friendly words
   to their neighbors
  while planning evil in
   their hearts. . . .*

*Praise the Lord!
  For he has heard my cry
   for mercy.
The Lord is my strength, my
   shield from every danger.
I trust in him with all my
   heart.
He helps me, and my heart
   is filled with joy.
I burst out in songs of
   thanksgiving.*

*The Lord protects his people
  and gives victory to his
   anointed king.
Save your people!
  Bless Israel, your special
   possession!
Lead them like a shepherd,
  and carry them forever
  in your arms.*

PSALM 28:1-3; 6-9

God gives strength

9 February

WHO'S YOUR BOSS?

FROM THE BIBLE:

Work hard and cheerfully at whatever you do, as though you were working for the Lord rather than for people. Remember that the Lord will give you an inheritance as your reward, and the Master you are serving is Christ. But if you do what is wrong, you will be paid back for the wrong you have done. For God has no favorites who can get away with evil.
COLOSSIANS 3:23-25

Don't follow bad examples

ERIC POUNDED his fist into his pillow. The whole thing was unfair. He was sent to his room for saying a bad word, but his father said those words, and no one punished *him*.

Hearing noises, Eric glanced out his open window. Three men were working on the road in front of his house. "How about another break?" suggested one.

"Sure thing, boss," answered the tallest one. The two men sat down under a tree, but the third, a dark-haired man, kept working. Soon the tall man came back and tried to persuade him to join them.

"I've already had my break," answered the dark-haired man.

"Haven't we all? But Harry says to take another one, and you know the foreman left him in charge today," argued the tall man.

"He doesn't have authority to give us extra time off, though," said the third man. "Mr. Grant wants the job finished today. We've got a lot to do."

"You're crazy," snorted the other man.

"Maybe it seems crazy," answered the dark-haired man pleasantly, "but it wouldn't be right for me to take time or anything else that isn't mine. Mr. Grant's my first boss, and I do my work for him."

Wow, what a guy! Eric thought. *He insists on working even when his temporary boss sets a bad example.* Then a new thought struck him. *I should do the same thing when it comes to using bad language. Even though other people say bad words, I should do what my first boss wants—and that's God.*

HOW ABOUT YOU? It's hard to do what's right when someone you love and respect is setting a poor example. But remember that, first of all, you serve Christ. Do what he approves of, not what others are doing. *C.E.Y.*

TO MEMORIZE: Remember that the Lord will give you an inheritance as your reward, and the Master you are serving is Christ. *Colossians 3:24*

JEREMY AND Samuel watched as the construction workers built a new apartment complex on the corner of their street. "It sure is tall," commented Jeremy. "I wonder how they get a tall building so straight."

"Let's go to the mall and ask Mr. Cohen," said Samuel. "He knows a lot about buildings."

The boys raced down the street to the mall. "So you want to know about buildings," said Mr. Cohen, who was their Sunday school teacher. "Tell me, do you know what a cornerstone is?"

"No," Jeremy replied. Samuel shrugged his shoulders.

"The cornerstone is a special stone or brick," said Mr. Cohen. "Accurate instruments are used to lay the cornerstone. All the other bricks in the building are lined up with it. If the cornerstone is laid straight, the rest of the building will be straight because the other bricks are laid one by one, using the cornerstone as a guide."

"Hey, that's cool!" said Samuel.

Mr. Cohen smiled. "The Bible tells us that Jesus is our cornerstone."

The boys looked surprised. "We aren't buildings," laughed Samuel.

"No, but the Bible uses the word *building* when referring to the church—that is, all the people who have trusted Jesus as their Savior," answered Mr. Cohen. "It says that Jesus is the cornerstone of his church. Our actions and attitudes must line up with his."

"So if we act and think like Jesus, we help to build his church the way he wants it. Right?" Jeremy asked.

"Right!" replied Mr. Cohen. "Always let Jesus be your guide."

HOW ABOUT YOU? Do you look to Jesus as your example when you are deciding how to act or think? If you line your actions up with Jesus, you'll be helping to build God's church his way. *D.L.R.*

TO MEMORIZE: We are his house, built on the foundation of the apostles and the prophets. And the cornerstone is Christ Jesus himself. *Ephesians 2:20*

THE CORNERSTONE

FROM THE BIBLE:

So now you Gentiles are no longer strangers and foreigners. You are citizens along with all of God's holy people. You are members of God's family. We are his house, built on the foundation of the apostles and the prophets. And the cornerstone is Christ Jesus himself. We who believe are carefully joined together, becoming a holy temple for the Lord. Through him you Gentiles are also joined together as part of this dwelling where God lives by his Spirit.
EPHESIANS 2:19-22

Live as Jesus would

11 February

SURPRISE DESSERT

FROM THE BIBLE:

I heard a loud shout from the throne, saying, "Look, the home of God is now among his people! He will live with them, and they will be his people. God himself will be with them. . . ."

The wall was made of jasper, and the city was pure gold, as clear as glass. . . .

The twelve gates were made of pearls—each gate from a single pearl! And the main street was pure gold, as clear as glass.

No temple could be seen in the city, for the Lord God Almighty and the Lamb are its temple. And the city has no need of sun or moon, for the glory of God illuminates the city, and the Lamb is its light.

REVELATION 21:3, 18, 21-23

Heaven is wonderful

BEN TOOK a bite of his chicken. "We learned about heaven in Sunday school today," he said, "but there's something I don't understand." He looked at Dad. "I know heaven is supposed to be wonderful. But won't it be boring?"

Dad smiled. "I don't think so," he said. "The Bible tells us that heaven is a joyful place, with no sadness, pain, or jealousy. But the most wonderful part will be getting to be with Jesus."

"Right," agreed Mom. "Think about how glad you always are to go to see Grandpa and Grandma. It will be even more exciting to see Jesus."

"I guess so." Jim shrugged as he ate his mashed potatoes. "I wonder why God didn't tell us more about heaven."

"It would be impossible for us to understand all the wonderful things he has planned for us," said Dad. He looked over at four-year-old Ashley. "Finish your carrots, Ashley. We're almost ready for dessert."

"What is it?" Ashley asked.

Mother smiled. "It's a surprise," she said.

"Can I have mine now, Mom?" asked Ben.

Mother shook her head. "Let's wait till Ashley's ready. If she sees it, she'll get so excited that she won't want to finish her carrots."

A short time later they were all enjoying strawberry shortcake. "I just thought of another reason God didn't tell us exactly what heaven will be like," Ben announced. "If we knew, we'd get so excited that we wouldn't want to finish doing the things God wants us to do now."

HOW ABOUT YOU? Do you wonder what heaven will be like? Until you get there, keep busy doing God's will on earth and telling others about Jesus so they can go to heaven, too! *S.L.K.*

TO MEMORIZE: You will show me the way of life, granting me the joy of your presence and the pleasures of living with you forever. *Psalm 16:11*

EVONNE WAS looking through the box of valentine cards left over from last year. "I just don't know what to do, Mom," she sighed. "Mrs. Thompson said we should bring a valentine for everyone in our class."

"That's not such a bad idea," answered Mom, "although you don't sound very happy about it."

"Well, it's not that I don't want to be friendly, but some of these cards are so mushy!" Evonne wrinkled her nose. "I don't want to give these cards to the boys!"

Mother nodded in agreement. "Why don't you *make* valentine cards to take to school? Then you could write whatever message you'd like. Come on, I'll help you get started."

Mom showed Evonne how to cut paper hearts by folding the paper in half. The table was soon full of pink, red, and white hearts. Next, they taped a piece of cinnamon gum to each heart. The red wrapper added just the right touch. They also used lace and little strawflowers to decorate the valentines. "This is fun, Mom! I think I know what I'd like to write on my valentines, too. I'll put 'God loves you! Happy Valentine's Day!' "

"That's a good idea," said Mom. "And a perfect opportunity to witness to your classmates."

"Yes," replied Evonne, "and it isn't mushy!"

HOW ABOUT YOU? What do you think of on Valentine's Day? Most people think of love. God's love for us is our greatest example of genuine love. He is the source of perfect love. Maybe you can write something about God's love on the valentines you distribute. *D.L.R.*

TO MEMORIZE: Dear friends, let us continue to love one another, for love comes from God. Anyone who loves is born of God and knows God. *1 John 4:7*

12 *February*

VALENTINE HEARTS

FROM THE BIBLE:

Dear friends, let us continue to love one another, for love comes from God. Anyone who loves is born of God and knows God. But anyone who does not love does not know God—for God is love.

God showed how much he loved us by sending his only Son into the world so that we might have eternal life through him. This is real love. It is not that we loved God, but that he loved us and sent his Son as a sacrifice to take away our sins.

Dear friends, since God loved us that much, we surely ought to love each other. No one has ever seen God. But if we love each other, God lives in us, and his love has been brought to full expression through us.

1 JOHN 4:7-12

Tell of God's love

13 February

TRUE LOVE

Love one another

KATRINA sighed happily as she walked into the living room. "I'm in love!" she announced. "Greg's such a wonderful guy. He's always so nice to me."

Mother frowned slightly. "*Love* is a pretty strong word."

Katrina's brother, Joel, laughed. "Katrina thinks that just because she's fifteen, she knows everything about love." He reached down to pat his dog. "Now, me and Ralph here—that's love. He does whatever I tell him. He's always ready to play, and he doesn't talk my ear off like some girl. That's true love."

Shortly afterwards Katrina had a phone call and came back looking upset. "That rotten Greg!" she said. "He took another girl to the basketball game last night and never even asked me! I'll never speak to him again!"

"Ha, ha!" laughed Joel. "All that true love went right down the drain!" Joel was laughing so hard that he didn't see Ralph sitting on the floor beside him. He stepped right on the dog's tail, and Ralph nipped Joel on the leg!

"Ouch! You bad dog!" scolded Joel.

Hearing the commotion, Mother hurried in. "I overheard what you two were talking about. Each of you felt certain that you'd found 'true love.' What happened?"

"Well, I thought I loved Greg, but he made me mad," said Katrina.

"Yeah, that's how I felt about Ralph," agreed Joel.

"I'm afraid that's the way it goes when we use the word *love* too loosely," Mother said. "Real love is constant, like God's love. I'm glad he never stops loving us."

HOW ABOUT YOU? Do you ever wonder what "true love" is? Some people think that love is a feeling, an emotional "high," something that just happens. But the Bible teaches that loving is something you decide to *do. S.L.K.*

TO MEMORIZE: So now I am giving you a new commandment: Love each other. Just as I have loved you, you should love each other. *John 13:34*

JASMINE AND BROOKE giggled as Jasmine slipped an envelope into the "valentine mailbox" their teacher had set up. "I've never seen such an ugly valentine," said Jasmine. "I can hardly wait to see Erin's face when she opens it."

When Jasmine arrived home that afternoon, her mother asked to see her valentines. "Oh, my! This is a pretty one," said Mother, picking one up. "It even has a chocolate heart on it! I'll bet this is your favorite. Who is it from?" She turned it over. "Oh, from Erin."

To her mother's surprise, Jasmine burst into tears. "Oh, Mother," she sobbed, "I've been so mean to Erin lately. I gave her an ugly valentine, and she gave me such a pretty one. She was nice to me today, even after she got my valentine."

Mother put her arm around Jasmine. "Are you sorry for the way you've been acting?" she asked.

Jasmine nodded and wiped her eyes. "I need to apologize. But what can I say?"

When Mother called Jasmine to set the table for supper, Judy bounced into the kitchen. "You seem happier now," observed Mother.

Jasmine smiled. "I called Erin. She said she felt bad when she read the valentine, but she forgave me. We're going to eat lunch together tomorrow. I still can't get over how nice she was to me when I was so mean to her."

"You know," said Mother, "Erin reminds me of Jesus. He loved us even when we were sinners."

HOW ABOUT YOU? Is it hard to admit you're a sinner? God says you are, but he loves you anyway. Confess your sin and receive his forgiveness. *H.W.M.*

TO MEMORIZE: But God showed his great love for us by sending Christ to die for us while we were still sinners. *Romans 5:8*

VALENTINES

FROM THE BIBLE:

Pay all your debts, except the debt of love for others. You can never finish paying that! If you love your neighbor, you will fulfill all the requirements of God's law. For the command- ments against adultery and murder and stealing and coveting—and any other commandment—are all summed up in this one commandment: "Love your neighbor as yourself." Love does no wrong to anyone, so love satisfies all of God's requirements.
ROMANS 13:8-10

Jesus loves you

15 February

THE EMPTY COCOON

FROM THE BIBLE:

Someone may ask, "How will the dead be raised? What kind of bodies will they have?" What a foolish question! When you put a seed into the ground, it doesn't grow into a plant unless it dies first. And what you put in the ground is not the plant that will grow, but only a dry little seed of wheat or whatever it is you are planting. Then God gives it a new body. . . .

There are bodies in the heavens, and there are bodies on earth. The glory of the heavenly bodies is different from the beauty of the earthly bodies. . . .

It is the same way for the resurrection of the dead. Our earthly bodies, which die and decay, will be different when they are resurrected, for they will never die. Our bodies now disappoint us, but when they are raised, they will be full of glory. They are weak now, but when they are raised, they will be full of power. They are natural human bodies now, but when they are raised, they will be spiritual bodies.

1 CORINTHIANS 15:35-38, 40, 42-44

Christians will have new bodies

"EEEEK!" Lisa ran up the porch steps screaming. Kyle chased her with a caterpillar cupped in his hands.

"I don't like caterpillars!" she yelled as she slammed the door behind her. Inside the house, Lisa saw her mother wiping tears from her eyes. "What's the matter, Mom?"

"I just got a phone call. Grannie Carter died."

"Oh, nooo!" Lisa moaned. Grannie Carter was one of her favorite people.

Mother smiled faintly. "Well, at least Grannie knew the Lord. She's happy."

Lisa and Kyle had never been to a funeral service before. When the time came, they found that, except for the casket and all the flowers, it wasn't too different from a regular church service. Afterwards, everyone went to the cemetery, where the casket was lowered into a hole in the ground.

Later that afternoon as Lisa, Kyle, and Mother ate lunch, Lisa said, "I thought Grannie was in heaven, but she was put in the ground." As Mother began to answer, Kyle pointed at a brown object hanging from a branch outside the window.

"What is that?" Lisa asked.

"It's an empty cocoon," said Kyle. "At one time, it was a caterpillar. It spun a cocoon around itself. After a while the cocoon burst open, and a beautiful butterfly came out."

"That's a good example of what has happened to Grannie Carter," said Mother. "She has left her cocoon, her earthly body. It was buried today, but the real Grannie has flown away to be with Jesus."

HOW ABOUT YOU? Has someone you love died and gone to heaven? Don't worry about the old body that was buried in a grave. God will give that person a wonderful new body someday. *B.J.W.*

TO MEMORIZE: Our bodies now disappoint us, but when they are raised, they will be full of glory. They are weak now, but when they are raised, they will be full of power. *1 Corinthians 15:43*

NO DIFFERENCE

AT A SPECIAL meeting at Jenny's church, Derek, one of the roughest boys at school, surprised everyone by becoming a Christian.

After the service, Jenny walked home with her friend Brittany, who had only recently started coming to their church. Jenny was surprised to hear her new friend's comments. "Maybe Derek's behavior will improve now that he's a Christian," said Brittany. "His family is very poor, you know, and his dad drinks. I'm glad I don't have a family like that. I'm glad I was born a Christian."

"Nobody is born a Christian," objected Jenny.

Brittany shrugged. "Oh, I know some people think that, but I don't agree."

The next week the circus came to their city. Brittany invited Jenny to go with her. The girls arrived just in time. "Oh no!" groaned Brittany as the gatekeeper waited for their tickets. "I forgot the tickets!" She explained the situation to the gatekeeper, asking if they could please go on in and bring the tickets later. As he shook his head, Brittany squared her shoulders and looked him straight in the eye. "Do you know who I am?" she asked haughtily. "I'm the mayor's daughter!"

"Well, Miss Mayor's Daughter, show me your ticket, and you can get in."

After walking away in silence, Jenny glanced at Brittany. "It didn't matter who you were, did it?" she asked quietly. "If the gatekeeper wouldn't let you into the circus even though you were the mayor's daughter, what makes you think God will let you into heaven just because you come from a Christian family?"

FROM THE BIBLE:

As the Scriptures say,

"No one is good—
   not even one.
No one has real understanding;
   no one is seeking God.
All have turned away from God;
   all have gone wrong.
No one does good,
   not even one."

ROMANS 3:10-12

You are a sinner

HOW ABOUT YOU? Do you think you were born a Christian? You weren't. The Bible says it makes no difference who you are. Whether you're from the best home in town or the worst, you need to accept Jesus into your heart. *H.W.M.*

TO MEMORIZE: All have sinned; all fall short of God's glorious standard. *Romans 3:23*

17 February

A HEAVY BURDEN

FROM THE BIBLE:

*Don't worry about anything;
instead, pray about everything.
Tell God what you need, and
thank him for all he has done. If
you do this, you will experience
God's peace, which is far more
wonderful than the human mind
can understand. His peace will
guard your hearts and minds as
you live in Christ Jesus.*
PHILIPPIANS 4:6-7

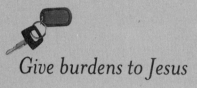

Give burdens to Jesus

"**MOM,** I wish Dad still lived here," said Roberto as he finished getting ready for school. "If I had just behaved better, maybe he wouldn't have left."

"Honey, Dad's leaving had nothing to do with you. He loves you as much as ever," Mom said patiently, putting an arm around Roberto. She and Dad had told Roberto this many times. He wanted to believe them, but he just couldn't.

Thoughts of his dad often popped up at school between the sentences Roberto was reading. He finally got his mind off his problems when his teacher showed the class an interesting book on wild animals. And he was thrilled when she said he could take it home for the evening.

Roberto tucked the heavy book under his arm and began walking home. As he walked, the book seemed to grow heavier and heavier. By the time he reached home, his arm ached.

Mom met him at the end of the driveway. "That book looks heavy," she said. "Let me help you." She reached down and took it. "Guilty feelings can also be heavy to carry," she continued. "The feeling that Dad left because of you is a burden too heavy for you to carry."

"I wish I didn't have that feeling," Roberto said. "It hurts."

"Yes, just like your arm hurts from carrying the book. Wouldn't you like Jesus to carry the burden for you?" Roberto nodded, and together they asked Jesus to carry Roberto's heavy burden.

HOW ABOUT YOU? Do you have a burden too heavy for you? If your parents are separated or divorced, do you wonder if it's your fault? Or perhaps secret worries about school or friends constantly fill your mind. It's important to talk about heavy burdens to an adult who can help you turn them over to Jesus. *K.R.A.*

TO MEMORIZE: Give all your worries and cares to God, for he cares about what happens to you.
1 Peter 5:7

HIGH FASHION

IT WAS Saturday afternoon, and Mandy was slumped in the rocker, trying to read. Her mom knelt on the floor, surrounded by fabric, pattern pieces, tape measure, scissors, and pins. She was cutting out a blouse to sew for herself. Mandy laid down her book and said, "I don't know how you do it, Mom. How do you turn all that confusion into something beautiful to wear?"

"I just follow the instructions," Mom said, holding up a printed paper. "See, this paper says which pieces to use and how to cut and fit them together. If I do what it says, my blouse will look like the one in the picture."

"That's because you're a good seamstress," Mandy answered. After a bit, she looked up again. "Hey, I wonder if that's what my teacher was talking about in Sunday school last week."

"What's that, Mandy?" her mother asked.

"She told us how God has in mind a plan for the wonderful person each of us could be. That's like the picture of the finished blouse on the pattern, isn't it? She also said that to become the person God wants us to be, we need to obey him and do what he tells us in the Bible. That's like following the instructions on the pattern."

"That's right!" exclaimed Mom. "God is fashioning us into something special. Even when things look impossible—like this blouse does to you now—we can know that he will make us into a beautiful finished product. That's a wonderful illustration, Mandy."

HOW ABOUT YOU? Are you letting God fashion you into the person you could be? Do you look for his instructions in his Word and ask him to help you follow them? *J.K.B.*

TO MEMORIZE: For we are God's masterpiece. He has created us anew in Christ Jesus, so that we can do the good things he planned for us long ago. *Ephesians 2:10*

FROM THE BIBLE:

You used to live just like the rest of the world, full of sin, obeying Satan, the mighty prince of the power of the air. He is the spirit at work in the hearts of those who refuse to obey God. All of us used to live that way, following the passions and desires of our evil nature. . . .

But God is so rich in mercy, and he loved us so very much, that even while we were dead because of our sins, he gave us life when he raised Christ from the dead. (It is only by God's special favor that you have been saved!) For he raised us from the dead along with Christ, and we are seated with him in the heavenly realms—all because we are one with Christ Jesus. And so God can always point to us as examples of the incredible wealth of his favor and kindness toward us, as shown in all he has done for us through Christ Jesus. . . .

For we are God's masterpiece. He has created us anew in Christ Jesus, so that we can do the good things he planned for us long ago.
EPHESIANS 2:2-7, 10

Follow God's instructions

19 February

THE ACTIVITY BOX

FROM THE BIBLE:

Then Jesus said, "Come to me, all of you who are weary and carry heavy burdens, and I will give you rest. Take my yoke upon you. Let me teach you, because I am humble and gentle, and you will find rest for your souls. For my yoke fits perfectly, and the burden I give you is light."
MATTHEW 11:28-30

Work cheerfully

AS MOM put bread in the toaster, she said brightly, "We have a lot to do."

"We always do on Saturday," Jessica complained.

"Yeah," murmured Justin. "I hate Saturdays!"

Dad poured a cup of coffee. "I don't like them, either, because they're days of whining and grumbling," he said.

Justin scowled. "Stop the work, and I'll stop the grumbling."

Dad ignored him. "Please find me a shoe box, Justin. Jessica, you can bring me some paper and a pencil." When they returned, Dad said, "Let's write everything we have to do today on slips of paper and put them in this box."

"Change the sheets. Vacuum the carpet. Clean the bathroom." Mom quickly named several tasks.

"Sweep the garage. Sweep the patio. Wash the car," added Dad. "Now, we'll take turns drawing out a slip."

"When the box is empty, we can have a picnic," suggested Mom.

"Yippee!" yelled the children.

"I want to pick first." Jessica reached for the box.

Dad held up his hand. "We forgot something," he said. "We need to give the Lord some time, too."

"Read a chapter in your Bible." Jessica wrote on a slip of paper.

"Stop and give thanks for our family," wrote Justin.

Then Dad held the box out to Jessica. "This is going to be the best Saturday we've had in a long time," she said as she drew out a slip and looked at it. Then she grinned. "Even if I do have to clean the bathroom!"

HOW ABOUT YOU? If your tasks have become boring, make an activity box. List on slips of paper everything you have to do. Then take out one paper at a time and do that task. Keep going until everything is done, and work cheerfully! *B.J.W.*

TO MEMORIZE: Whatever you do, do well. For when you go to the grave, there will be no work or planning or knowledge or wisdom. *Ecclesiastes 9:10*

BRENT NEVER FORGOT the day his new baby sister, Emily, came home from the hospital. Dad and Mom had told him that her spinal cord was damaged before she was born and she would never be able to walk.

Brent couldn't quite believe it. *Maybe if they all took really good care of Emily, her legs would become well,* he thought. When Brent mentioned this to his mother, she shook her head sadly. "No, the doctor said that her legs will never work. Instead of thinking about that, let's remember that this is God's plan for Emily and our family."

"How can it be God's plan?" Brent asked.

Mom sat down next to Brent. "Emily is going to need special care because her legs have no feeling," she said. "She will not know if they are hot or cold or if they have been bruised. That's where you and I fit into God's plan for her," said Mom. "It will take time and love to protect her and to help her learn about her disability."

"Oh," murmured Brent.

"Will you help Emily?" Brent's mother asked.

Brent was quiet for a while. Then he said, "I wish Emily could learn to walk. But since she can't, I want to help her."

"Great!" said Mom, squeezing his shoulder. "God knew Emily would need a big brother like you."

HOW ABOUT YOU? Do you have a brother, sister, or friend who is disabled? God has placed that person in your life as part of his plan for you. As you love and encourage your disabled sibling or friend, God will use you to be a blessing. Or, perhaps you have a disability yourself. God wants to use you to be a blessing, too. J.A.G.

TO MEMORIZE: Encourage those who are timid. Take tender care of those who are weak. Be patient with everyone. *1 Thessalonians 5:14*

20 February

GOD'S PLAN

FROM THE BIBLE:

Oh, what a wonderful God we have! How great are his riches and wisdom and knowledge! How impossible it is for us to understand his decisions and his methods! For who can know what the Lord is thinking? Who knows enough to be his counselor? And who could ever give him so much that he would have to pay it back? For everything comes from him; everything exists by his power and is intended for his glory. To him be glory evermore. Amen.

ROMANS 11:33-36

Accept God's plan

21 February

JUST LIKE JESUS
(PART 1)

FROM THE BIBLE:

*After washing their feet, he put
on his robe again and sat down
and asked, "Do you understand
what I was doing? You call me
'Teacher' and 'Lord,' and you
are right, because it is true. And
since I, the Lord and Teacher,
have washed your feet, you ought
to wash each other's feet. I have
given you an example to follow.
Do as I have done to you. How
true it is that a servant is not
greater than the master. Nor are
messengers more important than
the one who sends them. You
know these things—now do
them! That is the path of
blessing."*
JOHN 13:12-17

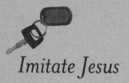

Imitate Jesus

BETHANY laughed as she watched her little brother, Nathan, playing in the living room. He had climbed up into Dad's favorite chair and was pretending to read the newspaper. He shouted, "I'm just like Daddy!"

Bethany just couldn't resist giving Nathan a big hug. "Wait right there so we can show Mommy what a big boy you are."

By the time Bethany returned to the living room with her mother, Nathan had put the paper down on his lap and was pretending to fall asleep. He was even leaning back with his hands behind his head; just like Dad did when he was finished reading the paper.

"Isn't that cute, Mom?" whispered Bethany, giggling. "He's trying to be just like Dad."

Mom smiled. "That's how children learn. They imitate people."

"Did I ever do that?" asked Bethany.

"Sure you did," replied Mom. "You used to pretend you were making dinner. You would get the pots and pans out of the cupboard and tell me that you were making mashed potatoes." Bethany went over to pick up her brother as Mom continued to speak. "That reminds me of an important lesson in the Bible, Bethany. As Christians, we need to imitate Jesus in order to learn how to live as mature Christians."

"But we can't see Jesus, so how can we imitate him?" Bethany asked. "Oh, wait—I know. We have the Bible. That tells us how he lived."

HOW ABOUT YOU? Are you learning to imitate Jesus? Studying God's Word will help you. Then when you are in a situation at school or at home, try to think of what Jesus would do if he were in your place. Imitate him. *D.L.R.*

TO MEMORIZE: Follow God's example in everything you do, because you are his dear children. *Ephesians 5:1*

JUST LIKE JESUS
(PART 2)

BETHANY gave a lot of thought to her mother's words about learning to be like Jesus, and she was eager to be more like him. She decided to read about Jesus in the Gospel of John. Every time she read about something Jesus did that she could follow, she wrote it down in a little notebook.

Thursday morning Mr. Singleton, the school principal, brought a new girl named Kim into Bethany's class. Some kids snickered because Kim's clothes were out of style, and she had straggly hair.

As Kim found a seat, Melissa slipped Bethany a note with a mean remark about Kim. Bethany smiled at her friend, but she wished that she hadn't. She had just read about how Jesus had been friendly to a Samaritan woman. Jesus was Jewish, and in those days Jewish people didn't associate with people from Samaria. But Jesus talked with her anyway. Bethany had written in her notebook: "Be friendly to everyone, even when others are not."

Dear Lord, she prayed silently, *I think you would want me to be Kim's friend. Please give me courage to make her feel welcome.*

As soon as the bell rang, Bethany made her way toward Kim. "Hi," she said, introducing herself. "Would you like to go to lunch with me?"

In the following days, Melissa and some of Bethany's other friends acted snobbishly toward Kim. But Bethany continued to treat her as a friend. It wasn't long before all of the girls accepted Kim, too.

HOW ABOUT YOU? Do you find it hard to make friends with someone who might seem different, especially when some of your other friends make fun of that person? Jesus would be friendly, though, and he wants you to be kind to others, too. Follow his example. Be friendly even if others are not. *D.L.R.*

TO MEMORIZE: Love each other with genuine affection, and take delight in honoring each other. *Romans 12:10*

FROM THE BIBLE:

Soon a Samaritan woman came to draw water, and Jesus said to her, "Please give me a drink." He was alone at the time because his disciples had gone into the village to buy some food.

The woman was surprised, for Jews refuse to have anything to do with Samaritans. She said to Jesus, "You are a Jew, and I am a Samaritan woman. Why are you asking me for a drink?"

Jesus replied, "If you only knew the gift God has for you and who I am, you would ask me, and I would give you living water."

"But sir, you don't have a rope or a bucket," she said, "and this is a very deep well. Where would you get this living water? And besides, are you greater than our ancestor Jacob who gave us this well? How can you offer better water than he and his sons and his cattle enjoyed?"

Jesus replied, "People soon become thirsty again after drinking this water. But the water I give them takes away thirst altogether. It becomes a perpetual spring within them, giving them eternal life." JOHN 4:7-14

Be friendly

23 February

CURIOSITY'S CAPTIVE

FROM THE BIBLE:

Later, as Jesus left the town, he saw a tax collector named Levi sitting at his tax-collection booth. "Come, be my disciple!" Jesus said to him. So Levi got up, left everything, and followed him.

Soon Levi held a banquet in his home with Jesus as the guest of honor. Many of Levi's fellow tax collectors and other guests were there. But the Pharisees and their teachers of religious law complained bitterly to Jesus' disciples, "Why do you eat and drink with such scum?"

Jesus answered them, "Healthy people don't need a doctor—sick people do."

LUKE 5:27-31

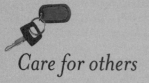

Care for others

"**UNCLE JERRY** makes me so mad!" said Jana as she slammed down the telephone. "That was Cheri, and she was crying. The electric company will turn off their electricity if they don't pay their bill by tomorrow. Uncle Jerry's out drinking with his buddies again."

Dad looked over the edge of the newspaper. "I feel sorry for Jerry," he said.

Jana huffed. "I feel sorry for his *family! Uncle Jerry is selfish and mean!*"

"We need to pray for him. He's in bondage to alcohol," Dad reminded her.

"He could get loose if he wanted to! He just—" Jana was interrupted by a banging sound from the garage. "What's that?"

"I don't know," Mother said, concerned. "We had better find out." When they opened the door, they saw their dog with a plastic pitcher over his head, bumping into everything.

Mother gathered the frightened dog in her arms. Dad got out his pocketknife and carefully cut the pitcher from the dog's neck.

"Rudy must have stuck his nose in the pitcher, then pushed it up against something as he pushed his head farther inside," said Jana.

Dad nodded. "Scolding him and telling him how foolish he was wouldn't have helped him at all," he observed. "He was caught and couldn't do anything to help himself. He needed us to help him. You know, Uncle Jerry is like Rudy. He is caught in a trap so powerful he cannot break loose. God can deliver him. And if God wants to use us to help, he will show us how."

HOW ABOUT YOU? Do you know people who are caught in the trap of sin? It might be alcohol or drugs or other things. Ask God to give you compassion for them, and pray for them. *B.J.W.*

TO MEMORIZE: Finally, all of you should be of one mind, full of sympathy toward each other, loving one another with tender hearts and humble minds. *1 Peter 3:8*

TWO CAMERAS

"**MY NEW** camera says 'automatic focus.' That means I don't have to focus it, right?" Jennifer asked.

"Correct," Dad told her. "No matter how close or how far you are from your subject, you won't have to adjust anything to get a clear picture."

"Oh, good! My old camera gave me a lot of trouble with that," exclaimed Jennifer. "I also had trouble making the right light adjustments."

Dad responded, "There's a mechanism on this camera that 'senses' how light it is. It opens or closes the shutter to let in more or less light."

"My science teacher said that our eyes work a lot like a camera does," Jennifer said. "The colored part of the eye called the iris is like the shutter. When the light is real bright, it makes the pupil get smaller. When it's dark, the iris opens wide to let in more light through the pupil."

"The eyes God has given us are very unique," added Dad. "And just as the pictures you take with your camera are recorded on a film, so the pictures taken by your eyes are recorded on your brain. That's why I don't let you read inappropriate books or watch offensive TV programs. I want your brain to be imprinted with better things."

"I hadn't thought about the eyes recording a picture on my brain," Jennifer said. "I'm going to be more careful with the camera in my head."

HOW ABOUT YOU? If you have the gift of sight, do you thank God for it? Close your eyes and think how different life would be if you could never open them again! You can thank God best by using your eyes to look at things that are good and wholesome and pure! *C.V.M.*

TO MEMORIZE: I will refuse to look at anything vile and vulgar. I hate all crooked dealings; I will have nothing to do with them. *Psalm 101:3*

FROM THE BIBLE:

*I will sing of your love and
    justice.
    I will praise you, Lord, with
    songs.
I will be careful to live a
    blameless life—
    when will you come to my
    aid?
I will lead a life of integrity
    in my own home.
I will refuse to look at
    anything vile and vulgar.
I hate all crooked dealings;
    I will have nothing to do with
    them.
I will reject perverse ideas
    and stay away from every evil.
I will not tolerate people who
    slander their neighbors.
    I will not endure conceit and
    pride.*

*I will keep a protective eye on the
    godly,
    so they may dwell with me in
    safety.
Only those who are above
    reproach
    will be allowed to serve me.
I will not allow deceivers to serve
    me,
    and liars will not be allowed
    to enter my presence.*
PSALM 101:1-7

Look at good things

25 February

THE ROAD TRIP

FROM THE BIBLE:

"I said, 'Plant the good seeds of righteousness, and you will harvest a crop of my love. Plow up the hard ground of your hearts, for now is the time to seek the Lord, that he may come and shower righteousness upon you.'

"But you have cultivated wickedness and raised a thriving crop of sins. You have eaten the fruit of lies—trusting in your military might, believing that great armies could make your nation safe!"

HOSEA 10:12-13

Talk pleasantly

AS THE JACKSON family traveled along, Tyrone and Tracy seemed to quarrel constantly. It was a relief when they reached Cripple Creek.

"This is an old gold mining town," Dad explained as he parked the car.

"May we ride the train?" Tyrone asked. Soon they were all seated on wooden benches in an open car behind an old steam engine. The engineer served as guide. As they entered a small valley, the train came to a stop. "This is Echo Valley," the engineer told them. "Listen."

He pulled the train's whistle. *Wuwoooooooo.* A few seconds later they heard a faint reply: *Wuwoooooooo.*

Tracy laughed. "Let me try." She cupped her hands around her mouth and called loudly, "Hello!"

"Hello," came the faint reply.

"My turn," said Tyrone. "Good-byeee!"

"Good-byeee," the echo repeated.

Later the family piled into the car. "Let's get cleaned up before dinner," Mom suggested.

"But I'm hungry now," whined Tracy.

"Big baby," Tyrone mocked.

"Big baby yourself!" said Tracy.

"Listen to the echoes." said Mom. "I hear ugly, hateful words echoing through this car. When we say mean words, we will hear mean words in return. When we send out nice, kind words, we get nice, kind words in return."

HOW ABOUT YOU? What kinds of words have you been sending out? Would you like them returned to you? *B.J.W.*

TO MEMORIZE: Give, and it will be given to you. A good measure, pressed down, shaken together and running over, will be poured into your lap. For with the measure you use, it will be measured to you. *Luke 6:38* (NIV)

"**AM I** doing this right, Grandma?"

Grandma examined the crocheted collar Amanda handed her. "Looks good to me," she said.

"What do I do next?" asked Amanda.

"Make the next row exactly like this one," Grandma replied. "By next week when I go to stay with your Aunt Denise and Darci, you should be able to follow the pattern by yourself."

"We wish you could stay with us all the time, don't we, Mittens?" Amanda brushed her bare toes over the fur of the cat at her feet. "Darci is so stuck-up. In fact, Darci is nothing but a spoiled brat. She . . ."

"That's enough, Amanda!" Grandma said sternly. "Remember, Darci is my granddaughter, and I love her as much as I love you."

"But you don't know what she did . . . ," began Amanda.

"Dinner is ready!" Mother's call from the kitchen interrupted Amanda.

After dinner, Amanda and Grandma returned to the family room. "I'm going to work on my— oh no! Look, Grandma!" Amanda pointed at the cat, who was playing with a mass of tangled thread. "Mittens unraveled all my hard work!"

Grandma smiled sympathetically. "It takes time and careful thought to crochet a lace collar, but anyone—even a cat—can unravel one."

"That's for sure," said Amanda, picking up the mess.

"It's like that with everything," Grandma continued. "It always takes more effort to build up than to tear down. It's easy to be hurtful and find fault with people, but God wants us to help build people up."

Amanda sighed. "I'll try to do better, Grandma. "Now, back to my collar."

HOW ABOUT YOU? Do you say hurtful things about others? This would be a good day to start building people up rather than tearing them down. *B.J.W.*

TO MEMORIZE: So encourage each other and build each other up, just as you are already doing. *1 Thessalonians 5:11*

HURTFUL WORDS

FROM THE BIBLE:

No one can tame the tongue. It is an uncontrollable evil, full of deadly poison. Sometimes it praises our Lord and Father, and sometimes it breaks out into curses against those who have been made in the image of God. And so blessing and cursing come pouring out of the same mouth. Surely, my brothers and sisters, this is not right! . . .

If you are wise and understand God's ways, live a life of steady goodness so that only good deeds will pour forth. And if you don't brag about the good you do, then you will be truly wise! But if you are bitterly jealous and there is selfish ambition in your hearts, don't brag about being wise. That is the worst kind of lie. For jealousy and selfishness are not God's kind of wisdom. Such things are earthly, unspiritual, and motivated by the Devil. . . .

But the wisdom that comes from heaven is first of all pure. It is also peace loving, gentle at all times, and willing to yield to others. It is full of mercy and good deeds. JAMES 3:8-17

Build up others

27 February

LISTEN AND LEARN

FROM THE BIBLE:

"Come to me with your ears wide open. Listen, for the life of your soul is at stake. . . ."

Seek the Lord while you can find him. Call on him now while he is near. Let the people turn from their wicked deeds. Let them banish from their minds the very thought of doing wrong! Let them turn to the Lord that he may have mercy on them. Yes, turn to our God, for he will abundantly pardon.

"My thoughts are completely different from yours," says the Lord. "And my ways are far beyond anything you could imagine. For just as the heavens are higher than the earth, so are my ways higher than your ways and my thoughts higher than your thoughts.

"The rain and snow come down from the heavens and stay on the ground to water the earth. They cause the grain to grow, producing seed for the farmer and bread for the hungry. It is the same with my word. I send it out, and it always produces fruit. It will accomplish all I want it to, and it will prosper everywhere I send it."

ISAIAH 55:3, 6-11

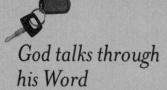

God talks through his Word

MOTHER CAME to tuck Kevin in, a nightly ritual in the Bronson home. "Kevin, you used to have your Bible propped on your lap when I came in to say good night," said Mother. "What's happened?"

"Well, I pray after you leave," replied Kevin. "But why should I read the Bible? I can't understand it." As he spoke, in came Ginger, his golden retriever. "Hey, Ginger, old girl," Kevin said, scratching her back. "Nice girl." Ginger wagged her tail and licked the air with her tongue as she tried to slobber Kevin's face. Suddenly she could contain herself no longer. She leaped onto Kevin's lap. Kevin fell back against the pillows laughing while Mother coaxed his pet out the door.

Mother came back and closed the door. "Kevin, when you talk to Ginger, does she understand every word you say?"

"No, but I like to talk to her anyway," replied Kevin. "She always listens. And she does understand a lot of things—like *come, sit, fetch, walk,* and *roll over.* She keeps learning new words, too."

Mother picked up Kevin's Bible. "Kevin, do you know that God talks to us through his Word?"

Kevin looked at the Bible in his mother's hand. He grinned. "I get the point, Mom. God likes to talk to me just as I like to talk to Ginger. And like Ginger, I don't understand everything, but I do understand some of God's commands. I need to keep learning new things from him."

HOW ABOUT YOU? Have you stopped reading God's Word just because you can't understand everything? The more you let God speak to you, the more you will understand. He's pleased when you "listen." *P.R.*

TO MEMORIZE: You must remain faithful to the things you have been taught. You know they are true, for you know you can trust those who taught you. *2 Timothy 3:14*

RICK AND Yolanda were helping their dad in his meat shop. Part of their job was to take the trash out to the big bin behind the store. Rick lifted the trash bin cover, then he slammed it back down quickly. "Yolanda, there's something in there!"

"You're just trying to scare me," laughed Yolanda.

"I'm telling the truth," Rick persisted, grabbing a stick. Bravely he pulled up the lid and poked at the rubbish with the stick. A high-pitched squeal jarred the air, and Yolanda screamed.

Dad rushed outside. "What's wrong?" he asked in alarm.

"Something's in the trash," Yolanda yelled.

Looking doubtful, Dad approached the trash bin and looked inside. "Why, it's a puppy!" he exclaimed. "Let's see if we can help him."

"Can we take him home, Dad?" Rick begged. "He looks like a stray."

"Ugh!" Yolanda made a face. "He smells! I bet Mom won't want him."

"He's a mess all right," said Dad. "We'll clean him up and see if we can find him a home."

When they arrived home, the children told their mother all about the puppy. At her suggestion they named him Ragamuffin. "You know, children, Ragamuffin would make a good illustration for my Sunday school lesson tomorrow," said Mom as she looked at the pup. "What you did for Ragamuffin, God did for us—and even more! God found us spiritually dirty, lost, and trapped in our sins. Yet he reached down to rescue us. He loved us when there was nothing lovable about us."

Ragamuffin barked and Yolanda laughed. "He agrees with you, Mom. I think Ragamuffin is glad he's been found!"

HOW ABOUT YOU? Have you been "found"? God sent Jesus to rescue you from sin. Have you accepted his forgiveness and trusted him as Savior? *J.L.H.*

TO MEMORIZE: When we were utterly helpless, Christ came at just the right time and died for us sinners. *Romans 5:6*

RAGAMUFFIN
(PART 1)

FROM THE BIBLE:

When we were utterly helpless, Christ came at just the right time and died for us sinners. Now, no one is likely to die for a good person, though someone might be willing to die for a person who is especially good. But God showed his great love for us by sending Christ to die for us while we were still sinners. And since we have been made right in God's sight by the blood of Christ, he will certainly save us from God's judgment. For since we were restored to friendship with God by the death of his Son while we were still his enemies, we will certainly be delivered from eternal punishment by his life. So now we can rejoice in our wonderful new relationship with God—all because of what our Lord Jesus Christ has done for us in making us friends of God.
ROMANS 5:6-11

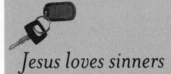

Jesus loves sinners

29 February

RAGAMUFFIN
(PART 2)

FROM THE BIBLE:

Praise the Lord!

I will thank the Lord with all my heart
*   as I meet with his godly people.*
How amazing are the deeds of the Lord!
*   All who delight in him should ponder them.*
Everything he does reveals his glory and majesty.
*   His righteousness never fails.*
Who can forget the wonders he performs?
*   How gracious and merciful is our Lord!*
He gives food to those who trust him;
*   he always remembers his covenant.*
He has shown his great power to his people
*   by giving them the lands of other nations.*
All he does is just and good,
*   and all his commandments are trustworthy.*
They are forever true,
*   to be obeyed faithfully and with integrity. . . .*
Reverence for the Lord is the foundation of true wisdom.
*   The rewards of wisdom come to all who obey him.*

Praise his name forever!
PSALM 111:1-10

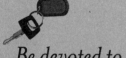

Be devoted to God

RICK AND Yolanda enjoyed romping with Ragamuffin, the stray puppy they found. They taught him tricks and took him on walks. They were delighted that no one answered the newspaper ad seeking Ragamuffin's owners.

But not everything was pleasant. Ragamuffin got into trouble. Sometimes he tracked mud into the house or knocked things over and broke them. Though Rick and Yolanda were patient, they often had to punish their puppy.

During dinner one day, the children scolded Ragamuffin for snitching food off the table. They worried that their dog might not like them after being punished. But Ragamuffin was as loyal as ever. He ran to meet them, wagging his tail and following them around. "Ragamuffin makes us feel like we're really important to him," observed Rick.

"You are," said Mom. "You rescued him and you take care of him. Ragamuffin knows that, and he loves you in return."

"Reminds me of someone who has rescued us," said Dad. Seeing the children's puzzled looks, he continued, "Our heavenly Father loves us. He saved us, and he provides for us. But I wonder if we remind God how important he is to us?"

"I never thought of it like that," Yolanda said. "I guess I sometimes act mad when God doesn't let things work out the way I want them to."

"And sometimes I get impatient when God doesn't answer my prayers right away," admitted Rick.

Mom nodded. "I'm afraid we're all guilty. We need to learn to give to God the kind of unconditional devotion that Ragamuffin gives to you."

HOW ABOUT YOU? Is God important to you? Do you give him your time? your love? your obedience? your service? Do you praise him with your lips and your life? Do you love and help others as he told you to? *J.L.H.*

TO MEMORIZE: We love each other as a result of his loving us first. *1 John 4:19*

1 March

BREENA hung up the phone. "We're trying to figure out what to do about Laura," she told her mother. "Laura is being a 'sometimes' friend. She only wants to be our friend when she needs help with homework. The rest of the time she acts as though we don't even exist."

As Breena crawled under the covers a little later, Mother appeared at her door. "Have you had your quiet time with the Lord today?" asked Mother.

Breena yawned and glanced at the Bible on the nightstand. "I'll read in the morning," she said. "I'm too tired tonight."

The next morning Breena overslept. As she hurried downstairs, she tripped. "Ouch!" she wailed. "My ankle!" Mother hurried to help. "Dear God," prayed Breena while Mother put ice packs on it, "please take the pain away."

Unable to walk, Breena stayed home from school. "Honey," said Mother after making her comfortable on the couch, "I was thinking about the problem with your 'sometimes' friend Laura."

Breena sighed. "What about it?"

"Well," Mother continued, "I wonder if you have become a 'sometimes' friend of God's. Last night you were too tired to talk to God. But you had time to talk to him when you needed help this morning."

"I think you're right, Mother. I need to be an all-the-time friend with God."

ALL-THE-TIME FRIEND

FROM THE BIBLE:

Always be joyful. Keep on praying. No matter what happens, always be thankful, for this is God's will for you who belong to Christ Jesus.
Do not stifle the Holy Spirit.
1 THESSALONIANS 5:16-19

Pray always

HOW ABOUT YOU? Do you talk to God as you do to a friend, or do you pray only when you have a need? Thank him for the things you see on your way to school. Share your thoughts about people and things that happen. *N.E.K.*

TO MEMORIZE: Keep on praying.
1 Thessalonians 5:17

2 March

THE BALLOON THAT BURST

FROM THE BIBLE:

He gives us more and more strength to stand against such evil desires. As the Scriptures say,

"God sets himself against the proud,
but he shows favor to the humble."

So humble yourselves before God. Resist the Devil, and he will flee from you. Draw close to God, and God will draw close to you. Wash your hands, you sinners; purify your hearts, you hypocrites. Let there be tears for the wrong things you have done. Let there be sorrow and deep grief. Let there be sadness instead of laughter, and gloom instead of joy. When you bow down before the Lord and admit your dependence on him, he will lift you up and give you honor.
JAMES 4:6-10

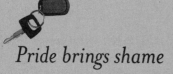

Pride brings shame

"**I WAS SURE** I'd win the Bible quiz contest last night," said Gayle with a sigh. "I can't figure out what went wrong."

"Yeah," agreed Kristen. "You always win everything."

"Now Debbie will be honored at the church party tonight instead of me," Gayle added.

Miss Lindsey came in the room with some crepe paper streamers. "Hurry, girls," she urged. "The party begins soon. You can hang these while I blow up some balloons. Tell me about the contest. I couldn't attend last night."

"I was awful," Gayle said as she taped a streamer to the ceiling. "I couldn't remember the answers, and I misquoted Bible verses."

"But she's smarter than Debbie," said Kristen.

"Sure I am," said Gayle confidently.

"Did you study for the contest?" asked Miss Lindsey.

"Oh, I don't need to study anymore," said Gayle. "I know the Bible."

"How much did you pray about the quiz?"

"Pray? Well, not much." Gayle was a little embarrassed.

Miss Lindsey looked at the balloon she was blowing up. She blew hard, and it grew bigger and bigger. Then, *BANG!* It burst into little pieces. "Well! The balloon was puffed up so much that it burst," observed Miss Lindsey. "You know, Gayle, I think that may be your trouble, too. You were puffed up with pride. You thought you were so smart you didn't need to study or pray."

Gayle picked up a fragment of the balloon. "I think you're right."

HOW ABOUT YOU? Being proud of our accomplishments is a good thing. But bragging about or using them as an excuse not to work hard is the wrong kind of pride. Which kind of pride do you have? *M.R.P.*

TO MEMORIZE: Pride ends in humiliation, while humility brings honor. *Proverbs 29:23*

"PAM, IT'S TIME to leave for the missionary meeting at church," called Mother. "Are you ready?" When Pam didn't respond, Mother headed for her room. Hearing her mother's footsteps approaching, Pam slipped a book under her pillow and quickly changed the dial on her radio. "What were you doing?" Mother asked.

"Oh, I was just looking for some good music," said Pam.

"Well, are you ready to leave for church?" asked Mother.

Pam reluctantly stood up. "I suppose," she muttered. But she was grouchy all the way to church because she really wanted to stay home.

Pam expected to be bored, but when the missionary showed slides, she watched intently. "Many of our people worship idols, practice black magic, and dabble in the spirit world," the missionary said. "When they accept Christ as Savior and become new creatures in him, they no longer want to do many of the things they did before. This last slide shows a big bonfire where they're burning their idols, magic books, and special potions. They're often persecuted for their stand, but Jesus means more to them than worldly possessions or popularity." He turned off the projector and waited for the lights to come on. Then he asked, "Is there anything you need to get rid of?"

Pam thought about the hard rock music she had been listening to earlier. She remembered the book she didn't want her mother to see. Pam bowed her head to pray. She, too, had some idols to destroy in her life.

NO MORE IDOLS

FROM THE BIBLE:

"Do not worship any other gods besides me.

"Do not make idols of any kind, whether in the shape of birds or animals or fish. You must never worship or bow down to them, for I, the Lord your God, am a jealous God who will not share your affection with any other god! I do not leave unpunished the sins of those who hate me, but I punish the children for the sins of their parents to the third and fourth generations."
EXODUS 20:3-5

Put away your idols

HOW ABOUT YOU? Does Jesus have first place in your life, or are you letting TV, video games, or friends control your thinking and actions? Are they coming before God? Examine your life. If there are some "idols" you need to put away, take care of it today.
J.L.H.

TO MEMORIZE: Dear children, keep away from anything that might take God's place in your hearts.
1 John 5:21

4 March

THE TEST

FROM THE BIBLE:

*O Lord my God, if I have
    done wrong
    or am guilty of injustice,
if I have betrayed a friend
    or plundered my enemy
    without cause,
then let my enemies capture me.
    Let them trample me into the
        ground.
    Let my honor be left in the dust.*

*Arise, O Lord, in anger!
    Stand up against the fury
        of my enemies!
    Wake up, my God, and bring
        justice!
Gather the nations before you.
    Sit on your throne high above
        them.
The Lord passes judgment on the
        nations.
    Declare me righteous, O Lord,
        for I am innocent, O Most
        High!
End the wickedness of the
        ungodly,
    but help all those who obey you.
For you look deep within the
        mind and heart,
    O righteous God.*

*God is my shield,
    saving those whose hearts are
        true and right.
God is a judge who is perfectly
        fair.
    He is angry with the wicked
        every day.*
PSALM 7:3-11

Always be honest

"HERE'S TEN DOLLARS. That should be enough," said Mother as she put money and a shopping list into Joey's hand. "You may keep the change."

After Joey finished buying the items for his mother, he left the store and pulled the change out of his pocket. "Wow, I was supposed to get a dollar and twenty-seven cents back," he mused, "but the cashier gave me *five* dollars and twenty-seven cents by mistake! Great! I'll have plenty of money for Saturday when I go to the video arcade with Steve."

After Joey got home, he worked on his model car while his mother ironed and listened to her favorite radio preacher. "I'd like to close my message today with a true story about honesty," said the speaker. Joey's ears perked up as the man told about a pastor who noticed that a bus driver had given him too much change. As he rode along, he was tempted to put the extra money in his wallet without saying anything. But he knew that would be wrong. So, as he left the bus, he returned the extra money to the driver. "You made a mistake," he said.

"That was no mistake," replied the bus driver. "That was a test. I visited your church last Sunday when you were preaching on honesty, and I wanted to see if you practice what you preach. I think I'll come to hear you again."

Wow, thought Joey. *Maybe God is giving me a test too. I'm going to take that extra money back to the store right now!*

HOW ABOUT YOU? Have you ever had the idea that no one would know when you did something dishonest? Be careful. You never know who may be watching you, perhaps even testing you. *P.R.*

TO MEMORIZE: The Lord passes judgment on the nations. Declare me righteous, O Lord, for I am innocent, O Most High! *Psalm 7:8*

"JOSH, you should be ashamed," declared Christy when her brother made a loud burp. "Your table manners are atrocious! And you've got syrup on your face!"

"Christy's right," Mother said. "Now, hurry, or we'll be late for Sunday school."

After Sunday school, Christy joined her family for the church service. She enjoyed the singing and listened to the message. But then she got restless. The Lord's Supper was being served, and it seemed to Christy that Pastor Grayson said the same thing every week. She poked Josh and whispered to him. But she quickly sat up straight when she saw her father frowning at her. Both she and Josh snickered as they watched a fly crawl up the back of Mrs. Martin, two rows ahead of them.

At the dinner table that noon, Christy carefully placed her napkin on her lap. "It's not polite to put your elbows on the table," she said, scolding her brother.

Dad looked at Josh and then at Christy. "Seems to me you both need to learn some good table manners," he said.

"Me?" asked Christy. "I'm sitting properly."

"I was thinking of a different table," said Dad. "The Lord's Table."

"That's right," agreed Mother. "Your manners there are even more important than your manners here at home. I think we'd better talk about it."

HOW ABOUT YOU? How do you behave at the Lord's Table? Even if you don't take Communion yet, remember Jesus at this special time. Listen to what the pastor says about what Jesus did on the cross for you. Thank God for what he did for you. Prayerfully examine your heart to see what sin may be in your life, and ask God to forgive you and help you turn away from it. *H.W.M.*

TO MEMORIZE: And when he had given thanks, he broke it and said, "This is my body, which is given for you. Do this in remembrance of me."
1 Corinthians 11:24

TABLE MANNERS

FROM THE BIBLE:

For this is what the Lord himself said, and I pass it on to you just as I received it. On the night when he was betrayed, the Lord Jesus took a loaf of bread, and when he had given thanks, he broke it and said, "This is my body, which is given for you. Do this in remembrance of me." In the same way, he took the cup of wine after supper, saying, "This cup is the new covenant between God and you, sealed by the shedding of my blood. Do this in remembrance of me as often as you drink it." For every time you eat this bread and drink this cup, you are announcing the Lord's death until he comes again.

So if anyone eats this bread or drinks this cup of the Lord unworthily, that person is guilty of sinning against the body and the blood of the Lord. That is why you should examine yourself before eating the bread and drinking from the cup. For if you eat the bread or drink the cup unworthily, not honoring the body of Christ, you are eating and drinking God's judgment upon yourself.
1 CORINTHIANS 11:23-29

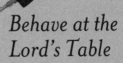

Behave at the Lord's Table

6 *March*

THE WRONG BOOK

FROM THE BIBLE:

In the beginning God created the heavens and the earth. The earth was empty, a formless mass cloaked in darkness. And the Spirit of God was hovering over its surface. Then God said, "Let there be light," and there was light. . . .

And God said, "Let there be space between the waters, to separate water from water." . . .

And God said, "Let the waters beneath the sky be gathered into one place so dry ground may appear." . . .

And God said, "Let bright lights appear in the sky to separate the day from the night. They will be signs to mark off the seasons, the days, and the years." . . .

And God said, "Let the waters swarm with fish and other life. Let the skies be filled with birds of every kind." . . .

And God said, "Let the earth bring forth every kind of animal. . . ." And so it was. . . .

Then God said, "Let us make people in our image, to be like ourselves. They will be masters over all life. . . ."

Then God looked over all he had made, and he saw that it was excellent in every way. This all happened on the sixth day.
GENESIS 1:1-3, 6, 9, 14, 20, 24, 26, 31

God made everything

GETTING OUT HIS SCIENCE BOOK, Scott sat down at the kitchen table to do some homework. *Wow!* he thought to himself after reading a few pages. *This sure doesn't sound like what it says in the Bible.* Feeling confused, he went to talk to his dad, who was replacing some spark plugs in the car. "Dad, my science book doesn't teach creation like the Bible does," said Scott. "According to my book, many scientists believe that the earth and people and everything just 'happened' to come into existence."

"Well, Son," said Dad, "you might as well know right now that some books are wrong. Man has written them, and man can sometimes make mistakes. But the Bible has no errors."

"Is that because the Bible was inspired by God?" Scott asked.

"That's right," Dad replied. "That's why we call it the Word of God—and it tells us that God created everything. In addition to that, our common sense tells us that people couldn't have just 'happened.' What if I told you this car just 'happened'—that nobody put the engine, the body, the seats, the wheels, and all the other parts of this car together, but they just all came together by themselves?"

Scott laughed. "I'd tell you that was crazy," he replied.

"You'd be absolutely right," Dad replied. "And the human body is far more complicated than this car. We're not accidents. We are part of God's plan and creation."

HOW ABOUT YOU? Have you heard people talk about evolution as if it were fact? Don't believe it! God made the whole world and everything in it. He made you, he loves you, and he has a wonderful plan and purpose for your life. *C.V.M.*

TO MEMORIZE: In the beginning God created the heavens and the earth. *Genesis 1:1*

JOY IN THE MORNING

SAMANTHA HAD a baby sister named Nicole. But soon after Mom brought the baby home, she had to take her back to the hospital. "Nicole's very sick," Mom told Samantha one day. "She needs a specialist in another city, so Dad and I are going to stay there with her for a while."

"Can I come, too?" asked Samantha.

"No. Aunt Ellie is going to come and stay with you for a few days."

"Mom, is Nicole going to get better?" Samantha asked.

"We don't know," Mom said, giving Samantha a hug.

Aunt Ellie came, but Samantha often worried when she thought about her baby sister. One morning when Samantha woke up, Mom was sitting in the chair beside her bed. "Mom! You're home! Is Nicole better?"

Mom held Samantha close. "Nicole died, honey," she said.

With tear-filled eyes, Samantha gazed up into her mother's face.

"Samantha, how did you feel when you woke up and saw me here?"

"Surprised and happy," Samantha replied.

"I think that's the way Nicole felt when she opened her eyes and saw Jesus." Mom's words were very quiet. "There's a Bible verse that says, 'Joy comes with the morning,' and that came true for Nicole this morning."

Samantha squeezed her mother's hand and said, "Oh, Mom, I'll miss Nicole so much, but I'm glad she's in heaven." Then Samantha and her mom cried together.

HOW ABOUT YOU? God's plan for you may include sadness. It may even include the death of someone you love. That should not frighten you. It's natural to feel sadness, but for those who love Jesus, joy does come with the morning. *P.I.K.*

TO MEMORIZE: His anger lasts for a moment, but his favor lasts a lifetime! Weeping may go on all night, but joy comes with the morning. *Psalm 30:5*

FROM THE BIBLE:

But let me tell you a wonderful secret God has revealed to us. Not all of us will die, but we will all be transformed. It will happen in a moment, in the blinking of an eye, when the last trumpet is blown. For when the trumpet sounds, the Christians who have died will be raised with transformed bodies. And then we who are living will be transformed so that we will never die. For our perishable earthly bodies must be transformed into heavenly bodies that will never die.

When this happens—when our perishable earthly bodies have been transformed into heavenly bodies that will never die—then at last the Scriptures will come true:

"Death is swallowed up in victory.
O death, where is your victory?
O death, where is your sting?"

For sin is the sting that results in death, and the law gives sin its power. How we thank God, who gives us victory over sin and death through Jesus Christ our Lord!

1 CORINTHIANS 15:51-57

Death can be joyful

8 March

CAN RIGHT BE WRONG?

FROM THE BIBLE:

It's true that we can't win God's approval by what we eat. We don't miss out on anything if we don't eat it, and we don't gain anything if we do. But you must be careful with this freedom of yours. Do not cause a brother or sister with a weaker conscience to stumble.

You see, this is what can happen: Weak Christians who think it is wrong to eat this food will see you eating in the temple of an idol. You know there's nothing wrong with it, but they will be encouraged to violate their conscience by eating food that has been dedicated to the idol. So because of your superior knowledge, a weak Christian, for whom Christ died, will be destroyed. And you are sinning against Christ when you sin against other Christians by encouraging them to do something they believe is wrong. If what I eat is going to make another Christian sin, I will never eat meat again as long as I live—for I don't want to make another Christian stumble.

1 CORINTHIANS 8:8-13

Don't be a stumbling block

DARRELL burst into the room. "Mom, guess what happened at Bible club!" he exclaimed. "Troy accepted Jesus as his Savior!"

"How wonderful!" Darrell's mother responded. "I'm happy Troy's a Christian, but I'm afraid he won't get much encouragement at home."

"I'll help Troy," Darrell said eagerly.

A few weeks later, Darrell wasn't so sure about that. "I asked Troy to go with me to Don's house to play pool," he grumbled, "but you know what he said? He said, 'Darrell, I thought you were a Christian!' Then he walked away! What's wrong with playing pool?"

Darrell's mother was thoughtful. "Maybe Troy's father plays a lot of pool in the bars, so Troy associates playing pool with drinking, wasting money, and being away from home too much—things his dad does. Troy probably doesn't understand that a quiet game of pool in somebody's basement can be OK. Darrell, I think you ought to stay away from playing pool so you're not a stumbling block to Troy."

"I don't see why I shouldn't play," objected Darrell.

His mother thought for a moment. "Troy's a baby Christian. Seeing you do something he considers wrong might hurt him spiritually. Joining you might lead him to play pool in the wrong place. As he grows in his Christian life, he'll learn how to handle his actions. But right now, pool playing is a problem for him."

Darrell nodded thoughtfully. "OK, Mom. I'll try."

HOW ABOUT YOU? Are there things you think are OK to do but which bother other people? Remember, a Christian's actions influence others. Do your activities draw people to Christ or turn them away? Refuse to be a "stumbling block." *J.L.H.*

TO MEMORIZE: You must be careful with this freedom of yours. Do not cause a brother or sister with a weaker conscience to stumble. *1 Corinthians 8:9*

GIVE AND GET

FROM THE BIBLE:

Let the words of Christ, in all their richness, live in your hearts and make you wise. Use his words to teach and counsel each other. Sing psalms and hymns and spiritual songs to God with thankful hearts. And whatever you do or say, let it be as a representative of the Lord Jesus, all the while giving thanks through him to God the Father.

You wives must submit to your husbands, as is fitting for those who belong to the Lord. And you husbands must love your wives and never treat them harshly.

You children must always obey your parents, for this is what pleases the Lord. Fathers, don't aggravate your children. If you do, they will become discouraged and quit trying.

COLOSSIANS 3:16-21

Do things enthusiastically

PAUL AND his brother Mike came into the house and hung up their coats. "How was Bible club?" their mother asked.

"I'm on the game committee for a party we're having next week," Mike replied. "We had a good lesson, too."

Mother looked at Paul as he turned on the TV. "Did you enjoy Bible club?" she asked. "What was the lesson about?"

"Huh?" Paul looked up. "Oh . . . uh . . . something about some queen." He turned his attention back to the TV.

"Are you on a committee for the party?" asked Mother.

"Naw," Paul mumbled. "Can I go over to Jim's?"

"Yes," said Mother, "but don't you have a Bible verse to learn?"

Paul shrugged. "I can do that later." He put on his coat and looked at himself in the hall mirror. His mother watched as he tipped his head and smiled. His reflection smiled back. Then he scowled, and the reflection scowled, too.

"Life is like a mirror," Mother said as she walked up behind Paul.

Paul's eyebrows shot up. "How's that?"

"Like a mirror, life gives back pretty much what you give to it," explained Mother. "If you give it a little, you get only a little out of it. If you put a lot into it, you'll find you enjoy it a lot more and get a lot out of it, too."

"You mean like Bible club?" he asked.

"Yes, like Bible club," Mother said.

HOW ABOUT YOU? Are you giving your best to the activities in which you're involved? When you do, you are serving God. *H.W.M.*

TO MEMORIZE: And whatever you do or say, let it be as a representative of the Lord Jesus, all the while giving thanks through him to God the Father. *Colossians 3:17*

10 March

'FESS UP

FROM THE BIBLE:

*Oh, what joy for those
    whose rebellion is forgiven,
    whose sin is put out of sight!
Yes, what joy for those
    whose record the Lord has
        cleared of sin,
    whose lives are lived in
        complete honesty!*

*When I refused to confess my
    sin,
    I was weak and miserable,
    and I groaned all day long.
Day and night your hand of
        discipline was heavy on me.
My strength evaporated like
        water in the summer heat.*

*Finally, I confessed all my sins
    to you
    and stopped trying to hide
    them.
I said to myself, "I will confess
    my rebellion to the Lord."
    And you forgave me! All my
    guilt is gone.*

*Therefore, let all the godly
    confess their rebellion to
    you while there is time,
    that they may not drown
    in the floodwaters of
    judgment.
For you are my hiding place;
    you protect me from trouble.
    You surround me with songs
    of victory.*

PSALM 32:1-7

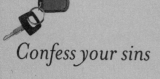

Confess your sins

ANTHONY GASPED and choked. Quickly, he turned away from Dave. He didn't want Dave to laugh at him.

"How'd ya like it?" Dave spoke to Anthony's back.

"Great," Anthony lied. He glanced at his watch. "Hey, I gotta run." Guilt tugged at his heart as he snuffed out the cigarette and hurried home.

When Anthony entered the house, he heard his little sister's voice. "Mommy, I didn't do it!" Anthony went down the hall toward his bedroom.

"Tiffany," Mom said, "don't lie to me."

As Anthony passed his parents' room, the smell of perfume almost choked him. Looking in, he saw that the carpet was sprinkled with powder, and tiny footprints led from the vanity to the door. "You'd better 'fess up," Anthony teased.

Tiffany began to sob. "I just wanted to smell pretty."

Her mother smiled. "Well, you certainly do that! The whole house is going to smell pretty. Go sit in your room while I clean up this mess." She turned toward Anthony. "And what have *you* been up to?"

"I . . . I . . . nothing," he stuttered, looking guilty.

Mom looked at him in surprise. She had been teasing, but now she realized Anthony really had been up to something. "Better, 'fess up, Son."

"Dave offered me a cigarette, and I tried smoking it," Anthony confessed.

"Oh, Anthony!" exclaimed his mother. "I'm sorry to hear that."

"It was terrible," admitted Anthony. "I'm glad I confessed. I feel so much better, and I think it will help me say no to Dave next time."

HOW ABOUT YOU? Is there something bothering your conscience? Do you need to 'fess up? If so, tell God, your parents, or whoever is involved. A clean conscience is a priceless possession. *B.J.W.*

TO MEMORIZE: But if we confess our sins to him, he is faithful and just to forgive us and to cleanse us from every wrong. *1 John 1:9*

SCHOOL BEGAN in the usual boring way for Roger. *We need some action around here,* Roger thought. He peeked into his desk to check on the little mouse he had in a small box.

A few minutes later Mrs. Madden had to go to the office. She appointed Jennifer to be class monitor. Quietly Roger took the mouse from his desk and released it.

"There's a mouse!" Many of the kids screamed and jumped up on their chairs.

"Take your seats," Jennifer instructed. "It won't hurt you." The mouse ran right over Jennifer's shoe. "Ahhhh!" she shrieked. She climbed onto her chair.

"Everyone sit down," Jennifer ordered. There's nothing to worry about." But she remained standing on her chair.

Just then Mrs. Madden returned to the chaos. She dismissed the class for an early lunch so that a janitor could remove the mouse.

After school Roger told his mother about Jennifer and the mouse. He told her everything except how the mouse got there. "It was pretty funny," he said. "Jennifer told the class to sit down because there was nothing to worry about, but she stayed standing on her chair."

"That's a good example of what we discussed in my Bible study this morning," said Mother. "Just as Jennifer's actions didn't match her words, Christians' actions don't always match what they say they believe."

Roger felt guilty. He knew that Jennifer wasn't the only one whose actions didn't match her words. He would need to talk to his mother and his teacher.

HOW ABOUT YOU? Do you say you believe in Jesus but carelessly lie, cheat, or treat others unkindly? Or do you act out your faith by living a godly life? Ask God to help you act according to your faith. *N.E.K.*

TO MEMORIZE: So you see, it isn't enough just to have faith. Faith that doesn't show itself by good deeds is no faith at all—it is dead and useless. *James 2:17*

ROGER'S MOUSE

FROM THE BIBLE:

Dear brothers and sisters, what's the use of saying you have faith if you don't prove it by your actions? That kind of faith can't save anyone. Suppose you see a brother or sister who needs food or clothing, and you say, "Well, good-bye and God bless you; stay warm and eat well"—but then you don't give that person any food or clothing. What good does that do?

So you see, it isn't enough just to have faith. Faith that doesn't show itself by good deeds is no faith at all—it is dead and useless.

Now someone may argue, "Some people have faith; others have good deeds." I say, "I can't see your faith if you don't have good deeds, but I will show you my faith through my good deeds."

Do you still think it's enough just to believe that there is one God? Well, even the demons believe this, and they tremble in terror! Fool! When will you ever learn that faith that does not result in good deeds is useless?
JAMES 2:14-20

Live what you believe

12 March

TRUE FREEDOM

FROM THE BIBLE:

My son, obey your father's commands, and don't neglect your mother's teaching. Keep their words always in your heart. Tie them around your neck. Wherever you walk, their counsel can lead you. When you sleep, they will protect you. When you wake up in the morning, they will advise you. For these commands and this teaching are a lamp to light the way ahead of you. The correction of discipline is the way to life.
PROVERBS 6:20-23

True freedom includes rules

CHRISTINA RAN into her bedroom and slammed the door. How unreasonable could her mother be! Christina wanted to go to the slumber party at Sarah's house, but her mother wouldn't let her go. "You know the girls are much older than you are and rather wild," Mother had said.

But Christina yelled, "You never give me any freedom."

She was still sniffling when she heard a sound at her window. Looking up, she saw a bird beating its wings against the glass. It seemed to be trying to get inside. As she watched, her mother knocked on the door. "I have some clean laundry, Christina."

As Mother set the clothes on the dresser, she saw the bird beating on the glass. "Christina," Mother said softly, "open the window and let the poor bird in. It's cruel to keep him out when he desperately wants to get in."

"Mother, he wouldn't know what to do once he got inside. He'd be trapped and frightened and wouldn't know how to get out again! He might get hurt."

"But don't you want him to have his freedom?" asked Mother.

"He's got more space and freedom outside," Christina said grumpily.

Mother smiled and nodded. "So by saying no, you're really giving him freedom and protecting him," she said. "That's what I'm trying to do for you."

HOW ABOUT YOU? Do you feel that your parents are restricting your freedom by giving you rules and expecting you to obey? In love, they are actually protecting you from situations or things that could harm you. Trust their judgment and obey their decisions. True freedom includes living within bounds set up by God. *J.L.H.*

TO MEMORIZE: For these commands and this teaching are a lamp to light the way ahead of you. The correction of discipline is the way to life. *Proverbs 6:23*

RACHEL THREW her books on the couch and with a loud groan plopped down beside them. "Was it that bad?" Grandma asked as she laid down her needlepoint. Grandma always had time to listen.

Glumly, Rachel nodded. "It was a terrible day, Gram. I can't do math. I've tried and tried, but I can't understand it. I even got a D on my last test."

"Have you asked your teacher for help?" asked Grandma.

"Mr. Fenski?" Rachel asked. "No way! He explains it in class, and if we don't understand, that's our problem. I'd be embarrassed to ask him for special help."

"I think you take after your grandpa," chuckled Grandma. "He hated to ask for help, too. He was too proud."

"I brought you a glass of iced tea, Gram," said Ricky as he came into the room carrying a tray that was almost too large for him to handle. As the glass wobbled, Rachel reached out to help. The little boy jerked the tray out of her reach. "No! I can do it all by my—"

"Oh! Look what you did!" Rachel cried as the glass toppled and tea splattered everywhere.

When things had settled down, Rachel said, "I guess I've been acting like Ricky and Grandpa, trying to do it by myself. Maybe I *will* ask Mr. Fenski for help."

Grandma nodded. "And don't forget to ask God to help you, too."

TOO PROUD

FROM THE BIBLE:

The Lord is far from the wicked, but he hears the prayers of the righteous.

A cheerful look brings joy to the heart; good news makes for good health.

If you listen to constructive criticism, you will be at home among the wise.

If you reject criticism, you only harm yourself; but if you listen to correction, you grow in understanding.

Fear of the Lord teaches a person to be wise; humility precedes honor.

PROVERBS 15:29-33

Ask for help

HOW ABOUT YOU? Is there an area in which you need help? Does a subject in school seem too difficult? Are your memory verses hard to learn? Is there a family situation you can't handle? Don't be too proud to ask for the help you need. Ask for God's help first, and then ask for the help of parents, friends, or teachers. *B.J.W.*

TO MEMORIZE: Pride leads to disgrace, but with humility comes wisdom. *Proverbs 11:2*

14 March

WHY COMPLAIN?

FROM THE BIBLE:

Yet true religion with contentment is great wealth. After all, we didn't bring anything with us when we came into the world, and we certainly cannot carry anything with us when we die. So if we have enough food and clothing, let us be content.

1 TIMOTHY 6:6-8

Enjoy what you have

IT WAS SPRING vacation, and Janie was bored. "Oh, Mom, what can I do?" she asked for the fourteenth time.

Her mother sighed. She had already made several suggestions, but nothing interested Janie. "I'll tell you what," Mom said finally. "I'll help you think of something that's fun to do if you'll do some jobs for me first."

"OK," Janie agreed. "Anything would be better than sitting around doing nothing." Mom wrote out a list of jobs. When Janie saw it, she groaned. It read: Vacuum the carpet and dust the furniture, wash the bathroom tile, and fold towels. "Is that enough?" she asked when she had finished doing everything.

"Not quite," said her mother. "Take these cookies to Mrs. Gumm's house."

"All the way over there?" Janie grumbled. But she went and came back.

"Now, how about having a cookie?" invited Mom. "Then maybe you could read for a while."

"Good idea!" said Janie. Then she laughed. "Isn't that silly? You suggested the same thing earlier, and it sounded boring then. Now it sounds like fun."

"The activity hasn't changed. You have," said Mom. "An old saying says 'The grass is always greener on the other side of the fence.' It's all a matter of *attitude*. You didn't appreciate your free time when you had it. I took it away from you for a while, and now you want it back again!"

"I'm sorry, Mom," said Janie. "I've been complaining and grumbling all morning. I know that's wrong. I think I will have that cookie now."

HOW ABOUT YOU? Are you a grumbler? Do you gripe and complain if you don't have someplace to go or something exciting to do? Do you often want what you don't have, instead of being thankful for what you do have? God wants to help you be content. *S.L.K.*

TO MEMORIZE: True religion with contentment is great wealth. *1 Timothy 6:6*

THE BEST HAMBURGER!

"DAD SURE LOOKS tired lately," said Bonita to her brother, Stephano. It was Saturday morning and the two children were playing catch in the front yard. Just a few minutes earlier, they had watched their dad slowly walk down the road to the bus stop. Even though it was Saturday, he had to go to the office.

"Dad's tired because of that big report he's writing for the convention next month," Stephano said.

"Mom's been busy, too," Bonita added. "It's not easy teaching full time and keeping the house straight. Wish we could help them."

"Well, we already helped Mom clean the house," said Stephano, "but there are some jobs kids just can't do!"

They threw the ball back and forth for a while, then Bonita spoke excitedly. "Stephano, how much money do you have?"

"I'm rich!" Stephano said, smiling. "All last week I helped Mr. Gonzales clean out the back room at his grocery store, remember?"

"I've got baby-sitting money saved up," said Bonita. "I thought we could take Dad and Mom out for dinner. It would let them know we appreciate them."

And that's just what Bonita and Stephano did! Their parents were very surprised. "You know," said Dad as they were eating, "this is the best hamburger I've ever tasted!"

"I agree," Mom said with a smile. "It's terrific to know that our children care about us!"

HOW ABOUT YOU? When was the last time you did something special for your dad and mom or told them how much you appreciate the hard work they do? Dads and moms sometimes become very busy and therefore very tired. Read 1 Corinthians 13, a chapter in which the apostle Paul talks about love. Then show that kind of love to your parents. *L.M.W.*

TO MEMORIZE: "Honor your father and mother." This is the first of the Ten Commandments that ends with a promise. *Ephesians 6:2*

FROM THE BIBLE:

If I could speak in any language in heaven or on earth but didn't love others, I would only be making meaningless noise like a loud gong or a clanging cymbal. If I had the gift of prophecy, and if I knew all the mysteries of the future and knew everything about everything, but didn't love others, what good would I be? And if I had the gift of faith so that I could speak to a mountain and make it move, without love I would be no good to anybody. If I gave everything I have to the poor and even sacrificed my body, I could boast about it; but if I didn't love others, I would be of no value whatsoever.

1 CORINTHIANS 13:1-3

Show love for parents

16 March

I APPRECIATE YOU!

FROM THE BIBLE:

Greet Priscilla and Aquila. They have been co-workers in my ministry for Christ Jesus. In fact, they risked their lives for me. I am not the only one who is thankful to them; so are all the Gentile churches. Please give my greetings to the church that meets in their home.

Greet my dear friend Epenetus. He was the very first person to become a Christian in the province of Asia. Give my greetings to Mary, who has worked so hard for your benefit. Then there are Andronicus and Junia, my relatives, who were in prison with me. They are respected among the apostles and became Christians before I did. Please give them my greetings. Say hello to Ampliatus, whom I love as one of the Lord's own children, and Urbanus, our co-worker in Christ, and beloved Stachys.

Give my greetings to Apelles, a good man whom Christ approves. And give my best regards to the members of the household of Aristobulus.

ROMANS 16:3-10

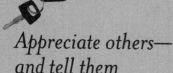

Appreciate others—and tell them

EVERY MORNING Michael read a chapter of the Bible and prayed. One morning he read Romans 16. *This is kind of a different chapter,* he thought. *It's mostly a list of the people Paul appreciated.* He studied it for a moment. *Maybe this chapter is in the Bible to show us how important it is to let others know how much we appreciate them.*

So at breakfast Michael said to his mother, "Thanks for cooking these eggs for me, Mom." Then when his brother Isaac came into the kitchen, Michael said, "Isaac, I appreciate you for letting me use your markers for my report." Both Mom and Isaac gave Michael such big smiles that he decided to keep on telling people how much they were appreciated.

At school, Michael said to his friend Keith, "Thanks for sticking up for me when those guys teased me yesterday. I appreciate that."

On the way home from school, Michael walked by his church. Pastor Jim was standing in the parking lot, talking to the organist. "Pastor," Michael called, "I want you to know I appreciate your messages. And Mrs. Harris, thanks for playing the organ each week." Michael received two more big smiles.

That night as Michael was getting ready for bed, he thought once again about appreciation. People needed to be appreciated. He could tell that by the big smiles he had been getting all day. He was glad he had learned a lesson from the apostle Paul.

HOW ABOUT YOU? You probably do appreciate all the people who do things for you, but do you let them know it? Make a list of five people whom you appreciate, and then tell them. You'll feel good because you will be helping others feel good. And don't forget to include Jesus on your list. He deserves the most appreciation of all! *L.M.W.*

TO MEMORIZE: Every time I think of you, I give thanks to my God. *Philippians 1:3*

"COME ON, SUE," Erika called. "It's time for choir."

Sue put her books in her locker and shut the door. "I decided not to go, Erika. It's such a nuisance having to stay after school twice a week."

"But, Sue, we planned on it," Erika said glancing at her watch.

"Erika, let's forget choir this year," urged Sue. "Let's go to my house and play my new video game instead."

Erika hesitated. She wanted to stay, but she didn't want to go to choir alone. She knew Sue wouldn't change her mind, either. "Well, OK," she agreed slowly.

That night Erika's mom asked how choir was. "Sue and I decided not to join this year," Erika explained.

"Was that really your choice or Sue's?" Mom asked.

Erika looked down. "You have a talent, Erika, and you've always said you wanted to use it for the Lord. The training you get at school will help you develop your talent, and besides, you had a lot of fun singing at the concerts last year. The main person you're hurting by not joining is yourself."

Erika thought about her mother's words. This wasn't the first time Sue had discouraged her from doing something she wanted to do.

"Mom, I'll join the choir next week," she said firmly. "I'm not going to let Sue talk me out of doing things anymore! I'll ask the Lord to help me make my own decisions."

HOW ABOUT YOU? Do you let others tell you what you should or shouldn't do? Sometimes friends can sound pretty convincing, and if you're not careful, they'll make your decisions for you. God wants you to make your own decisions. Ask him to help you have wisdom. *L.M.W.*

TO MEMORIZE: I can do everything with the help of Christ who gives me the strength I need. *Philippians 4:13*

HER OWN DECISION

FROM THE BIBLE:

After this, Absalom bought a chariot and horses, and he hired fifty footmen to run ahead of him. He got up early every morning and went out to the gate of the city. When people brought a case to the king for judgment, Absalom would ask where they were from, and they would tell him their tribe. Then Absalom would say, "You've really got a strong case here! It's too bad the king doesn't have anyone to hear it. I wish I were the judge. Then people could bring their problems to me, and I would give them justice!" And when people tried to bow before him, Absalom wouldn't let them. Instead, he took them by the hand and embraced them. So in this way, Absalom stole the hearts of all the people of Israel. 2 SAMUEL 15:1-6

Decide with God's help

18 March

T-SHIRT DAY

Meanwhile, as Peter was sitting outside in the courtyard, a servant girl came over and said to him, "You were one of those with Jesus the Galilean."

But Peter denied it in front of everyone. "I don't know what you are talking about," he said.

Later, out by the gate, another servant girl noticed him and said to those standing around, "This man was with Jesus of Nazareth."

Again Peter denied it, this time with an oath. "I don't even know the man," he said.

A little later some other bystanders came over to him and said, "You must be one of them; we can tell by your Galilean accent."

Peter said, "I swear by God, I don't know the man." And immediately the rooster crowed. Suddenly, Jesus' words flashed through Peter's mind: "Before the rooster crows, you will deny me three times." And he went away, crying bitterly.

MATTHEW 26:69-75

Don't be ashamed of Jesus

KARIN AND HER FAMILY were spending spring break at Mountain View Bible Camp, and Karin was having a wonderful time. "Can I please buy a camp T-shirt?" she begged one day. "Everyone else has one." Mother agreed, and Karin promptly put the shirt on. On the front was a picture of the chapel with the words "Proclaiming His Word to the World." On the back it said, "Mountain View Bible Camp." Karin wore the shirt almost every day that week, proud to be a part of the group.

Back home, Karin stuffed the shirt in a drawer and forgot about it. Mother didn't forget, though. From time to time she suggested that Karin wear it, but Karin always refused. "I like it," she insisted, "but it just wouldn't look right."

One Friday was declared T-Shirt day at school. Again Karin begged for a new shirt. "Not this time," Mother replied. "Wear your camp shirt. It's almost new."

"I can't wear that," protested Karin. "It wouldn't look right at school. Everyone else will wear shirts with cool sayings on them or they'll be from exciting vacation places like Yellowstone."

"Wasn't camp exciting?" asked Mother. "You loved your shirt before."

Karin bit her lip. "It was different at camp," she said.

"Yes, it was," Mother said. "It was comfortable to be identified as a Christian then, because others shared your faith."

Karin bristled. "Are you saying I'm ashamed to let others see that I'm a Christian?"

"Are you?" asked Mother softly.

Karin thought about it. "I guess maybe I have been," she confessed.

HOW ABOUT YOU? Do your friends and teachers know you're a Christian? Do you pray before you eat, witness when you can, and speak up for your faith in the classroom? Don't be ashamed of Jesus. Others need to know him, too. *J.L.H.*

TO MEMORIZE: You must never be ashamed to tell others about our Lord. *2 Timothy 1:8*

THE RIGHT NOSE

"I HATE THIS ugly nose!" wailed Heather as she looked into the mirror.

"Let's not worry about noses now," said Mom. "We've got to get going if we want to stop at the zoo today."

It was a beautiful sunny day. Heather and her mom enjoyed a leisurely stroll, looking at all the animals. "My! The elephants have long trunks, don't they?" commented Mom as they stopped to watch the great beasts. "I'm glad my nose isn't that long."

"That's what makes an elephant an elephant!" said Heather.

At the rhinoceros cage, Mom laughed as she pointed to the horns on their noses. "Oh, dear! That kind of nose would be even worse!" Heather gave her a curious look but said nothing. As they walked along, she noticed that her mother had a comment to make about almost every kind of animal's nose. When they reached the baboons, Mom turned to her. "Their noses are much too stubby, don't you think? Wouldn't they look better if they had noses more like the tigers?"

Heather was annoyed. "No, they wouldn't!" she snapped. "I like them just the way they are. The animals wouldn't be very interesting if they were all alike. Besides, you've told me yourself that God made them the way they are and that he knows best how they should look."

"Exactly," said Mother with a nod. "He knows best how animals should look, and he knows best how people should look."

"Oh!" exclaimed Heather as she clapped her hand over her nose. "I get it!"

HOW ABOUT YOU? Do you sometimes complain about the way you look? If everyone had the "perfect" nose, mouth, eyes, and teeth, we would all look alike! Remember, God made you, and he loves you just the way you are. *P.R.*

TO MEMORIZE: For the Spirit of God has made me, and the breath of the Almighty gives me life. *Job 33:4*

FROM THE BIBLE:

"So all the world from east to west will know there is no other God. I am the Lord, and there is no other. I am the one who creates the light and makes the darkness. I am the one who sends good times and bad times. I, the Lord, am the one who does these things. . . .

"Destruction is certain for those who argue with their Creator. Does a clay pot ever argue with its maker? Does the clay dispute with the one who shapes it, saying, 'Stop, you are doing it wrong!' Does the pot exclaim, 'How clumsy can you be!' How terrible it would be if a newborn baby said to its father and mother, 'Why was I born? Why did you make me this way?' "

This is what the Lord, the Creator and Holy One of Israel, says: "Do you question what I do? Do you give me orders about the work of my hands? I am the one who made the earth and created people to live on it. With my hands I stretched out the heavens. All the millions of stars are at my command."

ISAIAH 45:6-7, 9-12

God made me special

20 March

GRANDPA FORGETS
(PART 1)

FROM THE BIBLE:

"Pay attention, O Israel, for you are my servant. I, the Lord, made you, and I will not forget to help you."

"What is the price of five sparrows? A couple of pennies? Yet God does not forget a single one of them. And the very hairs on your head are all numbered. So don't be afraid; you are more valuable to him than a whole flock of sparrows."

ISAIAH 44:21; LUKE 12:6-7

God never forgets you

"HI, GRANDPA," exclaimed Denise. "Is Grandma here, too?" Denise had come to the supermarket with her father, who was picking up a cake mix and some ice cream for her birthday party the next day. But what was wrong with Grandpa? He didn't say anything. He just stared at her as if he didn't know her.

Just then Grandma appeared. She looked cross. "Robert, I told you to wait by the magazines," she scolded. Seeing Denise, she gave her a quick kiss. "Are you all ready for your birthday party?" she asked.

"Party?" asked Grandpa. "Who's having a party?"

"Denise is. We talked about it at breakfast," said Grandma patiently. "Don't you remember?" She took his arm. "Let's go buy a birthday present."

That night as Mother tucked her into bed, Denise told her about Grandpa's strange behavior. Mother looked concerned. "Grandpa isn't well," said Mother. "He has a disease called Alzheimer's. It causes people to forget names, places, even people they love."

Denise swallowed hard. "But Grandpa and I are friends—he said so himself. And friends aren't supposed to forget each other."

"I know," said Mother, giving Denise a hug, "but I'm afraid that earthly friends do sometimes forget. And Grandpa can't help it when he forgets," said Mother. "Thank God for the good times you've had together. Thank him, too, that Jesus is always there for you. Jesus is a friend who 'sticks closer than a brother'—or even a grandfather."

HOW ABOUT YOU? Do you feel sad because a friend moved away, chose someone else, or just simply forgot you? Aren't you glad God will never forget his own? Thank him for that, and let him fill the empty place in your life. *C.J.B.*

TO MEMORIZE: There are "friends" who destroy each other, but a real friend sticks closer than a brother. *Proverbs 18:24*

PINK AND YELLOW balloons hung around the living room. Many of Denise's aunts, uncles, and cousins were already there when Grandpa and Grandma arrived. But Grandpa stood by the door, a lost, confused expression on his face. "Who are these people?" he asked.

"They're your children and grandchildren," said Grandma.

Denise noticed that Grandma sounded like she was talking to a small child. *I guess that's because he has Alzheimer's disease and forgets a lot of things,* she thought. She went over and slipped her hand into his. "I'm glad you came, Grandpa."

Grandpa looked down at Denise, and a soft smile spread over his face. He patted her head clumsily, and then he said, "Is this your house, little girl?"

"Of course, Grandpa," Denise replied. "I'm Denise, remember?"

When Denise and Daddy helped clean the kitchen after the party, Denise closed the dishwasher door with a bang. "Why does Grandpa have Alzheimer's?" she muttered. "I can't think of a single reason why God let it happen."

"Neither can I," said Daddy. Denise's eyes widened. "That surprises you, doesn't it?" he asked. Denise nodded. "In life we have to expect sad things to happen as well as good things," continued Daddy. "Grandpa's Alzheimer's disease is sad. And just as he often can't understand what's happening around him, we can't understand why such sad things happen. God doesn't ask us to understand, but he does ask us to believe in him with all our hearts in spite of sad circumstances. He promises to be with us in difficult times."

HOW ABOUT YOU? Are you puzzled, wondering why God has allowed some sad thing to happen? He wants you to trust him, and he waits to give you comfort and help. *C.J.B.*

TO MEMORIZE: Each time he said, "My gracious favor is all you need. My power works best in your weakness." *2 Corinthians 12:9*

GRANDPA FORGETS
(PART 2)

FROM THE BIBLE:

*I look up to the mountains—does my help come from there?
My help comes from the Lord, who made the heavens and the earth!*

*He will not let you stumble and fall;
the one who watches over you will not sleep.
Indeed, he who watches over Israel never tires and never sleeps.*

*The Lord himself watches over you!
The Lord stands beside you as your protective shade.
The sun will not hurt you by day, nor the moon at night.
The Lord keeps you from all evil and preserves your life.
The Lord keeps watch over you as you come and go, both now and forever.*

PSALM 121:1-8

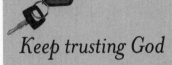

Keep trusting God

22 *March*

GRANDPA FORGETS
(PART 3)

FROM THE BIBLE:

Stay away from the love of money; be satisfied with what you have. For God has said,

"I will never fail you.
I will never forsake you."

That is why we can say with confidence,

"The Lord is my helper,
so I will not be afraid.
What can mere mortals do to me?"

Remember your leaders who first taught you the word of God. Think of all the good that has come from their lives, and trust the Lord as they do.
Jesus Christ is the same yesterday, today, and forever.
HEBREWS 13:5-8

God never changes

ONE SATURDAY, Denise woke up feeling grumpy and sad. In the kitchen she found her mother pouring the cereal. "How's Grandpa?" Denise asked.

"I don't know," replied Mother. "Do you want to go with your father and me to the nursing home this afternoon?"

Denise nodded. She sat down to eat, but the oatmeal stuck in her throat. Life was painful. First Grandpa had gotten Alzheimer's disease, and then he had fallen and broken his hip.

When they reached Grandpa's room that afternoon, Denise wished she hadn't come. Grandpa looked almost as white as his bedspread. His eyes were wild and frightened. "Help me. . . . please help me. . . . Will someone please help me?" he cried over and over. When a nurse came in, Denise's father took her hand and led her from the room. He smiled at her with understanding.

"I wish things could be the way they used to be," cried Denise. "Grandpa's so different. I want him to stay the same."

Father patted her hand and sighed. "Everything in life changes," he said. "Why, look at yourself—you've grown an inch since last summer. And Mother's new diet and exercise plan has helped her lose several pounds. As for me . . . well, I can't see it, of course, but they tell me I've gained a few."

Denise tried to smile. The transfer of weight from Mother to Father had been a family joke. Denise's father squeezed her hand. "I'll tell you what helps me accept the changes," he said. "It's the knowledge that I have a friend who never changes. And that friend is Jesus."

HOW ABOUT YOU? Are you frightened by the changes in your life? Perhaps someone close to you has died or moved away. Maybe someone you love is sick. Talk to God. He understands your confusion and hurt. *C.J.B.*

TO MEMORIZE: Jesus Christ is the same yesterday, today, and forever. *Hebrews 13:8*

LAN CLOSED her locker and hurried toward the door. Her first day in the new school had been just as she expected. She felt as if everyone stared at her because she looked different from most of the girls in her class. But then, they had not been born in Korea, and she had. She sighed. She was glad there were at least a few other Asian girls in the class, and she hoped she'd soon get to know them better.

"Lan," someone called. "Wait for me." Lan turned abruptly and saw a short blonde girl coming toward her. "I was hoping I'd get to meet you," the girl said. "My Sunday school teacher told me you and your folks just moved next door to her."

Lan nodded. "She wanted me to go to church with her yesterday," the Korean girl confessed. "But . . ."

"My name is Gina Ellers," the other girl said. "You would like our church. Lots of wonderful people go there."

Lan shook her head. "No," she said shyly. "They would just look at me and say I'm different."

"Oh, I don't think so," Gina replied. "They know that it doesn't matter how different we look on the outside because God sees the heart, and he knows that we're all the same inside," she explained. "We all need Jesus to be our Savior and friend."

"I never heard that before," Lan said thoughtfully. "Maybe I will come to your church and hear more about it. Or maybe you can tell me more."

HOW ABOUT YOU? Maybe you're a different nationality from others in your school. That makes no difference to God. He gave his Son for everyone, including you. Have you asked him to take away your sin and make you his child? *R.I.J.*

TO MEMORIZE: Anyone who calls on the name of the Lord will be saved. *Romans 10:13*

BEING DIFFERENT
(PART 1)

FROM THE BIBLE:

For if you confess with your mouth that Jesus is Lord and believe in your heart that God raised him from the dead, you will be saved. For it is by believing in your heart that you are made right with God, and it is by confessing with your mouth that you are saved. As the Scriptures tell us, "Anyone who believes in him will not be disappointed." Jew and Gentile are the same in this respect. They all have the same Lord, who generously gives his riches to all who ask for them. For "Anyone who calls on the name of the Lord will be saved."

ROMANS 10:9-13

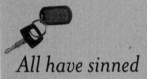

All have sinned

24 March

BEING DIFFERENT
(PART 2)

FROM THE BIBLE:

Then he called his disciples and the crowds to come over and listen. "If any of you wants to be my follower," he told them, "you must put aside your selfish ambition, shoulder your cross, and follow me. If you try to keep your life for yourself, you will lose it. But if you give up your life for my sake and for the sake of the Good News, you will find true life. And how do you benefit if you gain the whole world but lose your own soul in the process? Is anything worth more than your soul? If a person is ashamed of me and my message in these adulterous and sinful days, I, the Son of Man, will be ashamed of that person when I return in the glory of my Father with the holy angels."

MARK 8:34-38

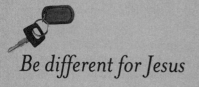

Be different for Jesus

GINA AND LAN became good friends, and it wasn't long before Lan accepted Jesus as her Savior. She was beginning to feel more at home in her new school, too. The two girls talked about it one day. "You know something?" said Gina. "You've been afraid of being different, and so have I."

Lan looked at her in surprise. "You? But you look just like all the other kids."

Gina nodded. "Maybe I look like most of them," she admitted, "but believing in Jesus makes me different from many of them. I hardly ever talk to anyone about church or God or anything like that because I'm afraid they might laugh at me."

"You mean you've never talked to anyone like you talked to me?" Lan asked in surprise.

Gina shook her head. "I've been a Christian for three years," she said, "and I've been ashamed to let anyone know about it." She paused for a long time. "Yesterday when our Sunday school teacher read about Jesus being ashamed of us if we are ashamed of him, I really felt terrible. I don't want him to be ashamed of me anymore."

Lan was not sure she understood everything Gina was saying. It was still all so new to her. But she did know what it meant to be different. She said slowly, "Maybe sometimes it's good to be different."

HOW ABOUT YOU? Are you afraid to let your Christian testimony show for fear that someone will think you are different? Maybe "being different" in your actions and speech will be the very thing that will cause someone to see that you are a Christian. Perhaps it will give you the opportunity to win someone to Christ. *R.I.J.*

TO MEMORIZE: Then he said to the crowd, "If any of you wants to be my follower, you must put aside your selfish ambition, shoulder your cross daily, and follow me." *Luke 9:23*

"WELL, GREG, what's on your schedule for tomorrow?" asked Dad as he sat down in an easy chair.

Greg snapped off the TV and picked up the paper. "Well," he said, "tomorrow afternoon we have a youth group party." He quickly read through the comic page while his dad took off his shoes. Then, handing Dad the newspaper, Greg added, "We're having a Bible quiz at the beginning of the party. Maybe I'll just go late."

"Oh?" asked Dad. "You used to enjoy quizzes. Why the change?"

Greg leafed through a sports magazine. "Joel always wins."

"Do you know what chapters the quiz will cover?"

"Yes," replied Greg, "but it doesn't matter. Joel will know everything. That guy really knows his Bible. The other day in science class, Joel and our teacher got into a discussion about Creation, and Joel did really good. He quoted verses from the Bible and talked about why he believed it was true. I wish I knew the Bible like that."

Dad asked, "How do you suppose Joel learned so much?" Greg shrugged. "Well," said Dad, "I don't think it came from reading magazines or newspapers or watching TV. If you want to know the Bible, you have to study the Bible."

Greg looked at Dad, then looked down at his magazine. Putting it down, he stood up. "Excuse me, please." He grinned at his dad. "I have to go study a couple chapters in my Bible. Joel's gonna get some competition tomorrow!"

HOW ABOUT YOU? Do you wish you had as much Bible knowledge as a friend? It's available to you, too, but it won't come automatically. Listen carefully when God's Word is taught in church and Sunday school. Also, study it for yourself. *H.W.M.*

TO MEMORIZE: Work hard so God can approve you. Be a good worker, one who does not need to be ashamed and who correctly explains the word of truth. *2 Timothy 2:15*

STUDY TO KNOW

FROM THE BIBLE:

But you must remain faithful to the things you have been taught. You know they are true, for you know you can trust those who taught you. You have been taught the holy Scriptures from childhood, and they have given you the wisdom to receive the salvation that comes by trusting in Christ Jesus. All Scripture is inspired by God and is useful to teach us what is true and to make us realize what is wrong in our lives. It straightens us out and teaches us to do what is right. It is God's way of preparing us in every way, fully equipped for every good thing God wants us to do.

2 TIMOTHY 3:14-17

Study the Bible

26 *March*

ARE YOU LISTENING?

FROM THE BIBLE:

The boy Samuel was serving the Lord by assisting Eli. . . .

One night . . . Samuel was sleeping in the Tabernacle near the Ark of God. Suddenly, the Lord called out, "Samuel! Samuel!"

"Yes?" Samuel replied. "What is it?" He jumped up and ran to Eli. "Here I am. What do you need?"

"I didn't call you," Eli replied. "Go on back to bed." So he did.

Then the Lord called out again, "Samuel!"

Again Samuel jumped up and ran to Eli. "Here I am," he said. "What do you need?"

"I didn't call you, my son," Eli said. "Go on back to bed."

. . . The Lord called a third time, and once more Samuel jumped up and ran to Eli. "Here I am," he said. "What do you need?"

Then Eli realized it was the Lord who was calling the boy. So he said to Samuel, "Go and lie down again, and if someone calls again, say, 'Yes, Lord, your servant is listening.'" So Samuel went back to bed.

And the Lord came and called as before, "Samuel! Samuel!"

And Samuel replied, "Yes, your servant is listening."

1 SAMUEL 3:1-10

Listen for God's voice

"HEARD THE LORD speak to me this morning," Dad said as the Jenkins family drove home from church.

"You did?" Four-year-old Jeremy was astonished. "I didn't hear him."

"I didn't hear him speak the same way you hear me," Dad explained, "but he spoke to my heart. I felt led to give more money to missions."

Mom nodded. "I felt the same way. Did you enjoy the message, Phil?"

Mom glanced at their older son in the backseat, but Phil looked blank. "Uhhh, I . . . well, I . . ."

Mom frowned. "Maybe you didn't hear the Lord because you weren't listening," she suggested.

Before Phil could defend himself, Dad said, "We're home."

As Mom fixed dinner, Dad watched the news on TV. The boys were sprawled on the living room carpet, looking at the Sunday paper together. "Ooohh!" Dad gasped. "That's terrible!" The boys looked up as the newscaster continued telling about a teenage boy who was in the hospital because he rode his bicycle in front of a train. "That's odd," observed Phil as Dad turned off the TV. "Even if he wasn't looking, he should have heard it coming."

"He didn't hear the train because he wasn't listening for it. He was wearing headphones and was listening to his portable radio."

"Sounds like me this morning in church!" said Phil. "I wasn't listening either."

HOW ABOUT YOU? The Lord often speaks to your heart in a still, small voice, simply impressing you with what you need to do. God speaks through your pastor, your teachers, your parents, and of course, the Bible. Don't let other things drown out the Lord's voice. *B.J.W.*

TO MEMORIZE: Look! Here I stand at the door and knock. If you hear me calling and open the door, I will come in, and we will share a meal as friends. *Revelation 3:20*

GARY SETTLED BACK in his seat as his science teacher began showing a movie about Adélie penguins.

Gary watched as the penguins swam toward the coast in the spring. They slid and waddled across the icy land, searching for a nesting place. How funny they looked! Soon they stopped at a rocky place, which was called a rookery. Large numbers of penguins would lay their eggs and raise their young there. A million penguins could live in a single rookery, but each penguin family had its own nest.

When the lights came on, Gary had several questions for his teacher. "If thousands of penguins live in one spot, how can a penguin tell which babies are hers?" he asked. "They all looked dressed alike to me." The class laughed.

"That's a good question, Gary," his teacher said. "Each penguin has a different voice. The parents can pick out their own children from thousands of other penguins just by the sound of their voices."

That evening Gary told his parents about the penguins. Dad smiled and nodded. "You know, God does the same thing for us," he said. "There are millions of people all over the world, but God knows those who belong to him. If they stray away from him, God calls them back to himself by his Word. He knows his own children, and he takes care of them."

"I'm glad I belong to Jesus," Gary said.

HOW ABOUT YOU? Do you wonder if God cares about you or your circumstances? If you've trusted Christ as your Savior, you belong to God. He knows you by name. He cares about every detail of your life. He has promised to care for you. Trust him. *J.L.H.*

TO MEMORIZE: But God's truth stands firm like a foundation stone with this inscription: "The Lord knows those who are his," and "Those who claim they belong to the Lord must turn away from all wickedness." *2 Timothy 2:19*

HE KNOWS HIS OWN
(PART 1)

FROM THE BIBLE:

"I assure you, anyone who sneaks over the wall of a sheepfold, rather than going through the gate, must surely be a thief and a robber! For a shepherd enters through the gate. The gatekeeper opens the gate for him, and the sheep hear his voice and come to him. He calls his own sheep by name and leads them out. After he has gathered his own flock, he walks ahead of them, and they follow him because they recognize his voice. They won't follow a stranger; they will run from him because they don't recognize his voice. . . .

"I am the good shepherd. The good shepherd lays down his life for the sheep. A hired hand will run when he sees a wolf coming. He will leave the sheep because they aren't his and he isn't their shepherd. And so the wolf attacks them and scatters the flock. The hired hand runs away because he is merely hired and has no real concern for the sheep.

"I am the good shepherd; I know my own sheep, and they know me."
JOHN 10:1-5, 11-14

God knows his own

28 March

HE KNOWS HIS OWN
(PART 2)

FROM THE BIBLE:

*Let us go right into the presence
of God, with true hearts fully
trusting him. For our evil
consciences have been sprinkled
with Christ's blood to make us
clean, and our bodies have been
washed with pure water.*

*Without wavering, let us hold
tightly to the hope we say we
have, for God can be trusted to
keep his promise. Think of ways
to encourage one another to
outbursts of love and good deeds.
And let us not neglect our
meeting together, as some people
do, but encourage and warn each
other, especially now that the day
of his coming back again is
drawing near.*
HEBREWS 10:22-25

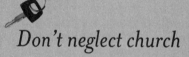

Don't neglect church

AFTER SEEING the movie about penguins, Gary
decided to do a report on them for extra credit.
He was reading a book on penguins when his
dad came into the family room. "How's your report coming, Gary?" Dad asked.

"Good, Dad. I'm learning some really neat
stuff," Gary replied. "Did you know that when
the penguins head for land and search for a nesting place, they march in single file for miles?
They don't have any landmarks to guide them,
but they never get lost. They use the sun to guide
them. Aren't they smart?"

"Yes, and it's because God gave them certain
instincts when he created them," Dad explained.
"God cares about his creation."

"Listen to this," Gary continued. "When the
penguin chicks are about three weeks old, they
get so hungry that both parents must go out and
hunt for food. Then the chicks gather into
groups of fifty or sixty. Each group is called a
crèche. In bad weather they huddle together to
keep warm. They stick together for safety, too. If
they wander off alone, a sea bird will try to capture them."

"That's a good illustration of Christians in a
local church," Dad said. "They need to band together for warmth and fellowship. The church
also gives them spiritual protection as they grow
in the faith."

"Wow! I'm getting lots of lessons from the
penguins. They sure are good teachers!" laughed
Gary.

HOW ABOUT YOU? Do you attend a good Bible-
believing church? Do you listen as the Bible is taught?
Do you make friends with the people there? These
friends can encourage you as you live for Jesus. *J.L.H.*

TO MEMORIZE: Let us not neglect our meeting
together, as some people do, but encourage and
warn each other, especially now that the day of his
coming back again is drawing near. *Hebrews 10:25*

BE STILL

AFTER DINNER one evening, Dad directed nine-year-old Micah, seven-year-old Caitlin, and Mom to three straight-backed chairs that stood in a row in the living room. The children looked puzzled but sat down as instructed. Next, Dad took his position in front of them, holding the most sought-after book—the computer catalog. Everyone listened attentively while Dad described the computer in which Micah was interested.

Suddenly Mom began to kick her legs while leaning against Micah's arm. Then she nudged him gently as she turned around in her seat. Next she bent forward in front of him to pick up a fallen paper.

Micah looked at Mom rather strangely as he tried to listen. He leaned forward so he wouldn't miss a word and so Mom's wiggling wouldn't bother him. Then Mom stood up and walked in front of him. She stopped at Caitlin's chair to ask in a loud whisper if Caitlin wanted her friend Alyssa to come over.

"Mom! How can I concentrate on what Dad's saying?" Micah exploded.

Caitlin suddenly began to giggle. "I know what you're trying to do. You're showing us how we act in church during the sermon!"

"Oh," Micah groaned. "Is that what you're doing?"

"You both are generally quiet in church," commented Dad, "but your wiggling can be just as disturbing as talking."

Micah rolled his eyes and looked at Mom. "I see what you mean," he said.

HOW ABOUT YOU? Do you wiggle, rattle papers, turn around, or whisper during church services? If you do, your mind is not concentrating on the message, and you may be keeping someone else from listening, too. Ask God to help you to "be silent" so you can learn more about him. *J.A.G.*

TO MEMORIZE: Be silent, and know that I am God! I will be honored by every nation. I will be honored throughout the world. *Psalm 46:10*

FROM THE BIBLE:

So on October 8 Ezra the priest brought the scroll of the law before the assembly, which included the men and women and all the children old enough to understand. He faced the square just inside the Water Gate from early morning until noon and read aloud to everyone who could understand. All the people paid close attention to the Book of the Law. . . . Ezra stood on the platform in full view of all the people. When they saw him open the book, they all rose to their feet.

Then Ezra praised the Lord, the great God, and all the people chanted, "Amen! Amen!" as they lifted their hands toward heaven. Then they bowed down and worshiped the Lord with their faces to the ground.

. . . They read from the Book of the Law of God and clearly explained the meaning of what was being read, helping the people understand each passage.
NEHEMIAH 8:1-3, 5-6, 8

Be still in church

THE SOLO PART

FROM THE BIBLE:

Once more he asked him, "Simon son of John, do you love me?"

Peter was grieved that Jesus asked the question a third time. He said, "Lord, you know everything. You know I love you."

Jesus said, "Then feed my sheep. The truth is, when you were young, you were able to do as you liked and go wherever you wanted to. But when you are old, you will stretch out your hands, and others will direct you and take you where you don't want to go." Jesus said this to let him know what kind of death he would die to glorify God. Then Jesus told him, "Follow me."

Peter turned around and saw the disciple Jesus loved following them—the one who had leaned over to Jesus during supper and asked, "Lord, who among us will betray you?" Peter asked Jesus, "What about him, Lord?"

Jesus replied, "If I want him to remain alive until I return, what is that to you? You follow me."

JOHN 21:17-22

Follow Jesus

"IT'S NOT FAIR!" Chris whined. "It's just not fair! I go to children's choir practice every Saturday. And I've been practicing the solo part for weeks, but now Mr. Widmark says that Mark will do the solo." The nine-year-old boy was fighting tears as he rode home with Mom.

"Now wait a minute, Chris," said Mom. "Did Mr. Widmark ever say that you were going to sing the solo?"

"Well, no," he said, "but I'm the most faithful boy in the choir. I just took it for granted that I'd get to sing it."

"You do have a nice voice, but evidently Mark does, too. Maybe Mr. Widmark is hoping that Mark's parents will come to church if he sings the solo. Or maybe Mark's voice is the best one for this song. Whatever the reason, it shouldn't matter to you who sings the solo part."

"But, Mom, doesn't being faithful for all these weeks of practice count for anything?" asked Chris. "Mark has only been coming for a few weeks."

"I understand how you feel," Mom said gently. "But remember the reason for being in the choir. You remind me of the apostle Peter at the end of the book of John. When Jesus explained how Peter would die, Peter wanted to know how John would have to die. Jesus said, 'What is that to you? You follow me!'"

Chris was quiet for a long time. Finally he said, "I guess I'll follow Jesus and not worry about what Mark does."

HOW ABOUT YOU? Have you ever been upset because, as you tried to serve the Lord, someone else got more attention than you? Peter had the same problem. Don't worry about what other people get to do. Your job is to follow Jesus. *M.R.P.*

TO MEMORIZE: Jesus replied, "If I want him to remain alive until I return, what is that to you? You follow me." *John 21:22*

ANDREA GLANCED around the Sunday school room. "I think I won the contest for bringing the most people to Sunday school this month," she whispered to Jana.

"I'm surprised to see Maria here," Jana said, looking at the lone figure seated in the back row. "Wouldn't she feel more comfortable in the special class?"

Andrea shrugged. "Maybe, but then she wouldn't count for me."

"Well, aren't you going to sit with Maria?" asked Jana.

Andrea raised her eyebrows. "Are you kidding?"

Renee joined them. "Andrea, you look so cute in my sweater," she gushed.

As Andrea took a front seat, her face felt like it was on fire. She felt humiliated! She wondered how many had heard Renee's comments. *I wish she'd never given me this stupid sweater!* Andrea fumed inwardly.

". . . and it's possible to do the right thing for the wrong reason." Miss Judy's words finally broke into Andrea's consciousness. "If we give so that others will praise us, it is wrong."

I hope Renee's listening! thought Andrea. *She just gave me her old clothes so she could act like Miss High-and-Mighty and put me down.*

". . . If we invite others just so we can win the contest, we are doing it for the wrong reason." Miss Judy's voice broke into Andrea's thoughts again.

Suddenly, Andrea remembered Maria in the back row. She gulped as she realized she was no better than Renee. "I'm sorry, Lord," she whispered. Rising quietly, she went to sit beside Maria.

HOW ABOUT YOU? Why do you give? Why do you pray? go to church? witness? Do you do it so others will say nice things about you, or because you love the Lord? Be sure to do the right things for the right reasons and you will be blessed. *B.J.W.*

TO MEMORIZE: Work hard and cheerfully at whatever you do, as though you were working for the Lord rather than for people. *Colossians 3:23*

RIGHT BUT WRONG

FROM THE BIBLE:

"Take care! Don't do your good deeds publicly, to be admired, because then you will lose the reward from your Father in heaven. When you give a gift to someone in need, don't shout about it as the hypocrites do— blowing trumpets in the synagogues and streets to call attention to their acts of charity! I assure you, they have received all the reward they will ever get. But when you give to someone, don't tell your left hand what your right hand is doing. Give your gifts in secret, and your Father, who knows all secrets, will reward you.

"And now about prayer. When you pray, don't be like the hypocrites who love to pray publicly on street corners and in the synagogues where everyone can see them. I assure you, that is all the reward they will ever get. But when you pray, go away by yourself, shut the door behind you, and pray to your Father secretly. Then your Father, who knows all secrets, will reward you."

MATTHEW 6:1-6

Have right motives

1 April

NO LOOKING BACK

FROM THE BIBLE:

As they were walking along someone said to Jesus, "I will follow you no matter where you go."

But Jesus replied, "Foxes have dens to live in, and birds have nests, but I, the Son of Man, have no home of my own, not even a place to lay my head."

He said to another person, "Come, be my disciple."

The man agreed, but he said, "Lord, first let me return home and bury my father."

Jesus replied, "Let those who are spiritually dead care for their own dead. Your duty is to go and preach the coming of the Kingdom of God."

Another said, "Yes, Lord, I will follow you, but first let me say good-bye to my family."

But Jesus told him, "Anyone who puts a hand to the plow and then looks back is not fit for the Kingdom of God."

LUKE 9:57-62

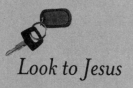

Look to Jesus

SCOTT HAD BEEN a Christian only a short time. His old friends kept after him to join them in doing things they used to do together.

"Scott, would you help me get my garden ready for spring planting?" asked Mr. Lockwood, Scott's Sunday school teacher.

"Sure," said Scott.

The next day Mr. Lockwood showed Scott how the garden tiller worked. "Start here, and don't take your eyes off that post down there," said Mr. Lockwood. "Make a straight row toward it. When you come back this way, you follow the furrow you've just made."

Scott's confidence began to build as row after row of neatly turned earth appeared. He was almost finished when he saw his teacher.

"Shut it off and take a break," shouted Mr. Lockwood.

Grinning, Scott turned back to shut off the machine. To his dismay, he saw that the tiller had made a big swerve to the right while he had been looking back. Mr. Lockwood saw what had happened, too. "Come and have your lemonade," he said, "and then we'll figure out how to straighten this last row."

As they sat under a tree, Scott talked about the problems he was having with his old friends.

Mr. Lockwood gazed over the garden. "Looking back messes up a field, and looking back can mess up a life, too. Sometimes we have to break friendships to follow God. Don't look back on your old life, Scott. Look to Jesus."

HOW ABOUT YOU? Do you have old friends who want you to join them in doing things that you know are wrong? Do those old ways seem attractive? Ask the Lord to help you not to look back. *R.E.P.*

TO MEMORIZE: But Jesus told him, "Anyone who puts a hand to the plow and then looks back is not fit for the Kingdom of God." *Luke 9:62*

DOUG WAS DELIGHTED when robins built a nest on a high ledge of the front porch. When the mother bird began sitting on it, he was sure there were eggs in it.

Doug waited eagerly for the eggs to hatch. Then one day he heard peeping sounds and saw the robins bringing worms to the nest. The baby birds had hatched! He was so excited that he called Grandpa to tell him about it.

"I'll be over to see the little family soon," Grandpa said.

A few days after the birds had hatched, Doug saw three bald little heads bob up every time a worm was brought to the nest. The babies were getting stronger. Soon he heard louder cheeps, and the little heads shot up with beaks wide open.

When Grandpa came over, Doug showed him the hungry little birds with their wide-open beaks just showing above the nest. "They've been getting stronger," Doug said.

"What do you think would happen if they wouldn't open those mouths for food?" asked Grandpa.

"Well, I guess they'd never get strong enough to fly," said Doug.

"Smart boy." Grandpa smiled. "Now, what do you think happens when Christians don't open up to take in God's Word—the spiritual food he gives to make us stronger Christians?"

Doug grinned. "Smart, Grandpa," he teased, then added, "I'm going to start 'opening wide' today by reading my Bible and praying."

HOW ABOUT YOU? Are you "opening wide" to take in the spiritual food God wants to give you? Spend time with God daily and grow strong in your Christian life. *C.E.Y.*

TO MEMORIZE: "It was I, the Lord your God, who rescued you from the land of Egypt. Open your mouth wide, and I will fill it with good things." *Psalm 81:10*

OPEN WIDE

FROM THE BIBLE:

*"For it was I, the Lord your God,
   who rescued you from the land
      of Egypt.
   Open your mouth wide, and I
      will fill it with good things.*

*"But no, my people wouldn't
      listen.
   Israel did not want me
      around.
So I let them follow their blind
      and stubborn way,
   living according to their own
      desires.
But oh, that my people would
      listen to me!
   Oh, that Israel would follow
      me, walking in my paths!
How quickly I would then
      subdue their enemies!
   How soon my hands would be
      upon their foes!
Those who hate the Lord would
      cringe before him;
   their desolation would last
      forever.
But I would feed you with the
      best of foods.
   I would satisfy you with wild
      honey from the rock."*

PSALM 81:10-16

Have daily devotions

FLYING HIGH

FROM THE BIBLE:

Don't worry about the wicked.
  Don't envy those who do
    wrong.
For like grass, they soon fade
    away.
  Like springtime flowers, they
    soon wither.

Trust in the Lord and do good.
  Then you will live safely in the
    land and prosper.
Take delight in the Lord,
  and he will give you your
    heart's desires.
Commit everything you do to the
    Lord.
  Trust him, and he will help
    you.
He will make your innocence as
    clear as the dawn,
  and the justice of your cause
    will shine like the noonday
    sun.

Be still in the presence of the
    Lord,
  and wait patiently for him to
    act.
Don't worry about evil people
    who prosper
  or fret about their wicked
    schemes.

Stop your anger!
  Turn from your rage!
Do not envy others—
  it only leads to harm.
PSALM 37:1-8

Submit to God's control

ANDY WATCHED the red kite soaring in the bright sky. His brother Mike grinned. "Looks like fun, huh, Andy? Would you like to be able to fly high like that?"

"Sure would!" Andy said, grinning back. "But if I were that kite, I'd want to break loose and fly away, high into the sky."

Mike laughed. "But if you broke loose, you'd crash to the ground instead of flying away," he said.

Andy turned to his father. "Would it, Dad?"

"Yep." Dad nodded. "It only flies because the wind pushes it against the resistance of the string. Without that string, it would soon fall."

"Oh." Andy held the spool of string even more tightly.

"You know," Dad mused, "in a way, we're something like that kite. The string guides the kite, and God guides us. Sometimes it's hard to act the way he wants us to, and we pull against the discipline that he uses to direct us. We try to break loose and fly our own way. But if God ever let us go, we would plunge right down, like a kite whose string has broken."

"That's pretty serious," said Mike.

"Would God ever let us go, Dad?" asked Andy.

"No, Andy. If you trust Jesus as your Lord and Savior, he'll never let you go," Dad assured him. "But it's important to submit ourselves to God's control."

HOW ABOUT YOU? Do you sometimes resent the "strings" you feel God has put on your life? Do you feel you'd like to be free to go wherever you want, to choose your own friends, or to pick your own TV programs? Everyone feels like that sometimes. But God has a reason for everything he allows to happen in your life. *J.K.B.*

TO MEMORIZE: Commit everything you do to the Lord. Trust him, and he will help you. *Psalm 37:5*

WHEN THE SCHOOL BELL rang, Tyson pushed past several children and hurried to the drinking fountain. He edged in at the front of the long line. "No cuts!" called several children, but Tyson took a long drink. When he went to hang up his coat, he found a coat on the hook nearest the door. He moved the coat to a place down the line and put his own coat in his favorite spot.

It was the start of a typical day. Tyson spent a lot of time daydreaming instead of studying. At recess he tried to be the first one out the door and the last one back in. "No fair," he grumbled when he had to stay inside to finish his work.

After school Tyson invited Jerry over to play. "I got a new detective set," he said. "Let's see if we can lift fingerprints."

The boys played until Tyson's dad came home from work. After Jerry left, Tyson told Dad about the "detective work" they had been doing. "You leave prints on everything you touch, you know," said Tyson.

"I know, Son," said Dad. "What kind of prints have you been leaving all day?"

Tyson squinted at his dad. "The same kind as always, of course," he said. "Your fingerprints don't change."

"True," agreed Dad, "but wherever you go, you leave other 'prints,' too. Let's call them 'lifeprints.' Everything you do makes an impression—or a 'lifeprint'—on other people. What kind of prints do you think you made today on your teacher and on the kids at school?"

HOW ABOUT YOU? What kind of "lifeprints" are you making? Do others see selfishness and laziness in your prints, or do they see kindness, courtesy, faithfulness, and friendliness? *H.W.M.*

TO MEMORIZE: Since God chose you to be the holy people whom he loves, you must clothe yourselves with tenderhearted mercy, kindness, humility, gentleness, and patience. *Colossians 3:12*

LIFEPRINTS

FROM THE BIBLE:

But now is the time to get rid of anger, rage, malicious behavior, slander, and dirty language. Don't lie to each other, for you have stripped off your old evil nature and all its wicked deeds. . . .

Since God chose you to be the holy people whom he loves, you must clothe yourselves with tenderhearted mercy, kindness, humility, gentleness, and patience. You must make allowance for each other's faults and forgive the person who offends you. Remember, the Lord forgave you, so you must forgive others. And the most important piece of clothing you must wear is love. Love is what binds us all together in perfect harmony.
COLOSSIANS 3:8-9, 12-14

Witness through actions

5 April

JUST A PEEK

FROM THE BIBLE:

He gives us more and more strength to stand against such evil desires. As the Scriptures say,

"God sets himself against the proud,
but he shows favor to the humble."

So humble yourselves before God. Resist the Devil, and he will flee from you. Draw close to God, and God will draw close to you. Wash your hands, you sinners; purify your hearts, you hypocrites. Let there be tears for the wrong things you have done. Let there be sorrow and deep grief. Let there be sadness instead of laughter, and gloom instead of joy. When you bow down before the Lord and admit your dependence on him, he will lift you up and give you honor.
JAMES 4:6-10

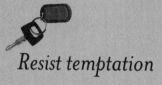

Resist temptation

"JUST BECAUSE the guys on that show use bad language, it doesn't mean I'm going to," complained Jack when his mother made him turn off the TV.

As Jack headed outdoors, he spied a plate of cookies on the counter. Mother had gone upstairs. *I'll just take a peek,* he thought. He reached out and picked up a piece. *I wonder if this one's mint.* He broke off a tiny corner and tasted it. *Yes!* He nibbled another corner. Soon the whole thing was gone. *Guess I'll try a little piece of fudge.* The fudge was delicious, too.

After dinner that evening, Mother said, "Wait till you see what Mrs. Anders gave us." She got the plate of sweets but looked puzzled. "This plate is lovely, but I guess there isn't enough to go around, so I'll pass. Everyone else can choose a piece."

Jack felt so guilty! "What's the trouble, Son?" Mother asked when she noticed how unhappy he appeared.

Tears filled Jack's eyes. He told how he ate the cookies and fudge.

"Do you see how, little by little, you gave in to temptation?" asked Mother. "How one small peek led to handling and smelling, then tasting and eating? That's how Satan works. He gets you to give in, just a little at a time."

Jack nodded. He thought of the TV show he had wanted to watch. Now he could see why it wasn't a good idea.

HOW ABOUT YOU? When you're not allowed to watch a TV show, do you "just look at" the beginning? When you pass magazines in a store, do you peek at the pictures in them that you know are harmful? Would you like to take "just one puff" on a cigarette or "just one sip" of an alcoholic drink? Say no right from the start. *H.W.M.*

TO MEMORIZE: So humble yourselves before God. Resist the Devil, and he will flee from you. *James 4:7*

"HURRY, MOM!" Sam urged. He was eager to get to his Little League game. "Can't you drive any faster?"

"I'm driving the speed limit," his mother assured him. Moments later Sam's heart sank as the car slowed down. "Oh, there's road construction ahead, and traffic's backing up," she said.

"Can't you drive on the shoulder or go across the median to get off and take another road?" asked Sam, sounding desperate.

"Sam, you're going to have to be patient," said Mom.

"I don't believe this," Sam muttered as his mother turned off the engine. "Can't you do something?"

"No, Son, I can't," answered Mom. She added gently. "Sam, you're getting more upset by the minute, and you haven't been speaking very kindly to me." Then she asked, "Do you know why I turned the engine off when I saw we were going to be delayed?"

"So you don't waste gas."

"Right," Mom replied. "I didn't want to waste energy. But you're wasting a lot of energy getting all upset about something we can't do anything about."

Sam was quiet. Then he said, "I'm sorry, Mom. I'll try to be more patient."

HOW ABOUT YOU? Do you become upset when things don't go the way you planned? Do you get angry at people for things that aren't their fault? God wants to help you develop patience. Ask him to help you. *D.K.*

TO MEMORIZE: Be humble and gentle. Be patient with each other, making allowance for each other's faults because of your love. *Ephesians 4:2*

ROAD CONSTRUCTION

FROM THE BIBLE:

Therefore I, a prisoner for serving the Lord, beg you to lead a life worthy of your calling, for you have been called by God. Be humble and gentle. Be patient with each other, making allowance for each other's faults because of your love. Always keep yourselves united in the Holy Spirit, and bind yourselves together with peace.

Dear brothers and sisters, whenever trouble comes your way, let it be an opportunity for joy. For when your faith is tested, your endurance has a chance to grow. So let it grow, for when your endurance is fully developed, you will be strong in character and ready for anything.

EPHESIANS 4:1-3; JAMES 1:2-4

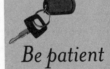

Be patient

7 April

THE RIGHT KEY

FROM THE BIBLE:

Around midnight, Paul and Silas were praying and singing hymns to God, and the other prisoners were listening. Suddenly, there was a great earthquake, and the prison was shaken to its foundations. All the doors flew open, and the chains of every prisoner fell off! The jailer woke up to see the prison doors wide open. He assumed the prisoners had escaped, so he drew his sword to kill himself. But Paul shouted to him, "Don't do it! We are all here!"

Trembling with fear, the jailer called for lights and ran to the dungeon and fell down before Paul and Silas. He brought them out and asked, "Sirs, what must I do to be saved?"

They replied, "Believe on the Lord Jesus and you will be saved, along with your entire household."

ACTS 16:25-31

Believe on Jesus

"LET'S SEE," murmured Danny, looking at the keys he held. The school bus had dropped him off at his grandparents' house. They'd be home after Grandma had her checkup at the doctor's office. In the meantime he planned to enjoy a snack. "Grandpa said to use the silver key with the round top. But I can't find it."

Danny tried each key in the lock, and none of them worked. Finally he walked around the house, checking every window and door. They were all locked.

After about forty minutes his grandparents arrived. "What took you so long?" Danny asked. "I couldn't get inside because you didn't give me the right key."

"Oh no!" exclaimed Grandpa. "Now I remember—I took it off that key ring when I had a duplicate made. I must have forgotten to put it back. I'm sorry."

After they entered with Grandma's key, Danny said, "It sure was tough sitting out there with all those keys and not having one that worked!"

Grandma nodded as she began to make supper. "But there's something even worse," she said. "It's expecting to get into heaven and then finding too late that you have the wrong key."

"You don't get into heaven with keys," said Danny.

"No, not actual keys," agreed Grandma. "But many people think being in a Christian family or living a good life will get them into heaven. These things are like wrong keys. The right key is to 'believe in the Lord Jesus Christ.'" She paused and then added, "I'm glad you have the right key, Danny."

"Me, too!" exclaimed Danny.

HOW ABOUT YOU? What "key" are you counting on for entering heaven? Good works? A Christian family? Your church? These are useless in opening heaven's door. Jesus is the Door to heaven. Believing in him as your Savior is the only key. *M.R.P.*

TO MEMORIZE: They replied, "Believe on the Lord Jesus and you will be saved, along with your entire household." *Acts 16:31*

JARED GLANCED nervously out the school window. All day it had looked stormy. He hoped there wasn't going to be another tornado alert today.

As Jared began the first math problem, a bell rang. "Tornado drill," said Miss Schultz. "Take a large book and file quietly into the hall." Quickly the students obeyed, taking their places in the school's inner hall. Then they put the books over their heads. But there was something different today. Jared could hear a siren signaling that a tornado funnel had been seen nearby.

Jared had never been so scared! But as he sat trembling, he remembered something Dad had said just the weekend before. They had gone swimming, and as Dad walked out into the deep water, Jared's little brother, Brian, hung on to Dad's shoulders. "Are you scared in the deep water, Brian?" Jared had asked.

Brian had said, "Nope, Dad's got me."

Dad had replied, "I'm glad you trust your father." Then he had added, "And remember that you can always trust your Father in heaven, too."

A few minutes later, Jared heard a roaring sound. It got louder and louder. It almost sounded like a train rushing by. He had heard that a tornado sounded that way. *I'm still scared,* Jared thought, *but not so awfully scared. God's my heavenly Father, and he's in control.*

After the "all clear" whistle sounded, the children returned to their classrooms and were soon dismissed to go home. They learned that a tornado had indeed passed by, but no one had been hurt.

HOW ABOUT YOU? Storms can be frightening, can't they? They are powerful and can cause a lot of damage. But God is even more powerful. Remember that God is in control. *H.W.M.*

TO MEMORIZE: And they were filled with awe and said among themselves, "Who is this man, that even the wind and waves obey him?" *Mark 4:41*

GOD'S STRENGTH
(PART 1)

FROM THE BIBLE:

He was already in the boat, so they started out, leaving the crowds behind (although other boats followed). But soon a fierce storm arose. High waves began to break into the boat until it was nearly full of water.

Jesus was sleeping at the back of the boat with his head on a cushion. Frantically they woke him up, shouting, "Teacher, don't you even care that we are going to drown?"

When he woke up, he rebuked the wind and said to the water, "Quiet down!" Suddenly the wind stopped, and there was a great calm. And he asked them, "Why are you so afraid? Do you still not have faith in me?"

And they were filled with awe and said among themselves, "Who is this man, that even the wind and waves obey him?"

MARK 4:36-41

God controls nature

9 April

GOD'S STRENGTH
(PART 2)

FROM THE BIBLE:

I don't want anyone to think more highly of me than what they can actually see in my life and my message, even though I have received wonderful revelations from God. But to keep me from getting puffed up, I was given a thorn in my flesh, a messenger from Satan to torment me and keep me from getting proud.

Three different times I begged the Lord to take it away. Each time he said, "My gracious favor is all you need. My power works best in your weakness." So now I am glad to boast about my weaknesses, so that the power of Christ may work through me. Since I know it is all for Christ's good, I am quite content with my weaknesses and with insults, hardships, persecutions, and calamities. For when I am weak, then I am strong.

2 CORINTHIANS 12:6-10

God gives power

THE TORNADO that passed close to Jared's town was the subject of conversation for many days.

One day Dad came home with a piece of a log. "What's that for?" asked Jared.

Dad held it out, and Jared saw a piece of straw, sticking out from the wood. "One of the fellows at work found this," said Dad. "Isn't it amazing how the wind could take that little straw and drive it into the wood?"

"Wow!" marveled Jared. "How could it do that."

"It took a special kind of power. I've been thinking about it all afternoon, and I've decided to teach that boys class at church."

"What's that got to do with this wood?" asked Jared.

"Well, I wanted to take the class," said Dad, "but I was afraid I wouldn't be able to handle it. This afternoon the Lord showed me that I have a special kind of power available to me—the Holy Spirit. This straw was weak, but when powered by the storm, it became very strong. I'm weak, too, but the Holy Spirit gives me power. So I believe I can help those boys. I thought about you, too."

"Me?" Jared was startled.

Dad nodded. "I heard the choir director asking you to sing a solo. Mr. Groppe said that you have a fine voice."

"But I get so nervous," began Jared, "and I . . ." He paused. "I have a special power available to me, too, don't I?"

HOW ABOUT YOU? Do you feel too weak to sing, give a testimony, make posters, or take part in some other activity for which God has given you a talent? If you're a Christian, a special power—God's power—is available to you. *H.W.M.*

TO MEMORIZE: Since I know it is all for Christ's good, I am quite content with my weaknesses and with insults, hardships, persecutions, and calamities. For when I am weak, then I am strong.
2 Corinthians 12:10

IDOL WORSHIP

"**WILL WE EVER** get to Uncle Pete's?" Kristen whined.

Mom looked at her watch. "It's about another hour. If you're bored you can study the Ten Commandments for Sunday school."

"OK," Kristen agreed, looking at the first one on the list. "You shall have no other gods before me," she read. "Our teacher says that even in America people worship false gods. What does that mean?"

"Another person, a job, money, clothes, popularity. Almost anything can become a god if we value it more than the true God," answered Mom.

The miles passed quickly as Kristen studied. Before long Uncle Pete and Aunt Jolene were coming to the van to meet them, followed by Kristen's cousin Rita. Rita sure looked different!

Kristen soon discovered the reason for the difference. Rita was doing her best to be just like the new rock star, Alicia. Rita walked like her, talked like her, and tried to sing like her. She fixed her hair like Alicia's, dressed like her, and even used the same toothpaste. Rita's room was plastered with posters of the rock star, and Rita played Alicia's new CD all day long.

By the time Mom had said her good-byes the next day, Kristen was ready to leave. "I am so sick and tired of hearing about Alicia—the wonderful, the beautiful, the marvelous!" Kristen exploded as soon as they pulled out of the driveway. "Rita worships that rock star! She's Rita's idol!"

"Now do you understand what the first commandment means?" Mom asked.

"I certainly do," Kristen replied.

HOW ABOUT YOU? What controls your thoughts, actions, and plans? Who is it that you want to be like? It's normal to have someone you admire and look up to, but be careful to pick someone who is following Jesus. And remember, don't make a "god" of him or her. *B.J.W.*

TO MEMORIZE: "Do not worship any other gods besides me." *Exodus 20:3*

FROM THE BIBLE:

Then God instructed the people as follows:

"I am the Lord your God, who rescued you from slavery in Egypt.

"Do not worship any other gods besides me.

"Do not make idols of any kind, whether in the shape of birds or animals or fish. You must never worship or bow down to them, for I, the Lord your God, am a jealous God who will not share your affection with any other god! I do not leave unpunished the sins of those who hate me, but I punish the children for the sins of their parents to the third and fourth generations. But I lavish my love on those who love me and obey my commands, even for a thousand generations."

EXODUS 20:1-6

Worship the true God

11 April

THE RED CELLOPHANE

FROM THE BIBLE:

*When we were utterly helpless,
Christ came at just the right
time and died for us sinners.
Now, no one is likely to die for a
good person, though someone
might be willing to die for a
person who is especially good.
But God showed his great love
for us by sending Christ to die
for us while we were still sinners.
And since we have been made
right in God's sight by the blood
of Christ, he will certainly save
us from God's judgment. For
since we were restored to
friendship with God by the death
of his Son while we were still his
enemies, we will certainly be
delivered from eternal punishment by his life. So now we can
rejoice in our wonderful new
relationship with God—all
because of what our Lord Jesus
Christ has done for us in making
us friends of God.*
ROMANS 5:6-11

*Jesus' blood
covers sin*

"WHAT'S THAT, Grandpa?" Sammy pointed to some small cards and pieces of shiny red paper on the kitchen table.

Grandpa smiled. "Grandma found these when she was cleaning the other day," he replied. "When I was a boy, we used to get these as prizes in cereal boxes."

"Wow!" Sammy was impressed. "What are all the shiny red papers for?"

"Ah, that's what makes these cards interesting," replied Grandpa. "Here's one with a picture of Babe Ruth. On the back of the card is this question: 'What was Babe Ruth's given name?' To find the answer, we put this shiny red paper—cellophane—over the question. Now what do you see?"

"It says 'George Herman Ruth,'" answered Sammy. "The question disappeared, and the answer showed up!"

"Right," said Grandpa. "This little piece of paper taught me a great lesson. When I was young, our church had revival meetings," began Grandpa. "One night the evangelist called me up to the platform. He asked if he could use this Babe Ruth card as an illustration. Then he put the red paper over the question and said, 'Now, read the question.' I said I couldn't see the question, only the answer. And he said, 'That's how it is with God. When you accept Jesus as Savior, the blood of Christ washes away your sin. Just as you can't see the question when it's covered by the red paper, God can no longer see your sin when it's covered by the blood of Christ.'"

HOW ABOUT YOU? What does God see when he looks at you? Does he see your sins, or are they covered by Jesus' blood so that he sees Christ in you? *P.R.*

TO MEMORIZE: I myself no longer live, but Christ lives in me. So I live my life in this earthly body by trusting in the Son of God, who loved me and gave himself for me. *Galatians 2:20*

"MOM, CAN I bake a cake?" asked Cindy.

Cindy's mother smiled. "Sure, Cindy, but I'm going to be busy, so I won't be able to help. Follow the directions exactly."

"Oh, I will," promised Cindy.

Cindy did follow the directions. So when the cake looked and tasted awful, she was almost in tears.

"What's up?" asked Dad, walking into the kitchen. Cindy explained about the ruined cake. "Oh no!" Dad said. "I know what happened. Last night when I put away the groceries, I dropped a box of salt, and it started to leak. I saw that the sugar canister was empty, so I poured the salt into it. I meant to mention it, but the phone rang and I forgot."

"So what I thought was sugar was really salt?" Cindy asked.

"I'm sorry, Cindy," Dad said, giving her a hug.

"What a perfect illustration for the verse in Isaiah where people called evil good," said Mom. "And they said light was darkness and bitter was sweet."

"Right," Dad said, nodding. "That canister said sugar, but it was really salt, so the cake was ruined. That's not so bad because you can make another cake. But if people say a thing is good when God says it's evil—and if they say things are evil when God says they're good—that can ruin an entire life."

HOW ABOUT YOU? Do you know what things God says are good? Do you know what things God says are evil? In today's world many people change it around so that the good seems to be evil and the evil seems to be good. Know what God says in his Word, and follow his guidelines. *L.M.W.*

TO MEMORIZE: Destruction is certain for those who say that evil is good and good is evil; that dark is light and light is dark; that bitter is sweet and sweet is bitter. *Isaiah 5:20*

THIS ISN'T SUGAR!

FROM THE BIBLE:

Destruction is certain for those who drag their sins behind them, tied with cords of falsehood. They even mock the Holy One of Israel and say, "Hurry up and do something! Quick, show us what you can do. We want to see what you have planned."

Destruction is certain for those who say that evil is good and good is evil; that dark is light and light is dark; that bitter is sweet and sweet is bitter.

Destruction is certain for those who think they are wise and consider themselves to be clever.

ISAIAH 5:18-21

Don't call evil "good"

13 April

THE WHISTLE

FROM THE BIBLE:

I know very well how foolish the message of the cross sounds to those who are on the road to destruction. But we who are being saved recognize this message as the very power of God. As the Scriptures say,

"I will destroy human wisdom and discard their most brilliant ideas."

So where does this leave the philosophers, the scholars, and the world's brilliant debaters? God . . . has shown their wisdom to be useless nonsense. Since God in his wisdom saw to it that the world would never find him through human wisdom, he has used our foolish preaching to save all who believe. God's way seems foolish to the Jews because they want a sign from heaven to prove it is true. And it is foolish to the Greeks because they believe only what agrees with their own wisdom. . . . But to those called by God to salvation, both Jews and Gentiles, Christ is the mighty power of God and the wonderful wisdom of God. This "foolish" plan of God is far wiser than the wisest of human plans.

1 CORINTHIANS 1:18-25

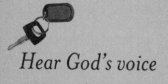

Hear God's voice

"WHERE'S MOLLY?" asked Dan. "I want to play with her." Dan had just come to spend a week with Grandpa, and he loved to play with Grandpa's collie.

Grandpa took a whistle from his pocket, put it to his mouth, and blew it. "It doesn't make any sound," said Dan. "It must be broken." But just then Molly came running from behind the barn.

Grandpa laughed. "The whistle emits a high-pitched sound that human ears can't hear, but a dog can hear it plainly," he explained.

Dan and Molly raced across the yard. Then Dan threw a stick for Molly to fetch. She brought it back, waiting eagerly for him to throw it again. When Dan was tired, he went to sit beside Grandpa on the porch, and Molly lay down nearby.

"May I play with the whistle, Grandpa?" Dan asked.

"No, Son," Grandpa shook his head. "We only use it when we want Molly to respond." He paused, then added, "As I watched you and Molly play, I thought of some ways God calls us when he wants our attention."

"God doesn't have a whistle," said Dan with a laugh.

Grandpa smiled. "No," he said, "but sometimes he speaks to us through our parents, teachers, and pastors. Sometimes he speaks through the Bible. And sometimes the Holy Spirit speaks silently through our consciences and minds."

"And we're the only ones who hear him, aren't we?" Dan asked thoughtfully.

"That's right," agreed Grandpa. "Only God's children can hear and understand what he says to them."

HOW ABOUT YOU? Has God "whistled" for you? Has he spoken to you through his Word? Has he spoken through a parent, a teacher, or a pastor? Has he pricked your conscience regarding something you should or should not do? Follow him. *B.K.*

TO MEMORIZE: My sheep recognize my voice; I know them, and they follow me. *John 10:27*

TAMMY LOVED to visit Grandpa Nelson's greenhouse. She loved working with Grandpa among the flowers and plants, learning to care for them and keep them healthy. But today she was confused. Grandpa had sent her into the storage room to get some potting soil. There, on a shelf, she saw some beautiful green plants. Grandpa had taught her that plants need light and water to grow, but these were being kept completely in the dark, and the soil in the pot was bone dry.

"Grandpa, those plants in the back room are going to die. Why did you put them there?" Tammy asked as she returned.

"Those are Easter cactus plants," Grandpa replied. "If you keep the plants in the dark for a month, they begin to bloom when you bring them out into the light. So we can have them bloom when we want them to."

"How strange," murmured Tammy.

"Yes, it is," agreed Grandpa. He put down his trowel and smiled. "You know, I think God sometimes puts us in the dark so we can bloom, too."

"You mean like when you were in the hospital?" Tammy asked.

Grandpa was glad Tammy understood. "At first I couldn't figure out why I had to be so sick," he told her. "But as I spent time praying and reading God's Word, I learned to relax and wait for God. You see, while I was 'in the dark,' the Lord gave me the 'bloom' of patience."

HOW ABOUT YOU? Have you ever wondered why you had to be "in the dark"? Why you had to be sick, or face a death or divorce in your family, or struggle with school problems? Sometimes the Lord allows problems in order to bring the "bloom" of patience or prayer into your life. *R.E.P.*

TO MEMORIZE: For when your faith is tested, your endurance has a chance to grow. *James 1:3*

BLOOMS OUT OF DARKNESS

FROM THE BIBLE:

Dear brothers and sisters, whenever trouble comes your way, let it be an opportunity for joy. For when your faith is tested, your endurance has a chance to grow. So let it grow, for when your endurance is fully developed, you will be strong in character and ready for anything.

If you need wisdom—if you want to know what God wants you to do—ask him, and he will gladly tell you. He will not resent your asking. . . .

God blesses the people who patiently endure testing. Afterward they will receive the crown of life that God has promised to those who love him.
JAMES 1:2-5, 12

God works through problems

15 April

THE LIVING GOD

FROM THE BIBLE:

But very early on Sunday morning the women came to the tomb, taking the spices they had prepared. They found that the stone covering the entrance had been rolled aside. So they went in, but they couldn't find the body of the Lord Jesus. They were puzzled, trying to think what could have happened to it. Suddenly, two men appeared to them, clothed in dazzling robes. The women were terrified and bowed low before them. Then the men asked, "Why are you looking in a tomb for someone who is alive? He isn't here! He has risen from the dead! Don't you remember what he told you back in Galilee, that the Son of Man must be betrayed into the hands of sinful men and be crucified, and that he would rise again the third day?"

Then they remembered that he had said this. So they rushed back to tell his eleven disciples—and everyone else—what had happened.

LUKE 24:1-9

God is alive

KARLA STARED at the screen as the missionary pictures were being shown. She saw people dressed like those in her own church. There were businessmen and housewives, schoolchildren and toddlers, all kneeling before a strange idol! They were praying. Karla knew that in some countries people worshiped wooden and stone gods, but these people were in a civilized area, a big city.

That evening she talked with her father and mother about it. "How do you know when you've got the right god?" she asked bluntly.

"What do you mean?" Karla's mother asked. "There is only one true God."

"Sure," Karla replied, "but all those people I saw in the pictures—they think they've got the right god, too."

"Yes," Dad said, "but the Bible tells us there is only one God. He is the Creator of the earth. He made everything in it, including man."

Karla was quiet for a long time. Finally she spoke. "So that's why we believe in him? Because he's so great?"

Dad shook his head. "Partly, but more than that."

Karla was thinking. "Is it because he sent his Son, Jesus, to die?" she suggested.

"There's still more," Dad told her. "Jesus—who is God—did more than die for us, as wonderful as that was! He also arose. And no other religion in the world has a living Savior."

Karla thought about that for a minute. There were wooden gods, stone gods, golden gods, and probably every other kind. But her God was different. He was alive! Only he could hear and answer her prayers.

HOW ABOUT YOU? Imagine what it would be like to pray to a stone or a piece of wood or to a person who is dead. If you are a Christian, give thanks for your risen, living Savior. Then tell others about him, too. *R.I.J.*

TO MEMORIZE: He isn't here! He has risen from the dead! *Luke 24:6*

WHEN ANGELA returned home from her friend's house, her hair was fixed a new way. "Kristine fixed it," Angela told her mother. "Do you like it?"

"It looks nice," said Mother. "It's fixed the same way Kristine wears hers, isn't it?" Angela nodded happily.

Her brother snorted. "You two might as well be twins," he said. "You're together every spare minute. You're even beginning to look alike." Angela smiled. She was happy to be just like Kristine.

The next day things didn't go well for Angela. She found herself getting angrier than usual over unimportant things. *What's wrong with me?* she wondered after being rude to a teacher who had irritated her.

"You sounded like Kristine," the girl next to Angela whispered. "I guess it's because you two hang around together so much."

Angela looked at her in surprise. She knew one of Kristine's faults was a quick temper. Was Angela taking on that characteristic, too? Perhaps she didn't want to be like Kristine after all.

"Oh, well. No one is perfect," Angela reminded herself with a shrug. But then she suddenly remembered something. *There's one person who is perfect—Jesus. He's the one I want to be like.* Angela knew she hadn't been "hanging around" with him nearly enough lately. *I'm sorry, Lord. We'll have that special time as soon as I get home,* she promised.

HOW ABOUT YOU? People often become like those with whom they spend the most time. It's easy to pick up the dress, language, and even mannerisms of those with whom one "hangs around." Do you spend enough time with Jesus to become like him? *K.R.A.*

TO MEMORIZE: Those who say they live in God should live their lives as Christ did. *1 John 2:6*

JUST ALIKE

FROM THE BIBLE:

"I am the vine; you are the branches. Those who remain in me, and I in them, will produce much fruit. For apart from me you can do nothing. Anyone who parts from me is thrown away like a useless branch and withers. Such branches are gathered into a pile to be burned. But if you stay joined to me and my words remain in you, you may ask any request you like, and it will be granted! My true disciples produce much fruit. This brings great glory to my Father.

"I have loved you even as the Father has loved me. Remain in my love. When you obey me, you remain in my love, just as I obey my Father and remain in his love. I have told you this so that you will be filled with my joy. Yes, your joy will overflow! I command you to love each other in the same way that I love you. And here is how to measure it— the greatest love is shown when people lay down their lives for their friends. You are my friends if you obey me."

JOHN 15:5-14

Be like Jesus

17 April

WHEN THE TREE NEEDS HELP

FROM THE BIBLE:

My son, obey your father's commands, and don't neglect your mother's teaching. Keep their words always in your heart. Tie them around your neck. Wherever you walk, their counsel can lead you. When you sleep, they will protect you. When you wake up in the morning, they will advise you. For these commands and this teaching are a lamp to light the way ahead of you. The correction of discipline is the way to life.
PROVERBS 6:20-23

Welcome help

DAVID WATCHED his father pull out the stake that had been wired to a small tree ever since it had been planted.

"A small tree often doesn't have the strength or ability to stand alone," Dad said. "This stake acted as a support, but now I believe the tree is big enough to take any winds that may come along. And it can teach us a lesson about life," added Dad.

"What do you mean?" David asked.

"When you were small, your mother and I held on to your hand every time you took a step," Dad explained. "We didn't want you to fall and get hurt. As you began to grow, we let you go by yourself, but we still watched you."

David nodded as he thought about it. Even now he often needed his parents' advice and help. He asked his father if he'd always have to depend on them.

"We're committed to helping you grow to be a strong follower of Jesus Christ," Dad replied, smiling. "As you grow up, you'll be ready someday to go on without us. Proverbs 22:6 is a verse that your mother and I try to follow as we raise you: 'Teach your children to choose the right path, and when they are older, they will remain upon it.'"

"Sort of like the tree, isn't it?" David asked. "When it was small and frail, you had to keep the stake beside it all the time. But now that it's old enough, it will keep growing straight without the supporting stake."

HOW ABOUT YOU? How do you feel when you are restricted in some way by your parents' rules and guidance? Don't get angry. Every young tree needs help to grow big and strong and straight. *R.I.J.*

TO MEMORIZE: My son, obey your father's commands, and don't neglect your mother's teaching. *Proverbs 6:20*

"OH NO!" Cory groaned when he opened his dresser drawer and saw he had no clean socks. It didn't help to know it was his own fault for not throwing his dirty things in the laundry basket. He groaned even louder when a button popped off his shirt. As he was tying his shoe, the shoelace broke. "Everything is going wrong!" he grumbled.

When Cory was finally dressed, he went to the kitchen and got a bowl of cereal and milk. While carrying the bowl to the table, it tipped, and the contents spilled over onto the floor. His face grew red with anger, and he yelled a bad word.

Even before Mother said anything, Cory felt guilty. Using a four-letter word had only made him feel worse. He and his mother talked it over as they cleaned up the mess. He told her about the things that had gone wrong that morning.

"Instead of getting more and more angry each time something went wrong, what if you had stopped to pray?" Mother asked.

Cory stirred a new bowl of cereal, thinking that over. "If I had prayed, I probably wouldn't have gotten so angry," he said slowly. "I'm going to pray right now for God's forgiveness," added Cory. "And if anything else goes wrong today, I'm going to pray about it just as soon as it happens so I won't end up saying a bad word again."

HOW ABOUT YOU? When everything seems to go wrong, do you get more and more upset until you swear? A better way to handle your anger is to talk to God about the things that are bothering you. Ask him to take your anger away. You may even be able to laugh about some of the annoying things that happen. *C.E.Y.*

TO MEMORIZE: If you keep your mouth shut, you will stay out of trouble. *Proverbs 21:23*

EVERYTHING'S WRONG

FROM THE BIBLE:

Whoever pursues godliness and unfailing love will find life, godliness, and honor.

The wise conquer the city of the strong and level the fortress in which they trust.

If you keep your mouth shut, you will stay out of trouble.

Mockers are proud and haughty; they act with boundless arrogance.

PROVERBS 21:21-24

Pray—don't swear

19 April

THE BROKEN WATCHES

FROM THE BIBLE:

"Listen to me, all you who are left in Israel. I created you and have cared for you since before you were born. I will be your God throughout your lifetime—until your hair is white with age. I made you, and I will care for you. I will carry you along and save you. . . .

"Do not forget this, you guilty ones. And do not forget the things I have done throughout history. For I am God—I alone! I am God, and there is no one else like me. Only I can tell you what is going to happen even before it happens. Everything I plan will come to pass, for I do whatever I wish."

ISAIAH 46:3-4, 8-10

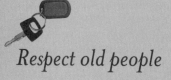

Respect old people

JUSTIN RAN into the house and slammed the front door. "Mom!" he called. "Dad said Grandpa is coming to visit again."

"Yes," replied Mom. "Dad is going to get Grandpa on Saturday morning." She sighed as she poked around in her jewelry box. "My watch is broken, and I was hoping one of my old ones would still work. Look, Justin." She held up a small, gold wristwatch. "This is my high school graduation present from Grandpa and Grandma. This one with the leather strap was my official nurse's watch. And the one I wear now—Dad bought this for me before we were married, but now it won't run either."

Justin nodded, then asked, "Why does Grandpa have to come? He spills things and talks funny."

"I thought you loved Grandpa," Mother said quietly.

"I do," Justin said, "or I did before he had that stroke. He used to do stuff with me. Now he just sits around and . . . gets in the way."

Mother pointed to the watches. "These watches won't run, but they bring back memories of happy times," she said. "I don't want to throw them out even though they don't have feelings the way people do." Justin looked at the floor. He knew she meant Grandpa. "I have many happy memories of growing up with Grandpa and Grandma," added Justin's mother. "Grandma is in heaven now, and Grandpa is old. But I don't want to throw him out. I love him too much."

Justin hugged his mother. "I'm sorry, Mom. I don't want to throw him out either."

HOW ABOUT YOU? Do you value old people? Never "throw them away" just because they can't do all the things they once could. Use every opportunity to show them that you do love and appreciate them. *B.K.*

TO MEMORIZE: Gray hair is a crown of glory; it is gained by living a godly life. *Proverbs 16:31*

THE RIGHT WAY TO SAY NO

"**OUR CLASS** is having a play," Tony told his parents during supper one evening. "There's a scene with the devil in it, and Miss Clark gave me that part, but I really don't want to do it."

"Did you tell her?" Mother asked as she placed some food on Carrie's plate.

"No, I was going to, but—"

Carrie interrupted Tony's explanation. "I don't want that!"

"Then you will not get any dessert," said Mother.

"I was going to tell Miss Clark," Tony continued, "but Christi was talking to her. Christi was telling her she refused to be a witch in the play, which didn't make Miss Clark too happy. I was afraid—"

This time Beth interrupted Tony. "Mother, could I eat extra vegetables instead of this casserole, please?" Mother hesitated. "I suppose so."

"What can I do about the play?" asked Tony.

Carrie spoke up again. "Why do I have to eat casserole if Beth doesn't?"

"Because your attitude is bad," Dad said sternly. "Beth asked politely if she could have a substitute. You declared that you were not going to eat yours."

Mother turned to Tony. "Maybe that's your answer," she said. "Did Christi ask Miss Clark to excuse her from the play, or did she just refuse to do it?"

"She just said she wouldn't do it," replied Tony.

"Whether or not our requests are granted often depends on *how* we ask rather than on *what* we ask," Dad said, as much to Carrie as to Tony.

HOW ABOUT YOU? When you are asked to do something you feel is wrong, don't be afraid to say no, but say it in the right way. Be respectful but firm, as Daniel was. *B.J.W.*

TO MEMORIZE: But Daniel made up his mind not to defile himself by eating the food and wine given to them by the king. He asked the chief official for permission to eat other things instead. *Daniel 1:8*

FROM THE BIBLE:

Then the king ordered Ashpenaz, who was in charge of the palace officials, to bring to the palace some of the young men of Judah's royal family and other noble families, who had been brought to Babylon as captives. "Select only strong, healthy, and good-looking young men," he said. "Make sure they are well versed in every branch of learning, are gifted with knowledge and good sense, and have the poise needed to serve in the royal palace. Teach these young men the language and literature of the Babylonians." The king assigned them a daily ration of the best food and wine from his own kitchens. They were to be trained for a three-year period, and then some of them would be made his advisers in the royal court. . . .

But Daniel made up his mind not to defile himself by eating the food and wine given to them by the king. He asked the chief official for permission to eat other things instead.

DANIEL 1:3-5, 8

Keep a pleasant attitude

21 April

GOOD-FOR-NOTHING JACOB

FROM THE BIBLE:

"You are the salt of the earth. But what good is salt if it has lost its flavor? Can you make it useful again? It will be thrown out and trampled underfoot as worthless. You are the light of the world—like a city on a mountain, glowing in the night for all to see. Don't hide your light under a basket! Instead, put it on a stand and let it shine for all. In the same way, let your good deeds shine out for all to see, so that everyone will praise your heavenly Father."

MATTHEW 5:13-16

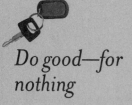

Do good—for nothing

IN THE EXPRESS LANE at the store, Jacob stood on one foot and then the other. He had promised Mrs. Moore he'd bring her some brown sugar.

The conversation of the two men in front of him caught his attention. "I'm telling you," complained one, "my grandson is good for nothin'. His folks hire someone to mow the lawn while that kid sits by his computer."

"Yep," the other agreed, "the younger generation is spoiled rotten." Jacob fumed.

When Jacob handed Mrs. Moore her brown sugar and change, she tried to return the change to him. "No thanks," said Jacob.

Mother was just getting her coat on when Jacob arrived home. "Jacob, watch Emily for me, please," she said. "I need to run a few errands." Jacob nodded. Then he watched Emily play on the swing set while he trimmed a hedge.

At the dinner table that evening, Jacob repeated the conversation he had heard at the supermarket. "Well, they did have a point," said Dad.

Mother looked up. "Don, are you saying that Jacob is good for nothing?"

"Well," said Dad, "today he ran an errand for Mrs. Moore. What did you get paid for that, Son?"

Jacob shrugged. "Nothing."

"And then you baby-sat Emily for your mother, and it looks like you trimmed the hedge for me. What did you get paid for those jobs?"

"Well, nothing," Jacob responded.

"Then I guess you're good for nothing, Jacob." Dad laughed. "And I reckon there are a lot more kids out there who are just as good for nothing as you are."

HOW ABOUT YOU? Do you expect to be paid for everything you do? Start doing at least one good deed a day for nothing. In heaven you will be rewarded for the things done for nothing. *B.J.W.*

TO MEMORIZE: Store your treasures in heaven, where they will never become moth-eaten or rusty and where they will be safe from thieves. *Matthew 6:20*

JUST OUTSIDE JILL'S WINDOW

THE MARRIS FAMILY lived in a two-story house surrounded by big trees. Jill especially liked the maple tree outside her bedroom window. She liked the sound of the leaves gently brushing against the glass.

One spring day Jill looked out the window and noticed a wren surveying the crook of a branch. Soon a second wren flew up. Jill stood still so she wouldn't frighten the birds. As she watched, they began to build a nest. The wrens made many trips, gathering twigs and bits of leaves. Jill had to laugh when she saw one of the wrens use a piece of hair ribbon that she had lost in the snow during the winter.

When the nest was finished, Jill checked each day to see if there was anything in it. One morning she saw small eggs in the straw. Soon there were baby wrens, too. The parents kept busy feeding the babies!

But one day there was a terrible thunderstorm. The branch swayed back and forth, and the nest swayed with it.

"How are the wrens, Jill?" asked Dad, as he was passing her room.

"The branch is swaying in the wind, but the mother wren is covering the babies," Jill answered. "It's great that God created her so she knows how to protect her babies."

"I'll tell you another great thing," said Dad, coming in to take a look. "God uses that very picture—a mother bird spreading her wings to protect the babies—as an example of how he cares for us, his children."

HOW ABOUT YOU? Have you ever seen a mother bird protect her young? The Bible often uses "word pictures" to illustrate God's love. Remember a mother bird's care for her babies, and you'll know how carefully God protects you. *L.M.W.*

TO MEMORIZE: He will shield you with his wings. He will shelter you with his feathers. His faithful promises are your armor and protection. *Psalm 91:4*

FROM THE BIBLE:

*Those who live in the shelter
    of the Most High
    will find rest in the shadow
    of the Almighty.
This I declare of the Lord:
    He alone is my refuge, my
    place of safety;
    he is my God, and I am
    trusting him. . . .
He will shield you with his
    wings.
    He will shelter you with his
    feathers.
    His faithful promises are your
    armor and protection.
Do not be afraid of the terrors
    of the night,
    nor fear the dangers of the
    day. . . .*

*If you make the Lord your refuge,
    if you make the Most High
    your shelter,
no evil will conquer you;
    no plague will come near
    your dwelling.
For he orders his angels
    to protect you wherever
    you go.
They will hold you with their
    hands
    to keep you from striking your
    foot on a stone. . . .*

*The Lord says, "I will rescue
    those who love me.
    I will protect those who trust
    in my name."*
PSALM 91:1-2, 4-5, 9-12, 14

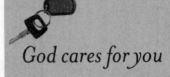

God cares for you

23 April

IN SHAPE

FROM THE BIBLE:

Then he said to the crowd, "If any of you wants to be my follower, you must put aside your selfish ambition, shoulder your cross daily, and follow me. If you try to keep your life for yourself, you will lose it. But if you give up your life for me, you will find true life. And how do you benefit if you gain the whole world but lose or forfeit your own soul in the process? If a person is ashamed of me and my message, I, the Son of Man, will be ashamed of that person when I return in my glory and in the glory of the Father and the holy angels.
LUKE 9:23-26

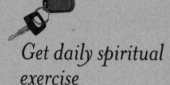

Get daily spiritual exercise

DAN had never been so glad to see the end of a week. Band camp had been fun, but for the most part there was too much work. What a way to spend Easter vacation!

Dan had played his trumpet so long and so hard that he'd split his lip. And every morning the band had marched for two hours. After the first day Dan felt like he never wanted to walk again! But by the end of the week his legs felt really strong.

Nevertheless, the very first day back at school, Dan twisted his ankle in gym class and had to stay off it for several days. Well, at least he didn't have to march with the band for a while! The band was preparing for a long parade, and Mr. Artz, the band director, was making them work hard.

Just as Dan was getting ready to rejoin the band, he got the flu. He began to get worried because he *did* want to march in that parade.

On the day of the parade Dan felt fine. But he couldn't believe how tired the parade made him!

At church the next day Pastor Steve talked about being spiritually strong. "Our spiritual lives are like our physical lives," said the pastor. "We don't have to do anything to get *out* of shape, but we must exercise daily to stay *in* shape."

Dan knew that if he wanted to be strong spiritually, he'd need to work hard like he had in band camp.

HOW ABOUT YOU? Is your spirit out of shape from lack of exercise? Doing nothing will get you out of shape very quickly, so discipline yourself to read the Bible, pray, and live for Jesus every day. *R.E.P.*

TO MEMORIZE: Because of this, I always try to maintain a clear conscience before God and everyone else. *Acts 24:16*

SARAH RUBBED her stomach as she eyed the cake Mother had just finished frosting. "Meredith and I sure are hungry!" Sarah's friend Meredith had come to spend the night, and the girls were looking for an after-school snack.

Mother laughed. "Help yourself," she invited.

After cutting and serving the cake, Sarah sat down beside her friend. She watched as Meredith picked at her piece. "Meredith, are you just going to eat the frosting?" she asked. "The cake is full of nuts and goodies."

"The frosting is all I ever eat," Meredith responded. She glanced at Sarah's mother. "I hope you aren't offended."

"No," Mother answered, "but I'm afraid you won't find the frosting very satisfying, and dinner won't be ready for a while. But, you're really leaving the best part. Why don't you take one taste and see if you like it?"

Meredith grimaced, but she took a tiny bite. She grinned. "It *is* good! I think I'll eat the rest."

That evening the girls were right in the middle of a game when Dad called them for family devotions. "Can we just read the story and skip the rest?" Sarah asked.

Dad frowned. "Skip the Bible reading and prayer?"

"Well, just this once," Sarah murmured, "so we can finish our game."

"That would be like eating the frosting and leaving the cake, wouldn't it?" Meredith asked.

"Yes," Mother answered, "If we simply read the story and skipped his Word, we'd be missing the best part."

HOW ABOUT YOU? Are you tempted to skip the Bible reading and read only the story in this book? Don't do it. The Scripture is the most important part. "Eat" the whole thing, and enjoy every bite. *B.J.W.*

TO MEMORIZE: Taste and see that the Lord is good. Oh, the joys of those who trust in him! *Psalm 34:8*

THE BEST PART

FROM THE BIBLE:

As Jesus and the disciples continued on their way to Jerusalem, they came to a village where a woman named Martha welcomed them into her home. Her sister, Mary, sat at the Lord's feet, listening to what he taught. But Martha was worrying over the big dinner she was preparing. She came to Jesus and said, "Lord, doesn't it seem unfair to you that my sister just sits here while I do all the work? Tell her to come and help me."

But the Lord said to her, "My dear Martha, you are so upset over all these details! There is really only one thing worth being concerned about. Mary has discovered it—and I won't take it away from her."

LUKE 10:38-42

Don't skip Bible reading

25 April

NEEDED: TIME TO LEARN

FROM THE BIBLE:

But when the Holy Spirit controls our lives, he will produce this kind of fruit in us: love, joy, peace, patience, kindness, goodness, faithfulness, gentleness, and self-control. Here there is no conflict with the law.

Those who belong to Christ Jesus have nailed the passions and desires of their sinful nature to his cross and crucified them there. If we are living now by the Holy Spirit, let us follow the Holy Spirit's leading in every part of our lives. Let us not become conceited, or irritate one another, or be jealous of one another.

Dear brothers and sisters, if another Christian is overcome by some sin, you who are godly should gently and humbly help that person back onto the right path. And be careful not to fall into the same temptation yourself.

GALATIANS 5:22–6:1

Be patient with new Christians

"IT SEEMS TO ME that if Mary Beth really meant it when she said she accepted Jesus, she'd be a little nicer at school," Nadine told her mother as they finished the dishes. As Nadine hung up the dishcloth, her yellow kitten jumped up on the counter. "Buddy! Get down from there!" yelled Nadine. Buddy jumped down. "Oh!" sputtered Nadine. "Now I've got to wash the counter again!"

"Now, now," sympathized Nadine's mother. "No need to get so upset. Just keep after Buddy, and he'll eventually learn that he's not allowed up there."

Nadine quickly wiped the counter, then tromped outside and plopped down on the steps. "Sometimes I wish I didn't even have a cat," she said, pouting.

"Honey," said Mother, sitting down next to her daughter, "you know you wouldn't give Buddy up. But you have to remember that he's still a baby. You need to train him and teach him the rules."

Purring loudly, Buddy rubbed up against Nadine, and she softened a little. "Like you do for me?" she asked.

"Yes," agreed Mother, "and like older Christians do for new Christians. Those who are babies in Christ can't be expected to immediately know the whole Bible or to do everything right. We must have lots of patience and teach them."

Nadine reached down and picked up Buddy. "I guess I can't expect you to know the rules completely yet," she murmured to him, "and I guess I shouldn't expect quite so much of Mary Beth, either."

HOW ABOUT YOU? Do you expect too much from those who are new Christians? Remember that one of the fruits of the Spirit is patience. As you pray for new Christians, also be patient with them. *V.L.R.*

TO MEMORIZE: But when the Holy Spirit controls our lives, he will produce this kind of fruit in us: love, joy, peace, patience, kindness, goodness, faithfulness, gentleness, and self-control. Here there is no conflict with the law. *Galatians 5:22-23*

THE LITTLEST MEMBER

BRANDON STRETCHED, yawned, and turned off the alarm. For several minutes he argued with himself. One voice said, "Get up. It's time for Sunday school." Another voice said, "Why? Your folks don't go." In the end the wrong voice won. "No one will miss me," Brandon mumbled, pulling the pillow over his head.

Later that week Brandon tripped over a tree stump and broke a toe. How it hurt! When the doorbell rang on Saturday, he hobbled to the door. "Oh, hi, Mr. Newman," he said, greeting his Sunday school teacher. "Come in."

Mr. Newman said, "I see you're limping, Brandon. Did you hurt your foot? Is that why you missed Sunday school?" Mr. Newman asked.

"I broke my little toe on Tuesday," Brandon answered. "I didn't come Sunday because . . . well . . . I just figured no one would miss me."

Mr. Newman shook his head. "Oh, Brandon, you *were* missed. You're important to the Lord, to our church, and to me. When you're absent, there's a big gap in our class." He pointed to Brandon's foot and asked, "When you broke your little toe, how did it affect the rest of your body?"

Brandon grimaced. "I couldn't do much of anything for a few days."

"So it is with the body of Christ, the people in church," Mr. Newman explained. "Every member is important, even those who think they're the 'little toe.' When one member hurts, we all hurt." He stood to leave. "You are important to our class, Brandon. Don't ever forget that."

HOW ABOUT YOU? Do you feel unimportant? Or do you know someone else who feels that way? If you're a Christian, you're a member of the body of Christ. You're not only important, you're needed! *B.J.W.*

TO MEMORIZE: The human body has many parts, but the many parts make up only one body. So it is with the body of Christ. *1 Corinthians 12:12*

FROM THE BIBLE:

The human body has many parts, but the many parts make up only one body. So it is with the body of Christ. . . .

But God made our bodies with many parts, and he has put each part just where he wants it. What a strange thing a body would be if it had only one part! Yes, there are many parts, but only one body. The eye can never say to the hand, "I don't need you." The head can't say to the feet, "I don't need you."

In fact, some of the parts that seem weakest and least important are really the most necessary. And the parts we regard as less honorable are those we clothe with the greatest care. So we carefully protect from the eyes of others those parts that should not be seen, while other parts do not require this special care. So God has put the body together in such a way that extra honor and care are given to those parts that have less dignity. This makes for harmony among the members, so that all the members care for each other equally.

1 CORINTHIANS 12:12, 18-25

Each member is important

27 April

A WAY TO SERVE

FROM THE BIBLE:

Now Samuel, though only a boy, was the Lord's helper. He wore a linen tunic just like that of a priest. Each year his mother made a small coat for him and brought it to him when she came with her husband for the sacrifice. . . .

Meanwhile, as young Samuel grew taller, he also continued to gain favor with the Lord and with the people.

1 SAMUEL 2:18-19, 26

Serve God by serving others

IT WAS SATURDAY, and Melinda lay across her bed as she read an exciting missionary story. *Wow,* she thought. *I wish I could serve God, but I'm only a kid.*

"Melinda, come here please," Mother called from the kitchen. "Mrs. Rodrigues is sick, and I want you to take this stew over there." Melinda sighed but did as Mother asked.

When she arrived, Melinda noticed that the breakfast and lunch dishes were still on the table. She loaded them into the dishwasher and set the table for dinner.

When Melinda got home, Mother asked her to run some magazines over to Mrs. Wilson. "You're a sweet girl, Melinda," Mrs. Wilson said.

When Melinda arrived home once again, she was singing. "Well, you seem to be in a good mood," Mother remarked. "Would you feed Robbie?"

"Sure," said Melinda.

At dinner Melinda's mood became heavy. "I wish I could grow up fast so I could serve the Lord," she said, "like the missionary I've been reading about."

Mother looked up in amazement. "Why, Melinda, you've been doing things for the Lord all afternoon."

"I have?" Melinda asked.

"You helped Mrs. Rodrigues," Mother pointed out. "You visited with Mrs. Wilson. You—"

"But, Mother, that was for *people*," sighed Melinda.

"How do you think missionaries serve the Lord?" asked Mother. "They do it by doing things for people. Everyone can serve God by serving others."

HOW ABOUT YOU? What have you done to serve God lately? You serve him by serving others. Make a list of two or three things you can do today to help others. *B.J.W.*

TO MEMORIZE: Worship the Lord with gladness. Come before him, singing with joy. *Psalm 100:2*

"**THERE WAS A NEW GIRL** at school today," remarked Gina as she cleared the table.

Mother looked up from loading the dishwasher. "I hope you were kind."

"But you should see this girl, Mother," Gina protested. "She's so backward. Some kids told me she probably has lice!"

The front door burst open. "Look what I found, everybody!" called Jeremy. "Isn't he cute?"

Mother shuddered. "That pup is filthy! Where did you find him?"

Jeremy patted the frightened, cowering animal. "He's been hanging around Stan's house, and his mother said they had to get rid of him. I'm sure he doesn't belong to anybody. Can I keep him, Mom? Please?" Jeremy begged.

Gina added her pleas. "We'll give him a bath and take good care of him, Mom."

Jeremy jumped up and down. "Can we keep him?"

Mom frowned. With dark, sad eyes the puppy looked at her and whined, and she weakened a little. "You'll have to ask your dad."

The children spent the next hour bathing, combing, feeding, and loving the pup. "He certainly looks better now," Mom remarked as she patted the puppy.

"All he needed was some tender, loving care," Gina said.

"Hmmm," murmured her mother. "I wonder what the new girl in your class would look like if someone gave her tender, loving care." Gina's mouth fell open as Mom continued, "Maybe all she needs is a friend."

HOW ABOUT YOU? Do you know someone who needs tender, loving care? Will you love that one as Christ loved you? Your love can make a big difference in a person's life. *B.J.W.*

TO MEMORIZE: Do for others as you would like them to do for you. *Luke 6:31*

THE STRAY

FROM THE BIBLE:

How thankful I am to Christ Jesus our Lord for considering me trustworthy and appointing me to serve him, even though I used to scoff at the name of Christ. I hunted down his people, harming them in every way I could. But God had mercy on me because I did it in ignorance and unbelief. Oh, how kind and gracious the Lord was! He filled me completely with faith and the love of Christ Jesus.

This is a true saying, and everyone should believe it: Christ Jesus came into the world to save sinners—and I was the worst of them all. But that is why God had mercy on me, so that Christ Jesus could use me as a prime example of his great patience with even the worst sinners. Then others will realize that they, too, can believe in him and receive eternal life.

1 TIMOTHY 1:12-16

Treat others with love

29 April

BETTER THAN APPLE BLOSSOMS

FROM THE BIBLE:

Remember that in a race everyone runs, but only one person gets the prize. You also must run in such a way that you will win. All athletes practice strict self-control. They do it to win a prize that will fade away, but we do it for an eternal prize. So I run straight to the goal with purpose in every step. I am not like a boxer who misses his punches. I discipline my body like an athlete, training it to do what it should. Otherwise, I fear that after preaching to others I myself might be disqualified.

1 CORINTHIANS 9:24-27

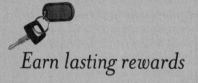

Earn lasting rewards

THE APPLE BLOSSOM FESTIVAL was held each spring in Amanda's town. She always looked forward to taking part in the games, and today was no exception. She especially loved the races, since she was a fast runner.

Amanda did well. She came in second in the first event. But she wanted to win a first-place ribbon so badly! In the third event it happened—she came in first. She skipped up to the judge's platform. The mayor gave her a blue ribbon and placed a wreath of apple blossoms on her head. It was so exciting!

The excitement didn't last very long, though. By the next day people were back to their regular routines. The booths were taken down, and Amanda's wreath of blossoms was already wilted. "I'm glad I won," Amanda told her parents, "but look at my wreath. It's already dead!"

For devotions that evening, Dad read 1 Corinthians 9. "The wreath you won at the races yesterday was a 'prize that will fade away,'" he said when he finished reading. "Paul reminds us that the race we run in life is for an 'eternal prize.' Things we do for the Lord will have lasting results. And there won't be just one winner. God will reward each of us according to how we have lived for him."

"Yes," said Mom, nodding. "The race you run as you live your life for the Lord is the most important race."

HOW ABOUT YOU? It's fun and exciting to win, isn't it? A "race" is the picture used by the apostle Paul to describe the Christian's life. Follow God's guidelines, and live for him. Then you will win a lasting reward. *L.M.W.*

TO MEMORIZE: Watch out, so that you do not lose the prize for which we have been working so hard. Be diligent so that you will receive your full reward. *2 John 8*

"**OH NO!** It looks like rain," Ben exclaimed, looking anxiously up at the sky one Saturday morning.

"It sure does," Dad agreed. "I think we'd better postpone our picnic."

Ben was very unhappy about the delay. As the raindrops began to fall, his eyebrows drew together in a frown. And when the rain poured down, he grew downright grumpy. "My whole day is spoiled," he complained.

"Shhhh. Listen," his sister Becky held up her finger. A clear, pure song came from a treetop outside. A robin was singing in the rain.

"Well, let the dumb bird sing. My day is ruined," Ben grumped.

"Why don't you get out one of your games, Ben? We may as well have some fun in spite of the rain," suggested Dad.

Ben grudgingly went to get a game. Soon he and Becky and Dad and Mom were all busy playing and laughing. The time flew by, and Ben forgot all about the rain spoiling his fun. Suddenly Dad looked up at the clock. "Can you believe it's nearly lunchtime?" he asked.

"We'll have a picnic right here on the floor," Mom decided. "Becky and I will get things ready, and you guys can clean up."

When the picnic food was brought in, they all sat on a blanket on the floor while they ate. "This is fun!" said Ben. "I even forgot about the rain. That robin had the right idea about singin' in the rain. I had as much fun as if I'd gone on a picnic—well, almost, anyway. I'm sorry I grumbled."

HOW ABOUT YOU? Do you grumble when it "rains" in your life—when things don't go your way? There are plenty of reasons to be happy and sing in spite of rain or other disappointments. And best of all, you please God by being cheerful even when you're disappointed. *C.E.Y.*

TO MEMORIZE: And don't grumble.
1 Corinthians 10:10

SINGING IN THE RAIN

FROM THE BIBLE:

Yet they kept on with their sin,
rebelling against the Most
High in the desert.
They willfully tested God in
their hearts,
demanding the foods they
craved.
They even spoke against God
himself, saying,
"God can't give us food in
the desert.
Yes, he can strike a rock so water
gushes out,
but he can't give his people
bread and meat."
When the Lord heard them,
he was angry.
The fire of his wrath burned
against Jacob.
Yes, his anger rose against Israel,
for they did not believe God
or trust him to care for them.
PSALM 78:17-22

Sing to the Lord always

1 May

A SAFE PLACE

FROM THE BIBLE:

Sing for joy, O heavens! Rejoice, O earth! Burst into song, O mountains! For the Lord has comforted his people and will have compassion on them in their sorrow.

Yet Jerusalem says, "The Lord has deserted us; the Lord has forgotten us."

"Never! Can a mother forget her nursing child? Can she feel no love for a child she has borne? But even if that were possible, I would not forget you! See, I have written your name on my hand. Ever before me is a picture of Jerusalem's walls in ruins."

ISAIAH 49:13-16

Accept Jesus as Savior

"WHAT DO YOU NEED, Mom?" asked Kayla. She was going to the store for her mother.

"A gallon of milk, a loaf of bread, and cheese slices," Mom replied. "Can you remember that?" She glanced at her daughter. "What are you doing?"

Kayla lifted her head and grinned at her mother. She turned her hand to show her mother what she had done. "I wrote the list on my hand with this pen," she said. "That way I'll be able to remember what you need."

"That's a unique idea, but you could have used a piece of paper," suggested Mom.

Kayla shook her head. "This is better. I might lose paper, but I can't lose my hand."

Mom laughed and gave Kayla a hug. "You're right," she agreed. "Wait a minute. I want to show you an interesting verse in the Bible." Walking over to her desk, Mother picked up her Bible and opened it to Isaiah 49. "Read this," she said.

Kayla read a verse aloud. "I have written your name on my hand." She looked up at her mother. "Hey, that's neat! God writes on his hand, too."

Mother nodded. "God said Israel's name was written on his hand, and I believe we can apply that to Christians, too. And God's writing will never come off."

Kayla looked down at the black writing on her hand. "That makes me feel good," she said. She closed her hand over the writing. "In God's hands—that's a safe place to be, isn't it?"

HOW ABOUT YOU? Have you ever written on your hand to remember a school assignment or someone's phone number? Your hand is a safe place for such things, isn't it? Is your name written on God's hand? God's hands are the safest place to be. *L.S.R.*

TO MEMORIZE: See, I have written your name on my hand. *Isaiah 49:16*

DERRICK LOVED FISHING. He went almost every Saturday and had read just about every book there was on the subject. Every time he went fishing, he would check his tackle box and his rod thoroughly. All his care paid off. It was very seldom that Derrick didn't come home with fresh fish.

One day he invited his friend Jon to go with him. Jon had never been fishing before and could hardly wait.

As they spent the day together, Derrick taught his friend all he could about fishing. Jon was a fast learner, and soon both had caught several fish.

That evening Derrick's mother noticed that he was unusually quiet at the supper table. When she asked if something was wrong, he replied, "Well, when Jon and I were eating lunch, he asked me why I bow my head and close my eyes before I eat. I told him I was praying. He asked why I did it."

"And what did you tell him?" asked Mother.

"I told him that praying was talking to God, and I was thanking him for the food. Then he asked me about church and God, and I didn't know what to say."

"Oh, I see." Mother was thoughtful. "Do you know what it means to be a 'fisher of people,' Derrick?"

"Sure," he answered. "It means to try to bring others to Jesus."

"Well," said Mother, "before you go fishing for fish, you're always very careful in your preparations. Be that way about fishing for people, too."

HOW ABOUT YOU? Have your friends ever asked you questions that you didn't know how to answer? Praying, reading your Bible, and memorizing Scripture will help prepare you for unexpected questions. And you will be a better "fisher of people." *D.S.M.*

TO MEMORIZE: Help me understand the meaning of your commandments, and I will meditate on your wonderful miracles. *Psalm 119:27*

A GOOD FISHERMAN

FROM THE BIBLE:

One day as Jesus was walking along the shore beside the Sea of Galilee, he saw two brothers— Simon, also called Peter, and Andrew—fishing with a net, for they were commercial fishermen. Jesus called out to them, "Come, be my disciples, and I will show you how to fish for people!" And they left their nets at once and went with him.

A little farther up the shore he saw two other brothers, James and John, sitting in a boat with their father, Zebedee, mending their nets. And he called them to come, too. They immediately followed him, leaving the boat and their father behind.

MATTHEW 4:18-22

Be ready to witness

3 May

WRONG INSTRUCTIONS

FROM THE BIBLE:

You slaves must obey your earthly masters in everything you do. Try to please them all the time, not just when they are watching you. Obey them willingly because of your reverent fear of the Lord. Work hard and cheerfully at whatever you do, as though you were working for the Lord rather than for people. Remember that the Lord will give you an inheritance as your reward, and the Master you are serving is Christ. But if you do what is wrong, you will be paid back for the wrong you have done. For God has no favorites who can get away with evil.
COLOSSIANS 3:22-25

Follow God's instructions

"I CAN DO IT, Dad. I know how." Mark was eager to help trim the hedge.

"OK, Son," agreed Dad. "I've got it started, so you can see how much I want cut off. I'm going to run to the store for grass seed. If you finish the hedge, you may cut just a little bit off the other bushes."

Mark took over the trimming, carefully cutting the hedge to the same level Dad had started. Then Barry, who lived in the house behind Mark's, came out. "You know what?" he said. "If you'd cut that down a little bit more, we could jump over it when we want to go to each other's house."

"You're right," Mark said. And he proceeded to follow Barry's advice.

Next Mark trimmed the bushes. Deb, his sister, came out of the house and surveyed his work. "I've always wished we could have these bushes trimmed so they go in points, like in formal gardens," she said. "Can you do them that way?"

"Sure," said Mark confidently, and he proceeded to show her. The results were not quite what he expected.

When Dad got home, he looked from Mark to the hedge, to the bushes, and back at Mark. "What happened?" he asked. "You didn't do things the way I told you." Mark explained about Barry's and Deb's suggestions. "Who are you working for?" Dad asked quietly. "Them or me?"

Mark was embarrassed and ashamed. "I'm sorry, Dad," he said.

HOW ABOUT YOU? Did you know that you are a servant of Christ? As his servant, you need to follow his instructions. Your friends may say, "It doesn't hurt to cheat just a little." But God says, "Be honest." The world says, "A little white lie is OK." God says, "You shall not lie." Shut out worldly advice and follow God's instructions. *H.W.M.*

TO MEMORIZE: Oh, that my actions would consistently reflect your principles! *Psalm 119:5*

THE MOST DANGEROUS ANIMAL

JASON and his parents were visiting the zoo, where Jason enjoyed seeing the lions, bears, and other dangerous animals. "Wow! Look at that bear yawn!" he exclaimed at one cage. "See all those teeth? I'll bet he could really do some damage if he came after you!" A short time later he was equally impressed with a tiger that scowled at them. Jason shivered. "Imagine something like that sneaking up on you in the jungle!" he exclaimed. On the way home he asked, "Dad, which animal do you think is the most dangerous?"

"That's a good question," replied Dad. "I think I'll vote for the lion, but there's something even more dangerous to people. Look out the window, Son. What do you see?"

"Well, we're right in the middle of the city!" replied Jason. "There are a lot of bars. Over there, a police officer is talking to a drunk man. And it looks like there's an accident up ahead, next to that burned-out building with the broken windows."

"This surely has become a poor section of town," murmured Jason's mother.

"But there aren't any animals here, Dad."

"Literally speaking, you're right," admitted Dad. "But this street shows the effects of sin on people. And sin is the work of Satan. More people die and more hearts and homes are broken because of people's sin than from all the animals put together. As much as we need to beware of dangerous animals like the ones we saw in the zoo, we need to be far more cautious about getting close to sin. Sin is the most dangerous 'animal' there is!"

HOW ABOUT YOU? Would you be frightened if a lion or bear crossed your path? You should be much more frightened of things that you know are wrong. Be smart. Stay away from sin! *S.L.K.*

TO MEMORIZE: Be careful! Watch out for attacks from the Devil, your great enemy. *1 Peter 5:8*

FROM THE BIBLE:

As the Scriptures say,

No one is good—
not even one.
No one has real understanding;
no one is seeking God.
All have turned away from God;
all have gone wrong.
No one does good,
not even one."
"Their talk is foul, like the
stench from an open grave.
Their speech is filled with
lies."
"The poison of a deadly snake
drips from their lips."
"Their mouths are full of
cursing and bitterness."
"They are quick to commit
murder.
Wherever they go, destruction
and misery follow them.
They do not know what true
peace is."
"They have no fear of God to
restrain them."
ROMANS 3:10-18

Beware of sin

5 May

THE LIGHTHOUSE

FROM THE BIBLE:

For God is working in you, giving you the desire to obey him and the power to do what pleases him.

In everything you do, stay away from complaining and arguing, so that no one can speak a word of blame against you. You are to live clean, innocent lives as children of God in a dark world full of crooked and perverse people. Let your lives shine brightly before them. Hold tightly to the word of life, so that when Christ returns, I will be proud that I did not lose the race and that my work was not useless.

PHILIPPIANS 2:13-16

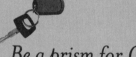

Be a prism for God

JEFF'S CLASS was on a field trip to a lighthouse, and the caretaker took them up to the top room to see the powerful light. "This big light runs on electricity," he said, indicating the heavy cables that went into the light. Walking over to a counter, he pointed to an old lamp about one-fourth the size of the modern one. "This kerosene lamp was used before they had electricity," he continued.

"But that light is smaller," one of the kids piped up. "Could it shine very far over the ocean?"

"Actually, the old lamp shone just as far as the modern one does," the caretaker answered. He picked up two odd-shaped pieces of glass from the counter. "These are prisms. They are cut to bend the rays of light that hit them and to reflect that light back—not once, but several times. By using prisms, the beam of the kerosene lamp could be magnified up to a thousand times. A sailor far out at sea could see the beam of reflected light."

That night all Jeff could talk about was his visit to the lighthouse. "They used a small kerosene lamp in the old days," he said. "They used prisms to reflect the beam of light to make it strong."

Mother smiled. "Prisms remind me of how the Bible says Jesus is the light of the world. And because we are Christians, it's our job to reflect that light for everyone to see."

HOW ABOUT YOU? What are you doing to reflect the light of Jesus? Are you using the talents he has given you to glorify him? Are you telling others about him? Are you kind and loving? *D.S.M.*

TO MEMORIZE: You are to live clean, innocent lives as children of God in a dark world full of crooked and perverse people. Let your lives shine brightly before them. *Philippians 2:15*

JENNA AND JILL. People who didn't know them thought they were twins. The two girls seemed inseparable. But one day that all changed.

"Jill, aren't you going to stay for pep assembly?" Jenna asked.

"No, I don't feel well," Jill said. "I called my mom to come and get me."

"See you tomorrow then," said Jenna.

But Jill didn't come to school the next day. Jenna stopped to see her at home, but she was resting. Jill did come back to school the next week, but she seemed very tired. And before long, she was in the hospital.

Jenna went there and brought their favorite flower, a pink rose. She could tell Jill liked the rose even though she didn't say much. She was hooked to several tubes, and nurses kept checking her.

The longer Jill stayed in the hospital, the less Jenna visited her.

"Jenna, who's your best friend?" asked Mother one day.

Jenna looked puzzled. "Jill, of course!"

"I thought best friends liked to be together," Mother answered. "You haven't seen Jill in days."

Jenna burst into tears. "Mom, I can't go there. Jill can barely talk. And she looks so different. What can I say?"

"You don't need to say anything," answered Mother. "Just be there. Or take your Bible along and read to her. Jill really needs a friend now. Her mom told me that she thinks you no longer care about her."

"But I do, Mom!" exclaimed Jenna. "I care so much it hurts!"

"Then go be with her," encouraged Jenna's mother. "Show her you still care."

HOW ABOUT YOU? Do you know someone who is ill? Be a comforter. Visit if possible. Read a few comforting Bible verses. Send a card, a note, flowers, or a favorite item. *J.L.H.*

TO MEMORIZE: He comforts us in all our troubles so that we can comfort others. *2 Corinthians 1:4*

A COMFORTER

FROM THE BIBLE:

All praise to the God and Father of our Lord Jesus Christ. He is the source of every mercy and the God who comforts us. He comforts us in all our troubles so that we can comfort others. When others are troubled, we will be able to give them the same comfort God has given us. You can be sure that the more we suffer for Christ, the more God will shower us with his comfort through Christ. . . .

We are confident that as you share in suffering, you will also share God's comfort.

2 CORINTHIANS 1:3-5, 7

Comfort the ill

7 May

TRIED AND TRUE

FROM THE BIBLE:

*How amazing are the deeds of
the Lord!
All who delight in him should
ponder them.
Everything he does reveals his
glory and majesty.
His righteousness never fails.
Who can forget the wonders he
performs?
How gracious and merciful is
our Lord!
He gives food to those who trust
him;
he always remembers his
covenant.
He has shown his great power to
his people
by giving them the lands of
other nations.
All he does is just and good,
and all his commandments
are trustworthy.
They are forever true,
to be obeyed faithfully and
with integrity.
He has paid a full ransom for his
people.
He has guaranteed his
covenant with them forever.
What a holy, awe-inspiring
name he has!
Reverence for the Lord is the
foundation of true wisdom.
The rewards of wisdom come
to all who obey him.*

Praise his name forever!
PSALM 111:2-10

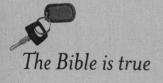

The Bible is true

LORI CAREFULLY measured a cup of sugar into a bowl. "I like making cookies," she said.

"You do a good job," Mom agreed, "and I appreciate your taking that task off my hands today. I need time to prepare for my Bible study."

"Mom, is everything in the Bible really true? Jamie's father is a preacher, and they believe most of the Bible," said Lori. "But her father says some of the things just couldn't have happened. Like some of the miracles. He says God has set up certain laws of nature."

"God did establish laws of nature," agreed Lori's mother, "and he can also set them aside as he sees fit." She paused as she watched Lori take the baking soda from the cupboard. "Lori," said Mom, "why don't you put in extra soda today?"

Lori stood still. "How come?"

Mom shrugged. "It might make the cookies taste better. And if you'd add an extra cup of milk, you might get some nice soft cookies."

Lori stared at her mother, then she laughed. "Are you trying to ruin my cookies?" she asked. "Won't work, Mom! I've used this recipe often enough to know it's right the way it is."

"In other words, you've tested it and found it to be accurate," said Mom. Then she pointed to the Bible lying on a kitchen shelf. "There's another book that's been tried and proven to be accurate. All it says is true."

HOW ABOUT YOU? Have you wondered if the Bible is really true? It is. Many events the Bible said would come to pass have already happened. The Bible has changed the lives of people throughout the world. Even science, as it has developed, proves the truth of the Bible. *H.W.M.*

TO MEMORIZE: The grass withers, and the flowers fade, but the word of our God stands forever. *Isaiah 40:8*

KYLE LIKED to visit his great-uncle's dairy farm. He liked to throw down feed from the silo. He liked to swing on ropes in the hayloft. He liked to ride on the tractor. But most of all, he liked to work with Uncle Hank on the old Model T car in the shed behind the tractor barn.

Uncle Hank was working to restore it to its original condition. It had been taken apart piece by piece, then each part had been cleaned. Worn parts had been repaired or replaced. The old paint had been stripped off the body, the rust removed, and a new coat of paint had been applied. Now the work was nearly done. Kyle would polish the car until it shone as Uncle Hank put the engine back together.

As they were working on the car one day, Uncle Hank turned to Kyle and asked, "How would you like to have this car?" Kyle grinned, and his eyes lit up. Uncle Hank smiled. "Someday it will be yours," he said. "It's going to be your inheritance from me."

That evening Kyle excitedly told his parents about Uncle Hank's decision. Mom smiled. "What a nice thing for Great-Uncle Hank to do," she said.

Dad nodded. "It certainly is," he said. After a moment he added, "You know, this reminds me of what God has done for us. He has promised that whoever trusts in his Son, Jesus Christ, will someday enjoy all the blessings of heaven, just as you'll someday enjoy owning that car. Aren't you glad you belong to him?"

HOW ABOUT YOU? Is there an inheritance waiting in heaven for you? There is if you've asked Jesus Christ to be your Savior. Want to know more? Ask a trusted friend or adult. *T.V.B.*

TO MEMORIZE: Now we live with a wonderful expectation because Jesus Christ rose again from the dead. *1 Peter 1:3*

AN INHERITANCE
(PART 1)

FROM THE BIBLE:

All honor to the God and Father of our Lord Jesus Christ, for it is by his boundless mercy that God has given us the privilege of being born again. Now we live with a wonderful expectation because Jesus Christ rose again from the dead. For God has reserved a priceless inheritance for his children. It is kept in heaven for you, pure and undefiled, beyond the reach of change and decay. And God, in his mighty power, will protect you until you receive this salvation, because you are trusting him. It will be revealed on the last day for all to see.

1 PETER 1:3-5

Receive God's inheritance

9 May

AN INHERITANCE
(PART 2)

FROM THE BIBLE:

Furthermore, because of Christ, we have received an inheritance from God, for he chose us from the beginning, and all things happen just as he decided long ago. God's purpose was that we who were the first to trust in Christ should praise our glorious God. And now you also have heard the truth, the Good News that God saves you. And when you believed in Christ, he identified you as his own by giving you the Holy Spirit, whom he promised long ago. The Spirit is God's guarantee that he will give us everything he promised and that he has purchased us to be his own people. This is just one more reason for us to praise our glorious God.
EPHESIANS 1:11-14

Christians have the Holy Spirit

AS SOON AS he could, Kyle visited Great-Uncle Hank and helped him work on the Model T again. After a while, Uncle Hank stuck his head out from under the hood and looked at Kyle. "I want you to know my will states that you will inherit this car," he said. "I'd like you to have a set of keys for it now."

"Wow!" Kyle's eyes glistened as he thanked his uncle.

That night Kyle showed his parents the keys. "So you're really going to own that car," said Dad with a smile.

Kyle nodded, but he had a question. "You said Christians will receive the blessings of heaven as an inheritance from God. How can we be sure of that?"

"Well," replied Dad, "how can you be sure Uncle Hank will give you the car?"

Kyle answered, "I trust him because I've never heard him lie. He even gave me keys to prove that he intends to give me the car."

"That's right," answered Dad, "and we can trust God to do what he said, too, because he has never lied. He also sends the Holy Spirit to live in us to prove that we really belong to him."

"How can we know the Holy Spirit is living in us?" asked Kyle.

Dad answered, "Galatians 5:22-23 says the proof or fruit of the Spirit is love, joy, peace, patience, kindness, goodness, faithfulness, gentleness, and self-control."

Mom nodded. "I also know I'm God's child because the Holy Spirit causes me to be interested in the things of God. And he gives me peace in my heart."

HOW ABOUT YOU? Has the Holy Spirit given you assurance that you are a child of God? Is he changing your life? Is there evidence of his presence in your life? *T.V.B.*

TO MEMORIZE: For his Holy Spirit speaks to us deep in our hearts and tells us that we are God's children. *Romans 8:16*

EQUIPPED AND READY

"WHERE'S YOUR BIBLE, Jeff?" asked Dad as Jeff and his sister, Jasmine, climbed into the car one Sunday morning.

"I dunno," mumbled Jeff. "I can't find it."

"If you had been reading it, you'd know where it is," whispered Jasmine. Jeff glared at her. "Do you know your memory verse?" Jasmine continued.

Jeff shook his head. "I was too busy this week."

The next evening Jeff was going with his dad to play golf. They had just started backing out of the driveway when Jeff noticed Dad's golf bag standing in the garage. "Hold it!" he called. "You forgot your golfing equipment!"

"Oh, that," said Dad. "I thought we'd try golfing without it."

"Dad, that's crazy!" protested Jeff.

"Think so?" asked Dad. "Is it any crazier than you saying you want to tell people about the Lord but not taking the time to read the Bible and memorize verses?"

"Well," mumbled Jeff weakly, "I guess not."

"After the special youth services last month, you said that you dedicated your life to the Lord," Dad reminded Jeff. "The Bible says we are to be 'fully equipped for every good thing.' I can't be properly equipped for golf without my clubs and golf balls. You can't be properly equipped as a Christian without a knowledge of God's Word. You need to study it regularly and spend time in prayer."

"I guess I never thought of it that way, Dad," admitted Jeff.

HOW ABOUT YOU? Are you properly equipped as a Christian? Do you study and memorize God's Word so you can share his love with others? Do you spend time talking to the Lord? Don't try to "play the game"—to live a Christian life—without the equipment you need. *L.M.W.*

TO MEMORIZE: It is God's way of preparing us in every way, fully equipped for every good thing God wants us to do. *2 Timothy 3:17*

FROM THE BIBLE:

But you must remain faithful to the things you have been taught. You know they are true, for you know you can trust those who taught you. You have been taught the holy Scriptures from childhood, and they have given you the wisdom to receive the salvation that comes by trusting in Christ Jesus. All Scripture is inspired by God and is useful to teach us what is true and to make us realize what is wrong in our lives. It straightens us out and teaches us to do what is right. It is God's way of preparing us in every way, fully equipped for every good thing God wants us to do.

2 TIMOTHY 3:14-17

Be prepared to serve God

11 May

TWENTY-TWENTY VISION

FROM THE BIBLE:

Children, obey your parents because you belong to the Lord, for this is the right thing to do. "Honor your father and mother." This is the first of the Ten Commandments that ends with a promise. And this is the promise: If you honor your father and mother, "you will live a long life, full of blessing."
EPHESIANS 6:1-3

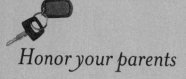

Honor your parents

"HEY, DAD, I went to the eye doctor today, and he said my vision was 20/20," announced David at dinner. "That's perfect, you know!"

"That's right," agreed Mom as she passed the salad. Loud voices, a slamming door, and squealing tires next door interrupted her. When it was quiet again, she murmured, "Poor Mrs. Marley."

"Yes, I'm afraid Chad is worrying her to death," Dad said with a nod.

"I don't know why everybody's on Chad's case," David protested.

"In some ways he's a nice boy," said Mom, "but I don't approve of the way he's been acting lately. The way he talks to his parents is disgraceful!"

"He called his mother 'stupid old woman' the other day," Cheri reported. "That's not nice."

"It certainly isn't," agreed Dad. "It's too bad Chad doesn't have 20/20 vision. He seems to be going blind."

"Chad's going blind?" David was horrified.

"Well, in a manner of speaking he is," answered Dad. "He is blind to how his actions are hurting himself and his parents."

As Mom cleared the breakfast table the next morning, she told David, "Chad wrecked his folks' car and was charged with drunken driving last night."

"Oooooh!" David exhaled. "Maybe he is going blind like Dad said." Before leaving for school, David paused long enough to pray and ask God to help Chad.

HOW ABOUT YOU? How's your spiritual eyesight? One way to check it is to take a look at your attitude toward your parents. Do you honor and obey them? To speak disrespectfully of them or to them is a sign of serious problems. *B.J.W.*

TO MEMORIZE: Honor your father and mother. *Exodus 20:12*

"I'M THE ONLY GIRL in my class who has to ride a bicycle!" Kim stormed as she picked up her library book. "The other girls' parents take them wherever they need to go! And the other girls get to date, too."

Mom looked up. "Kim, we've been through this before. Let's talk."

But Kim headed for the door. "I have to get to the library," she grumbled. She went out to the garage, slamming the door behind her.

Mom sighed. "Well, we might as well enjoy a few minutes of quiet," she said. "Jason's taking a nap."

Dad nodded. "Might be a good time to clean the garage," he suggested.

For an hour they worked in silence. Then, just as Kim rode her bike into the garage, a voice rang out from the house. "Mommy?"

"Peace and quiet just ended," Mom said. She called out, "Jason, we're—"

"Mommy!" The little boy's scream drowned out her words.

Mom tried again. "We're in—"

"MOMMY!" a terrified wail split the air. Mom, Dad, and Kim ran into the house. Jason was standing in the kitchen. "I thought you left me," he sobbed.

"If you'd listened, you could have heard Mom," Kim scolded.

Dad nodded. "That's true, Kim. Looks like we have two children not listening to their parents." Kim blushed. "We ask the Lord daily to help us make the right decisions concerning you, Kim," Dad continued. "I think we all need to do a better listening job. Why don't we practice our listening skills by talking about this dating thing."

HOW ABOUT YOU? Do you feel that your parents don't understand you? Have you tried to understand them? Have you really listened to what they say? God has given them the responsibility of using their wisdom in guiding you. They're worth listening to. *B.J.W.*

TO MEMORIZE: Listen, my child, to what your father teaches you. Don't neglect your mother's teaching. *Proverbs 1:8*

WORTH LISTENING

FROM THE BIBLE:

Fear of the Lord is the beginning of knowledge. Only fools despise wisdom and discipline.

Listen, my child, to what your father teaches you. Don't neglect your mother's teaching. What you learn from them will crown you with grace and clothe you with honor.
PROVERBS 1:7-9

Listen to your parents

13 May

THANKS!

FROM THE BIBLE:

Who can find a virtuous and capable wife? She is worth more than precious rubies. . . .

When she speaks, her words are wise, and kindness is the rule when she gives instructions. She carefully watches all that goes on in her household and does not have to bear the consequences of laziness.

Her children stand and bless her. Her husband praises her.
PROVERBS 31:10, 26-28

Thank God for your mother

THE STUDENTS in Mrs. Green's fifth-grade class were planning a party for their teacher's birthday. They wanted to surprise her with cake and ice cream. "But who will make the cake?" Tyler asked his friends.

"Count my mom out," Andrew spoke up. "She hates to cook!"

"My mom can't do it, either," Jessica said. "She works. The last time I asked her if I could bring cookies to school, she got really angry!"

"Well, I guess it's up to my mom, then," said Tyler when no one else offered. His mom worked as secretary in the family business and was busy, too. She wouldn't have time to make a fancy masterpiece, but Tyler thought she'd probably be willing to make a cake from a mix.

Tyler was right. Even though his mother was in the midst of organizing tax records, she said she'd make a cake for the class. In return, Tyler agreed to do the dishes and to help in any way he could. "You're special, Mom." Tyler gave her a hug. "None of the other mothers would take time to bake for us."

"Don't be too critical," Tyler's mother told him. "Sometimes parents are too busy to take on an added responsibility." She paused and then continued. "Not all children are as helpful as you are, either, nor as appreciative. Maybe that makes a difference."

"Well, thanks for being such a great mom," Tyler said.

HOW ABOUT YOU? When was the last time you thanked your mom for doing something special for you? When was the last time you told her how much you liked the supper she cooked? And did you thank God for her? You're very special to her, but sometimes it takes a great deal of effort to be a mom. Let her—and God—know how much you appreciate her. *L.M.W.*

TO MEMORIZE: Her children stand and bless her. *Proverbs 31:28*

GREG FUMBLED for the snooze button on the alarm clock and burrowed deeper into his blanket. When the alarm roused him again, he hit the snooze button once more and nestled back in his bed. Several minutes later Mother called, "Get up, Greg. Hurry or you'll miss your bus."

Greg sat up quickly, then stumbled from his bed. "I'll hurry." He did, and he was ready just in time to catch the bus.

"My alarm didn't go off this morning," Greg complained at the dinner table that evening. "I almost missed my bus."

Mother laughed. "It went off all right," she assured him. "I heard it. But you kept hitting the snooze button. So I finally called you myself."

"You sound like some Christians I know," said Dad. He grinned at Greg's quizzical look and reached for his Bible. "Why don't you read Romans 13 for us, Greg? It tells us that Christians need to 'wake up'."

When Greg finished reading, Dad nodded and said, "God is sounding an 'alarm' here. He says we'd better wake up and live as we should because our time here is getting shorter and shorter. Soon it will be too late to win people to Jesus or to do other things God wants us to do. But so often we hit the 'snooze button' and ignore the warning. We don't even realize what's happening. We need to wake up and live for the Lord."

HOW ABOUT YOU? Have you hit the "snooze button" in your Christian life? Time is passing quickly. It's time to wake up and do the things you know God wants you to do. *H.W.M.*

TO MEMORIZE: Another reason for right living is that you know how late it is; time is running out. Wake up, for the coming of our salvation is nearer now than when we first believed. *Romans 13:11*

THE ALARM

FROM THE BIBLE:

Pay all your debts, except the debt of love for others. You can never finish paying that! If you love your neighbor, you will fulfill all the requirements of God's law. For the commandments . . . are all summed up in this one commandment: "Love your neighbor as yourself." Love does no wrong to anyone, so love satisfies all of God's requirements.

Another reason for right living is that you know how late it is; time is running out. Wake up, for the coming of our salvation is nearer now than when we first believed. The night is almost gone; the day of salvation will soon be here. So don't live in darkness. Get rid of your evil deeds. Shed them like dirty clothes. Clothe yourselves with the armor of right living, as those who live in the light. We should be decent and true in everything we do, so that everyone can approve of our behavior. Don't participate in wild parties and getting drunk, or in adultery and immoral living, or in fighting and jealousy. But let the Lord Jesus Christ take control of you.
ROMANS 13:8-14

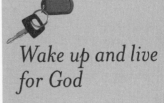

Wake up and live for God

15 May

JUST LIKE DORCAS

FROM THE BIBLE:

There was a believer in Joppa named Tabitha (which in Greek is Dorcas). She was always doing kind things for others and helping the poor. About this time she became ill and died. Her friends prepared her for burial and laid her in an upstairs room. But they had heard that Peter was nearby at Lydda, so they sent two men to beg him, "Please come as soon as possible!"

So Peter returned with them; and as soon as he arrived, they took him to the upstairs room. The room was filled with widows who were weeping and showing him the coats and other garments Dorcas had made for them. But Peter asked them all to leave the room; then he knelt and prayed. Turning to the body he said, "Get up, Tabitha." And she opened her eyes! When she saw Peter, she sat up! He gave her his hand and helped her up. Then he called in the widows and all the believers, and he showed them that she was alive.

The news raced through the whole town, and many believed in the Lord.

ACTS 9:36-42

Help others

"**WHAT ARE YOU MAKING,** Mom?" Jody asked.

"I'm making a baby sweater for one of the ladies at church," answered Mom.

"How come you do so many things like that for other people?" Jody asked.

"I enjoy making things, and I enjoy giving them away." Jody's mother smiled. "When you make something at school, you enjoy bringing it home to me, don't you?"

Jody nodded. "Sure, but you do things for people you hardly know."

"Not as much as Dorcas did," answered Mom.

"Dorcas?" Jody asked. "Who's she?"

"The book of Acts tells about Dorcas," explained Jody's mother. "She was probably one of the first women inspired by Christ to be active in works of love. She knew how to sew, and she made clothes for widows and poor people."

"Oh, I remember hearing about her in Sunday school," Jody said thoughtfully.

Mom smiled. "When Dorcas died, everyone was very sad. Do you remember what happened then?"

Jody thought for a moment. "She was raised from the dead!"

"That's right," said Mom. "The apostle Peter was in town at the time, and when he was told about it, he prayed, and God raised her to life."

"When I get older I'm going to do things for other people, too—like Dorcas and you," Jody decided.

"You don't have to wait that long," Mom said. "Let's think of something you can do for others right now."

HOW ABOUT YOU? What can you do for someone? Could you draw a picture or make a small gift and give it to your grandparents? Could you help them by dusting or cleaning? Or help your mother make cookies for someone who is ill? Make a card for a shut-in? Mow the lawn for an elderly neighbor? When you help others, you please the Lord, too! *V.L.C.*

TO MEMORIZE: She extends a helping hand to the poor and opens her arms to the needy.
Proverbs 31:20

NOW LET US ASSUME

"**I HOPE** you don't get upset with me, Dad," said Trent, "but, what Darwin says about evolution sounds logical to me."

Dad smiled. "I'm not at all upset with you, Son," he said. "I gave that a lot of thought when I was young, too." As he talked, he walked over to the bookshelves and pulled out a book. "Most kids your age don't get to see this book," he said as he held it out to Trent. "It's about evolution, and it's pretty hard to understand. But I'd like you to look through it and see how many times you can find such words as *let us assume, perhaps, or probably*—words indicating uncertainty. I'll come back in a few minutes to see what you've found."

Trent opened the book as he sat down in a nearby chair. Soon he was busily reading. He looked up as his dad walked into the room sometime later. "Nine times, Dad," Trent said, even before his dad could ask a question. "Nine times in ten minutes."

Dad took the book. "Imagine how often you'd find such words if you read this from cover to cover," he said. "To *assume* means to suppose or pretend. Trent, wouldn't you rather *know*?" Dad handed him another book. "Here's the world's best textbook, the Bible! It tells how we can know our Creator. We can know where we came from and where we're going."

HOW ABOUT YOU? Do you know the God who created you? You can know him through his book, the Bible. It proves itself through fulfilled prophecy and changed lives. It has stood the test of time. It tells how you can have a personal relationship with God through his Son, Jesus Christ. *P.R.*

TO MEMORIZE: I know the one in whom I trust, and I am sure that he is able to guard what I have entrusted to him. *2 Timothy 1:12*

FROM THE BIBLE:

It is God who saved us and chose us to live a holy life. He did this not because we deserved it, but because that was his plan long before the world began—to show his love and kindness to us through Christ Jesus. And now he has made all of this plain to us by the coming of Christ Jesus, our Savior, who broke the power of death and showed us the way to everlasting life through the Good News. And God chose me to be a preacher, an apostle, and a teacher of this Good News.

And that is why I am suffering here in prison. But I am not ashamed of it, for I know the one in whom I trust, and I am sure that he is able to guard what I have entrusted to him until the day of his return.

Hold on to the pattern of right teaching you learned from me. And remember to live in the faith and love that you have in Christ Jesus. With the help of the Holy Spirit who lives within us, carefully guard what has been entrusted to you.
2 TIMOTHY 1:9-14

You can know God

17 May

GROW, GROW, GROW

FROM THE BIBLE:

Every year Jesus' parents went to Jerusalem for the Passover festival. When Jesus was twelve years old, they attended the festival as usual. After the celebration was over . . . Jesus stayed behind in Jerusalem. His parents . . . assumed he was with friends among the other travelers. But when he didn't show up that evening, they started to look for him. . . . Three days later they finally discovered him. He was in the Temple, sitting among the religious teachers, discussing deep questions with them. And all who heard him were amazed at his understanding and his answers.

His parents didn't know what to think. "Son!" his mother said to him. "Why have you done this to us? Your father and I have been frantic, searching for you everywhere."

"But why did you need to search?" he asked. "You should have known that I would be in my Father's house." . . .

Then he returned to Nazareth with them and was obedient to them. . . .So Jesus grew both in height and in wisdom, and he was loved by God and by all who knew him.

LUKE 2:42-52

Check your spiritual growth

"WILL YOU MEASURE me, Danielle?" Jeff asked his older sister.

"I just measured you yesterday," protested Danielle. At his pleading look, she gave in. "Well, all right. Stand straight."

"Have I grown any?" Jeff asked anxiously.

"Nope, you're still the same height," said Danielle. Jeff looked puzzled.

In Sunday school the next day, Jeff really didn't want to sing one of the songs. He joined in, but the words seemed to stick in his throat. "Read your Bible, pray every day . . . and you'll grow, grow, grow," went the words of the song. *It's not true,* thought Jeff. *I've read my Bible every day, but I haven't grown at all.* He was tempted to quit reading, but what if the other verse of the song were true? It went, "Neglect your Bible, forget to pray . . . and you'll shrink, shrink, shrink."

That afternoon Jeff and his parents visited his great-grandmother at the nursing home. "Jeff, you're growing to be more like your father every day," Grandma Owens said. "You talk like him."

Jeff thought about that on the way home. Maybe there were more ways to grow than just getting taller. His great-grandma had said he was growing to be more like his father. Maybe the words in the song meant growing in another way. He decided to ask his parents. Mom answered. "Reading the Bible and praying makes a person grow more like Jesus."

Jeff thought, *This week I'll measure myself in a different way. I'll see if I've grown to be more like Jesus.*

HOW ABOUT YOU? How much have you grown this year? It's fun to get measured and see how much you've grown physically, but have you checked to see if you've grown in your Christian life? *C.E.Y.*

TO MEMORIZE: Instead, we will hold to the truth in love, becoming more and more in every way like Christ, who is the head of his body, the church. *Ephesians 4:15*

"HI THERE, MICHAEL. What are you doing?" The booming voice startled Michael. He glanced up to find his uncle looking over his shoulder. Quickly, Michael put behind his back the magazine he had been reading.

"Uncle Walter! I didn't hear you coming."

Uncle Walter raised his eyebrows. "So I noticed. Would you like to go with me to the construction site of the new bank?"

"Would I ever!" Michael jumped up from the porch. Uncle Walter turned toward the car. Michael started to follow him, then remembered the magazine. "Uncle Walter, wait a minute. I've . . . ahhh . . . I'm thirsty." Quickly, he slipped into the house. After hiding the magazine under the pillow on his bed, he stopped by the kitchen for a drink.

Later, at the construction site, Michael and his uncle put on hard hats. Shielding his eyes, Michael looked up, up, up the steel frame. "Look at those men working on the steel beams. That looks scary!" he exclaimed.

"It does," Uncle Walter agreed.

Michael couldn't keep his eyes off the men above him. "They have to watch every step."

"Watching these steel workers reminds me of a Bible verse: 'So, be careful how you live.' That means to be very, very careful," Uncle Walter explained. "The verse ends by saying, 'not as fools, but as those who are wise.'"

Michael slowly lowered his gaze and saw that Uncle Walter was watching him closely. "You saw the magazine I was reading. I can't hide anything from you."

"Or from God," Uncle Walter reminded him.

HOW ABOUT YOU? When people talk about your "walk," it is often referring to your life. As a Christian, you need to walk very carefully. Watch your steps—your reading material, your habits, your language, your friends, every part of your life! *B.J.W.*

TO MEMORIZE: Be careful how you live, not as fools but as those who are wise. *Ephesians 5:15*

WATCH YOUR STEP!

FROM THE BIBLE:

"Do for others what you would like them to do for you. This is a summary of all that is taught in the law and the prophets.

"You can enter God's Kingdom only through the narrow gate. The highway to hell is broad, and its gate is wide for the many who choose the easy way. But the gateway to life is small, and the road is narrow, and only a few ever find it."

MATTHEW 7:12-14

Walk carefully

19 May

SIN BUGS

FROM THE BIBLE:

"Then the King will turn to those on the left and say, 'Away with you, you cursed ones, into the eternal fire prepared for the Devil and his demons! For I was hungry, and you didn't feed me. I was thirsty, and you didn't give me anything to drink. I was a stranger, and you didn't invite me into your home. I was naked, and you gave me no clothing. I was sick and in prison, and you didn't visit me.'

"Then they will reply, 'Lord, when did we ever see you hungry or thirsty or a stranger or naked or sick or in prison, and not help you?' And he will answer, 'I assure you, when you refused to help the least of these my brothers and sisters, you were refusing to help me.'"

MATTHEW 25:41-45

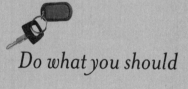

Do what you should

AS HANNAH TURNED a rock over in the backyard, she drew back. "Yuck, Mom! Look at all these icky bugs hiding under this rock!"

Mother watched the bugs scurry around. "Those are pill bugs," she said.

"They don't seem to like the sun. I think they're looking for a dark place to hide," observed Hannah.

"They're a little like us then, aren't they?" Mother said thoughtfully.

Hannah glanced at her mother in surprise. "Huh?"

"Well, just as these bugs are scrambling for hiding places, we sometimes scramble to find hiding places for the sin in our hearts," explained Mother. "We try to keep it in the dark, but God sees it."

"My Sunday school teacher was talking about sin last week. She says there are two kinds, sins of 'commission' and sins of 'omission.'"

"And do you know what that means?" said Mother, smiling.

"The sins of commission are the bad things we think or do," answered Hannah. "It's a sin to lie or say something to hurt somebody."

"That's right," said Mother, nodding. "And what are the sins of omission?"

"That's when we don't do things we should do," answered Hannah, "like not calling a friend when we know she's sad."

"Good for you!" said Mother. "You remembered that lesson very well. It's even more important to remember that God sees every sin."

Hannah nodded as she watched the last of the insects disappear. "I'll think of these as 'sin bugs' from now on." She shuddered. "They'll be a reminder that I don't want sin in my heart."

HOW ABOUT YOU? Are *sins of commission* and *sins of omission* new terms to you? It's sometimes easy to recognize the things we do wrong, but it's harder to realize that "not doing" something may be a sin, too. *V.L.C.*

TO MEMORIZE: Remember, it is sin to know what you ought to do and then not do it. *James 4:17*

"I'M NEVER going to speak to Michelle again!" stormed Tonya, slamming the door behind her.

Her mother frowned. "Never is a long time."

"I don't care how long it is," Tonya snapped. Tonya's words faded as she ran down the hall to her room.

"Tonya!" Mother called after her. "Let's go visit Aunt Margaret!"

A short trip across town brought Tonya and her mother to the Colonial Plaza Nursing Home. As she walked beside her mother down the hall, Tonya's mind was still churning with angry thoughts about Michelle.

"Aunt Margaret, what's the matter?" Mother's startled cry brought Tonya back to reality. Mother knelt beside the old lady's wheelchair.

In Aunt Margaret's hand was a crumpled letter. Tears were streaming down her cheeks. "Oh, Betty," she sobbed. "I've been so stubborn."

"Stubborn about what?" Mother questioned.

"Too stubborn to say 'I'm sorry.' " Aunt Margaret's voice quivered as she spoke.

It was some time before Tonya and her mother made sense out of what Aunt Margaret was saying. When they finally left, Tonya was wiping her eyes. In the car she turned to her mother. "You mean Aunt Margaret and Aunt Sarah had not spoken to one another for twenty years?"

Mother nodded. "Yes, and now Aunt Sarah has asked Aunt Margaret to forgive her. They can't even remember why they quarreled. I'm glad they have finally decided to forgive each other. Unforgiveness is a heavy burden to carry for all those years."

Tonya gulped. "When we get home, I'd better call Michelle. Never is a long time—too long."

HOW ABOUT YOU? Do you sometimes say things you don't really mean? Is there someone to whom you need to apologize? *B.J.W.*

TO MEMORIZE: You must make allowance for each other's faults and forgive the person who offends you. *Colossians 3:13*

NEVER IS A LONG TIME

FROM THE BIBLE:

But now is the time to get rid of anger, rage, malicious behavior, slander, and dirty language. Don't lie to each other, for you have stripped off your old evil nature and all its wicked deeds. In its place you have clothed yourselves with a brand-new nature that is continually being renewed as you learn more and more about Christ, who created this new nature within you. In this new life, it doesn't matter if you are a Jew or a Gentile, circumcised or uncircumcised, barbaric, uncivilized, slave, or free. Christ is all that matters, and he lives in all of us.

Since God chose you to be the holy people whom he loves, you must clothe yourselves with tenderhearted mercy, kindness, humility, gentleness, and patience. You must make allowance for each other's faults and forgive the person who offends you. Remember, the Lord forgave you, so you must forgive others.
COLOSSIANS 3:8-13

Forgive others

21 May

A DIFFICULT MOVE

FROM THE BIBLE:

After the death of Moses the Lord's servant, the Lord spoke to Joshua son of Nun, Moses' assistant. He said, "Now that my servant Moses is dead, you must lead my people across the Jordan River into the land I am giving them. I promise you what I promised Moses: 'Everywhere you go, you will be on land I have given you—from the Negev Desert in the south to the Lebanon mountains in the north, from the Euphrates River on the east to the Mediterranean Sea on the west, and all the land of the Hittites.' No one will be able to stand their ground against you as long as you live. For I will be with you as I was with Moses. I will not fail you or abandon you."

JOSHUA 1:1-5

Accept God's leading

AT THE CLOSE of the church service, Carrie listened in disbelief as Pastor Allen said, "After much prayer, the Lord is calling our family to serve him at an Indian reservation. We'll be leaving in a month." Carrie was upset by the news. Her best friend was Becky, the pastor's daughter.

When the service ended, Carrie dashed out to the car. She was too angry to even speak to Becky. "How could Pastor Allen do this?" Carrie sobbed on the way home.

"He must obey the Lord's leading," Dad said gently.

"But I don't want him to leave," Carrie wailed. "Becky's my best friend."

Carrie was upset all day. At bedtime Mom gave her a hug. "Honey," she said, "your old crib is set up in the guest room. How would you feel about sleeping in it tonight?"

Carrie laughed. "I don't want to sleep in a crib. Besides, I wouldn't fit."

Mom smiled. "That's true," she agreed. "Part of growing up means leaving behind old things and adjusting to new ways. You left your crib a long time ago, and that was good. People sometimes leave their homes, and that can be good, too. When friends leave, God is still with us, planning things for our good. And keeping the Allens here apparently doesn't fit into God's plan."

"Right," said Dad. "Let's thank God for the good years we've had with them and make their last days at our church extra special."

HOW ABOUT YOU? Are you faced with a move, a new family member, or a new church or school? Are you angry about changes or new circumstances in your life? It isn't easy to let the familiar go, but God will still be with you in your new situation. *J.L.H.*

TO MEMORIZE: I will be with you as I was with Moses. I will not fail you or abandon you. *Joshua 1:5*

THE LYING CEREAL BOX

"CAN I GET the prize out?" Gina asked Dad eagerly, pointing to the back of her cereal box. The picture showed colored candy pouring out of a package.

Dad shook the box. He reached in and brought out the prize—a small, sample-size package of candy. He tossed it to Gina.

When Gina tore open the package a little later, she poured out the candy. She counted every piece—only twenty-six. She counted the pieces in the picture on the cereal box. There were one hundred pieces. "I thought I would get as much candy as there was in the picture," she told Dad.

"The people who make the cereal wanted you to think that so you'd buy the cereal," explained Dad. "They deceived you."

Gina frowned. "What does *deceive* mean?"

"Leading someone to believe something that isn't true," explained Dad.

That afternoon Gina's friend Ashley came to play. Gina had recently begun taking piano lessons, so she showed Ashley what she had been learning. "I'll be your pupil," said Ashley. They pretended that Gina was the teacher.

Soon Gina's friend Beth came to the door. "Do you want to play?" Beth asked.

Gina didn't want to play. "We're having a piano lesson," she said.

After Beth left, Dad asked, "Did you tell Beth the truth?"

Gina shrugged. "I didn't lie about it," she said.

"Do you think you deceived her?" persisted Dad.

"Yes," Gina answered. Then she hurried to the front door. "Come back, Beth," she called. "You can be in on our piano lesson, too."

FROM THE BIBLE:

An honest witness tells the truth; a false witness tells lies.

Some people make cutting remarks, but the words of the wise bring healing.

Truth stands the test of time; lies are soon exposed.

Deceit fills hearts that are plotting evil; joy fills hearts that are planning peace!

No real harm befalls the godly, but the wicked have their fill of trouble.

The Lord hates those who don't keep their word, but he delights in those who do.

PROVERBS 12:17-22

Don't deceive

HOW ABOUT YOU? Do you ever deceive someone by giving the wrong idea? Do you give your parents the impression you're one place when you're actually somewhere else? Do you get out of doing something by making excuses that aren't quite accurate? You can lie in ways other than *saying* something that isn't true. *K.R.A.*

TO MEMORIZE: Do not steal. Do not cheat one another. Do not lie. *Leviticus 19:11*

23 May

TOO MUCH FOOT

FROM THE BIBLE:

Then Job spoke again:
"I have heard all this before.
What miserable comforters you
are! Won't you ever stop your
flow of foolish words? What
have I said that makes you speak
so endlessly? I could say the
same things if you were in my
place. I could spout off my
criticisms against you and shake
my head at you. But that's not
what I would do. I would speak
in a way that helps you. I would
try to take away your grief. But
as it is, my grief remains no
matter how I defend myself. And
it does not help if I refuse to
speak.
"O God, you have ground me
down and devastated my
family."
JOB 16:1-7

Don't become a pest

"**HEY, HOLLY,** can you play today?" asked Karen.

Holly hesitated. "Well, I don't know. I have quite a few things to do."

"Aw, come on," begged Karen. "What do you have to do? I could help you."

Holly shook her head. "Not really. I have to practice the piano."

"I could just come in and listen," persisted Karen.

"Karen," said Holly, "we were together last night after school and Monday night, too. I like playing with you, but I really will be busy."

"Well, OK," agreed Karen glumly.

Holly breathed a sigh of relief as she walked up the steps to the house. She found her mother in the kitchen starting supper. "Karen wanted to play again today, but I told her I had a lot of things to do. I hope she's not mad."

"Why would she be mad?" asked Mother. "You've been spending most afternoons with her lately."

"I know," sighed Holly. "I'm glad she's my friend, but sometimes I like being alone. I like to read and draw and write letters."

Mother nodded. "Did you know there's a verse in the Bible about this?"

"In the Bible? What verse?" asked Holly in surprise.

"Proverbs 25:17 says, 'Don't visit your neighbors too often, or you will wear out your welcome,'" quoted Mother. "See, Holly, the Lord who created friendship understands your problem. Friends do need to give each other time to develop different interests."

"Thanks, Mom!" exclaimed Holly. "I feel better about it now! I wish Karen could understand that verse, too."

HOW ABOUT YOU? Do you spend lots of time with only one friend? Reach out to other people and make new friends, too. Spend time alone and do a creative project or read a book. *L.M.W.*

TO MEMORIZE: Don't visit your neighbors too often, or you will wear out your welcome. *Proverbs 25:17*

A SPECIAL DIET
(PART 1)

"MOTHER, HOW COME Christians have such different ideas about right and wrong?" asked Joan one day.

Mother was silent for a while. "That's not an easy question to answer," she replied. "Let's see . . . we're having Uncle Phil and Aunt Sue over for dinner tonight, right? We'll each eat quite differently. Aunt Sue has diabetes and can't have food with sugar in it. Uncle Phil is on a low-cholesterol diet for his heart, so I'm cooking chicken without the skin for him."

"And Daddy needs to lose weight," giggled Joan, "so he'll eat a big salad."

"Do you see what I'm getting at, honey?" asked Mother. "People have different conditions, so they have different dietary needs. Christians have different backgrounds and different levels of maturity, so they have different spiritual needs."

Joan nodded seriously. "You mean, what's right for one person may not be right for another?"

"In a way that's true," agreed Mother. "God may convict one believer about a certain activity because it would cause others to stumble. Or someone may have a tender conscience about a particular activity."

Joan was thoughtful. "Then it's up to each person to decide right and wrong?"

"Well," said Mother, "some things are spelled out clearly in the Bible. And even those things that aren't specifically forbidden may not always be the best choice. We must avoid anything that would hurt God's cause or harm others."

FROM THE BIBLE:

Accept Christians who are weak in faith, and don't argue with them about what they think is right or wrong. For instance, one person believes it is all right to eat anything. But another believer who has a sensitive conscience will eat only vegetables. Those who think it is all right to eat anything must not look down on those who won't. And those who won't eat certain foods must not condemn those who do, for God has accepted them. Who are you to condemn God's servants? They are responsible to the Lord, so let him tell them whether they are right or wrong. The Lord's power will help them do as they should.

In the same way, some think one day is more holy than another day, while others think every day is alike. Each person should have a personal conviction about this matter. . . .

So why do you condemn another Christian? Why do you look down on another Christian? Remember, each of us will stand personally before the judgment seat of God.
ROMANS 14:1-5, 10

Develop convictions

HOW ABOUT YOU? Do you ask God to show you what things you should not do? Don't be critical of others regarding issues not spelled out in the Bible. On the other hand, don't do something if you have doubts about it. *S.L.K.*

TO MEMORIZE: In the same way, some think one day is more holy than another day, while others think every day is alike. Each person should have a personal conviction about this matter. *Romans 14:5*

25 May

A SPECIAL DIET
(PART 2)

FROM THE BIBLE:

So don't condemn each other anymore. Decide instead to live in such a way that you will not put an obstacle in another Christian's path.

I know and am perfectly sure on the authority of the Lord Jesus that no food, in and of itself, is wrong to eat. But if someone believes it is wrong, then for that person it is wrong. And if another Christian is distressed by what you eat, you are not acting in love if you eat it. Don't let your eating ruin someone for whom Christ died. Then you will not be condemned for doing something you know is all right.

For the Kingdom of God is not a matter of what we eat or drink, but of living a life of goodness and peace and joy in the Holy Spirit. If you serve Christ with this attitude, you will please God. And other people will approve of you, too. So then, let us aim for harmony in the church and try to build each other up.

Don't tear apart the work of God over what you eat.
ROMANS 14:13-20

Respect convictions of others

"C'MON, LET'S PLAY catch with my new softball," suggested Joan's brother, Rick, one Sunday afternoon following church.

After the children had thrown the ball back and forth for just a few minutes, they heard a voice from next door. "I'm surprised at you children—playing ball on Sunday!" said their neighbor Mrs. White. "And your parents call themselves Christians!" With that, she stalked off into her house.

Joan and Rick looked at each other in dismay and then hurried in to ask their parents what they should do. "Can you believe that?" grumbled Rick.

Mother sighed. "Don't be disrespectful, Son," she said. "She was brought up to believe any kind of outdoor recreation is wrong on the Lord's Day."

Joan scowled. "Wow! That reminds me of what you told me about 'special diets,' Mother—that what's wrong for one person may be fine for someone else."

"Yes, but it's important to respect the 'special diets,' or convictions, of others," Mother replied. "Besides, it's not a bad idea to choose activities on Sunday that keep your mind on the Savior."

Dad nodded. "Since Mrs. White feels that playing sports on Sundays is wrong, I think you should do something else. Why don't you play that Bible board game we bought you?"

"Why should we have to change what we do, just because of what she believes?" grumbled Rick.

"I can think of one good reason," Dad replied. "It offends Mrs. White."

Rick replied, "I guess you're right."

HOW ABOUT YOU? Do you respect the convictions of others? You don't have to agree with what everyone else believes, but you can modify your actions, whenever possible, so that you don't offend people unnecessarily. *S.L.K.*

TO MEMORIZE: So don't condemn each other anymore. Decide instead to live in such a way that you will not put an obstacle in another Christian's path. *Romans 14:13*

"**I WANT** a volunteer to sign this paper." Miss Rito showed her Sunday school class a blank sheet. "When you sign it, you will be agreeing to obey whatever I write on the paper. I could ask you to mow my lawn or to give me your allowance next week. I can write anything I want on this paper." There were no volunteers. "Don't you trust me?" asked Miss Rito.

Finally Gia raised her hand. "I'll sign it."

After Gia signed her name, Miss Rito took the paper again and began writing. Everyone waited breathlessly. She gave the paper back to Gia. "Read it out loud," she instructed.

"Go to the table," Gia read. "Pick up the Bible, and keep whatever you find under it." Quickly, Gia obeyed. "Ooh," she squealed as she lifted the Bible. On the table was a dollar bill!

"Thank you, Gia, for trusting me," Miss Rito replied.

Then Miss Rito told the class, "When we give our lives to Jesus, it's like signing a blank sheet of paper. We say, 'Lord, I am surrendering my life to you. You write in the orders.' Before Gia could receive her prize, what did she have to do?"

"She had to sign the paper," said Lena.

"And she had to do what it said," Brent added.

"Right." Miss Rito nodded. "She had to trust me, and she had to obey me. So we must trust God and obey him, handing our lives over to him. He has many rewards for those who do."

HOW ABOUT YOU? Are you afraid to yield your life to God? Don't fret. Surrender your life to him. You'll be surprised at all the good things he has in store for you. *B.J.W.*

TO MEMORIZE: Your goodness is so great! You have stored up great blessings for those who honor you. *Psalm 31:19*

THE BLANK PIECE OF PAPER

FROM THE BIBLE:

So, dear brothers and sisters, you have no obligation whatsoever to do what your sinful nature urges you to do. For if you keep on following it, you will perish. But if through the power of the Holy Spirit you turn from it and its evil deeds, you will live. For all who are led by the Spirit of God are children of God.

So you should not be like cowering, fearful slaves. You should behave instead like God's very own children, adopted into his family—calling him "Father, dear Father." For his Holy Spirit speaks to us deep in our hearts and tells us that we are God's children. And since we are his children, we will share his treasures—for everything God gives to his Son, Christ, is ours, too. But if we are to share his glory, we must also share his suffering.

Yet what we suffer now is nothing compared to the glory he will give us later.

ROMANS 8:12-18

Trust and obey

27 May

A PROMISE IS A PROMISE

FROM THE BIBLE:

*Look here, you people who say,
"Today or tomorrow we are
going to a certain town and will
stay there a year. We will do
business there and make a
profit." How do you know what
will happen tomorrow? For your
life is like the morning fog—it's
here a little while, then it's gone.
What you ought to say is, "If the
Lord wants us to, we will live
and do this or that."*

JAMES 4:13-15

Accept changed plans

"IT'S SO SUNNY out today, I wish we could go to our cabin," said Felicia at the breakfast table.

"I was thinking the same thing," answered Dad. "Let's do it. We'll plan to leave as soon as I get home from work tonight—if you help your mother pack."

"Sure thing!" Felicia gave her dad a big kiss.

While Felicia was helping her mother prepare for the trip, her father called from the office. "I'm so sorry," he apologized, "but we have a big project that has to be completed by tomorrow afternoon. We'll have to postpone our trip."

Felicia slammed down the receiver. "It's not fair!" she stormed. "Dad promised we could go."

"When Dad's boss asks him to work longer, there's nothing he can do," Mom answered.

"But he promised!" wailed Felicia.

"Now just a minute," interrupted her mother. "He didn't exactly promise. He did say we'd plan to go, but you have to realize that sometimes it's difficult, or even impossible, to carry out our plans. We get sick, or circumstances change, and there's nothing we can do about it."

Felicia scowled. "Well, if I can't count on my own dad, who can I count on?"

"You can always count on God. He has made many promises to us, and because he is God, we know that we can trust him completely." Mom smiled. "I know you're disappointed, but I'm sure Dad is disappointed, too."

HOW ABOUT YOU? Are you careful to only make promises that you should be able to keep? Are you careful not to accuse Mom and Dad of "promising" things when they are merely "planning" them? Learn to accept changing circumstances and plans. *L.M.W.*

TO MEMORIZE: What you ought to say is, "If the Lord wants us to, we will live and do this or that." Otherwise, you will be boasting about your own plans, and all such boasting is evil. *James 4:15-16*

CALEB AND CAMILLE tucked pansies and geraniums into the soil. They were helping Dad decorate their grandparents' graves. "Look at all the flags waving in the breeze," said Caleb as he glanced around the cemetery.

Camille looked up from her work. "Daddy, how come only some graves have flags flying beside them?" she asked.

"Those flags honor the soldiers who gave their lives to protect our country's freedom," Dad explained.

"They paid a big price to keep us free, didn't they?" Caleb asked thoughtfully.

"Yes, they did," agreed Dad. He gathered the tools they had been using. "But someone else paid a greater price for our freedom than the soldiers did," he observed as they started toward the car.

Caleb and Camille looked puzzled. "Who?"

"Jesus. He died on the cross to free us from the penalty of sin," answered Dad. "He arose from the dead and is alive in heaven now, so there's no need to decorate a grave for him. But there is a way we can remember his sacrifice."

"How?" Caleb asked.

"By participating in the Communion service at church," Dad explained. "When believers take Communion, they remember Christ's sacrifice on the cross. They are also looking forward to Christ's return. The Communion service and all that it means should fill our hearts with thanksgiving."

HOW ABOUT YOU? Before you celebrate the Lord's Supper in church, make sure you are a Christian. Then examine your heart by asking yourself these questions: Am I obeying the Lord in my life? Have I confessed all known sin? If you have done anything that would hurt your fellowship with the Lord, confess it to him before you take Communion. Then participate with a joyful and grateful heart. *J.L.H.*

TO MEMORIZE: For every time you eat this bread and drink this cup, you are announcing the Lord's death until he comes again. *1 Corinthians 11:26*

IN REMEMBRANCE

FROM THE BIBLE:

For this is what the Lord himself said, and I pass it on to you just as I received it. On the night when he was betrayed, the Lord Jesus took a loaf of bread, and when he had given thanks, he broke it and said, "This is my body, which is given for you. Do this in remembrance of me." In the same way, he took the cup of wine after supper, saying, "This cup is the new covenant between God and you, sealed by the shedding of my blood. Do this in remembrance of me as often as you drink it." For every time you eat this bread and drink this cup, you are announcing the Lord's death until he comes again.

So if anyone eats this bread or drinks this cup of the Lord unworthily, that person is guilty of sinning against the body and the blood of the Lord. That is why you should examine yourself before eating the bread and drinking from the cup.

1 CORINTHIANS 11:23-28

Remember Christ's sacrifice

29 May

WEIGHT WATCHERS

FROM THE BIBLE:

Remember that in a race everyone runs, but only one person gets the prize. You also must run in such a way that you will win. All athletes practice strict self-control. They do it to win a prize that will fade away, but we do it for an eternal prize. So I run straight to the goal with purpose in every step. I am not like a boxer who misses his punches. I discipline my body like an athlete, training it to do what it should. Otherwise, I fear that after preaching to others I myself might be disqualified.
1 CORINTHIANS 9:24-27

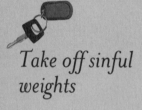

Take off sinful weights

"**MAY I HAVE** another piece of cake?" Brian asked.

"You've been unusually quiet," his mother remarked as she cut the cake. "Is something bothering you?"

"I came in third in track today," Brian blurted out. "I was always first last year. I don't know what's the matter with me."

"I do," said Stephanie. "You're too fat."

"Stephanie!" Dad reprimanded. "That was not kind."

"Is she *ever* kind?" Brian asked sarcastically.

"That's enough! You are both wrong—and right," Mom sighed. "It's wrong to say hurtful things about one another, but it's true Brian has gained weight. And Stephanie, you're not the kind, sweet girl you used to be."

"Yes," Dad agreed. "You have changed in the last couple of months, Stephanie. Are you still resentful that Jill was chosen as captain of the sixth-grade basketball team?"

"If it weren't for her sneaky ways, I'd be the captain," Stephanie protested.

"Stephanie, even as Brian needs to take off weight to run well, so you need to lay aside that weight of bitterness," said Dad. "It's hindering you from being a winner in your life as a Christian."

HOW ABOUT YOU? Are you carrying some "weights" that are hindering your Christian race—a bad attitude, a sharp tongue, a bitter or rebellious spirit? These are things that bring defeat into the life of a Christian. Anything that keeps you from praying, reading your Bible, and overcoming sin needs to be "laid aside." Check your life now for "weights." *B.J.W.*

TO MEMORIZE: Therefore, since we are surrounded by such a huge crowd of witnesses to the life of faith, let us strip off every weight that slows us down, especially the sin that so easily hinders our progress. *Hebrews 12:1*

WITH HANDS in his pockets and teeth clenched, Tony walked toward home. He was having trouble with Quentin and his gang. Looking over his shoulder, he saw the four boys about half a block behind him. They were pointing at him and laughing.

Tony's heart shifted gears. What could he do? He was six blocks from home. If he ran, they would pounce on him. He knew they wanted him to run. They had been teasing him about being a sissy Christian. But how could he fight four bullies?

He quickened his steps as the voices behind him grew closer. "O Lord, what can I do? Help me," he pleaded. Then he remembered the Scripture his dad had read that morning. The people of Judah had also been outnumbered. The Lord had told King Jehoshaphat not to be afraid. "Would you fight my battle, too?" Tony asked God.

Then he remembered what the people of Judah did. They sang praises. Quietly, he started singing a chorus.

Glancing back, he saw the bullies were getting closer. He sang louder. When he looked around again, he was surprised to see that Quentin and his gang had stopped. They were shouting at one another. Suddenly Quentin grabbed one boy by the collar, and a fight was on. Tony watched in amazement for a minute. Then with a big grin, he ran home singing.

He ran into the house. "Mom!" he called. "You're not going to believe this!"

HOW ABOUT YOU? Are there times when you are outnumbered? Does it seem like everyone is against you? Don't worry. Praise the Lord. Let him fight your battles. He may not cause your enemies to fight one another, but he has a way of solving your problems when you praise him. *B.J.W.*

TO MEMORIZE: This what the Lord says: Do not be afraid! Don't be discouraged by this mighty army, for the battle is not yours, but God's. *2 Chronicles 20:15*

PRAISE THE LORD

FROM THE BIBLE:

After this, the armies of the Moabites, Ammonites, and some of the Meunites declared war on Jehoshaphat. Messengers came and told Jehoshaphat, "A vast army from Edom is marching against you from beyond the Dead Sea. They are already at Hazazon-tamar." (This was another name for En-gedi.) Jehoshaphat was alarmed by this news and sought the Lord for guidance. He also gave orders that everyone throughout Judah should observe a fast. So people from all the towns of Judah came to Jerusalem to seek the Lord. . . .

The Spirit of the Lord came upon one of the men standing there. His name was Jahaziel son of Zechariah, son of Benaiah, son of Jeiel, son of Mattaniah, a Levite who was a descendant of Asaph. He said, "Listen, King Jehoshaphat! Listen, all you people of Judah and Jerusalem! This is what the Lord says: Do not be afraid! Don't be discouraged by this mighty army, for the battle is not yours, but God's."

2 CHRONICLES 20:1-4, 14-15

Don't worry—praise God!

31 May

AUNT JOY'S GARDEN GATE

FROM THE BIBLE:

So he explained it to them. "I assure you, I am the gate for the sheep," he said. "All others who came before me were thieves and robbers. But the true sheep did not listen to them. Yes, I am the gate. Those who come in through me will be saved. Wherever they go, they will find green pastures. The thief's purpose is to steal and kill and destroy. My purpose is to give life in all its fullness.

"I am the good shepherd. The good shepherd lays down his life for the sheep. A hired hand will run when he sees a wolf coming. He will leave the sheep because they aren't his and he isn't their shepherd. And so the wolf attacks them and scatters the flock. The hired hand runs away because he is merely hired and has no real concern for the sheep.

"I am the good shepherd; I know my own sheep, and they know me, just as my Father knows me and I know the Father. And I lay down my life for the sheep."
JOHN 10:7-15

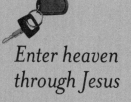

Enter heaven through Jesus

ANGELA SKIPPED up the sidewalk to Aunt Joy's home. She liked the way her aunt treated her—like a friend rather than just a child—although she did feel that Aunt Joy talked about God too much. Angela rang the doorbell, and Aunt Joy opened the door to let her come inside. After chatting with her aunt a few minutes, she asked, "May I go see the flowers?"

"Of course," agreed Aunt Joy.

Angela especially liked going into the flower garden, which was surrounded by a white fence. The only way to get in was through a charming gate. When she lifted the latch on the gate, hanging chimes tinkled. And just inside the gate, flowers of every color seemed to nod hello as they gently bobbed in the breeze.

After a little while, Angela ran back to the porch where her aunt was pouring tea and had set out some cookies. "Did you like my flowers?" Aunt Joy asked.

"Oh, I love your garden!" Angela exclaimed. "I love the gate, too."

Aunt Joy smiled. "What if you didn't go through the gate?" she asked. "What if you just stood outside?"

"Then I'd miss seeing all the beautiful flowers," answered Angela promptly. She bit into a cookie. "That would be silly."

"Remember what I've been telling you about God's home in heaven?" asked Aunt Joy. "It's even lovelier than my garden. But you can get into God's beautiful heaven only through a special gate, the Lord Jesus—only by having your sins forgiven through him. Would you like to hear more?"

Angela looked thoughtful. "Yes."

HOW ABOUT YOU? The Bible often uses an illustration that helps you understand a truth. When Jesus says he's a "door" or "gate," he means that you can get into heaven by asking him to forgive your sins and come into your heart. Would you like to open the door of your heart to him? *C.E.Y.*

TO MEMORIZE: Yes, I am the gate. Those who come in through me will be saved. *John 10:9*

ORDINARY DAYS

THE MURRAYS were concluding their family devotions by reading from an exciting missionary book. "The jungle closed in around Pedro," read Dad. "He knew his enemies were looking for him. Since Pedro had become a Christian, other members of his tribe were determined to kill him. Pedro prayed as he ran."

"This is so scary," Mary whispered.

Dad continued reading. "Suddenly a dark-skinned man stepped out of the bushes just ahead. He motioned for Pedro to follow him. *Should I follow him?* Pedro thought. *Is this man an enemy, too?* Pedro didn't know what to do." Dad looked up, put a marker in the book and closed it. "Bedtime!" he said.

"Oh no!" groaned Kurt.

"Just one more page?" pleaded Mary.

Mom shook her head. "There's school tomorrow."

Kurt stretched. "Boy, some people live such exciting lives, and mine is so ordinary. School, practicing trumpet, studying, eating, sleeping, and school again."

"Well, I suspect Pedro was glad when his life became somewhat ordinary after he escaped from his enemies," Dad said.

"Then he does get away!" Kurt laughed heartily at his unexpected discovery. "Well, I still think my days are pretty dull."

"God planned for ordinary days in our lives," said Dad. "He knows we need them. Even men of the Bible had ordinary days. Daniel didn't face lions every day. He also worked in the king's court doing many ordinary jobs. And Paul was a tentmaker. He no doubt spent many days sewing, measuring, and cutting. We need to see all those ordinary days as gifts from God."

HOW ABOUT YOU? Do you sometimes feel that the exciting things are happening to everyone else? Ordinary days of going to school, eating, and sleeping are a part of God's plan for you. Think of each day as a gift from God. *J.A.G.*

TO MEMORIZE: There is a time for everything, a season for every activity under heaven. *Ecclesiastes 3:1*

FROM THE BIBLE:

God has made everything beautiful for its own time. He has planted eternity in the human heart, but even so, people cannot see the whole scope of God's work from beginning to end. So I concluded that there is nothing better for people than to be happy and to enjoy themselves as long as they can. And people should eat and drink and enjoy the fruits of their labor, for these are gifts from God.

And I know that whatever God does is final. Nothing can be added to it or taken from it. God's purpose in this is that people should fear him.
ECCLESIASTES 3:11-14

Thank God for each day

2 June

PUMPED UP

FROM THE BIBLE:

And so, dear brothers and sisters, we can boldly enter heaven's Most Holy Place because of the blood of Jesus. This is the new, life-giving way that Christ has opened up for us through the sacred curtain, by means of his death for us.

And since we have a great High Priest who rules over God's people, let us go right into the presence of God, with true hearts fully trusting him. For our evil consciences have been sprinkled with Christ's blood to make us clean, and our bodies have been washed with pure water.

Without wavering, let us hold tightly to the hope we say we have, for God can be trusted to keep his promise. Think of ways to encourage one another to outbursts of love and good deeds. And let us not neglect our meeting together, as some people do, but encourage and warn each other, especially now that the day of his coming back again is drawing near.

HEBREWS 10:19-25

Go to church

EVERY SUNDAY morning Bart grumbled about going to church. He complained about having to get up early, about his clothes, and about anything else he could think of. "Why must we always go to church?" he whined.

Dad rumpled Bart's hair as he walked by. "It's good for you," he said.

That afternoon Bart and his dad decided to take a bike ride. "My tires are a little soft," said Bart as they started out. "I meant to pump them up at the gas station yesterday, but I forgot. I think they'll be fine, though."

"We could pump them up before we go," suggested Dad.

"I don't feel like bothering," replied Bart. "They'll be fine. Let's go."

Before long, Bart began to get tired. "Whew, it's hard to peddle with soft tires," he exclaimed. He was glad when they finally reached home. He ran and got the tire pump. After the tires were filled, Bart tried the bike. "It pedals easy as pie now," he said.

Dad nodded. "Good," he said. "But now it's time to put your bike away and get ready for the evening service."

"Aw, Dad," whined Bart. "It seems like we just got back from church. I was thinking of taking another spin on my bike."

"I was thinking, too," said Dad. "Just as it's hard work to ride a bike with soft tires, it's hard work to live for God without the things we learn in church and Sunday school. It's hard work to live without the encouragement we get from other Christians. We need to get 'pumped up' regularly with God's Word and with Christian fellowship. It pays to take time to do that."

HOW ABOUT YOU? Do you sometimes complain about having to go to church? You need constant encouragement to live as God wants you to live. *C.E.Y.*

TO MEMORIZE: Think of ways to encourage one another to outbursts of love and good deeds. *Hebrews 10:24*

"I'LL HOOK UP the hose to rinse off the car," said Philip. He screwed the end of a hose onto the faucet. "All set," he called.

"Turn it on harder," instructed his father. "I'm not getting much water."

"But it's on all the way," objected Philip.

Dad looked up and laughed. "Look at all the leaks—they look like tiny fountains!" he said.

"Maybe we can fix the hose," suggested Philip. He ran into the house and returned carrying a roll of tape. Leaving the water on so he could see the leaks, he wrapped tape around one of the biggest holes. But that just made the other "fountains" jump higher!

"That's not going to work," Dad said, smiling. "By the time you fix the last leak, the first one will be leaking again." Then he added, "This reminds me of you, Philip. You've been getting into a lot of trouble lately. Although you're always sorry, you're soon in some other trouble."

Philip sighed. "What's the leaky hose got to do with that?"

"Trying to 'be good'—to get rid of your sins through your own efforts—is like trying to plug up all these holes with tape," explained Dad. "It won't work! We need a new hose. And what you need is a new heart. I'm not talking about a flesh-and-blood heart. I mean a new spiritual heart—a new nature that helps you want to obey God. Only Jesus can give it to you."

HOW ABOUT YOU? Have you been trying to get rid of sin through your own efforts? It will never work. Come to Jesus just as you are. Let him cleanse you and give you a new heart. *S.L.K.*

TO MEMORIZE: Those who become Christians become new persons. They are not the same anymore, for the old life is gone. A new life has begun! *2 Corinthians 5:17*

THE HOSE WITH HOLES
(PART 1)

FROM THE BIBLE:

Whatever we do, it is because Christ's love controls us. Since we believe that Christ died for everyone, we also believe that we have all died to the old life we used to live. He died for everyone so that those who receive his new life will no longer live to please themselves. Instead, they will live to please Christ, who died and was raised for them.

So we have stopped evaluating others by what the world thinks about them. Once I mistakenly thought of Christ that way, as though he were merely a human being. How differently I think about him now! What this means is that those who become Christians become new persons. They are not the same anymore, for the old life is gone. A new life has begun!

All this newness of life is from God, who brought us back to himself through what Christ did. And God has given us the task of reconciling people to him. For God was in Christ, reconciling the world to himself, no longer counting people's sins against them. This is the wonderful message he has given us to tell others."

2 CORINTHIANS 5:14-19

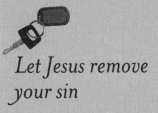

Let Jesus remove your sin

4 June

THE HOSE WITH HOLES
(PART 2)

FROM THE BIBLE:

I don't understand myself at all, for I really want to do what is right, but I don't do it. Instead, I do the very thing I hate. I know perfectly well that what I am doing is wrong, and my bad conscience shows that I agree that the law is good. But I can't help myself, because it is sin inside me that makes me do these evil things.

I know I am rotten through and through so far as my old sinful nature is concerned. No matter which way I turn, I can't make myself do right. I want to, but I can't. When I want to do good, I don't. And when I try not to do wrong, I do it anyway. . . .

But there is another law at work within me that is at war with my mind. This law wins the fight and makes me a slave to the sin that is still within me. Oh, what a miserable person I am! Who will free me from this life that is dominated by sin? Thank God! The answer is in Jesus Christ our Lord.
ROMANS 7:15-19, 23-25

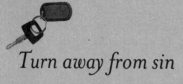

Turn away from sin

ONE EVENING after Philip had accepted Jesus as Savior, his dad found him on the couch in the living room, frowning. "What's wrong?" asked Dad.

Philip looked up and sighed. "Well, I thought that after I accepted Jesus, I would have a new nature," he explained. "But I still do wrong things. Why do I still sin?"

Dad thought for a moment. "I have to wash the car again. We can talk while we work." Once outside Dad said, "Here," handing Philip the hose. "Hook it up."

When Philip turned the water on he yelled, "Dad, this is the same old hose! Did you think it was the new one?"

Dad smiled. "Not exactly," he admitted, watching the familiar "fountain display" of the leaky old hose. "I want you to understand why a Christian can still sin. Even though we bought a new hose, it's still possible to try using the old one. In the same way it's possible for a Christian to turn back to his old sin nature. When that happens, we need to admit our sin to God and turn from it. We'll have to fight our old nature until we get to heaven."

Philip sighed. "It sounds like a lot of work to me."

Dad nodded. "Sometimes it is," he agreed, "but we can ask the Lord to help us daily. And just as I'm going to get rid of this hose, someday we'll get rid of our old sinful natures—for good!"

HOW ABOUT YOU? Do you wonder why you still have a problem with sin even though you're a Christian? It's because your old nature still wants to be in control. Trust Jesus daily to help you live for him. *S.L.K.*

TO MEMORIZE: Our old sinful selves were crucified with Christ so that sin might lose its power in our lives. We are no longer slaves to sin. *Romans 6:6*

NO NEED OF SHOES

"**IS GREAT-GRANDPA** wearing his shoes?" asked eight-year-old Amy. Mom patted Amy's arm and went on talking. The room was full of people talking. And, of course, there was Great-Grandpa. He lay, with his eyes closed and his hands folded, in a long box lined with satin—a casket. The funeral home was filled with the smell of flowers. Amy felt out of place. Then someone put a hand on her shoulder. It was Daddy. He took her hand and led her to a sofa. Amy's lips trembled. "Does Great-Grandpa have his shoes on?" she asked again.

"Yes, he does," said Daddy. Amy felt a teeny bit better. Daddy seemed to understand how strange she felt. "Remember when you helped me plant the garden last spring?" Daddy asked. Amy nodded. She had planted all the radishes and half the beans. "What happened to the seeds you planted?" asked Daddy.

Amy smiled. "Beans and radishes grew where I planted them," she answered.

Daddy nodded. "Those tiny seeds died, but then vegetables grew. There was new life in the garden. Great-Grandpa was a Christian, so when his body died he went to be with Jesus. Now he has new life, too," Daddy explained. "His body is here, but the real person is in heaven with Jesus."

Amy thought about it. "Does he need his cane there?"

Daddy shook his head. "No. Heaven is a perfect place where he has everything he needs or wants."

HOW ABOUT YOU? Have you visited a funeral home? Did it give you a strange feeling? Death is hard to understand, but it helps to remember that it's only the body that has died. The real person inside has moved on to another place. For a Christian, that place is heaven, where Jesus is. *C.J.B.*

TO MEMORIZE: He will swallow up death forever! The Sovereign Lord will wipe away all tears. *Isaiah 25:8*

FROM THE BIBLE:

What I am saying, dear brothers and sisters, is that flesh and blood cannot inherit the Kingdom of God. These perishable bodies of ours are not able to live forever.

But let me tell you a wonderful secret God has revealed to us. Not all of us will die, but we will all be transformed. It will happen in a moment, in the blinking of an eye, when the last trumpet is blown. For when the trumpet sounds, the Christians who have died will be raised with transformed bodies. And then we who are living will be transformed so that we will never die. For our perishable earthly bodies must be transformed into heavenly bodies that will never die.

When this happens—when our perishable earthly bodies have been transformed into heavenly bodies that will never die—then at last the Scriptures will come true:

"Death is swallowed up in victory."

1 CORINTHIANS 15:50-54

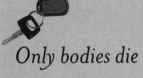

Only bodies die

6 June

THE GUEST BOOK

FROM THE BIBLE:

No temple could be seen in the city, for the Lord God Almighty and the Lamb are its temple. And the city has no need of sun or moon, for the glory of God illuminates the city, and the Lamb is its light. The nations of the earth will walk in its light, and the rulers of the world will come and bring their glory to it. Its gates never close at the end of day because there is no night. And all the nations will bring their glory and honor into the city. Nothing evil will be allowed to enter—no one who practices shameful idolatry and dishonesty— but only those whose names are written in the Lamb's Book of Life.

REVELATION 21:22-27

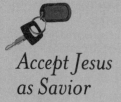

*Accept Jesus
as Savior*

MARIA WAS in charge of the guest book at her Aunt Stephina's wedding. As the guests filed past, she politely asked each one, "Will you sign the guest book, please?"

Suddenly a big, deep voice boomed out, "Well, here's my little niece, nearly all grown up." It was Uncle Pedro, who was in the army. He was her favorite relative, and today he looked more handsome than ever in his uniform. "I see they have you on guest book duty," said Uncle Pedro with a smile. "That's a mighty important job. Here's a riddle for you: Where is the most important 'guest book' of all? You have until after you get off duty to think about it."

After the wedding, Maria sat down beside her uncle. "I've got the answer," she said. "The most important guest book is in the White House."

Uncle Pedro laughed and shook his head. "Good try," he said, "but wrong. The most important guest book is in heaven."

"There's a guest book in heaven?" asked Maria.

"The Bible tells us of a Book of Life," replied Uncle Pedro. "It says that to enter heaven, our names must be written in that book."

"Do we write them in when we get there?" Maria asked.

"Oh no," said Uncle Pedro. "Your name has to be there so you can get into heaven."

"Well, how do we get it written there?" asked Maria.

"By believing in the Lord Jesus Christ," replied Uncle Pedro. "Have you asked Jesus to be your Savior and Lord?" Maria nodded and Uncle Pedro smiled. "Then it's there!" he said.

HOW ABOUT YOU? Have you asked Jesus to forgive your sin and be your Savior? He wants to write your name in the Book of Life so that you may someday join him in heaven and be happy forever. *C.E.Y.*

TO MEMORIZE: Rejoice because your names are registered as citizens of heaven. *Luke 10:20*

A "SOMETIMES CHRISTIAN"

WHEN HIS MOTHER called, John left his game reluctantly. "What do you want?" he asked irritably.

"Please sweep up the cookie crumbs you left on the floor," said Mother. "And don't eat any more cookies. I have just enough for the meeting at church."

His sister, Kara, came into the room while he was sweeping. Surprised, she asked why he was doing that. "Scram!" John growled.

"Excuse me!" said Kara dramatically. "I came to tell you something, but now I don't know if I will." When John punched her in the shoulder, she ran behind the table. "Mr. Williams, your coach, called today," she said. "He wants to hire you to do some yard work. He said to be sure to tell Mom he appreciated your respectful attitude at school! What a laugh!"

"What's so funny?" John asked. "I try to be a good Christian at school."

"Well," retorted Kara, "don't invite any of your friends or teachers home. If they saw how you act around here, they'd know what a phony you are."

After Kara left, John felt bad. *Could Kara be right?* he wondered. At school he tried to be an example of Christian living. But when he got home, he seemed to forget about being a Christian. "Lord, forgive me," he prayed. "Help me to behave like a Christian all the time." Then he went to apologize to his mother and sister.

HOW ABOUT YOU? Are you as kind to your brothers and sisters as you are to your friends? Do you speak as respectfully to your parents as you do to your teachers? Sometimes we can fool people with nice words and good deeds, but our families know whether or not we are really letting Christ's love flow through us. *C.R.*

TO MEMORIZE: In the same way, let your good deeds shine out for all to see, so that everyone will praise your heavenly Father. *Matthew 5:16*

FROM THE BIBLE:

If I could speak in any language in heaven or on earth but didn't love others, I would only be making meaningless noise like a loud gong or a clanging cymbal. If I had the gift of prophecy, and if I knew all the mysteries of the future and knew everything about everything, but didn't love others, what good would I be? And if I had the gift of faith so that I could speak to a mountain and make it move, without love I would be no good to anybody. If I gave everything I have to the poor and even sacrificed my body, I could boast about it; but if I didn't love others, I would be of no value whatsoever.

Love is patient and kind. Love is not jealous or boastful or proud or rude. Love does not demand its own way. Love is not irritable, and it keeps no record of when it has been wronged.

1 CORINTHIANS 13:1-5

Live for Christ at home

8 June

JUST IN TIME

FROM THE BIBLE:

Don't let the excitement of youth cause you to forget your Creator. Honor him in your youth before you grow old and no longer enjoy living. It will be too late then to remember him, when the light of the sun and moon and stars is dim to your old eyes, and there is no silver lining left among the clouds. Your limbs will tremble with age, and your strong legs will grow weak. Your teeth will be too few to do their work, and you will be blind, too. And when your teeth are gone, keep your lips tightly closed when you eat! Even the chirping of birds will wake you up. But you yourself will be deaf and tuneless, with a quavering voice. You will be afraid of heights and of falling, white-haired and withered, dragging along without any sexual desire. You will be standing at death's door. And as you near your everlasting home, the mourners will walk along the streets.

ECCLESIASTES 12:1-5

Accept Christ

GLEN PULLED a brightly colored paper from his pocket. *What's this?* he wondered. It was a coupon for a free candy bar. He had cut it out of the newspaper and then forgotten about it. Eager to get the candy, he hurried to the store, picked up the candy bar, and handed the coupon to the sales clerk.

The clerk smiled at Glen and looked at the coupon. "Oh, you made it just in time," she said. "It expires tomorrow." Glen was relieved.

On the way home, Glen decided to stop at his aunt Carrie's house. He told her about the almost-expired coupon.

"Why don't you sit down and have some lemonade with me?" As she handed him a glass, she said, "Your experience reminds me of something else that we can have for free, but it also has an expiration date."

"What's that," asked Glen.

"Salvation," Aunt Carrie answered. "God's gift of eternal life is free to those who accept it because Jesus paid the price by dying for our sins."

"I know that," answered Glen. "But what about the expiration date? I never heard about that before."

"Why, it is the day your life on earth ends," said Aunt Carrie. "God gives us a whole lifetime to accept Jesus as our Lord and Savior. But once this earthly life is over, the free offer of eternal life expires."

"I'm glad I have already accepted God's free gift of salvation," said Glen with a smile.

"Me, too," said Aunt Carrie. "It's good to become a Christian when you are young."

HOW ABOUT YOU? Have you accepted Christ as your Lord and Savior? If not, talk to a trusted Christian friend or adult who can help answer questions you might have about becoming a Christian. *C.E.Y.*

TO MEMORIZE: The Father who sent me gave me his own instructions as to what I should say. And I know his instructions lead to eternal life. *John 12:49-50*

TODD QUICKLY scribbled a note for his mother— "Gone fishin'. Todd." Then he grabbed his pole and bait and hurried out the door. As Todd reached the river, he saw a boy sitting in his favorite fishing spot. "Catchin' anything?" he asked.

The boy looked up and mumbled, "Naw, this isn't a very good spot."

Todd couldn't believe his ears! This was the best spot on the whole river! "Well, you gotta be patient when you're fishin'," he reminded the boy.

"Patient! I've been sitting here all morning without any bites," the boy complained, giving his pole such a jerk that his line popped out of the water.

"How often do you pop your line out of the water like that?" Todd asked.

"Oh, every few minutes—just to see if a fish has eaten the worm yet," the boy replied.

"You fish much?" asked Todd.

"My first time," the boy answered.

"What's your name?" Todd asked.

"Pete Fisher," came the reply.

Todd sat down. "Pete," he said, "we've gotta talk."

At dinner that night, Todd told his family about Pete. "We sure had fun! He's learnin' to fish so he can live up to his name."

"That's funny," Dad said, smiling. "It reminds me of the Peter in the Bible. He was a fisherman, too. And one day Jesus said to Peter, 'Come, be my disciples, and I will show you how to fish for people!' Todd, you have a perfect opportunity to 'fish' for Pete. Your friendship could help lead Pete to Christ."

HOW ABOUT YOU? Do you go fishing? You should if you're following Jesus. This kind of fishing doesn't even require handling wiggly worms! It requires a smile or maybe an invitation to play with you. Ask God to show you how you can become a fisher of people. *L.M.W.*

TO MEMORIZE: Jesus called out to them, "Come, be my disciples, and I will show you how to fish for people!" *Matthew 4:19*

GONE FISHIN'
(PART 1)

FROM THE BIBLE:

From then on, Jesus began to preach, "Turn from your sins and turn to God, because the Kingdom of Heaven is near."

One day as Jesus was walking along the shore beside the Sea of Galilee, he saw two brothers— Simon, also called Peter, and Andrew—fishing with a net, for they were commercial fishermen. Jesus called out to them, "Come, be my disciples, and I will show you how to fish for people!" And they left their nets at once and went with him.

A little farther up the shore he saw two other brothers, James and John, sitting in a boat with their father, Zebedee, mending their nets. And he called them to come, too. They immediately followed him, leaving the boat and their father behind.

MATTHEW 4:17-22

Be a fisher of men

10 June

FROM THE BIBLE:

Dear brothers and sisters, you must be patient as you wait for the Lord's return. Consider the farmers who eagerly look for the rains in the fall and in the spring. They patiently wait for the precious harvest to ripen. You, too, must be patient. And take courage, for the coming of the Lord is near.
JAMES 5:7-8

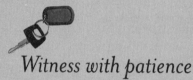

Witness with patience

TODD LAY IN BED, thinking of what his dad had said about being a fisher of people. He knew that if he was going to use God's Word he would need to have it in his heart and mind. He worked hard at learning Bible verses so he could share them with his new friend, Pete.

Many times he asked Pete to go to church, but Pete always refused. And Pete didn't seemed interested when Todd tried to talk about God either. Todd was frustrated. "I give up, Dad," he said. "Pete never wants to come to church."

"Todd," Dad reminded him, "you have to be patient when you're fishing, remember? You can't keep popping your line out of the water."

"Huh?" grunted Todd.

"You don't have to ask Pete to go to church with you so often," said Dad. "I suggest that you first strengthen your friendship with Pete. Tell him what you enjoy at church and the fun you have with the other kids. Then maybe Pete will become interested enough to come sometime. Remember, though, don't lie to make it sound like it's just all fun. You must be honest."

For the next three weeks, Todd practiced what his dad had suggested. Finally, he felt the nibble he'd been waiting for. "Dad!" he shouted as he burst into the house. "Guess what happened today?"

"I found your note about going fishing, so I'd say you caught a fish." Dad smiled.

"Did I ever!" Todd beamed. "And his name is Pete! You were right, Dad. A good fisherman must be patient if he really wants to catch a fish."

HOW ABOUT YOU? Are you an impatient "fisher of people"? Does it seem as though you're never going to get a bite? Don't give up. The salvation of a friend is worth waiting for. *L.M.W.*

TO MEMORIZE: You, too, must be patient.
James 5:8

"LOOK BEHIND YOU, Mom," said Rita as she and her mother picked raspberries. "There are some berries you missed."

"Oh, and they're nice ones." Mom bent to pick them.

"There are more in the bush behind them," said Rita.

Mom looked as Rita pointed, but she shook her head. "No, those aren't ripe yet. But I see some in the bush you just finished."

"I guess we should pick each other's bushes," laughed Rita. "This is fun. Remember when Carla and her mom used to come with us?"

"Yes," Mom sighed. "How is Carla doing since her mother left home?"

"Oh, she whines all the time. I get sick of hearing about it," said Rita. "After all, she's better off with her dad."

"I guess it all depends on your viewpoint," suggested Mom. "You see Carla's problems from a distance, so you see things she doesn't see. But don't forget that she also can see things you can't see. It's like these berries—we miss some good ones and mistake others for good, depending on how we view them."

Rita nodded slowly. "I see what you mean."

"As Christians, we need to be more understanding and less critical of others," added Mom. "Tell me, what bothers Carla most now that her mother's gone?"

Rita thought for a minute. "Well, she says she misses her mom. They were so close. She could tell her anything."

"God can use you to help make this change easier for her," said Mom. "Show her good things about her situation, and help her with the hard ones."

HOW ABOUT YOU? Are you annoyed when your friends talk about their troubles? Does it bug you because it spoils your fun to hear them talk? Remember, the Bible says, "A friend loves at all times." *A.G.L.*

TO MEMORIZE: Give me an understanding mind so that I can govern your people well and know the difference between right and wrong. *1 Kings 3:9*

THE VIEWPOINT

FROM THE BIBLE:

Since God chose you to be the holy people whom he loves, you must clothe yourselves with tenderhearted mercy, kindness, humility, gentleness, and patience. You must make allowance for each other's faults and forgive the person who offends you. Remember, the Lord forgave you, so you must forgive others. And the most important piece of clothing you must wear is love. Love is what binds us all together in perfect harmony. And let the peace that comes from Christ rule in your hearts. For as members of one body you are all called to live in peace. And always be thankful.

Let the words of Christ, in all their richness, live in your hearts and make you wise. Use his words to teach and counsel each other. Sing psalms and hymns and spiritual songs to God with thankful hearts. And whatever you do or say, let it be as a representative of the Lord Jesus, all the while giving thanks through him to God the Father.
COLOSSIANS 3:12-17

Be understanding

12 June

JANA'S PASSPORT

FROM THE BIBLE:

Yet I could have confidence in myself if anyone could. If others have reason for confidence in their own efforts, I have even more! For I was . . . born into a pure-blooded Jewish family that is a branch of the tribe of Benjamin. So I am a real Jew if there ever was one! What's more, I was a member of the Pharisees, who demand the strictest obedience to the Jewish law. And zealous? Yes, in fact, I harshly persecuted the church. And I obeyed the Jewish law so carefully that I was never accused of any fault.

I once thought all these things were so very important, but now I consider them worthless because of what Christ has done. Yes, everything else is worthless when compared with the priceless gain of knowing Christ Jesus my Lord. I have discarded everything else, counting it all as garbage, so that I may have Christ and become one with him. I no longer count on my own goodness or my ability to obey God's law, but I trust Christ to save me. For God's way of making us right with himself depends on faith.

PHILIPPIANS 3:4-9

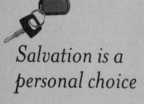

Salvation is a personal choice

TED AND JANA were going to spend the summer in England with their older sister. "Did you forget anything?" Dad asked when they were on their way to the airport. "If so, now is the time to remember before we get too far from home."

"Do you have the tickets and passports?" Mom asked.

"Right here." Jana patted her purse. "But I hate my passport picture."

"Let me see it again." Ted held out his hand.

"No way!" Jana held her purse tightly.

"Well, give me my ticket and passport," Ted insisted.

Jana opened her purse and took them out. "Oh no!"

Dad took his foot off the accelerator. "What's wrong?"

"I have Mom's passport instead of mine," wailed Jana.

"It's a good thing you discovered it!" Dad looked for a place to turn around.

Mom looked thoughtful. "Hmmmm," she mused. "I'm going to have to tell Mrs. Lewis about this experience. I've had a couple of opportunities to witness to her, and whenever I ask if she has accepted Christ, she tells me about the wonderful Christian parents she had. She seems to think that makes her a Christian, too."

"I see what your mom is getting at," said Dad as he headed back home. "Maybe when Mrs. Lewis hears about this, she'll see that just as your mother's passport won't get Jana into England, the salvation of her parents won't get her into heaven."

HOW ABOUT YOU? Do you have your "passport" to heaven? Your own righteousness—your fine family, your Christian parents, your own good works—will not get you to heaven. You must receive God's righteousness by accepting Jesus as your Savior. It's a decision you must make for yourself. *B.J.W.*

TO MEMORIZE: I no longer count on my own goodness or my ability to obey God's law, but I trust Christ to save me. *Philippians 3:9*

"IT'S TOO HOT to mow the lawn," groaned Josh.

"Well, it's not going to get cooler. You'd better start now," advised Mother.

"The Bible says, 'Don't make your children angry by the way you treat them.' And I feel angry right now," grumbled Josh.

"You're taking that verse out of context, Son," said Mother firmly. "The same chapter says, 'Children, obey your parents.'"

Later that day Josh played with his little brother, Nick. Soon Mother heard Nick crying, so she went outside. "Josh pushed me down," sobbed the little boy.

"Well, he ran into me," Josh defended himself. "The Bible says, 'If an eye is injured, injure the eye of the person who did it.'"

"There you go again, taking a verse out of context. The Bible also says, 'Be kind to one another,'" Mother replied sternly.

"What does context mean?" Josh asked. "You said that earlier today."

"Taking something out of its context means to take it out of its proper surroundings," Mother explained. "If you do that to Goldy, your gold fish—you take it out of water—it will soon die. If you take a Bible verse out of its proper surroundings—that is, if you use it any way you want, without considering other Bible verses—you can make it seem like the verse is saying something different from what it really means."

HOW ABOUT YOU? Do you use Bible verses to try and get your own way? God's Word is sacred, and you should never use it in a wrong way. Don't use it in a way that doesn't agree with the principles taught in the Bible. *S.L.N.*

TO MEMORIZE: When the Spirit of truth comes, he will guide you into all truth. *John 16:13*

LESSON IN A FISHBOWL

FROM THE BIBLE:

"You have heard that the law of Moses says, 'If an eye is injured, injure the eye of the person who did it. If a tooth gets knocked out, knock out the tooth of the person who did it.' But I say, don't resist an evil person! If you are slapped on the right cheek, turn the other, too. If you are ordered to court and your shirt is taken from you, give your coat, too. If a soldier demands that you carry his gear for a mile, carry it two miles. Give to those who ask, and don't turn away from those who want to borrow.

"You have heard that the law of Moses says, 'Love your neighbor' and hate your enemy. But I say, love your enemies! Pray for those who persecute you! In that way, you will be acting as true children of your Father in heaven. For he gives his sunlight to both the evil and the good, and he sends rain on the just and on the unjust, too. If you love only those who love you, what good is that? . . . If you are kind only to your friends, how are you different from anyone else?"

MATTHEW 5:38-47

Use God's Word carefully

14 June

A SAD STORY

FROM THE BIBLE:

So they arrested him and led him to the high priest's residence, and Peter was following far behind. The guards lit a fire in the courtyard and sat around it, and Peter joined them there. A servant girl noticed him in the firelight and began staring at him. Finally she said, "This man was one of Jesus' followers!"

Peter denied it. "Woman," he said, "I don't even know the man!"

After a while someone else looked at him and said, "You must be one of them!"

"No, man, I'm not!" Peter replied.

About an hour later someone else insisted, "This must be one of Jesus' disciples because he is a Galilean, too."

But Peter said, "Man, I don't know what you are talking about." And as soon as he said these words, the rooster crowed. At that moment the Lord turned and looked at Peter. Then Peter remembered that the Lord had said, "Before the rooster crows tomorrow morning, you will deny me three times." And Peter left the courtyard, crying bitterly.
LUKE 22:54-62

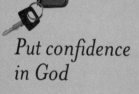

Put confidence in God

DAVID'S Sunday school teacher was Bob Carson, a young man who had recently graduated from college. He often spent his Saturdays taking his class of sixth-grade boys fishing, miniature golfing, or doing some other activity. David constantly talked about "Mr. Bob." Through his teaching David had grown spiritually, and his parents were thankful for that. Sometimes they were concerned, however, that David talked about Mr. Bob too much.

One Sunday another man taught the class. Where was Mr. Bob? No one seemed to know.

That afternoon the pastor called David's father. When he got off the phone, Dad put his hand on David's shoulder. "Son, I have very sad news for you. Last night Bob Carson was arrested for drunk driving."

At first David refused to believe the news, but he finally realized it must be true. "How could he do such a thing!" he exclaimed angrily.

"David, we all have sinful natures within us," Dad replied. "Because we are human, we sometimes let people down. That's why the Bible tells us to put our confidence and trust in God rather than in another person. People fail. God doesn't! Be thankful for the help Mr. Bob has given you through his teaching. At the same time, recognize that he has a serious problem and pray that he will seek the Lord's help to overcome this."

HOW ABOUT YOU? Has an adult Christian let you down by doing something contrary to God's teaching? Because they are human, Christians do sometimes sin. Even Peter, who walked with Jesus for three years, denied him. It's good that we can learn about God through other Christians, but our final authority and pattern for life should be Jesus. *L.M.W.*

TO MEMORIZE: It is better to trust the Lord than to put confidence in people. *Psalm 118:8*

NISHA SHOT from her chair and raced out to the pool. Her younger brother had just run in and reported that a small neighbor boy had fallen into the water. "Jack can't swim," Raul had gasped, "and neither can I."

Without a thought for herself, Nisha dove into the pool. Jack was thrashing around, trying in vain to stay above the water. His life was in Nisha's hands. She knew she had to rescue Jacque or he would probably drown.

By the time Mother ran out, Nisha was lying on the cement beside Jack, exhausted. Because of Nisha's quick action, he would be fine.

That evening they were still quite excited about what had happened, but Nisha was rather quiet. "Were you scared?" Raul asked for at least the sixth time.

Nisha shook her head. "I took that lifesaving course, so I knew what to do," she said. She looked thoughtfully at her parents. "Last Sunday my teacher said that people are 'drowning in sin' and that Christians know how they can be saved. I've been thinking about that. I didn't worry about whether Jack would like the methods I used to save him. If I had held back, he might have died. But so often I don't tell my friends about Jesus because I'm afraid they wouldn't like me to do that. I need to start helping them, too."

HOW ABOUT YOU? If you could save someone from drowning, would you do it? Of course you would. Telling people about Jesus and praying for them is another way to help drowning people—those who are drowning in their sins. If you are not sure how to do this, ask a Christian friend or trusted adult to help you. *V.L.R.*

TO MEMORIZE: Therefore, go and make disciples of all the nations. *Matthew 28:19*

LIFESAVING

FROM THE BIBLE:

This is why I remind you to fan into flames the spiritual gift God gave you when I laid my hands on you. For God has not given us a spirit of fear and timidity, but of power, love, and self-discipline. So you must never be ashamed to tell others about our Lord. And don't be ashamed of me, either, even though I'm in prison for Christ. With the strength God gives you, be ready to suffer with me for the proclamation of the Good News.

It is God who saved us and chose us to live a holy life. He did this not because we deserved it, but because that was his plan long before the world began—to show his love and kindness to us through Christ Jesus. And now he has made all of this plain to us by the coming of Christ Jesus, our Savior, who broke the power of death and showed us the way to everlasting life through the Good News. And God chose me to be a preacher, an apostle, and a teacher of this Good News. 2 TIMOTHY 1:6-11

Tell someone about Jesus

16 June

STILL MORE SANDING

FROM THE BIBLE:

Let the whole world bless our
* God*
* and sing aloud his praises.*
Our lives are in his hands,
* and he keeps our feet from*
* stumbling.*
You have tested us, O God;
* you have purified us like silver*
* melted in a crucible.*
You captured us in your net
* and laid the burden of slavery*
* on our backs.*
You sent troops to ride across our
* broken bodies.*
* We went through fire and*
* flood.*
* But you brought us to a place*
* of great abundance.*
PSALM 66:8-12

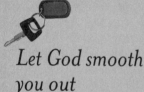

Let God smooth you out

GREG WATCHED as his father began refinishing the old table. Dad put a new piece of sandpaper in his electric sander and began to work.

"You're spoiling it," Greg said when Dad finally stopped the sander. "You're making it look like it has all kinds of scratches."

"I'm not through with it yet," Dad answered, turning on the sander once more.

Greg watched for a long time. His father finally stopped sanding and began applying stain. When he had finished staining the wood, the table did look pretty. But the next day he put a new piece of sandpaper in the sander and once again began sanding the tabletop.

"Dad," Greg called out, "you've already put the stain on."

Dad turned off the machine and began to explain. "It still has some flaws in it," he said taking Greg's hand and rubbing it over the tabletop so he could feel the rough spots. "I'll just keep sanding until it's perfect."

When the table was finished, Greg admired the finished product. But he was surprised to hear Dad say, "We're a lot like this table."

Greg laughed. "I sure hope you're not planning to use the sander on me!"

Dad smiled. "God sometimes uses difficult situations to smooth out our rough places," Dad explained.

Greg nodded. He thought of the time he broke his arm. He had learned patience as he had to learn to write with his left hand. He would ask God to help him grow and become a better Christian through whatever circumstances came into his life.

HOW ABOUT YOU? Have you had difficult experiences? Perhaps there has been a death or a divorce in your family. Maybe you or someone you love is sick. Whatever your experience, let God use it to help you grow. *R.I.J.*

TO MEMORIZE: When he has tested me like gold in a fire, he will pronounce me innocent. *Job 23:10*

REASON FOR DISCIPLINE

ROBERT WATCHED as his dad pounded a post into the ground close to the tree and then ripped old pieces of cloth into strips, getting ready to tie the tree to the post. "Why do you have to do that?" Robert asked.

Dad answered, "This tree is beginning to lean to the left. If I don't correct that now, it will lean more and more until it'll be too late to correct."

When Dad finished the job, Robert patted the tree. "Don't take it too hard, little tree," he said playfully. "It might hurt now, but you'll be glad later."

"Is that the way you feel when I have to straighten you out on certain things?" his father asked with a smile.

"What do you mean?" Robert asked in surprise.

"Well, when I see you doing things that aren't right, it's my responsibility to help you to change," explained Dad. "Are you glad I do that?"

Robert did not answer immediately. He could remember several spankings he had received when he was younger. He hadn't liked that, but he guessed they had worked. Remembering the sting of the spankings had been enough to keep him from repeating his wrongdoings. Now that he was older, he feared other types of punishment, too—being grounded or not being allowed to watch TV. Those things still helped to keep him from doing wrong.

"I don't particularly like to discipline you," Dad was saying. "But if you're going to be the kind of person God wants you to be, it's sometimes necessary."

HOW ABOUT YOU? How do you feel when your parents must correct you for wrongdoing? Do you get angry and resentful? God says correction is necessary to help you be what you ought to be—more like Christ. *B.J.W.*

TO MEMORIZE: Discipline your children while there is hope. If you don't, you will ruin their lives. *Proverbs 19:18*

FROM THE BIBLE:

And have you entirely forgotten the encouraging words God spoke to you, his children? He said,

"My child, don't ignore it when the Lord disciplines you,
and don't be discouraged when he corrects you.
For the Lord disciplines those he loves,
and he punishes those he accepts as his children."

As you endure this divine discipline, remember that God is treating you as his own children. Whoever heard of a child who was never disciplined? If God doesn't discipline you as he does all of his children, it means that you are illegitimate and are not really his children after all. Since we respect our earthly fathers who disciplined us, should we not all the more cheerfully submit to the discipline of our heavenly Father and live forever?

For our earthly fathers disciplined us for a few years, doing the best they knew how. But God's discipline is always right and good for us because it means we will share in his holiness.
HEBREWS 12:5-10

Be thankful for discipline

18 June

LIKE JINX

FROM THE BIBLE:

Children, obey your parents because you belong to the Lord, for this is the right thing to do. "Honor your father and mother." This is the first of the Ten Commandments that ends with a promise. And this is the promise: If you honor your father and mother, "you will live a long life, full of blessing."
EPHESIANS 6:1-3

Obey parents

SARA OVERHEARD her mother telling Dad that Sara had failed to clean out her closet. "I even gave her a box to put the outgrown clothes into," said Mom.

Sara went outside and sat on her swing. Her collie, Jinx, came over to her, but Sara ignored her pet. She thought of all the things she did do right. She made her bed before school. She set the table for dinner each afternoon and dried the dishes her mother washed each evening. She would clean that closet later. Why did it have to be done right now?

Soon Dad was sitting on the other swing. "Sara, you need to clean your closet," he said.

"I'm going to do it," replied Sara. "I wanted to see that special on TV first."

Dad picked up a stick and threw it. "Get it, Jinx," he said. The dog was off at a gallop to retrieve the stick. Dad turned his attention back to Sara. "Now that is quick obedience. Jinx didn't say, 'I'll do it when I get around to it.' He just obeyed." After a pause, Dad added, "A truck collecting clothing for needy people stopped here today, Sara. None of your outgrown clothes got put on it because you didn't obey your mother."

Now Sara felt bad. "Why didn't Mom tell me the truck was coming?" she asked. "I would've cleaned the closet right away if I'd known."

"We want you to be willing to obey us without always asking for reasons," said Dad quietly.

HOW ABOUT YOU? When your parents tell you to do something, do you put it off? Do you demand reasons? Or do you try to argue that you will do it later when you've nothing else to do? The only true obedience is *immediate* obedience. *R.E.P.*

TO MEMORIZE: Children, obey your parents because you belong to the Lord, for this is the right thing to do. *Ephesians 6:1*

"DAD, MY FISHING LINE is pulling!" shouted Ron.

Dad laughed. "That's because there's a fish on the end. Start reeling him in."

Soon the little sunfish was lying on the sand, but it was too small to keep. Reluctantly Ron put it back into the water. It flipped its tail, and in a moment it had disappeared.

"Whoa!" said Dad as Ron tossed his line back into the lake. "Aren't you forgetting something?" Ron looked at him, puzzled. "The bait," Dad explained.

Ron laughed. "Oh yeah," he said pulling his line back in. "I guess no fish would be dumb enough to bite on the bare hook, would he? I'll disguise it and make it look good with this juicy worm. The fish won't know there's any danger, so he'll open his mouth and swallow the hook. Then I'll have him!"

"That reminds me of the way Satan works," Dad mused.

Ron was curious. "What do you mean, Dad?"

"Satan tries to make sin look attractive," explained Dad. "Sometimes we're uneasy about something, or maybe we've been warned that it's wrong. Yet it looks good or our friends are doing it, and we're tempted to try it. Satan is a master at disguising sin and making bad things look good. So when you're tempted by a questionable activity, remember the fish. He wouldn't have gotten caught if he had stayed away from the hook."

HOW ABOUT YOU? Does Satan catch your attention with a "good" movie so that you become careless about what you watch? Does he make playing video games so much fun that you do it even though you know you're spending too much time and money? What other methods does he use? Be careful. *P.R.*

TO MEMORIZE: Put on all of God's armor so that you will be able to stand firm against all strategies and tricks of the Devil. *Ephesians 6:11*

ATTRACTIVE BAIT

FROM THE BIBLE:

Be careful! Watch out for attacks from the Devil, your great enemy. He prowls around like a roaring lion, looking for some victim to devour. Take a firm stand against him, and be strong in your faith. Remember that your Christian brothers and sisters all over the world are going through the same kind of suffering you are.

In his kindness God called you to his eternal glory by means of Jesus Christ. After you have suffered a little while, he will restore, support, and strengthen you, and he will place you on a firm foundation. All power is his forever and ever. Amen.

1 PETER 5:8-11

Avoid Satan's bait

20 June

WHINER OR WINNER?

FROM THE BIBLE:

There was a man named Job. . . . He feared God and stayed away from evil. . . .

One day . . . a messenger arrived at Job's home with this news: "Your oxen were plowing, with the donkeys feeding beside them, when the Sabeans raided us. They stole all the animals and killed all the farmhands. . . ."

While he was still speaking, another messenger arrived with this news: "Your sons and daughters were feasting in their oldest brother's home. Suddenly, a powerful wind swept in from the desert. . . . The house collapsed, and all your children are dead. . . ."

Job stood up and tore his robe in grief. Then he shaved his head and fell to the ground before God. He said,

"I came naked from my mother's womb,
    and I will be stripped of everything when I die.
The Lord gave me everything I had,
    and the Lord has taken it away.
Praise the name of the Lord!"

In all of this, Job did not sin by blaming God.
JOB 1:1, 13-15, 18-22

Have right attitudes

"YOU HAVE SCOLIOSIS, which is a curved spine, Debi," Dr. Bryant said. He turned toward Mother. "A specialist will decide how it should be treated. Exercises may help, or Debi may have to wear a brace or have surgery."

In the following days Debi prayed and prayed. Oh, how she wanted God to straighten her spine. "God can heal you, Debi," Mother said one night, "but if he doesn't, it's because he has other good plans for you."

"How can wearing an ugly brace be good?" Debi sobbed.

"Even though it will be difficult, wearing a brace can teach you compassion," Mother answered.

To her dismay, Debi did need the brace. "You'll still be able to do almost everything you've always done," Dr. Roberts told her.

"A few days later, Mother told Debi, "You need to clean your room."

"But my brace is so awkward," whined Debi. "I can't."

Mother frowned. "I'm sorry, but you will have to adjust."

Later Mother heard Debi on the phone. "I couldn't do that, Pam," she whined.

"What can't you do?" Mother asked later.

"I can't go hiking," Debi answered.

"You certainly can," Mother insisted. "Debi, a brace on your back does not make you an invalid. Your physical problem can make you a whiner or a winner."

Debi sniffed. "How can I be a winner?"

"By having the right attitude," answered Mother. "Remember Job? Everything went wrong in his life—everything but his attitude. He came out a winner. Now, call Pam back and tell her you're going hiking."

HOW ABOUT YOU? The question is not, What's your problem? The question is, How's your attitude? Everyone has problems. You can become a whiner or a winner. It's up to you. What's your choice? *R.I.J.*

TO MEMORIZE: The Lord gave me everything I had, and the Lord has taken it away. Praise the name of the Lord! *Job 1:21*

JEREMY AND ALICIA were watching a television show when their parents arrived home. "What's on?" Dad asked as he sat down in his recliner.

"Oh, some show about an undercover policeman who's trying to break the mob's secret code." Jeremy kept his eyes glued to the television set.

"Oh, wow! Look at that!" Alicia, too, kept her eyes fastened on the TV. "He's breaking into the mob's warehouse where they store their drugs. He's got a gun, and he's going to blast the bad guys."

"There's his girlfriend. Do you think they're going to kill her?" Jeremy asked.

"I hope not! They just fell in love at the beginning of the show," replied Alicia. Just then a loud burst of gunfire pierced the stillness of the living room, followed by a torrent of machine-gun fire. The mobsters began to fall to the ground while the hero continued to shoot around the warehouse.

Right at that moment Dad turned the TV off. "I thought you knew better than to watch such a program," he said. "Doesn't that violence bother you?"

"It's not real," Alicia protested weakly.

"Real or not, this is wrong," replied Dad. "In fact, just this morning I read some verses in Psalm 101 that talk about these kinds of television shows."

"Aw, Dad, the Bible doesn't mention TV shows," protested Jeremy.

"Well," said Dad, "Psalm 101 says, 'I will be careful to live a blameless life.' Wouldn't you say that could be applied to TV programs?"

"I guess you're right," Jeremy said soberly. "We didn't make a wise choice when we picked that show."

HOW ABOUT YOU? Are the TV programs you watch filled with violence or inappropriate suggestions? Do they make sin look glamorous and desirable? Do they make you forget God and his principles? Be very careful about what you choose to look at. *L.S.R.*

TO MEMORIZE: I will be careful to live a blameless life. *Psalm 101:2*

NO WICKED THING

FROM THE BIBLE:

*I will sing of your love and
  justice.
  I will praise you, Lord,
    with songs.
I will be careful to live a
    blameless life—
  when will you come to
    my aid?
I will lead a life of integrity
  in my own home.
I will refuse to look at
  anything vile and vulgar.
I hate all crooked dealings;
  I will have nothing to do
    with them.
I will reject perverse ideas
  and stay away from every evil.
I will not tolerate people who
    slander their neighbors.
  I will not endure conceit
    and pride.*

*I will keep a protective eye on the
    godly,
  so they may dwell with me
    in safety.
Only those who are above
    reproach
  will be allowed to serve me.
I will not allow deceivers to
    serve me,
  and liars will not be allowed
    to enter my presence.
My daily task will be to ferret
    out criminals
  and free the city of the Lord
    from their grip.*

PSALM 101:1-8

Watch only good TV

22 June

HOW TO BEAT BOREDOM

FROM THE BIBLE:

"The King will say to those on the right, 'Come . . . inherit the Kingdom. . . . For I was hungry, and you fed me. I was thirsty, and you gave me a drink. I was a stranger, and you invited me into your home. I was naked, and you gave me clothing. I was sick, and you cared for me. I was in prison, and you visited me.' . . .

"'I assure you, when you did it to one of the least of these my brothers and sisters, you were doing it to me!'

"Then the King will turn to those on the left and say, 'Away with you . . . into the eternal fire prepared for the Devil and his demons! For I was hungry, and you didn't feed me. I was thirsty, and you didn't give me anything to drink. I was a stranger, and you didn't invite me into your home. I was naked, and you gave me no clothing. I was sick and in prison, and you didn't visit me.'

". . . 'I assure you, when you refused to help the least of these my brothers and sisters, you were refusing to help me.'"

MATTHEW 25:34-36, 40-45

Serve one another

MATT SAT IDLY on the porch swing. When Jerry came riding by on his bicycle at top speed, Matt almost didn't see him. "Hey, Jerry," he called to his friend's back, "where's the fire?"

Jerry slammed on his brakes. "No fire," he responded. "I've just got a lot to do today."

"Boy, I don't," Matt grumbled. "I'm so bored."

"Nothing to do?" echoed Jerry. "I'm really busy! I'm on my way to mow Mr. Norton's lawn. Want to help me?"

"Sure," Matt answered. "How much will we get paid?"

"Nothing." Jerry grinned. "I'm doing it for the Lord and for fun."

"For the Lord and for fun?" Matt slapped his forehead. "You're mowing a lawn for fun? Does Mr. Norton have a riding mower or something?"

Jerry shook his head. "No, I'm doing it because it's fun to help others. And besides, Jesus said when I do something for others, I'm doing it for him."

Matt raised his eyebrows and moaned. But because he didn't have anything else to do, he went with Jerry. He also went with him the next day—and the next day, too—as Jerry "worked for the Lord."

"Say, this is fun," Matt told Jerry as they cleaned his dad's garage without having been asked to do so.

"My mom says we get bored because we think about ourselves too much," Jerry told Matt. "She says it's less likely to happen when we're busy helping others."

HOW ABOUT YOU? Is "I'm bored" your theme song? Could that be because you're thinking too much about yourself? There are many things you can do to keep busy and help others. *B.J.W.*

TO MEMORIZE: And the King will tell them, "I assure you, when you did it to one of the least of these my brothers and sisters, you were doing it to me!" *Matthew 25:40*

MARIA CLIMBED slowly into the car. "Hi, honey," said her dad. "It sure was a beautiful day for your picnic."

"Yeah," mumbled Maria.

"Did you have a good time?" Dad asked.

"Oh, sure," she answered after a moment of silence.

Dad glanced at her curiously. "You don't sound very happy. What's wrong?"

"Oh, Dad," moaned Maria, "I blew it! While we were on the swing, Joni asked me about being a Christian, and I couldn't answer her questions very well."

"Oh, I see," Dad said thoughtfully. As they pulled into the driveway, he spoke again. "I've got something in the garage I want to show you."

"All right," Maria agreed glumly.

Dad walked to his workbench and handed Maria a knife and a piece of wood. "Here," he said. "This is one of my wood-carving knives. Would you cut this stick in half for me, please?"

Maria tried to do as he directed. "I can't," she complained. "It's dull!"

"You're right," agreed Dad. "It's been away from the sharpener a long time. This knife has to be sharpened often to be of much use. And if we want God to be able to use us, we have to be 'sharpened' by spending time with him."

Maria looked from her dad to the knife. "You gave me a dull knife on purpose, didn't you, Dad?" she asked. "You want me to see that I'm like this knife—I'm dull! You're right, too. I haven't been reading my Bible very often or even praying for my friends. I hope I'll be 'sharper' the next time Joni asks questions."

HOW ABOUT YOU? Are you faithful in spending time with the Lord and studying his Word? Are you ready to answer when someone asks you questions about God? If not, it's time to "sharpen up." *S.L.N.*

TO MEMORIZE: If you are asked about your Christian hope, always be ready to explain it. *1 Peter 3:15*

BE SHARP

FROM THE BIBLE:

Oh, how I love your law!
I think about it all day long.
Your commands make me wiser
than my enemies,
for your commands are my
constant guide.
Yes, I have more insight than my
teachers,
for I am always thinking of
your decrees.
I am even wiser than my elders,
for I have kept your
commandments.
I have refused to walk on any
path of evil,
that I may remain obedient to
your word.
I haven't turned away from your
laws,
for you have taught me well.
How sweet are your words to my
taste;
they are sweeter than honey.
Your commandments give me
understanding;
no wonder I hate every false
way of life.
PSALM 119:97-104

Be ready to witness

24 June

JUST THE SHELL
(PART 1)

FROM THE BIBLE:

For we know that when this earthly tent we live in is taken down—when we die and leave these bodies—we will have a home in heaven, an eternal body made for us by God himself and not by human hands. We grow weary in our present bodies, and we long for the day when we will put on our heavenly bodies like new clothing. . . .

So we are always confident, even though we know that as long as we live in these bodies we are not at home with the Lord. That is why we live by believing and not by seeing. Yes, we are fully confident, and we would rather be away from these bodies, for then we will be at home with the Lord.

2 CORINTHIANS 5:1-2, 6-8

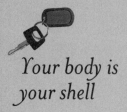

Your body is your shell

DAVID ALWAYS LIKED IT when the family went to the beach. He had been able to get a good-sized collection of shells from their trips. And now, here they were again, he and his father, walking up and down the sandy beach, looking for more shells. Suddenly he stopped and called, "Dad, come here! I found something, but I don't know what it is."

Dad soon joined David, who pointed at a strange-looking sea creature. At least that is what David thought it was. Dad knelt down and looked carefully at David's find. As he did so, David begged him to be careful. He didn't want his father to be bitten. "This one will never bite," Dad said. "There's no life in it."

"How come?" David wanted to know.

David's father picked it up. "Because this is just a shell," he explained, turning it over so David could see what it looked like. "It's a lobster shell. There comes a time in the lobster's life when he squeezes out and leaves his shell."

Before David could ask any more questions, his father asked if he remembered when Grandpa Jones died. "Do you remember how I explained that Grandpa had gone to heaven?" Dad asked.

David nodded. "But I didn't understand how he could be in the casket and be in heaven, too," David replied.

"It's very much like this shell that you just found. The lobster is gone," Dad said. "This is just his shell. In the same way, when Grandpa died, he left his body and went to live with Jesus because he was a Christian."

HOW ABOUT YOU? Do you have a Christian relative or friend who has died recently? If so, that Christian has simply left his body and has gone to be with Jesus. Your body is just the house in which your soul lives. *R.I.J.*

TO MEMORIZE: Yes, we are fully confident, and we would rather be away from these bodies, for then we will be at home with the Lord. *2 Corinthians 5:8*

DAVID SHOWED his mother the shells he and his dad had found on the beach. Then he told her about the lobster that had gone away and had left his shell behind. All that evening David was very quiet.

Just before he went to bed, he had more questions. "Doesn't Grandpa miss us?" he wanted to know. "Is he happy in heaven?"

"Absolutely," replied Dad. "Grandpa isn't sick like he was here because there's no sickness in heaven. Heaven is a perfect place. There's no sin, and no one even cries!"

"Mom cried at Grandpa's funeral," David reminded his father.

"That's right," Dad admitted. "That's because she knew she would miss him."

"But she wanted him to go to heaven, didn't she?" David asked.

David's father nodded. "That's right. She knew he would be happier there than he was here," he explained. "Here he had lots of pain. There he wouldn't have any pain. Mom also knew that she would be going to heaven someday, so she would see Grandpa again. Jesus gave her comfort in knowing these things."

David nodded. "I'm glad we all will get to see Grandpa again."

HOW ABOUT YOU? Would you like to be ready for heaven? Ask a trusted friend or adult how you can become a Christian. *R.I.J.*

TO MEMORIZE: For God so loved the world that he gave his one and only Son, that whoever believes in him shall not perish but have eternal life. *John 3:16* (NIV)

JUST THE SHELL
(PART 2)

FROM THE BIBLE:

Jesus made these statements while he was teaching in the section of the Temple known as the Treasury. But he was not arrested, because his time had not yet come.

Later Jesus said to them again, "I am going away. You will search for me and die in your sin. You cannot come where I am going."

The Jewish leaders asked, "Is he planning to commit suicide? What does he mean, 'You cannot come where I am going'?"

Then he said to them, "You are from below; I am from above. You are of this world; I am not. That is why I said that you will die in your sins; for unless you believe that I am who I say I am, you will die in your sins."

JOHN 8:20-24

Be saved

26 June

SPECIAL SERVANTS

FROM THE BIBLE:

I will praise the Lord at all
*   times.*
*   I will constantly speak his*
*   praises.*
I will boast only in the Lord;
*   let all who are discouraged*
*   take heart.*
Come, let us tell of the Lord's
*   greatness;*
*   let us exalt his name together.*

I prayed to the Lord, and he
*   answered me,*
*   freeing me from all my fears.*
Those who look to him for help
*   will be radiant with joy;*
*   no shadow of shame will*
*   darken their faces.*
I cried out to the Lord in my
*   suffering, and he heard me.*
*   He set me free from all my*
*   fears.*
For the angel of the Lord guards
*   all who fear him,*
*   and he rescues them.*

Taste and see that the Lord is
*   good.*
*   Oh, the joys of those who trust*
*   in him!*
PSALM 34:1-8

Angels protect
Christians

AS SAMANTHA and her brother, Matthew, raced across the field, something suddenly moved in the long grass ahead of them!

"Oh!" exclaimed Samantha. "What is it?"

Matthew came up, panting from the run. "It's a bird that's hurt!"

They watched the bird slowly hop away, dragging one wing. "Let's catch it," suggested Samantha. As she reached down to touch the bird, it ran ahead, crying.

Again and again the children got almost close enough to catch it, and each time it struggled forward, just out of reach. At the edge of the field, it suddenly flapped both wings and soared into the air. Samantha and Matthew were both surprised.

At the dinner table that evening, Samantha and Matthew told their parents what had happened. "That bird was probably a killdeer," said Dad. "More than likely it had a nest in the grass and was leading you away from its babies."

"Well, it did a good job of protecting them," laughed Matthew.

"God provided a unique way for those young killdeers to be protected," observed Mom. "And did you know that both of you are protected in a special way, too? Angels watch over you."

"Like they watched over Daniel in the lions' den!" said Samantha.

"And Peter in prison!" added Matthew

"You're both right," approved Dad. "Of course, Jesus is always with us. But it's comforting to know we have angels watching over us also."

HOW ABOUT YOU? Did you know that God has provided angels to watch over his children? They are special servants of his. They give comfort to Christians, and they are happy when people repent and become Christians. Angels also protect Christians, which means that nothing can happen to you unless God allows it. *C.E.Y.*

TO MEMORIZE: For the angel of the Lord guards all who fear him, and he rescues them. *Psalm 34:7*

"OUCH!" yelled Mary as she trimmed a dead branch off a rosebush. "How come dead branches can still hurt like that?"

"They don't lose their thorns when they die," said Mom. "They can still inflict pain." She looked at Mary and then asked, "Have you heard of William Shakespeare?"

"Oh, sure, Mom," said Mary. "Miss Abbott read some of his poetry in English class. Sometimes it's hard to figure out what he means, though."

"In one of his plays someone said, 'The evil that men do lives after them.'"

"What does that mean?" Mary asked.

"Even after someone dies, the bad things he has done live on and continue to inflict pain," explained Mom. "I had an aunt with a bad temper. When I was a little girl, I heard her arguing with my mother—her sister. She said some terrible things that were not true. And even though that was a long time ago, my aunt's words still hurt my mother."

During family devotions that night, Mary said what she and her mother had talked about. Dad turned in the Bible to Ecclesiastes 10. "King Solomon had some wise things to say about our speech, too," he said. "I believe he's telling us that a fool speaks without thinking, and no one can say what will happen to those words. But the words of a wise person are gracious."

"I just thought of something," said Mary with a smile. "I have a pressed rose in my Bible. It's dead, but it's still pretty. I want my words to be like that—something nice to remember for a long time."

HOW ABOUT YOU? Are your words pleasant to remember, or are they thorns that will hurt someone? Words are often long remembered. Let your words be gracious. *A.G.L.*

TO MEMORIZE: It is pleasant to listen to wise words, but the speech of fools brings them to ruin. *Ecclesiastes 10:12*

THORNY WORDS

FROM THE BIBLE:

It does no good to charm a snake after it has bitten you.

It is pleasant to listen to wise words, but the speech of fools brings them to ruin.

Since fools base their thoughts on foolish premises, their conclusions will be wicked madness.

Foolish people claim to know all about the future and tell everyone the details! But who can really know what is going to happen?

ECCLESIASTES 10:11-14

Words last a long time

28 June

SOME FRIEND!

FROM THE BIBLE:

"And I assure you of this: If anyone acknowledges me publicly here on earth, I, the Son of Man, will openly acknowledge that person in the presence of God's angels. But if anyone denies me here on earth, I will deny that person before God's angels. Yet those who speak against the Son of Man may be forgiven, but anyone who speaks blasphemies against the Holy Spirit will never be forgiven.

"And when you are brought to trial in the synagogues and before rulers and authorities, don't worry about what to say in your defense, for the Holy Spirit will teach you what needs to be said even as you are standing there."
LUKE 12:8-12

Speak up for Jesus

THE POLICE CAR pulled up to the curb where Joel was standing with some other children. "Do you kids know Jason Connor?" the officer asked.

"No, sir," answered one of the children.

"I need to find him in a hurry," the policeman said, then drove away.

When Joel later told his friend Kurt what had happened, Kurt said, "You should have told him that you know Jason."

"But what if he's in trouble?" asked Joel.

"Some friend you are!" scolded Kurt. "Seems like you should stand by him, not act like you don't know him."

Later both boys were sorry to learn that Jason's parents had been in a car accident and were hospitalized.

As Kurt and Joel stood in a checkout lane at the supermarket the next day, two men behind them began talking. "I hear the Connors were in an accident," said one.

"They sure were," replied the other. "They'll both be out of work at least a month. That will give them time to wonder where their God was when they got hit." He glanced down at Kurt. "Don't let anybody fool you about a loving God, kid. There isn't any."

Kurt looked away and said nothing, but Joel smiled at the man and said, "Sir, I know the Connors. God is their friend, and mine, too. He was with them when they got hurt, and he'll take care of them. Right, Kurt?"

"Right, Joel," Kurt agreed. With shame Kurt realized that by his silence he had denied knowing Jesus, just as Joel had refused earlier to admit knowing Jason.

HOW ABOUT YOU? Do you speak up for the Lord when you have an opportunity? Or, by your silence, do you deny that you even know him? Ask God to give you the courage to speak up for him. *A.G.L.*

TO MEMORIZE: The Holy Spirit will teach you what needs to be said even as you are standing there. *Luke 12:12*

JENNIFER WATCHED in horror as elderly Mrs. Carlson tripped over the curb and fell to the ground. Jennifer ran out of the house to see if her neighbor was hurt. "Don't move," she said when she saw that Mrs. Carlson was in great pain. "I'll get a blanket and call an ambulance." With that, she ran into the house.

When Jennifer returned, Mrs. Carlson looked up and smiled weakly. "I'm so glad you were here," she said. "You seemed to know exactly what to do. Thank you."

Soon the ambulance arrived, and Jennifer watched as the paramedics carefully lifted Mrs. Carlson into the vehicle. As Jennifer turned to go back into the house, she prayed.

The next Sunday Jennifer told her Sunday school teacher about the incident. "I'm sure glad I took a first-aid class," she said. "I knew just what to do."

"Great!" exclaimed Miss Berry. "It's good to know what to do in emergencies." She paused briefly. "There's a good spiritual lesson in this," she added. "Just as we should be prepared to give physical help, we should also be prepared to help someone find Christ."

Jennifer was quiet. She had lots of friends who didn't know Jesus, but she didn't know what to say or how to talk with them about accepting Christ. Actually, she was embarrassed to talk with them about it. She admitted this to her teacher. "I understand how you feel," Miss Berry replied. "But you've experienced salvation, and so have I. We need to tell our friends and neighbors what happened to us as well as show them what a change Christ has brought into our lives. I know the Lord will help us find the right words to use."

HOW ABOUT YOU? Do your friends know that you are a Christian? Have you ever talked with them about the life you have in Christ? Don't be ashamed of sharing your testimony. Your friends need Jesus, too. *R.I.J.*

TO MEMORIZE: I am not ashamed of this Good News about Christ. *Romans 1:16*

READY TO HELP

FROM THE BIBLE:

*"I take joy in doing your will,
 my God,
for your law is written on my
 heart."*

*I have told all your people about
 your justice.
 I have not been afraid to speak
 out,
 as you, O Lord, well know.
I have not kept this good news
 hidden in my heart;
 I have talked about your
 faithfulness and saving
 power.
I have told everyone in the great
 assembly
 of your unfailing love and
 faithfulness.*
PSALM 40:8-10

Be ready to help

30 June

THE MYSTERIOUS WITNESS

FROM THE BIBLE:

Oh, what joy for those
whose rebellion is forgiven,
whose sin is put out of sight!
Yes, what joy for those
whose record the Lord has
cleared of sin,
whose lives are lived in
complete honesty!

When I refused to confess
my sin,
I was weak and miserable,
and I groaned all day long.
Day and night your hand of
discipline was heavy on
me. . . .

Finally, I confessed all my sins
to you
and stopped trying to hide
them. . . .
And you forgave me! All my
guilt is gone. . . .

[The Lord says,] "Do not be like
a senseless horse or mule
that needs a bit and bridle to
keep it under control."

Many sorrows come to the
wicked,
but unfailing love surrounds
those who trust the Lord.
PSALM 32:1-6, 9-10

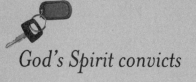

God's Spirit convicts

THE RED NUMBERS on the watch flashed eerily in the darkness. Carl sighed and stuffed it under his pillow. Oh, why had he stolen it?

Carl had never owned a watch. When he saw this one displayed on the store counter he slipped it into his pocket. Now he realized what a foolish thing he had done. He couldn't wear the watch for fear his folks would notice it. And he wondered if anyone at the store had seen him steal it.

Maybe things will seem better tomorrow, he thought. But at lunchtime, he noticed several teachers talking together. One of them seemed to glance in Carl's direction.

That night as he lay in his bed, Carl heard footsteps in the hallway. "Who's there?" he whispered hoarsely.

The door swung open, and Carl's father stepped in. "I just got up for a drink of water, Son. Is everything all right?"

Something inside Carl seemed to snap. "It's in my top drawer," he sobbed.

Carl poured out the whole story, ending with his impression that everybody seemed to know what he had done. Dad nodded. "I think I know what you mean," he said. "Actually, someone did see you steal that watch, and he has been bothering you about it ever since."

"But who, Dad?" Carl wondered.

"The Holy Spirit, Son," explained Dad. "When the Spirit convicts people of sin, they often have the miserable feeling that someone is after them. You'll have no rest until you stop running from God and do the right thing."

HOW ABOUT YOU? Have you ever had the miserable feeling that Carl described after you did something wrong? If so, then you know how uncomfortable it feels to do wrong. Remember that feeling the next time you think about doing something you know you shouldn't do. *S.K.L.*

TO MEMORIZE: The wicked run away when no one is chasing them, but the godly are as bold as lions. *Proverbs 28:1*

"HI, MOM!" Tina hugged her mother, who had come to the scout leader's home to pick her up.

"It's great to have you back from camp," Mom said. There was a sudden blast of music from the scout leader's porch. "What's all that noise?"

"Oh, somebody's radio," answered Tina. "We listened to it a lot on the bus."

Mom raised her eyebrows. "You know, Tina, Dad and I don't approve of that kind of music."

"Oh, Mom!" Tina frowned. "It's just music. No one listens to the words."

Later that day Tina told her mother all about camp. "We sang a lot of songs around the campfire," Tina said. "But one song was strange! The scout leader said it was a 'Bible song' about Abraham, Isaac, and Jacob, but the song said they were 'fishermen' who 'sailed to Jericho.'"

"So? What's wrong with that?" Mom asked, to Tina's surprise.

"Mom!" Tina couldn't believe her ears. "Those men weren't fishermen. The song's not true."

"Does it matter?" asked Mom.

"Of course it matters when you are singing about the Bible," replied Tina.

Mom smiled. "Well, I'm glad you realize that the words of the songs we use are important. That goes for all music, not just campfire songs."

Tina was quiet. "You mean that stuff on the radio?" she said finally.

Mom nodded. "Many of those songs talk about drugs, sex outside of marriage, suicide, Satan worship, and all kinds of things the Bible teaches against. Often they have bad language in them as well. We need to avoid such things."

HOW ABOUT YOU? Are you careful about the music you hear? There are many songs with "nice tunes," but the words or messages may be evil. Listen to the words. If they are not good or true, turn them off. *S.L.N.*

TO MEMORIZE: Then you will sing psalms and hymns and spiritual songs among yourselves, making music to the Lord in your hearts. *Ephesians 5:19*

ABRAHAM, A FISHERMAN?

FROM THE BIBLE:

Sing a new song to the Lord,
for he has done wonderful
deeds.
He has won a mighty victory
by his power and holiness. . . .
He has remembered his promise
to love and be faithful to
Israel.
The whole earth has seen the
salvation of our God.

Shout to the Lord, all the earth;
break out in praise and sing
for joy!
Sing your praise to the Lord with
the harp,
with the harp and melodious
song,
with trumpets and the sound
of the ram's horn.
Make a joyful symphony before
the Lord, the King!

Let the sea and everything in it
shout his praise!
Let the earth and all living
things join in.
Let the rivers clap their hands
in glee!
Let the hills sing out their
songs of joy before the Lord.
For the Lord is coming to judge
the earth.
He will judge the world with
justice,
and the nations with fairness.
PSALM 98:1-9

Choose music carefully

2 July

ONCE IS TOO OFTEN

FROM THE BIBLE:

Wisdom shouts in the streets. She cries out in the public square. She calls out to the crowds along the main street, and to those in front of city hall. "You simpletons!" she cries. "How long will you go on being simpleminded? How long will you mockers relish your mocking? How long will you fools fight the facts? Come here and listen to me! I'll pour out the spirit of wisdom upon you and make you wise.

"I called you so often, but you didn't come. I reached out to you, but you paid no attention. You ignored my advice and rejected the correction I offered. So I will laugh when you are in trouble! I will mock you when disaster overtakes you—when calamity overcomes you like a storm, when you are engulfed by trouble, and when anguish and distress overwhelm you.

"I will not answer when they cry for help. Even though they anxiously search for me, they will not find me."

PROVERBS 1:20-28

Don't try drugs

"UNCLE RANDY was in a motorcycle accident," said Mother as she hung up the phone. "He had apparently been taking drugs." Lisa and Kristen didn't know what to say. After a moment Mother continued. "You know, the first time Uncle Randy took drugs he said he just wanted to get high once, but he never quit." Mother turned to leave the room. "I'd like some time alone."

"Sure, Mother," the girls answered.

After a few moments Mother heard a crash. She went to investigate and saw pieces of china dolls on the floor. "Girls, you know you're not to handle those dolls. They're antique and very fragile."

"Lisa said it wouldn't hurt to play with them just once," murmured Kristen.

Lisa picked up the pieces. "Can't we fix them?" she asked.

"We'll try," said Mother, "but they'll never be the same. And it won't change your punishment for disobeying."

Mother got the glue, and they went to work. "The cracks still show," observed Lisa.

"They look like scars," Kristen added.

"I'm doing my best," Mother answered. "You know, girls, as I try to repair these, I keep thinking of Uncle Randy. His life is full of scars because of drugs. He never finished school, he lost several jobs, and he had this accident." As she set one doll down to dry, she said to her daughters, "When you look at these dolls, I hope you'll think about the results of doing wrong—even one time."

HOW ABOUT YOU? Have you been tempted to try drugs "just once" to see what it's like? Once is too often. "Doing drugs" for pleasure is wrong in God's sight. It's destructive to the body, and taking them "once" could hurt you for life. *S.L.N.*

TO MEMORIZE: For God bought you with a high price. So you must honor God with your body. *1 Corinthians 6:20*

THE TATTERED TREASURE

THE HAMILTONS were moving. Beth came into the bedroom just as her mother pulled a box from the closet. "What's in that box, Mom?"

Beth's mother smiled. "It's full of old keepsakes—letters from your dad, school albums, report cards, things like that."

"Look at this old flag," Beth said, pulling a tattered piece of red and white cloth from the box. "Why don't you throw it away, Mom?"

A faraway look came into her mother's eyes. "That flag was draped over my grandpa's casket when he was shipped home from the war. He died for that flag."

"Died for this flag?" Beth asked.

"I mean he died so we would have the right to fly the flag," Mom replied. "He died for the freedom of our country. For years my grandmother flew that flag on every holiday. My mother was just a little girl when her father died. All she ever had of him was this flag. It meant a lot to her, and it means a lot to me."

"I know something that's even more valuable than this flag," Beth said quietly. "It's the Bible. We talked in Sunday school about how many people have died so we could have God's Word."

"You're right, Beth," Mom agreed. "Even today some people are martyred for obeying the Bible."

Mom lovingly folded the flag. "How blessed we are to live in a country where we can have God's Word in our homes and hearts. We would have lost our freedom if men like Grandpa had not been willing to die for our flag," said Mom. "But we'd lose more if we didn't have the Word of God."

HOW ABOUT YOU? Do you realize the value of your Bible? It cost more than dollars and cents. It cost some people their lives. Treasure the Word. It's valuable! *B.J.W.*

TO MEMORIZE: How can a young person stay pure? By obeying your word and following its rules. *Psalm 119:9*

Treasure your Bible

4 July

NO LIMIT

FROM THE BIBLE:

Then Jesus said, "Come to me, all of you who are weary and carry heavy burdens, and I will give you rest. Take my yoke upon you. Let me teach you, because I am humble and gentle, and you will find rest for your souls. For my yoke fits perfectly, and the burden I give you is light."
MATTHEW 11:28-30

Become a citizen of heaven

THE WIND whipped through Tucker's hair, and salt water washed his face as the boat approached Liberty Island. "Look! There she is," he yelled.

"The Statue of Liberty is beautiful!" exclaimed Mother.

As they docked, Tucker skipped down the gangplank. He couldn't wait to get inside the Statue of Liberty.

After they had enjoyed a guided tour, they headed back to their hotel. "I can remember my grandparents telling what it was like to come to America from Holland," said Dad. "They said the Statue of Liberty was the first sight to welcome them in a strange land."

"I'll bet they were glad to get here," said Tucker.

"Yes, they were," Dad replied. "They were also glad when they became citizens of this country and could finally call America their home."

"Do immigrants still come to America?" Tucker asked.

"Yes," Dad answered, "but not as many as in times past."

"Why?" asked Tucker.

"Things have changed," said Dad. "The poem on the statue says, 'Give me your tired, your poor, your huddled masses yearning to breathe free,' but the door is no longer open to everyone. Since so many people have wanted to come to America, our government has had to put restrictions on the invitation. Criminals and the insane aren't accepted, and there's a quota now on the number that can come each year from any one region. It seems sad, but I suppose it's necessary."

"That reminds me of another gateway to freedom," said Mother, "and it is still open to everyone. Jesus invites all to come to him. He offers freedom from sin and grants citizenship in heaven to anybody who will come."

HOW ABOUT YOU? Have you accepted the invitation of Jesus? Is your citizenship in heaven? His offer is open to everyone. *J.L.H.*

TO MEMORIZE: We are citizens of heaven, where the Lord Jesus Christ lives. And we are eagerly waiting for him to return as our Savior. *Philippians 3:20*

"I TOLD ALL my friends I was going to Niagara Falls and Canada," whined Mindy, "and now—"

"Dad said he was sorry," interrupted twelve-year-old Jeff. "He can't help it that his job made it necessary to change our plans."

"I think we have two choices here," said Mom. "We can mope around all summer feeling sorry for ourselves, or we can be thankful for the things we *are* able to do. We can have a 'celebration summer' with mini-vacations."

"How?" Jeff and Mindy wanted to know. "What would we celebrate?"

"We can celebrate having good health and being together," suggested Dad. "We can enjoy the beauty of God's creation around us."

"And we can do special little things—things we have always planned to do 'someday,'" added Mom.

"Things like touring the pottery factory?" Mindy asked.

Mother nodded. "Yes, and the museum and the bakery."

"And this year we'll make time to go to the County Fair and the steam-engine show," Dad promised.

"Let's take Grandpa James with us," Mindy added. "He would love it."

Mom smiled. "That's a splendid idea. Why don't we include someone on each one of our mini-vacations?"

"Boy, this sounds like fun," Jeff said.

HOW ABOUT YOU? Is your family unable to take a big vacation this year? Why not have mini-vacations? And even if that doesn't work out, you'll be surprised at the good times you can have in your own neighborhood. Enjoy the things around you. And in your planning, don't forget to include someone who may be lonely. Most of all don't forget to thank God. *B.J.W.*

TO MEMORIZE: Praise the Lord; praise God our Savior! For each day he carries us in his arms. *Psalm 68:19*

CELEBRATION SUMMER

FROM THE BIBLE:

*Praise the Lord, I tell myself,
and never forget the good
things he does for me.
He forgives all my sins
and heals all my diseases.
He ransoms me from death
and surrounds me with love
and tender mercies.
He fills my life with good things.
My youth is renewed like the
eagle's! . . .
The Lord is merciful and
gracious;
he is slow to get angry and full
of unfailing love.
He will not constantly accuse us,
nor remain angry forever.
He has not punished us for all
our sins,
nor does he deal with us as we
deserve.
For his unfailing love toward
those who fear him
is as great as the height of the
heavens above the earth.
He has removed our rebellious
acts
as far away from us as the
east is from the west.
The Lord is like a father to his
children,
tender and compassionate to
those who fear him.*

PSALM 103:2-5, 8-13

Enjoy blessings around you

PATCH IT UP

FROM THE BIBLE:

The words of the godly lead to life; evil people cover up their harmful intentions.

Hatred stirs up quarrels, but love covers all offenses.

Wise words come from the lips of people with understanding, but fools will be punished with a rod.

Wise people treasure knowledge, but the babbling of a fool invites trouble.

The wealth of the rich is their fortress; the poverty of the poor is their calamity.

The earnings of the godly enhance their lives, but evil people squander their money on sin.

People who accept correction are on the pathway to life, but those who ignore it will lead others astray.

To hide hatred is to be a liar; to slander is to be a fool.

Don't talk too much, for it fosters sin.

Be sensible and turn off the flow!

The words of the godly are like sterling silver; the heart of a fool is worthless.

The godly give good advice, but fools are destroyed by their lack of common sense.

PROVERBS 10:11-21

Don't make problems worse

ANGELA LOOKED at her brother. "There's a hole in your pants!" She said.

Mom shook her head and sighed. "His only good pair is in the wash, so he'll have to wear these," she said. "Just make sure you don't pick at the hole and make it bigger, Jason."

Angela pouted. "Why do we have to wear such worn-out clothes?"

Mom sighed again. "You know we can't afford new clothes since the divorce, honey," she said. "I could work more hours, but then I wouldn't have much time left for you kids. I think family life is more important than clothes."

"Maybe if you had been a better wife, Dad wouldn't have left us," grumbled Angela. She tried not to see the tears in her mother's eyes.

On the way home from school, Angela noticed that the hole in Jason's pants was bigger. "You've been picking at that hole," she scolded. "Every time you pick at it, you only make it harder for Mom to patch it up."

Jason looked ashamed. "I don't want to make things harder for Mom." He paused, then added, "You do the same thing, you know."

"I do not!" retorted his sister.

"I'm talking about the way you treat Mom," explained Jason. "You always pick at her about getting divorced and not having much money."

Angela was silent for a few moments. "I guess I do," she admitted.

"Mom will patch my jeans tonight," Jason said, "and I think we should do some patching, too. Let's try to 'patch up' our family problems rather than making them worse."

HOW ABOUT YOU? Do you have a problem at home? Instead of feeling angry or discouraged, do what you can to make the situation better. Pray about it, be as cheerful as possible, and be supportive and loving toward others. *S.L.K.*

TO MEMORIZE: Don't talk too much, for it fosters sin. Be sensible and turn off the flow! *Proverbs 10:19*

STARFISH AND PEOPLE

BEING a pastor's daughter didn't make it any easier for Becky to move to a new home, but her father felt the Lord wanted them on an Indian reservation in Florida. She longed to return to the city where her father's church had been filled with people every Sunday. Here, only one Indian family seemed interested in church.

One Saturday Becky's family went to the beach for the day. They were all amazed to see numerous starfish lying on the beach. "Perhaps they got stranded by the tide," suggested Dad, "or maybe they got washed up during the storm."

As they walked, they saw a man putting starfish back into the ocean. The man said, "If they don't get into the water, they'll die!"

Becky looked at all the starfish on the sand. "But there are so many!" she exclaimed. "What difference will it make if you save just a few?"

The man smiled as he put a starfish in the water. "It will make a difference to this one," he said.

That evening as Becky sat on the front steps, she saw an Indian girl coming down the path. *I suppose I should invite her to church,* she thought, *but even if she does come, the church will still be practically empty.* Then she remembered the starfish and ran toward the girl. "Hi," she said with a smile. "I'm Becky. My dad preaches in that church over there, and we have such a good time. Will you come tomorrow?"

HOW ABOUT YOU? Do you ever complain about being the lone Christian at home? in your neighborhood? in your classroom? Does winning others to the Lord seem like too big a task? Maybe God has put you there because he wants to use you to make a difference in just one life. *J.L.H.*

TO MEMORIZE: In the same way, there is joy in the presence of God's angels when even one sinner repents. *Luke 15:10*

FROM THE BIBLE:

So Jesus used this illustration: "If you had one hundred sheep, and one of them strayed away and was lost in the wilderness, wouldn't you leave the ninety-nine others to go and search for the lost one until you found it? And then you would joyfully carry it home on your shoulders. When you arrived, you would call together your friends and neighbors to rejoice with you because your lost sheep was found. In the same way, heaven will be happier over one lost sinner who returns to God than over ninety-nine others who are righteous and haven't strayed away!

"Or suppose a woman has ten valuable silver coins and loses one. Won't she light a lamp and look in every corner of the house and sweep every nook and cranny until she finds it? And when she finds it, she will call in her friends and neighbors to rejoice with her because she has found her lost coin. In the same way, there is joy in the presence of God's angels when even one sinner repents."

LUKE 15:3-10

Every person is important

8 July

THE MISSING PIECE

FROM THE BIBLE:

From the depths of despair,
O Lord,
I call for your help.
Hear my cry, O Lord.
Pay attention to my prayer.

Lord, if you kept a record of our
sins,
who, O Lord, could ever
survive?
But you offer forgiveness,
that we might learn to fear
you.

I am counting on the Lord;
yes, I am counting on him.
I have put my hope in his
word. . . .

O Israel, hope in the Lord;
for with the Lord there is
unfailing love
and an overflowing supply of
salvation.
He himself will free Israel
from every kind of sin.

Lord, my heart is not proud;
my eyes are not haughty.
I don't concern myself with
matters too great
or awesome for me.
But I have stilled and quieted
myself,
just as a small child is quiet
with its mother.
Yes, like a small child is my
soul within me.
PSALM 130:1–131:2

Don't insist on your
own way

KAREN HUNG UP the phone and walked over to her parents, who were assembling a jigsaw puzzle. "Cindy Lawson got the summer baby-sitting job at the Tylers," she announced. "Isn't that awful?"

Mom looked puzzled. "That's a nice opportunity for Cindy."

"But I wanted the job," grumbled Karen.

"You should be glad for your friend," said Dad. "Besides, you'll find other things to do this summer."

"No, I won't," Karen pouted. Then her face brightened. "Maybe if I call Cindy back and tell her how much I wanted the job, she'll let me have it."

"I think you should let the matter drop," said Mom.

"But I'm sure God wants *me* to have this job," whined Karen. Then she glanced at her father curiously. He had picked up a puzzle piece and had gotten out a pair of scissors. He seemed to be considering cutting the puzzle piece. "Dad, what are you doing?"

"I'm trying to fit this piece into this empty spot," explained Dad. "If I cut off this bump here and glue it onto the other side, I can make it fit."

"You know that won't work," scolded Karen. "Besides, you'll need that piece somewhere else."

Karen's mother laughed. "I think I know what your father is trying to say, Karen. That puzzle piece represents you."

"Right," said Dad. "Trying to jam that piece into a place where it doesn't fit is like you trying to get your way about that job. Even if you succeeded, you would miss out on whatever God really wanted you to do."

HOW ABOUT YOU? Do you get upset when things don't go the way you want? Remember that God is in control, and he knows what's best for you. Let him put you in the right place at the right time. *S.L.K.*

TO MEMORIZE: I long for the Lord more than sentries long for the dawn, yes, more than sentries long for the dawn. *Psalm 130:6*

AS PAULA PACKED her suitcase, memories came flooding into her mind of her wonderful week at church camp the previous summer. She remembered meeting Bethany and Ellen. She remembered swimming, ball games, and craft times. But the best memory was the night she had asked Jesus to come into her heart. She started to sing the camp theme song at the top of her lungs.

"Whoa, little sister! You sure are happy today." It was Paula's brother, Michael, who was home from Bible college for the summer. "I'm glad you can go back to camp, where you met the Lord."

That evening Michael led family devotions. He read about Jacob's two trips to Bethel. And he explained that El-Bethel—the name Jacob called the place on the second trip—meant "God of Bethel." When he prayed, he asked the Lord to give Paula a wonderful time and great blessing at camp. "But help us all to learn, like Jacob did, that it's the *God* of the place, not the *place*, that we worship," he finished.

When Paula arrived at camp, everything seemed wrong. There was a new chapel. Bethany and Ellen hadn't come back. There was a different speaker. Paula didn't feel close to God as she had thought she would.

It wasn't until they sang "Into My Heart" at the close of the evening service that Paula realized it was the God of Camp Carlson, not the camp that had changed her life. Camp was a place where she would learn more about him and have more wonderful times. But it was God she worshiped, and he was still the same.

HOW ABOUT YOU? Is there a special place where you feel close to God? While it's nice to go back to that place, you can worship God any place. *R.E.P.*

TO MEMORIZE: Jesus replied, "The Scriptures say, 'You must worship the Lord your God; serve him only.'" *Luke 4:8*

THE GOD OF CAMP CARLSON

FROM THE BIBLE:

Then Jacob woke up and said, "Surely the Lord is in this place, and I wasn't even aware of it." He was afraid and said, "What an awesome place this is! It is none other than the house of God—the gateway to heaven!" The next morning he got up very early. He took the stone he had used as a pillow and set it upright as a memorial pillar. Then he poured olive oil over it. He named the place Bethel— "house of God"—though the name of the nearby village was Luz. . . .

God said to Jacob, "Now move on to Bethel and settle there. Build an altar there to worship me—the God who appeared to you when you fled from your brother, Esau." . . .

Jacob built an altar there and named it El-bethel, because God had appeared to him there at Bethel when he was fleeing from Esau.
GENESIS 28:16-19; 35:1, 7

Worship God, not a place

10 July

A FISH OUT OF WATER

FROM THE BIBLE:

Now there are different kinds of spiritual gifts, but it is the same Holy Spirit who is the source of them all. There are different kinds of service in the church, but it is the same Lord we are serving. There are different ways God works in our lives, but it is the same God who does the work through all of us. A spiritual gift is given to each of us as a means of helping the entire church.

To one person the Spirit gives the ability to give wise advice; to another he gives the gift of special knowledge. The Spirit gives special faith to another, and to someone else he gives the power to heal the sick. He gives one person the power to perform miracles, and to another the ability to prophesy. He gives someone else the ability to know whether it is really the Spirit of God or another spirit that is speaking. Still another person is given the ability to speak in unknown languages. . . .

But we have all been baptized into Christ's body by one Spirit, and we have all received the same Spirit.

1 CORINTHIANS 12:4-10, 13

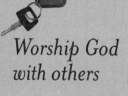

Worship God with others

AS THE SMALL ROWBOAT rocked with the gentle motion of the water, Nicholas watched his father cast his fishing line. "Dad," said Nicholas, "I don't want to go to the new church tomorrow."

"Really?" asked Dad. "Why not?"

"All my friends are back at our old church," replied Nicholas.

Nicholas's dad slowly reeled in his line a little. "I know we're going to miss everybody," he said, "but we had to move, and we still need to go to church."

"Can't we just have church at home?" asked Nicholas. "We could sing and read from the Bible."

"I've got a bite," said Dad. In a few moments he held up a small fish. "What would happen if we threw this fish in the boat and left it there?"

"It would die," said Nicholas.

"And if we throw it back?" asked Dad as he threw the fish into the lake.

"Well, now it will live."

"What if we took the fish to another lake?" Dad asked next. "Would it be able to live there?"

Nicholas thought a moment. "I think so," he said.

"Well," said Dad, "our family is a little like a fish that's been taken from one lake and put into another. We're in a new place where we have everything we need to go on living—food, clothes, a home." He paused. "But as Christians, we also need to be around other Christians. If we don't go to church, we can begin to die spiritually—like a fish out of water. Besides, we please God when we're part of a church family that cares for one another."

HOW ABOUT YOU? Have you felt out of place when you had to change churches? Remember, meeting with other Christians is an important part of worshiping God. *D.A.B.*

TO MEMORIZE: Yes, the body has many different parts, not just one part. *1 Corinthians 12:14*

SARITA WAS so happy! When she opened her birthday present, she found a beautiful doll! Every day after that, Sarita played with her doll. She treated it like a real baby, pretending to feed it and put it to bed.

One day Sarita wanted her mother to play a game with her instead of spending so much time with the new baby. "Please, Mother," begged Sarita, "will you play with me?"

"Not now, dear," answered Mother. "Play with your doll until I finish giving the baby her bath. Then I'll play with you."

So Sarita pretended to rock her doll to sleep. But she felt lonely because her doll couldn't talk to her.

Finally Mother said, "Ready, Sarita?" Together they sat down on the floor and began the game. Sarita was happy now. It felt so good to be able to talk and laugh with Mother. She gave a contented sigh.

Mother put her arms around Sarita and asked, "Were you feeling lonely?"

"Yes, I was. But I'm not now," answered Sarita.

"Don't you love your doll anymore?" asked Mother.

"Oh yes," said Sarita. "I still love her as much as I ever did. But I needed someone to love me back."

"Oh, Sarita," said Mother, giving her a kiss. "I love you very much. You know, I think God must feel the same way you do. He could have made us like dolls that can't talk or show love. But he made us real people so we'd be able to love him back."

HOW ABOUT YOU? God shows you every day how much he loves you. Do you show him that you love him back? One way to do this is by obeying his commands. Another is by telling him in prayer that you love him. *C.E.Y.*

TO MEMORIZE: We know how much God loves us, and we have put our trust in him. *1 John 4:16*

LOVE RETURNED

FROM THE BIBLE:

We know how much God loves us, and we have put our trust in him.

God is love, and all who live in love live in God, and God lives in them. And as we live in God, our love grows more perfect. So we will not be afraid on the day of judgment, but we can face him with confidence because we are like Christ here in this world.

Such love has no fear because perfect love expels all fear. If we are afraid, it is for fear of judgment, and this shows that his love has not been perfected in us. We love each other as a result of his loving us first.

If someone says, "I love God," but hates a Christian brother or sister, that person is a liar; for if we don't love people we can see, how can we love God, whom we have not seen? And God himself has commanded that we must love not only him but our Christian brothers and sisters, too.

1 JOHN 4:16-21

Tell God you love him

12 July

MORE THAN SAND

FROM THE BIBLE:

*O Lord my God, you have done
    many miracles for us.
    Your plans for us are too
    numerous to list.
If I tried to recite all your
    wonderful deeds,
    I would never come to the end
    of them. . . .*

*Thank you for making me so
    wonderfully complex!
    Your workmanship is
    marvelous—and how well I
    know it.
You watched me as I was being
    formed in utter seclusion,
    as I was woven together in the
    dark of the womb.
You saw me before I was born.
    Every day of my life was
    recorded in your book.
Every moment was laid out
    before a single day had passed.*

*How precious are your thoughts
    about me, O God!
    They are innumerable!
I can't even count them;
    they outnumber the grains
    of sand!
And when I wake up in the
    morning,
    you are still with me!*

PSALM 40:5; 139:14-18

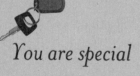

You are special

"NINE, TEN, ELEVEN," Julie painstakingly separated tiny pieces of sand from the pile she held in her hand and dropped them, grain by grain, into her pail.

"Are you just going to sit on this beach blanket, trying to count sand?" asked her brother Rick.

"There must be more sand than anything else in the whole world," Julie exclaimed, ignoring her brother. Rick rolled his eyes and headed toward the water.

Julie stayed on the blanket, counting sand. After a little while her father looked up from the book he was reading. "How's the counting? Do you think you'll be able to finish the whole beach this afternoon?" he teased.

Julie sprinkled the remaining sand she held over her feet. "I give up," she said. "I can't even count one handful. How much sand is there, Dad?"

Dad laughed. "There is no way we could begin to count all the sand in the world," he said. "Isn't that wonderful?"

Julie was puzzled. "*Wonderful?*" she asked. "Why is that wonderful?"

Dad reached into the tote bag packed with books, towels, and lotion. He took out a small Bible and turned to Psalm 139. "It says here that God's thoughts concerning us outnumber the grains of sand," he said. "Just think of that!"

Julie filled her bucket to the top with sand. Then she tipped it over and watched the millions of grains pour out. "Yes," she agreed. "It is wonderful."

HOW ABOUT YOU? Do other kids sometimes say things that leave you feeling worthless? God made each person special. The next time you feel less than special, think about all the sand there is. Then thank God that you are so special to him that his thoughts about you are far more than all the grains of sand in the world. *N.E.K.*

TO MEMORIZE: How precious are your thoughts about me, O God! *Psalm 139:17*

"THE NEW GUY across the street is cool!" Jason told his mother. "His name is Tim, and he's got two dogs."

"I've noticed that Sam Wellman is often there," observed Jason's mother. "Is Tim anything like Sam? I know Sam is often in trouble at school."

"Oh, Mom," sighed Jason. "He's OK." So Tim and Jason began spending a lot of time together.

A few weeks later Jason arranged for Tim to keep his dog, Midget, while he and his parents were away for a weekend. When they returned, Jason brought the dog home. As he came in the door, he stubbed his toe and let out a bad word. "Jason!" said Mom.

Jason hopped around on one foot. "I'm sorry. I guess I picked that word up from Tim."

"Then it may be time to choose a better friend," said Mom.

That evening Midget scratched and scratched. Dad looked up. "Does that dog have fleas?"

Jason checked. "She does have fleas!"

"Sprinkle her with flea powder," Mom ordered. "And we're going to have to spray the house. Midget must have gotten those fleas from Tim's dogs."

Dad added, "And that, Jason, is why we've been concerned about your friendship with Tim."

"You were afraid I'd get fleas?" Jason asked.

"No, not fleas," Dad replied, "but sin is contagious, too. For instance, you can pick up bad words without even realizing it—until they slip out."

HOW ABOUT YOU? Are you associating with the wrong crowd? Be careful. Your friends influence you by their talk and actions whether you realize it or not. Make sure they're the kind of friends whose influence makes you a better person. *B.J.W.*

TO MEMORIZE: Bad company corrupts good character. *1 Corinthians 15:33*

IT'S CATCHING

FROM THE BIBLE:

Keep away from angry, short-tempered people, or you will learn to be like them and endanger your soul. . . .

Don't envy evil people; don't desire their company. For they spend their days plotting violence, and their words are always stirring up trouble.
PROVERBS 22:24-25; 24:1-2

Choose friends carefully

14 July

SLIVERS AND SANDING

As you endure this divine discipline, remember that God is treating you as his own children. Whoever heard of a child who was never disciplined? If God doesn't discipline you as he does all of his children, it means that you are illegitimate and are not really his children after all. Since we respect our earthly fathers who disciplined us, should we not all the more cheerfully submit to the discipline of our heavenly Father and live forever?

For our earthly fathers disciplined us for a few years, doing the best they knew how. But God's discipline is always right and good for us because it means we will share in his holiness. No discipline is enjoyable while it is happening—it is painful! But afterward there will be a quiet harvest of right living for those who are trained in this way.

HEBREWS 12:7-11

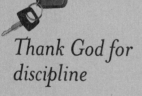

Thank God for discipline

"OUCH!" Benjamin stopped sanding the birdhouse he was making and looked at the sliver in his finger. He went to find his mother.

She met him at the kitchen door. "I was coming to look for you," she said. "I was just informed that you've been teasing Todd Berry. Is this true?"

"Eric started it," murmured Benjamin. "Besides, Todd is such a sissy!" Suddenly he remembered the sliver. He held up his finger. "Look, Mom. The rough wood of my birdhouse did this to me."

"We'd better get that out before it starts to fester," Mom said. She got a needle and tweezers, and gently worked on Benjamin's finger. Finally she held the sliver up in triumph.

Benjamin looked at his sore finger. "Thanks, Mom," he said. "I'll go sand down that old birdhouse so it won't do that again!"

"You know," said Mom, "just as the rough wood gave you a sliver, you gave Todd a 'sliver.' You hurt him by your words and actions. Can you think of a way to remove that 'sliver'?"

Benjamin looked down. "I'm sorry," he said finally. "I'll tell Todd I'm sorry, too."

"That should help," said Mom. "You also need to confess what you've done to God and ask his forgiveness. And there's one more thing: Your father and I have talked with you about this problem before. This time we'll have to do a little 'sanding' to help you avoid giving any more 'slivers.' That means being grounded for a few days."

HOW ABOUT YOU? Do you have rough edges that give "slivers" to other people? Do you say unkind things? refuse to share? snub others? Thank God for parents who help "sand you" into a better person. *H.W.M.*

TO MEMORIZE: No discipline is enjoyable while it is happening—it is painful! But afterward there will be a quiet harvest of right living for those who are trained in this way. *Hebrews 12:11*

"LOOKS GOOD, GUYS." Brent stood back and surveyed the side of the barn. He and his younger brothers, Eric and Nate, were busy painting, and Brent was in charge. He had helped Dad paint before, so now he was showing his brothers how to do it.

As they worked, the boys' conversation turned to their friend Keith, who lived nearby. "Keith asked me some questions about our church," said Nate.

"Maybe we should ask the pastor to call on his family," suggested Brent.

"Yeah," agreed Eric. "It's the pastor's job to tell them about Jesus."

Soon Mother came out with a tray of cookies and milk. "Brent," she said, "since you were the only one who knew how to paint, why didn't Dad tell you to paint the barn alone?"

"Because the job was too big for one person," said Brent.

"Dad figured Brent could teach Nate and me to paint," Eric added.

"That's right," Mother answered. "But I overheard you say that it's the pastor's job to tell people about Jesus. That job is also too big for one person. The Bible says the pastor's primary job is to teach the people in his church how to tell others about Jesus."

"He does that in his sermons," observed Nate.

Mother nodded. "The pastor teaches us how to tell others about Jesus, just like Brent taught the you, Nate and Eric, how to paint the barn."

"That makes sense," said Brent. "We better pay more attention so we'll be ready to answer Keith's questions."

THE WITNESS
(PART 1)

FROM THE BIBLE:

He is the one who gave these gifts to the church: the apostles, the prophets, the evangelists, and the pastors and teachers. Their responsibility is to equip God's people to do his work and build up the church, the body of Christ, until we come to such unity in our faith and knowledge of God's Son that we will be mature and full grown in the Lord, measuring up to the full stature of Christ.
EPHESIANS 4:11-13

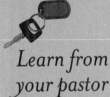

Learn from your pastor

HOW ABOUT YOU? Do you listen carefully to your pastor? Are you doing your best to serve God? You need to be equipped, or prepared, to serve, too. The Lord uses pastors to help with much of that preparation. *T.V.B.*

TO MEMORIZE: He is the one who gave these gifts to the church: the apostles, the prophets, the evangelists, and the pastors and teachers. *Ephesians 4:11-12*

16 July

THE WITNESS
(PART 2)

FROM THE BIBLE:

"As I was on the road, nearing Damascus, about noon a very bright light from heaven suddenly shone around me. I fell to the ground and heard a voice saying to me, 'Saul, Saul, why are you persecuting me?'

"'Who are you, sir?' I asked. And he replied, 'I am Jesus of Nazareth, the one you are persecuting.' The people with me saw the light but didn't hear the voice.

"I said, 'What shall I do, Lord?' And the Lord told me, 'Get up and go into Damascus, and there you will be told all that you are to do.'

". . . A man named Ananias lived there. He was a godly man in his devotion to the law, and he was well thought of by all the Jews of Damascus. He came to me and stood beside me and said, 'Brother Saul, receive your sight.' And that very hour I could see him!

"Then he told me, 'The God of our ancestors has chosen you. . . . You are to take his message everywhere, telling the whole world what you have seen and heard.'"
ACTS 22:6-15

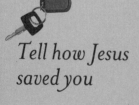

Tell how Jesus saved you

BRENT RAN excitedly into the house. "I'm going over to play with Keith, Mother," he said. "How can I help him be sure he's going to heaven?"

"Well," said Mother, "how did you help your brothers know how to paint the barn? Did you tell them how some of the world's great artists mix colors? Or did you explain various types of strokes and painting techniques?"

"Of course not." Brent gave her a puzzled look. "I just told them what Dad told me and showed them how I did it."

Mother nodded. "You started with your own experience, didn't you? Why not do that when you talk to Keith about the Lord?" she suggested. "Tell him how you became a Christian. That's what the apostle Paul often did."

Later that day Brent went over to Keith's house. "Hi, Brent," said Keith. "Come on in and see the model airplane I've been working on."

Brent looked at the model. "Wow!" he exclaimed. "Where did you get it?"

"My uncle Fred gave it to me. He was going to help me build it, but he had a heart attack and died before we could get started," said Keith sadly. "I sure miss him."

"I'm sorry your uncle died," replied Brent. "Once you told me you were sure he went to heaven. Why did you say that?"

"He told me," Keith replied. "It had something to do with Jesus, but I never listened very well. I wish I had."

"I'm sure I'm going to heaven when I die," Brent replied. "Would you like me to tell you why?"

"Sure!" Keith exclaimed.

HOW ABOUT YOU? Do you tell your friends about Jesus? The words in today's memory verse were given to the apostle Paul. Learn and apply them to yourself, too. Tell your friends what Jesus did for you. *T.V.B.*

TO MEMORIZE: You are to take his message everywhere, telling the whole world what you have seen and heard. *Acts 22:15*

"OH, THIS LETTER to Grandma is so messy," Sarah wailed.

Mother looked at the paper Sarah was holding up. "How did it get so messed up?" she asked.

"I erased a whole paragraph and did it over," explained Sarah.

"Well, if you want to send it today, you'll have to leave it the way it is," replied Mother. "Grandma will understand." So Sarah sealed the envelope and put it in the mailbox.

Later Sarah looked unhappy. Mother asked, "Is something bothering you, honey?"

Sarah's voice shook as she replied, "I don't think Jana likes me anymore. Ever since I took her doll, she doesn't really want to play with me. I gave it back and told her how sorry I was. She said she forgave me, but she doesn't act like it." A tear rolled down Sarah's cheek.

"Have you told Jesus that you really were sorry?" asked Mother. Sarah nodded. "Then," said Mother, "God has forgiven you. And I believe Jana has too, but it may take time to gain her trust again." Mother put an arm around Sarah. "Remember how you erased part of your letter to Grandma and the page was messy? Life is like that. We are writing a page in our lives each day. Sometimes we sin and need Jesus to erase those sins. But the people we know still see the messy pages. So be patient with Jana. Show her that you can be trusted."

HOW ABOUT YOU? Have you messed up a page in your life? If you're truly sorry and confess your sin to God, he will forgive you. As far as he is concerned, that sin is totally blotted out. Yet sin does leave its mark. Be patient when others need time before they can fully trust you again. *H.W.M.*

TO MEMORIZE: So then, let us aim for harmony in the church and try to build each other up. *Romans 14:19*

THE MESSY PAGE

FROM THE BIBLE:

For we are not our own masters when we live or when we die. While we live, we live to please the Lord. And when we die, we go to be with the Lord. So in life and in death, we belong to the Lord. . . .

For the Kingdom of God is not a matter of what we eat or drink, but of living a life of goodness and peace and joy in the Holy Spirit. If you serve Christ with this attitude, you will please God. And other people will approve of you, too. So then, let us aim for harmony in the church and try to build each other up.
ROMANS 14:7-8, 17-19

Sin leaves its mark

18 July

REFLECTIONS

FROM THE BIBLE:

When Moses came down the mountain carrying the stone tablets inscribed with the terms of the covenant, he wasn't aware that his face glowed because he had spoken to the Lord face to face. And when Aaron and the people of Israel saw the radiance of Moses' face, they were afraid to come near him.

But Moses called to them and asked Aaron and the community leaders to come over and talk with him. Then all the people came, and Moses gave them the instructions the Lord had given him on Mount Sinai. When Moses had finished speaking with them, he put a veil over his face. But whenever he went into the Tent of Meeting to speak with the Lord, he removed the veil until he came out again. Then he would give the people whatever instructions the Lord had given him, and the people would see his face aglow. Afterward he would put the veil on again until he returned to speak with the Lord.
EXODUS 34:29-35

Reflect Jesus

"WELL?" Lisa looked at her sister, Beth. "Do I look like Tara?" Lisa held a picture in a magazine under her chin as she gazed into the mirror. She had worked a long time to get her hair arranged like that of the movie star.

Beth shrugged. "A little, maybe. Come on, we've got to go." They were on their way to the lake before Lisa mentioned the movie star again.

"Tara's so beautiful." Lisa sighed.

"Why do you want to be like her?" asked Beth.

"Hasn't she been married several times?" asked Mom.

"But this magazine says she has the most exciting life in the world," Lisa said.

When they reached the lake, everyone piled out of the car. Soon they were enjoying a picnic lunch. "The lake's lovely. Look how blue it is," Mom observed.

"The water isn't really blue, though," said Dad. "It is reflecting the sky."

After the picnic they had fun hiking, fishing, and swimming. "It looks like rain," said Dad when he noticed the gathering clouds. "We'd better go."

"Look at the lake now." Mom pointed toward the water.

"It's gray now. It's reflecting the clouds," said Beth.

"And it isn't beautiful anymore," added Lisa.

"The lake doesn't have a choice about what it reflects," said Mom, "but in our lives, we can choose."

Lisa knew Mom was thinking about Tara Tarton. *Tara's life is gray compared to the beautiful life of Jesus,* Lisa admitted to herself. *I should be reflecting him.*

HOW ABOUT YOU? Is your life reflecting the beauty of Jesus? Compared to him, the life of any singer or ball player, or of any friend or relative, is gray. Reflect Jesus and his way of life, not that of someone else. *K.R.A.*

TO MEMORIZE: And all of us have had that veil removed so that we can be mirrors that brightly reflect the glory of the Lord. *2 Corinthians 3:18*

I WISH THIS *feeling would never end,* Juliana thought as she sat under the stars with her youth group friends. As she and her Christian friends sang God's praises, she felt closer to him than ever before. But she'd been to retreats before, and she knew that on Monday morning she wouldn't feel the same. *If I don't feel close to God on Monday, maybe he isn't real at all.* Juliana tried to forget these ideas, but she couldn't.

When Juliana arrived home the next day, Mom was busy with dinner preparations. "My cousin, Pauline, is coming for dinner," Mom explained.

"I didn't know you had a cousin," said Juliana as she began to help.

Pauline entertained the family all during dinner with funny stories about Mom's childhood. "I'm glad I got to know you," Juliana told her. "And just think, a few hours ago I didn't know you existed."

"Shame on your mom for not mentioning me," Pauline said with a wink. "But I've been here all along."

The words stuck with Juliana. Cousin Pauline's existence wasn't dependent on Juliana knowing about her or "feeling her presence." It was the same with God. Juliana had doubted God was real because she didn't always feel his presence.

"Tell us about the retreat," suggested Mom.

"It was great," Juliana said. "Really great."

HOW ABOUT YOU? Have you ever felt God to be especially close, only to be doubtful of his presence when you no longer felt that way? It's nice to feel God's presence, but it's important to know he is there whether you have the "feeling" or not. *K.R.A.*

TO MEMORIZE: Then Jesus told him, "You believe because you have seen me. Blessed are those who haven't seen me and believe anyway." *John 20:29*

NO MORE DOUBTS

FROM THE BIBLE:

One of the disciples, Thomas (nicknamed the Twin), was not with the others when Jesus came. They told him, "We have seen the Lord!" But he replied, "I won't believe it unless I see the nail wounds in his hands, put my fingers into them, and place my hand into the wound in his side."

Eight days later the disciples were together again, and this time Thomas was with them. The doors were locked; but suddenly, as before, Jesus was standing among them. He said, "Peace be with you." Then he said to Thomas, "Put your finger here and see my hands. Put your hand into the wound in my side. Don't be faithless any longer. Believe!"

"My Lord and my God!" Thomas exclaimed.

Then Jesus told him, "You believe because you have seen me. Blessed are those who haven't seen me and believe anyway."

Jesus' disciples saw him do many other miraculous signs besides the ones recorded in this book.

JOHN 20:24-30

Trust God's Word, not your feelings

20 July

DRIP-DRY GIVER

FROM THE BIBLE:

Remember this—a farmer who plants only a few seeds will get a small crop. But the one who plants generously will get a generous crop. You must each make up your own mind as to how much you should give. Don't give reluctantly or in response to pressure. For God loves the person who gives cheerfully. And God will generously provide all you need. Then you will always have everything you need and plenty left over to share with others. As the Scriptures say,

"Godly people give generously to the poor.
Their good deeds will never be forgotten."

2 CORINTHIANS 9:6-9

Give cheerfully

"CAMPING IS FUN, but it's sure easier to do the washing at home, isn't it?" observed Jody.

"Yes," agreed Mom as she wrung out a beaded shirt, twisting it tightly. "Would you hang this up for me, please?"

"Sure." Jody hung the shirt on the clothesline. "Can I wring out this sweater now?" she asked.

"Oh, don't wring that," said her mother. "Just squeeze it gently and then roll it in a towel. Wringing wouldn't be good for the material." She turned to a third group of clothes. "Now these," she said, "are drip-dry. Just hang them up."

Later that day Dad gave Jody her allowance. She looked at the money in her hand. "Would it be OK if I put all of this in the missionary offering in church tomorrow?" she asked suddenly. "Since we're camping, I don't really need any of it this week."

Mom smiled. "You've come a long way in your giving. Remember when you first got your allowance? We insisted that you give a tenth to the Lord, so you did. But you weren't happy about it," Mom reminded her. "It was kind of 'wrung out' of you, like I wrung the water out of the beaded shirt this morning. Later, you gave your tenth willingly, but that's all you'd give. It was as though you were 'gently squeezed' into giving that much. I'm aware that now you often give extra money. That reminds me of the drip-dry clothes where the water freely runs off."

"That's the kind of giver God prefers, too," added Dad. "The one who gives freely."

HOW ABOUT YOU? What kind of giver are you? Do you give only because you have to? Or do you gladly give a portion of your money to the Lord? *H.W.M.*

TO MEMORIZE: Remember this—a farmer who plants only a few seeds will get a small crop. But the one who plants generously will get a generous crop. *2 Corinthians 9:6*

"VALERIE, OVER HERE!" Valerie looked up in surprise as she heard her mother's voice. Why was Mom picking her up after school? "I thought you might like to go to the gift shop with me," said Mom.

They had gone several blocks when Valerie blurted out, "Mom, I'm the only one in my class who doesn't watch horror movies. I don't like being the oddball."

"I know it's not easy to be different, Val," agreed Mom as she drove into the parking lot.

Valerie sighed. "Our verse on Sunday was about being 'a chosen people.'"

Mom laughed. "Chosen means 'a special purchase'—a rare treasure to God," she explained as they got out of the car. Inside the shop Mom said, "Let's look at the vases. I'd like to make a new flower arrangement for the piano."

Valerie immediately saw the vase she wanted.

After looking at the price tag, Mom laughed. "Leave it to you to pick out the most expensive one in the shop."

"Why is it so expensive?" asked Valerie.

"It's handcrafted," her mother explained. "These others were made in molds, and basically they're all alike. This vase is one of a kind."

"Just like me," Valerie grinned. "A rare treasure—a special purchase."

"Right. And don't ever let the world squeeze you into its mold." Mom picked up the vase. "Let's buy this one. It will be a reminder of how special we are to God."

HOW ABOUT YOU? Do you ever feel like an oddball because you have to take a stand for what's right? Just remember you are God's special treasure. It's OK to be different. *B.J.W.*

TO MEMORIZE: You are a chosen people. You are a kingdom of priests, God's holy nation, his very own possession. This is so you can show others the goodness of God, for he called you out of the darkness into his wonderful light. *1 Peter 2:9*

A SPECIAL PURCHASE

FROM THE BIBLE:

God's truth stands firm like a foundation stone with this inscription: "The Lord knows those who are his," and "Those who claim they belong to the Lord must turn away from all wickedness."

In a wealthy home some utensils are made of gold and silver, and some are made of wood and clay. The expensive utensils are used for special occasions, and the cheap ones are for everyday use. If you keep yourself pure, you will be a utensil God can use for his purpose. Your life will be clean, and you will be ready for the Master to use you for every good work.

Run from anything that stimulates youthful lust. Follow anything that makes you want to do right. Pursue faith and love and peace, and enjoy the companionship of those who call on the Lord with pure hearts.

2 TIMOTHY 2:19-22

Dare to be different

22 July

VACATION LESSONS
(PART 1)

FROM THE BIBLE:

"Yes, the way to identify a tree or a person is by the kind of fruit that is produced.

"Not all people who sound religious are really godly. They may refer to me as 'Lord,' but they still won't enter the Kingdom of Heaven. The decisive issue is whether they obey my Father in heaven. On judgment day many will tell me, 'Lord, Lord, we prophesied in your name and cast out demons in your name and performed many miracles in your name.' But I will reply, 'I never knew you. Go away; the things you did were unauthorized.'"

MATTHEW 7:20-23

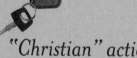

"Christian" actions can't save you

KAREN HAD LOOKED forward to spending part of her summer vacation with her aunt in Colorado. Not only was Aunt Dee her very favorite aunt, but she owned a jewelry store where Karen loved to roam around, looking at all the beautiful gems. "Is this a ruby?" Karen asked the first day she visited the store. "It looks like the one you gave Mom for her birthday."

"It's not exactly the same," Aunt Dee replied. "Your mother's is the real thing. This one is synthetic."

Taking the ring, Karen looked at it carefully. "What's synthetic?"

Aunt Dee laughed. "Well, I guess you could call it a fake. It's not a real ruby. It looks like a ruby, and most people can't tell the difference. But a trained eye will tell you that it's not the real thing."

"Lots of people could be fooled," commented Karen, as she put the ring back.

After a moment Aunt Dee asked, "Did you know that there are synthetic Christians?"

"Synthetic Christians?" Karen repeated. "What do you mean?"

"The Bible tells us that some people are not really born again," explained Aunt Dee. "They just pretend to be Christians. They act like it on the outside, but there has not been a change inside. They are fakes—synthetic. But God knows who's real and who's faking it."

Karen thought about that. She was glad she could say she was really a Christian and not just a synthetic.

HOW ABOUT YOU? Do you think you're a Christian because your parents are Christians or because you live a "good" life and do all the things you see other Christians do? That won't do it. The way to be born again is by making a personal commitment to Christ. *R.I.J.*

TO MEMORIZE: Not all people who sound religious are really godly. . . . The decisive issue is whether they obey my Father in heaven." *Matthew 7:21*

"WE'RE GOING to have company tonight," Aunt Dee called to Karen, "so take out the good silver and set the table, will you, please?"

Karen went to the closet where she knew her aunt kept the good silverware and took it out carefully. A look of surprise came over her face when she opened the box. "Aunt Dee," she called, "the silverware is all black and ugly looking."

Aunt Dee came into the dining room and looked at the silverware. "Oh, of course," she said. "It hasn't been used for some time. We'll have to clean it before we can use it. I'll help you."

Karen and her aunt began to polish the tarnished silverware. "If silver is such a precious metal, how come it turns black like this?" asked Karen.

"I don't know exactly why it does that," answered Aunt Dee, "but I do know that the longer it sits around in a box or drawer without being used, the more likely it is to tarnish. Fortunately, it can be polished again."

"Sort of like Christians," Karen said softly. She recalled a sermon about how Christians should be kept clean and shining, ready for the Lord to use. She mentioned the illustration to her aunt.

"That is so right," Aunt Dee agreed. "We should go daily to the Lord, confessing our sin and asking him to help us keep from becoming tarnished."

HOW ABOUT YOU? If God wants you to do something for him, are you ready for his work? Don't allow sin to come into your life and stay there. You need to confess your sin and receive God's forgiveness. You must not go back to that sin but rather turn from it. Then you're ready to do whatever task God has for you. *R.I.J.*

TO MEMORIZE: You must warn each other every day, as long as it is called "today," so that none of you will be deceived by sin and hardened against God. *Hebrews 3:13*

VACATION LESSONS
(PART 2)

FROM THE BIBLE:

What harmony can there be between Christ and the Devil? How can a believer be a partner with an unbeliever? And what union can there be between God's temple and idols? For we are the temple of the living God. As God said:

"I will live in them
*   and walk among them.*
I will be their God,
*   and they will be my people.*
Therefore, come out from them
*   and separate yourselves from*
*   them, says the Lord.*
Don't touch their filthy things,
*   and I will welcome you.*
And I will be your Father,
*   and you will be my sons and*
*   daughters,*
*   says the Lord Almighty."*

Because we have these promises, dear friends, let us cleanse ourselves from everything that can defile our body or spirit. And let us work toward complete purity because we fear God.
2 CORINTHIANS 6:15–7:1

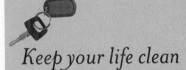

Keep your life clean

24 July

VACATION LESSONS
(PART 3)

FROM THE BIBLE:

When Moses failed to come back down the mountain right away, the people went to Aaron. "Look," they said, "make us some gods who can lead us. This man Moses, who brought us here from Egypt, has disappeared. We don't know what has happened to him."

So Aaron said, "Tell your wives and sons and daughters to take off their gold earrings, and then bring them to me."

All the people obeyed Aaron and brought him their gold earrings. Then Aaron took the gold, melted it down, and molded and tooled it into the shape of a calf. The people exclaimed, "O Israel, these are the gods who brought you out of Egypt!"
EXODUS 32:1-4

God first—things later

KAREN CONTINUED to spend a lot of time in her aunt's jewelry store, and she read several books about gems. "Did you read this book?" her aunt asked one evening. "I think it's my favorite."

Karen shook her head. "What's it about?"

Aunt Dee began to turn the pages of the book. "It's sort of a history of gems," she explained. "For instance, in this chapter it tells how gems became so important in ancient days. It tells how carvings and inscriptions were made in the harder stones—those that would not chip or break easily. That made them very valuable. But then something terrible happened."

"What happened?" Karen asked.

"People started using these gems in their worship," Aunt Dee explained. "In fact, they began to worship the gems rather than worshiping God."

"Oh, that is terrible," agreed Karen.

Aunt Dee nodded. "Even today Christians worship things instead of God."

Karen could hardly believe that. "I wouldn't put anything before the Lord, would you?"

Her aunt shook her head. "I don't mean to," she said, "but I must admit that sometimes things become so important to me that I get my priorities mixed up. Often the things themselves are not evil, but sometimes I let work, television, clothes, or a lot of other things become so important to me that I forget that I belong to God. I should give my loyalty to him."

HOW ABOUT YOU? It's unlikely that you would ever make an idol that you would actually worship in the way the Israelites did. And you probably won't choose any objects to bow down to, either. But do things in your life become so important that you forget God? Check yourself! *R.I.J.*

TO MEMORIZE: This world is fading away, along with everything it craves. But if you do the will of God, you will live forever. *1 John 2:17*

KAREN HAD ENJOYED her vacation, but now it was time to go home. The day she left, Aunt Dee gave her a little gold pendant with a real diamond chip! Karen squealed in delight and gave her aunt a hug. The ring on Aunt Dee's own finger sparkled brilliantly in the light.

Karen had never examined Aunt Dee's diamond ring. Now she held her aunt's hand, turning it until the light made the diamond sparkle even more. "My mom has a diamond, too," she said, "and that's what I want someday!"

Aunt Dee laughed. "A young man may show his love for you by giving you a diamond, but I hope it won't be for a long time!" She paused in thought. "God gave us much more than a diamond. He gave us his Son. That's how much he loved us."

Karen had learned a verse a long time ago that seemed to fit with what her aunt was saying. "'For God so loved the world that he gave his only Son, so that everyone who believes in him will not perish but have eternal life.'" She quoted it to her aunt. "That's John 3:16," she added.

"Yes, and that shows how much God loves us," Aunt Dee said. "Men give beautiful diamonds to the women they love, but God gave us his very own Son."

HOW ABOUT YOU? Do you ever think seriously about what God gave to this world? to you? It wasn't something man made. It wasn't something you have to buy. It wasn't something that only had a sparkle. It was his own Son, Jesus. Have you accepted his gift of love? Have you ever really thanked him for that wonderful and priceless gift? *R.I.J.*

TO MEMORIZE: This is real love. It is not that we loved God, but that he loved us and sent his Son as a sacrifice to take away our sins. *1 John 4:10*

VACATION LESSONS
(PART 4)

FROM THE BIBLE:

And as Moses lifted up the bronze snake on a pole in the wilderness, so I, the Son of Man, must be lifted up on a pole, so that everyone who believes in me will have eternal life.

"For God so loved the world that he gave his only Son, so that everyone who believes in him will not perish but have eternal life. God did not send his Son into the world to condemn it, but to save it.

"There is no judgment awaiting those who trust him. But those who do not trust him have already been judged for not believing in the only Son of God."

JOHN 3:14-18

God gave us Jesus

26 July

BALANCING THE ACCOUNT

FROM THE BIBLE:

"You have heard that the law of Moses says, 'If an eye is injured, injure the eye of the person who did it. If a tooth gets knocked out, knock out the tooth of the person who did it.' But I say, don't resist an evil person! If you are slapped on the right cheek, turn the other, too. If you are ordered to court and your shirt is taken from you, give your coat, too. If a soldier demands that you carry his gear for a mile, carry it two miles. Give to those who ask, and don't turn away from those who want to borrow.

"You have heard that the law of Moses says, 'Love your neighbor' and hate your enemy. But I say, love your enemies! Pray for those who persecute you! In that way, you will be acting as true children of your Father in heaven. For he gives his sunlight to both the evil and the good, and he sends rain on the just and on the unjust, too. If you love only those who love you . . . how are you different from anyone else?"

MATTHEW 5:38-47

Return good for evil

"OOOOHHHH! I just can't get this checkbook to balance with the bank statement," moaned Mother.

Father looked over her shoulder. "Last week I wrote a check for twenty dollars to Hanson's Hardware," he said. "Is it listed in the checkbook?"

Mother quickly scanned the check register. "No, it's not. That helps, but it still doesn't balance."

"Mother! Mother!" Stephen burst into the room. "Melissa hit me!"

"But he hit me first!" yelled Melissa.

"Well, I owed you one from last time," Stephen roared. "The Bible says if someone hits you, you have the right to hit him back!"

Mother gasped. "Why, Son! That's not what the Bible teaches at all."

"Yes, it is," replied Stephen firmly. "The Old Testament says, 'Whatever anyone does to hurt another person must be paid back in kind.'"

"Sit down," ordered Father. "That passage isn't talking about personal vengeance. It was meant as a civil law, to ensure justice in the nation of Israel. People who return blow for blow find the score is never settled."

Mother sighed. "That sounds like my checkbook. The account never balances."

Father nodded. "Jesus did away with the law of revenge. He told us to return good for evil. That's the only way to settle the score."

"You mean when Stephen hits me, I'm supposed to do something good for him?" Melissa asked. "That's too hard!"

Father nodded again. "God says to overcome evil with good."

Stephen and Melissa looked at each other and sighed. "We'll try," they said in unison.

HOW ABOUT YOU? Are you keeping score of the wrongs others do to you? Are you figuring out how you can get back at them? God's way to settle the score is to do something good for them. Try it. *B.J.W.*

TO MEMORIZE: Don't let evil get the best of you, but conquer evil by doing good. *Romans 12:21*

CARLA STIRRED Jell-O into boiling water, added some ice cubes, and put the bowl with the watery mixture in the refrigerator to set. "What can I do now?" she asked her mother after a while. "I wish I had a good Christian friend to play with."

"Isn't Daniella a Christian?" asked Mother.

Carla nodded. "Yeah, but I'm beginning to think she's hopeless. She always wants her own way, and she says mean things about other kids."

"That's too bad," said Mother. "Well, maybe it's time to check your Jell-O."

Carla went to the refrigerator. "It's getting there," she said. "It's ready for the fruit." She added bananas while she continued to complain about Daniella.

"Tell me something," said Mother. "Has she improved at all since she became a Christian?"

"Oh, sure," Carla said, nodding, "but not enough. She still has a long way to go."

"Like the Jell-O," said Mother.

"The Jell-O?" questioned Carla. "What do you mean?"

"The Jell-O has improved since you started it, but it has a long way to go, too," explained Mother. "In time it will be set and ready to eat. It reminds me of Christians. They don't usually 'set' all at once. It takes time. As they grow in the Lord, they improve in outward behavior. We need to be patient with them."

HOW ABOUT YOU? Do you know Christians who need a lot of improvement? Are you praying for them? Are you helping them by being friendly and encouraging them to attend church and study God's Word? Do you set a good example for them? God finishes what he starts. He'll finish what he has begun in them—and in you. *H.W.M.*

TO MEMORIZE: I am sure that God, who began the good work within you, will continue his work until it is finally finished on that day when Christ Jesus comes back again. *Philippians 1:6*

NOT HOPELESS

FROM THE BIBLE:

Every time I think of you, I give thanks to my God. I always pray for you, and I make my requests with a heart full of joy because you have been my partners in spreading the Good News about Christ from the time you first heard it until now. And I am sure that God, who began the good work within you, will continue his work until it is finally finished on that day when Christ Jesus comes back again.

It is right that I should feel as I do about all of you, for you have a very special place in my heart. We have shared together the blessings of God. . . . I pray that your love for each other will overflow more and more, and that you will keep on growing in your knowledge and understanding. For I want you to understand what really matters, so that you may live pure and blameless lives until Christ returns. May you always be filled with the fruit of your salvation—those good things that are produced in your life by Jesus Christ—for this will bring much glory and praise to God.
PHILIPPIANS 1:3-11

God finishes what he started

WHERE'S JENNA?

FROM THE BIBLE:

O Lord, you have examined my
heart
and know everything about me.
You know when I sit down or
stand up.
You know my every thought
when far away.
You chart the path ahead of me
and tell me where to stop and
rest.
Every moment you know
where I am.
You know what I am going to say
even before I say it, Lord.
You both precede and follow me.
You place your hand of
blessing on my head. . . .

I can never escape from your spirit!
I can never get away from
your presence! . . .
If I ride the wings of the morning,
if I dwell by the farthest oceans,
even there your hand will guide
me,
and your strength will support
me.
I could ask the darkness to hide
me
and the light around me to
become night—
but even in darkness I cannot
hide from you.
To you the night shines as bright
as day.
Darkness and light are both
alike to you.

PSALM 139:1-12

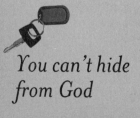

You can't hide
from God

"WHERE IS JENNA?" called Marcia in a singsong voice as she played with her baby sister one afternoon. "Where is Jenna hiding?" Jenna peeked through the chubby little fingers she was holding in front of her face. Suddenly she dropped her hand. "There she is!" exclaimed Marcia. "There's Jenna!" The baby squealed in delight and promptly placed her fingers back over her eyes, ready to play the game again. Marcia laughed, too. "You really think you're hiding from me, don't you?" she said. "Babies are silly, aren't they, Mother?"

"Sometimes they are," agreed Mother. "Almost as silly as adults."

Marcia looked at her mother suspiciously. "What do you mean?" she asked.

"I was just thinking of how we sometimes try to hide from God," said Mother. "We do something wrong, and we think nobody knows about it. Isn't that silly? We tend to forget that God sees and knows all about it."

Marcia nodded. "I know I try to hide sometimes," she admitted. She laughed as she saw Jenna once again peeking through her fingers. "Next time I'm tempted to think that way, I'll remember how silly it is."

HOW ABOUT YOU? Do you think nobody knows you broke that dish or toy? told that lie? snitched a cookie? Whatever you've done, God knows about it. Admit your sin to him and to the person you've wronged. Ask for forgiveness. *H.W.M.*

TO MEMORIZE: "Can anyone hide from me? Am I not everywhere in all the heavens and earth?" asks the Lord. *Jeremiah 23:24*

THE "WHITE" T-SHIRT

JASON QUICKLY RAN to the telephone. It was his friend Tucker. "I'm sorry, Tucker, but I can't come over now," said Jason. "My mother needs my help with the laundry." Jason hung up the phone and began helping his mom fold clothes.

"Jason, why did you tell Tucker I needed you?" asked Mom.

"Don't you want me to help you?" Jason asked.

"That would be nice," agreed his mother. "But what you told Tucker wasn't true."

"In a way it was true," argued Jason. "If you needed me to help, I would. Besides, it's not so bad to say things that aren't completely true."

"Jason," said Mom, "hand me that T-shirt from the top of the laundry basket, please. What color is it?"

"It's white," replied Jason. "All of Dad's T-shirts are white."

"Now dig to the bottom of the basket and get me another T-shirt," Mom directed. Jason looked puzzled but did as he was told. "What color is that one?" asked Mom.

Jason looked at it. "It's white, too," he said, "but next to this one, the first one looks yellowish."

"That's right, Jason," Mom nodded. "Until you had a really white T-shirt, you couldn't tell the first one was actually old and yellowed. It's the same with us. If we compare ourselves with the people around us, we seem to be doing all right. But when we compare ourselves with Jesus, we see how sinful we are. People may think it's all right to tell 'little white lies,' but God says his Son, Jesus, never lied or sinned in any way. Be careful to use Jesus as your example instead of watching how others play with sin."

FROM THE BIBLE:

This suffering is all part of what God has called you to. Christ, who suffered for you, is your example. Follow in his steps. He never sinned, and he never deceived anyone. He did not retaliate when he was insulted. When he suffered, he did not threaten to get even. He left his case in the hands of God, who always judges fairly. He personally carried away our sins in his own body on the cross so we can be dead to sin and live for what is right. You have been healed by his wounds! Once you were wandering like lost sheep. But now you have turned to your Shepherd, the Guardian of your souls.

1 PETER 2:21-25

Follow Jesus' example

HOW ABOUT YOU? Do you try to live like Jesus? His is the only pattern after which to shape your life. *B.B.*

TO MEMORIZE: Christ, who suffered for you, is your example. Follow in his steps. *1 Peter 2:21*

30 July

BELIEVE IT OR NOT

FROM THE BIBLE:

"What do you mean?" Nico-
demus asked.

Jesus replied, "You are a
respected Jewish teacher, and yet
you don't understand these things?
I assure you, I am telling you what
we know and have seen, and yet
you won't believe us. But if you
don't even believe me when I tell
you about things that happen here
on earth, how can you possibly
believe if I tell you what is going
on in heaven? For only I, the Son
of Man, have come to earth and
will return to heaven again. And
as Moses lifted up the bronze
snake on a pole in the wilderness,
so I, the Son of Man, must be
lifted up on a pole, so that
everyone who believes in me
will have eternal life."

JOHN 3:9-15

God's Word is true

JEFF WAS SPENDING summer vacation with his cousin Rada, and every day was action-packed. Jeff loved it! But each evening when they had family devotions, Jeff endured the Bible reading and prayer. "You don't really believe all that religious stuff, do you?" he asked Rada one night.

"Sure I do, and it's not 'religious' stuff"! retorted Rada.

Jeff shrugged. "Well, I don't see how anyone could believe some of these Bible stories. Imagine men walking in fire and not being burned or a man walking on water," Jeff snorted.

One day as they drove into town, Rada read a bumper sticker. "If Jesus said it, I believe it, and it's so."

"It should say, 'If Jesus said it, it's so,'" his dad commented. "It's so whether I believe it or not."

One day Rada's dad took them on a canoe trip. "The water's not very deep," said Jeff as they floated peacefully downstream. "I can see the bottom."

"It's deeper than it looks, Jeff," chuckled Rada's dad. "It's over your head."

"Aw, I don't believe it," Jeff scoffed just as they went under a low-hanging branch. Over they went into the water. All three came up spitting and sputtering.

"Stand up, Jeff," said Rada, grinning.

"I can't! I can't touch the bottom." Jeff swam toward the overturned canoe.

Soon the canoe was righted, and they again floated downstream. "The water was deep whether you believed it or not, Jeff," commented Rada's dad. "Believing it or not believing it doesn't change it. The same is true of God's Word."

HOW ABOUT YOU? Do you believe the Word of God? Do you believe *all* of it? God says if you believe in Jesus, you will have eternal life. *B.J.W.*

TO MEMORIZE: Though everyone else in the world is a liar, God is true. *Romans 3:4*

IT WAS Kurt's and Kristen's responsibility to see that the swimming pool got the proper amount of chlorine and other chemicals, but they hadn't done their job. Now the water was green. This meant they couldn't swim for two days.

"I'll bet these are going to be the two hottest days all summer," moaned Kurt, as he wiped the sweat off his forehead. "I can't believe that the water turned green so fast. It didn't look bad yesterday."

"You're right," sighed Kristen, fanning herself. "We should have used the water tester. By the time we could see that the algae was growing, it was too late to prevent it with chemicals."

"Did you say you haven't been using the water tester to see whether or not you needed to add chemicals?" Mother asked.

"Yeah," replied Kurt. "We thought we'd be able to tell if the water was getting dirty just by looking at it."

"How could all of that green stuff get in the pool overnight?" asked Kristen.

"You didn't *see* it yesterday," responded Mother. "The algae was there, but you needed to use the water tester so that you would know that it was there. That reminds me of some sins," she remarked. "There are little actions that don't seem like sin at all, but given a chance to grow, they can become very ugly."

"Too bad we don't have a guide to tell us when there's a problem—like we have the water tester for the pool," observed Kristen.

"We do!" exclaimed Kurt. "The Bible is our guide to help us know when our actions aren't right, so we can change them."

HOW ABOUT YOU? Do you ever have trouble with "little" sins getting out of control? The Bible is the guide to test your actions. Use it daily. *D.L.R.*

TO MEMORIZE: Make me walk along the path of your commands, for that is where my happiness is found. *Psalm 119:35*

THE WATER TESTER

FROM THE BIBLE:

The law of the Lord is perfect,
reviving the soul.
The decrees of the Lord are trustworthy,
making wise the simple.
The commandments of the Lord are right,
bringing joy to the heart.
The commands of the Lord are clear,
giving insight to life.
Reverence for the Lord is pure,
lasting forever.
The laws of the Lord are true;
each one is fair.
They are more desirable than gold,
even the finest gold.
They are sweeter than honey,
even honey dripping from the comb.
They are a warning to those who hear them;
there is great reward for those who obey them.

How can I know all the sins lurking in my heart?
Cleanse me from these hidden faults.
Keep me from deliberate sins!
Don't let them control me.
Then I will be free of guilt
and innocent of great sin.

May the words of my mouth and the thoughts of my heart
be pleasing to you,
O Lord, my rock and my redeemer.

PSALM 19:7-14

The Bible is our guide

1 August

OUT OF TUNE

FROM THE BIBLE:

Is there any encouragement from belonging to Christ? Any comfort from his love? Any fellowship together in the Spirit? Are your hearts tender and sympathetic? Then make me truly happy by agreeing wholeheartedly with each other, loving one another, and working together with one heart and purpose.

Don't be selfish; don't live to make a good impression on others. Be humble, thinking of others as better than yourself. Don't think only about your own affairs, but be interested in others, too, and what they are doing.

Your attitude should be the same that Christ Jesus had.

PHILIPPIANS 2:1-5

Get in tune with God

"WHERE'S my guitar pick?" demanded James. "You've been in my room again, haven't you, Mandy. I left my pick on my dresser, and now it's gone."

"I didn't take it," said Mandy. "And I don't go in your room."

"Well, someone took it!" James stomped down the hall and slammed his bedroom door. Mandy's brother had been acting like this often in recent weeks.

Later that evening James sat at the piano, tuning his guitar. "Where did you find your pick?" asked Mother. "Mandy told me you thought she had taken it."

"It was in my pocket," James muttered. He struck a piano key with one finger. *Plunk! Plunk!* Then he plucked a guitar string. *Ping! Ping! Plunk!* After a few more twists and turns his guitar was in tune.

"You're getting pretty good, Son," said Dad.

"Why do you always listen to the piano and the guitar together?" asked Mandy.

"If all the strings aren't in tune with the piano, they don't sound good with each other, either," explained James.

Mother looked at James. "Just like each of your guitar strings has to be in tune with the piano, so every member of the family needs to be in harmony with God. Otherwise, they are out of tune with each other," she said thoughtfully.

Dad nodded. "I've been hearing angry words around here. Could it be someone is out of tune?"

James sighed. "All right—I know it's me," he admitted. "I'm sorry."

HOW ABOUT YOU? Are you out of tune with God? Do you have trouble getting along with your family and friends? Now's the time to have a little "prayer meeting" all by yourself, and let God get you back in tune. *B.J.W.*

TO MEMORIZE: How wonderful it is, how pleasant, when brothers live together in harmony! *Psalm 133:1*

"YOUR HOT DOG'S almost done, Dave," Aaron told his little brother. Aaron twirled the long fork once more before withdrawing it from the fire. He placed the hot dog on a bun and handed it to Ellis. Then he began to roast one for himself.

"Know what, Dad?" Aaron said to his father, who was roasting two hot dogs at a time. "I think Devon, the new boy at school, is a Christian. I know he goes to church, and he never swears or blows his cool. He's not like most of the guys."

"Well, that sounds promising," replied Dad, who moved to the picnic table and handed one of the hot dogs to Mom.

Aaron followed. "Dave, you're not eating the hot dog I roasted for you," he complained, looking at the untouched meat on Dave's plate.

"Am too. See?" Dave held up a half-eaten hot dog bun, thickly spread with catsup. "I like hot dogs."

"That's just bread," said Aaron. "It's not a hot dog unless the meat's in it."

"Aaron's right," said Dad. "And here's something else to remember—just as a hot dog roll without the meat isn't a hot dog, a person isn't a Christian without Christ. He's like that empty roll. Take your friend Devon, for instance. I'm glad he's such a nice young man, Aaron, but none of the things you mentioned make him a Christian. He is a Christian only if he's accepted Christ into his life."

HOW ABOUT YOU? Have you asked Jesus Christ to come into your life? You may be a very nice person—but a very nice person without Christ is not a Christian. Don't be like an "empty roll." *H.W.M.*

TO MEMORIZE: I myself no longer live, but Christ lives in me. So I live my life in this earthly body by trusting in the Son of God, who loved me and gave himself for me. *Galatians 2:20*

THE EMPTY ROLL

FROM THE BIBLE:

"And yet we Jewish Christians know that we become right with God, not by doing what the law commands, but by faith in Jesus Christ. So we have believed in Christ Jesus, that we might be accepted by God because of our faith in Christ—and not because we have obeyed the law. For no one will ever be saved by obeying the law."

But what if we seek to be made right with God through faith in Christ and then find out that we are still sinners? Has Christ led us into sin? Of course not! Rather, I make myself guilty if I rebuild the old system I already tore down. For when I tried to keep the law, I realized I could never earn God's approval. So I died to the law so that I might live for God. I have been crucified with Christ. I myself no longer live, but Christ lives in me. So I live my life in this earthly body by trusting in the Son of God, who loved me and gave himself for me.
GALATIANS 2:16-20

A Christian has Christ

3 August

CHRISTIAN SAYS

FROM THE BIBLE:

We know what real love is because Christ gave up his life for us. And so we also ought to give up our lives for our Christian brothers and sisters. But if anyone has enough money to live well and sees a brother or sister in need and refuses to help—how can God's love be in that person?

Dear children, let us stop just saying we love each other; let us really show it by our actions. . . .

And this is his commandment: We must believe in the name of his Son, Jesus Christ, and love one another, just as he commanded us. Those who obey God's commandments live in fellowship with him, and he with them. And we know he lives in us because the Holy Spirit lives in us.

1 JOHN 3:16-18, 23-24

Don't just "say"— but "do"

"I'M SIMON—and remember, you must always do what Simon *says*." Miss Elrojo, Anthony's teacher, was speaking.

"Simon says, 'Thumbs up,'" said Miss Elrojo. So Anthony turned his thumbs up. "Simon says, 'Step forward,'" Miss Elrojo instructed as she stepped forward. All the children followed her example. "Simon says, 'Snap your fingers.'" But Miss Elrojo clapped her hands instead, and before Anthony could stop himself, he clapped his hands, too.

After supper Anthony's family learned a Bible verse during evening devotions. "We'll learn 1 John 3:18," said Dad. "Dear children, let us stop just saying we love each other; let us really show it by our actions." They repeated it together, and Dad explained it. "Our actions should match our words," he said.

"Hey," laughed Anthony, "Simon should learn this verse."

"Simon?" asked Mother. "What do you mean?" So Anthony explained the trouble he had when "Simon" said one thing and did another.

"That brings up a good point," observed Dad. "As Christians, we sometimes act like we're playing a game. Maybe it could be called 'Christians Say.' Sometimes Christians say one thing and do another. Can you think of examples?"

"Christians say, 'Read your Bible,' and then they only open it on Sunday," suggested Mother.

"Christians say, 'Go to church,' and then they stay home to read the newspaper," said Anthony's brother.

"Christians say, 'Be helpful,' and then they don't do chores," added Anthony.

"You've got the idea," said Dad.

HOW ABOUT YOU? Do you play "Christian Says"? Remember that people will often follow what you do rather than what you say. Listen to what God says, and love others in deed, not just in word. *H.W.M.*

TO MEMORIZE: Dear children, let us stop just saying we love each other; let us really show it by our actions. *1 John 3:18*

ALMOST!

EVER SINCE SUNDAY David had been thinking off and on about the pastor's sermon. He knew he needed to ask Jesus to be his Savior, and he had almost made that decision last Sunday. But right now he had other things on his mind—baseball, for instance. Becoming a Christian could wait.

David shook the thoughts from his mind as he got out of bed. Today was the big day! His team, the Lions, would be playing the Bears, a team from the south side of town, for the city championship. David was the shortstop for his team, and he was eager to play.

The coaches had been saying that the two teams were equal in ability, and it soon became obvious that this was true. First the Lions were ahead, then the Bears, then the Lions again. Unfortunately for David and his teammates, the Bears scored two runs in the bottom of the ninth inning and won the championship.

"That was a good game!" Dad said later.

"But, Dad, we lost!" David protested.

"You still can feel good about it," Mom said. "Being the second-place team in the city is an honor, too!"

"Yeah, David," his sister agreed. "You almost won!"

"Almost isn't enough!" David complained.

Dad gave him a thoughtful look. "That's true, David. Almost isn't enough—not in winning baseball games, nor in getting to heaven."

David was startled. He hadn't thought about it that way before! He knew he needed to make the decision to become a Christian, and he was almost ready to do it. Now he realized that almost being a Christian wasn't enough.

FROM THE BIBLE:

Then Agrippa said to Paul, "You may speak in your defense."

So Paul, with a gesture of his hand, started his defense: "I am fortunate, King Agrippa, that you are the one hearing my defense against all these accusations made by the Jewish leaders. . . .

"King Agrippa, do you believe the prophets? I know you do—"

Agrippa interrupted him. "Do you think you can make me a Christian so quickly?"

Paul replied, "Whether quickly or not, I pray to God that both you and everyone here in this audience might become the same as I am, except for these chains."

ACTS 26:1-2, 27-29

Accept Christ

HOW ABOUT YOU? Are you "almost" a Christian? Perhaps you listen to your parents, your pastor, and your Sunday school teacher talk about Christ. What's holding you back? Why not become a Christian today? *L.M.W.*

TO MEMORIZE: Agrippa interrupted him, "Do you think you can make me a Christian so quickly?" *Acts 26:28*

5 August

NO LONGER TRASH

FROM THE BIBLE:

Remind your people to submit to the government and its officers. They should be obedient, always ready to do what is good. They must not speak evil of anyone, and they must avoid quarreling. Instead, they should be gentle and show true humility to everyone. . . .

These things I have told you are all true. I want you to insist on them so that everyone who trusts in God will be careful to do good deeds all the time. These things are good and beneficial for everyone. . . .

For our people should not have unproductive lives. They must learn to do good by helping others who have urgent needs.
TITUS 3:1-2, 8, 14

You're saved to serve

"MOTHER, CAN YOU take me to my Bible club today?" asked Tia one afternoon. "I'm late."

"OK," agreed Mother, "but you'll have to walk home." They went to the car. "Do we need to stop for anyone else?" asked Mother. "Have you invited any of your friends?" Tia shook her head. "The Carsellos are coming over this evening," continued Mother. "Your father and I hope we'll have an opportunity to witness to them. I thought you could tell some Bible stories to Lina."

Tia squirmed. *I wish Mother would quit suggesting stuff like that, she thought. I don't want the kids to think I'm weird.*

When Tia returned home late that afternoon, Mother asked her to empty the trash. Tia took it out to the garage. Then she brought an empty white meat tray back into the house and rinsed the tray out. .

"I need this for a Bible club craft," Tia explained. "I'm going to use it as frame for my shell picture."

"OK," said Mother. "I see you've rescued that tray for a purpose." She paused, then added thoughtfully, "It's a bit like us. God rescued us for a purpose, too. We can worship him and serve him and bring others to him. Your shell picture will be a good reminder of that."

Tia looked at the tray and nodded. She was a Christian, but she wondered if she'd done much about fulfilling the purpose for which she'd been saved. *Tonight will be a good time to start, she* thought. *I'll tell those stories to Lina.*

HOW ABOUT YOU? Are you a Christian? Good works could never have saved you, but now that you are saved, God wants you to work for him. *H.W.M.*

TO MEMORIZE: Our people should not have unproductive lives. They must learn to do good by helping others who have urgent needs. *Titus 3:14*

"LINDA LOUISE LINCOLN, get down here!" called Mom. "We're waiting for you." Linda hurried out to the car.

"What's in that box you're carrying?" asked Dad.

"My new necklace. I want to wear it on Sunday," said Linda.

"A necklace!" bellowed her brother, Rob. "You made us wait for a piece of jewelry? We're going to a camp, not a fashion show!"

A few hours later the Lincolns arrived at the campground. The next couple days were filled with fishing, swimming, and boating. When Sunday came, they got ready to attend the church service at the camp pavilion. "Grab your Bibles," said Dad.

"Bibles?" Linda looked startled. "I didn't bring mine."

Mom, Dad, and Rob all looked at her in surprise.

""You can look on with one of us," Dad told her.

"I'm glad you folks have not taken a vacation from God this week," said the pastor. "I'm reading from Jeremiah 2 in the New Living Translation. 'Does a young woman forget her jewelry? Does a bride hide her wedding dress? No! Yet for years on end my people have forgotten me.'"

Linda blushed when her brother poked her with his elbow. She knew he was remembering, as she was, that she had brought her jewelry to camp but had forgotten her Bible. All week she had neglected to spend time with the Lord. She didn't want to forget to spend time with God again.

FORGOTTEN JEWEL

FROM THE BIBLE:

"But that is the time to be careful! Beware that in your plenty you do not forget the Lord your God and disobey his commands, regulations, and laws. For when you have become full and prosperous and have built fine homes to live in, and when your flocks and herds have become very large and your silver and gold have multiplied along with everything else, that is the time to be careful. Do not become proud at that time and forget the Lord your God, who rescued you from slavery in the land of Egypt. Do not forget that he led you through the great and terrifying wilderness with poisonous snakes and scorpions, where it was so hot and dry. He gave you water from the rock! He fed you with manna in the wilderness, a food unknown to your ancestors. He did this to humble you and test you for your own good."
DEUTERONOMY 8:11-16

Don't forget God

HOW ABOUT YOU? Have you forgotten God? Perhaps it isn't jewelry that you put ahead of the Lord, but how about TV? or baseball? or a bicycle? God wants you to put him first. *P.R.*

TO MEMORIZE: Does a young woman forget her jewelry? Does a bride hide her wedding dress? No! Yet for years on end my people have forgotten me *Jeremiah 2:32*

7 August

FISHERS OF MEN

FROM THE BIBLE:

One day as Jesus was walking along the shore beside the Sea of Galilee, he saw two brothers—Simon, also called Peter, and Andrew—fishing with a net, for they were commercial fishermen. Jesus called out to them, "Come, be my disciples, and I will show you how to fish for people!" And they left their nets at once and went with him.

A little farther up the shore he saw two other brothers, James and John, sitting in a boat with their father, Zebedee, mending their nets. And he called them to come, too. They immediately followed him, leaving the boat and their father behind.

MATTHEW 4:18-22

Keep witnessing

GRANDPA STRETCHED out lazily on the creek bank. Tamara shifted restlessly. "The fish aren't biting here. Let's try another spot, Grandpa," she suggested.

"This is the third spot we've tried," Grandpa reminded her. "Relax."

Tamara sighed. As her cork rocked on the gentle waves, she sighed again.

"Something bothering you?" asked Grandpa.

"Yeah," said Tamara. "I've invited six girls to church this week, and not one is going to come. I think I'll quit inviting anybody to church." Grandpa wrinkled his brow as he looked at Tamara. Then he sat up and started reeling in his line. Tamara jumped up. "You got a bite?" she asked excitedly.

Grandpa shook his head. "No. I'm quittin'."

"But Grandpa, we've got all afternoon," Tamara argued.

"Yeah, but we've been here long enough, and we haven't caught one fish. I'm giving up fishing for good." He stood up. "Pull in your line."

"Please, let's wait a little longer," Tamara pleaded.

As Grandpa checked his bait, he gave his granddaughter a crooked grin. "Well, if you're sure. I just thought you were ready to quit. If you give up that easy fishing for people, I reckoned you would soon tire of fishing for fish, too."

Tamara smiled. "I get the message, Grandpa. When we get home, I'll call Louisa and invite her to church."

Grandpa tossed his line back into the water. "That's more like it," he said. "Just because the fish aren't biting today, it doesn't mean we give up fishing."

HOW ABOUT YOU? Does it seem like you're wasting your time inviting your friends to church or witnessing in other ways? Don't be discouraged. Sooner or later someone will "take the bait." Just keep on fishing. *B.J.W.*

TO MEMORIZE: Jesus called out to them, "Come be my disciples, and I will show you how to fish for people!" *Mark 1:17*

"MOTHER, I FINISHED cleaning the front window for you," reported Kyle.

When Mother looked through the window she said, "Kyle, look at all those smudges! Please do that over. The Patels are coming for dinner, you know."

Kyle looked at the window. "Oh," he said, "the inside is clean. All those spots are on the outside. I'll clean them, too."

As Kyle was eating dinner, Mother quietly advised him to use his napkin. A little later Father frowned when Kyle interrupted Mr. Patel. Finally Mother said, "If you're finished Kyle, you may play in your room." Kyle knew that look of Mother's, so he went to his room.

After the visitors left, Mother came to talk with him. "Kyle, your table manners were bad tonight," she told him. "You forgot to use your napkin, and you slurped your spaghetti. Besides that, you kept interrupting your father and Mr. Patel."

"I just wasn't thinking," he said. "I'm sorry."

Mother smiled. "I appreciate your attitude, Son," she said. "You know, this is like your window cleaning today. It was important to clean the window inside, just like it's important for us to keep our inside thoughts clean from sins like selfishness and greed. But you also needed to clean the outside of the window, and we need to keep the outside part of our lives clean—to get rid of bad habits and manners that others can see. It will help the light of Christ really shine through."

HOW ABOUT YOU? Do you have bad habits you need to overcome? These things may not be sinful in themselves, but you should work at eliminating habits that bother others. *S.L.K.*

TO MEMORIZE: I try to please everybody in every way. For I am not seeking my own good but the good of many, so that they may be saved. *1 Corinthians 10:33* (NIV)

BOTH SIDES

FROM THE BIBLE:

You say, "I am allowed to do anything"—but not everything is helpful. You say, "I am allowed to do anything"—but not everything is beneficial. Don't think only of your own good. Think of other Christians and what is best for them. . . .

Whatever you eat or drink or whatever you do, you must do all for the glory of God. Don't give offense to Jews or Gentiles or the church of God. That is the plan I follow, too. I try to please everyone in everything I do. I don't just do what I like or what is best for me, but what is best for them so they may be saved.
1 CORINTHIANS 10:23-24, 31-33

Get rid of bad habits

9 August

THE RIGHT PROGRAM

FROM THE BIBLE:

Always be full of joy in the Lord. I say it again—rejoice! Let everyone see that you are considerate in all you do. Remember, the Lord is coming soon.

Don't worry about anything; instead, pray about everything. Tell God what you need, and thank him for all he has done. If you do this, you will experience God's peace, which is far more wonderful than the human mind can understand. His peace will guard your hearts and minds as you live in Christ Jesus.

And now, dear brothers and sisters, let me say one more thing as I close this letter. Fix your thoughts on what is true and honorable and right. Think about things that are pure and lovely and admirable. Think about things that are excellent and worthy of praise. Keep putting into practice all you learned from me and heard from me and saw me doing, and the God of peace will be with you.
PHILIPPIANS 4:4-9

Put right things in your mind

HANNAH'S SCREAMS brought Mom running. As she picked up her little girl, Mom demanded, "What have you done now, boys?"

"Oh, she's such a baby," Josh said. "She's scared of a little worm."

The sound of a car in the driveway drew everyone's attention. "It's Dad with our new computer!" yelled Jeremy. The boys raced to the garage.

Dad brought the computer into the house and plugged it in. While he read the instructions, the boys pushed several keys. But nothing happened. "Dad, this doesn't work," complained Josh.

Dad looked up. "It will." He slipped a disk into the computer and pushed a button. There was a *whirrr* and a *click*, and a game appeared on the screen. "A computer can only do what it's programmed to do," said Dad.

"Look at the monster, Hannah!" Jeremy teased, pointing to the screen.

Mom instantly turned off the computer. "Before you play one game, listen to me," she said firmly. "When we are born, our minds are like this computer. We have great potential, but what we become depends on how we are programmed. That is why we have family devotions and provide good reading materials and tapes. That is why we talk about good things. But you two are programming fear into Hannah, and it has to stop."

"We're sorry," the boys said in unison.

"If you're truly sorry, you'll stop," Dad declared.

HOW ABOUT YOU? Are you programming the wrong things into a little brother or sister? And what are you programming into yourself? What you read, watch, and hear "programs" your mind. *B.J.W.*

TO MEMORIZE: This is the new covenant I will make with the people of Israel on that day, says the Lord: I will put my laws in their minds so they will understand them, and I will write them on their hearts so they will obey them. I will be their God and they will be my people. *Hebrews 8:10*

SANYO SAT on the porch steps, his chin propped up in his hand. There was a baseball game on TV, but Sanyo didn't even care. All he could think about was Roberto! Just the week before, the boys had taken a hike around the park. Now Roberto was in the hospital, seriously sick. When Sanyo's mom had talked to Roberto's mom that morning, Mrs. Joakim said the doctors had told them Roberto might not get well. That was scary! Sanyo sat and thought about his friend.

The screen door opened behind him, and Sanyo's mother brought out a glass of lemonade. "I thought you might be thirsty," she said.

Sanyo drank the lemonade without even noticing how good it tasted. "Mom, why did Roberto get sick?"

"Well," replied Mom, "all the bad things that happen to us are a result of sin entering the world. It's because of sin that the world is out of balance. Death will come to all of us sooner or later—through sickness, through car accidents, or other ways. The important thing is that God cares about us, and he cares about Roberto. He is there to give comfort to the Joakim family. He is there to help Roberto face the situation. We should pray that Roberto senses the comfort that the Lord can provide."

"Mom, could we pray right now?" Sanyo asked.

So Mom sat on the step next to Sanyo, and together they prayed for Roberto.

HOW ABOUT YOU? Has there been a time when one of your friends or a relative was very sick? Sickness and death are a result of sin entering the world. But God gives comfort to Christians! He promises them an eternal home in heaven. Through him you can have peace, even in the most difficult times. *L.M.W.*

TO MEMORIZE: Yet what we suffer now is nothing compared to the glory he will give us later. *Romans 8:18*

A SICK FRIEND
(PART 1)

FROM THE BIBLE:

Yet what we suffer now is nothing compared to the glory he will give us later. For all creation is waiting eagerly for that future day when God will reveal who his children really are. Against its will, everything on earth was subjected to God's curse. All creation anticipates the day when it will join God's children in glorious freedom from death and decay. For we know that all creation has been groaning as in the pains of childbirth right up to the present time. And even we Christians, although we have the Holy Spirit within us as a foretaste of future glory, also groan to be released from pain and suffering. We, too, wait anxiously for that day when God will give us our full rights as his children, including the new bodies he has promised us.
ROMANS 8:18-23

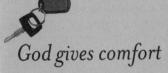

God gives comfort

11 August

A SICK FRIEND
(PART 2)

FROM THE BIBLE:

This letter is from Paul, appointed by God to be an apostle of Christ Jesus, and from our dear brother Timothy.

We are writing to God's church in Corinth and to all the Christians throughout Greece.

May God our Father and the Lord Jesus Christ give you his grace and peace.

All praise to the God and Father of our Lord Jesus Christ. He is the source of every mercy and the God who comforts us. He comforts us in all our troubles so that we can comfort others. When others are troubled, we will be able to give them the same comfort God has given us. You can be sure that the more we suffer for Christ, the more God will shower us with his comfort through Christ. So when we are weighed down with troubles, it is for your benefit and salvation! For when God comforts us, it is so that we, in turn, can be an encouragement to you. Then you can patiently endure the same things we suffer. We are confident that as you share in suffering, you will also share God's comfort.

2 CORINTHIANS 1:1-7

Encourage those in need

ONE DAY Sanyo's mom again talked to Mrs. Joakim on the phone. After she hung up she said, "Roberto is feeling a little better and would like some company. How would you like to go to the hospital to see him?"

Sanyo hesitated. "But Mom, what would I say?"

"Talk about the things you usually talk about—baseball, school, or hiking," suggested Mom.

Sanyo looked worried. "But what if Roberto wants to talk about being sick?"

"Let him," Mom advised. "Sometimes the kindest thing to do for someone in the hospital is to listen."

Sanyo was thoughtful. "I'm glad Roberto is a Christian," he said finally.

"Yes, that is comforting." Sanyo's mother paused and then said, "Remember, you can't pretend to understand what Roberto is going through. You've never been faced with a serious illness. You can, however, remind Roberto that the Lord loves him and cares for him very much."

Sanyo got his jacket. He was still scared to go, but he knew he should. He was certainly glad he knew the Lord as his personal Savior. The Lord could help him know what to say when he visited his friend.

HOW ABOUT YOU? Are you afraid to visit a sick person because you don't know what to say? Even adults are often nervous about visiting someone who is ill. But don't stay away! Let that person know you care. If you've been in the same circumstances, you can talk about that. Just listening to your friend will be helpful. Tell what's been happening in school and church. Remind the person that God cares. *L.M.W.*

TO MEMORIZE: You can be sure that the more we suffer for Christ, the more God will shower us with his comfort through Christ. *2 Corinthians 1:5*

"SPECIAL BULLETIN!" the radio blared. "There will be no school at Brookside today. The school was vandalized last night. Windows were broken, desks smashed, and rooms sprayed with paint. Damage is estimated to be . . ."

"Vandalized!" Megan exclaimed. "Who would want to do that?"

"Whoever did it was really dumb," declared Eric.

"I bet someone who hated school did it," Megan guessed.

"It's sad when someone has no respect for property or the rights of others," said Dad. "Unless that person changes, I fear that he or she is headed for real trouble."

Several days later the vandal was arrested. He was a fifteen-year-old named Keith. He had been in trouble with the law many times before. When his case was tried, he was found guilty.

"The judge sent Keith to reform school," Megan said that evening. "It must be awful to go to a place like that."

"Yes, but sin has a penalty too," Dad reminded her. "In a sense, the judge didn't send Keith to reform school. Keith sent himself. He knew the rules, and he chose to disobey. Now he has to face the consequences. You know, people also have the choice to accept or reject what Jesus did for us."

"I never thought of that," said Eric. "But you're right, Dad. We do have to make our own choice."

HOW ABOUT YOU? What choice have you made? You have sinned, but Jesus died so that you may have eternal life. You must confess your sins, ask forgiveness, and accept Christ as your Savior. Have you done that? *J.L.H.*

TO MEMORIZE: If you are unwilling to serve the Lord, then choose today whom you will serve. . . . But as for me and my family, we will serve the Lord. *Joshua 24:15*

KEITH'S CHOICE

FROM THE BIBLE:

"And as Moses lifted up the bronze snake on a pole in the wilderness, so I, the Son of Man, must be lifted up on a pole, so that everyone who believes in me will have eternal life.

"For God so loved the world that he gave his only Son, so that everyone who believes in him will not perish but have eternal life. God did not send his Son into the world to condemn it, but to save it.

"There is no judgment awaiting those who trust him. But those who do not trust him have already been judged for not believing in the only Son of God."

JOHN 3:14-18

Choose salvation

13 August

NO ROOM

FROM THE BIBLE:

"Not all people who sound religious are really godly. They may refer to me as 'Lord,' but they still won't enter the Kingdom of Heaven. The decisive issue is whether they obey my Father in heaven. On judgment day many will tell me, 'Lord, Lord, we prophesied in your name and cast out demons in your name and performed many miracles in your name.' But I will reply, 'I never knew you. Go away; the things you did were unauthorized.'

"Anyone who listens to my teaching and obeys me is wise, like a person who builds a house on solid rock. Though the rain comes in torrents and the floodwaters rise and the winds beat against that house, it won't collapse, because it is built on rock. But anyone who hears my teaching and ignores it is foolish, like a person who builds a house on sand. When the rains and floods come and the winds beat against that house, it will fall with a mighty crash."

MATTHEW 7:21-27

Be registered in heaven

"ARE WE almost there? It's been such a long ride!" exclaimed Jessica. She and her sister, Kelley, could hardly wait to get to Sea World and the motel.

"Two whole days in a motel with a pool!" Kelley giggled.

"We're here, girls," announced Dad. He turned toward the motel.

Inside, Dad approached the desk. "My name is Gardiner," he said. "We have reservations."

The receptionist checked the computer. "I'm sorry," she said uncertainly. "I can't find your name here."

"Please look again," Dad said. After another search, the receptionist shook her head slowly. "Well, do you have a room with two double beds?" asked Dad.

"No, I don't. I'm really sorry," the lady replied. "There's a convention in town, and all motels are full."

"It would be awful to go back home now," wailed Jessica.

Dad nodded. "There's been a mistake," he said, "but don't fret. Let's go have some ice cream while we think about what to do next."

Seated in the restaurant, Dad said, "If this seems bad, think how it would be if we should arrive in heaven someday and discover that our names have never been registered there."

"But, Daddy," Jessica said thoughtfully, "that won't happen. The Bible says Jesus has gone ahead of us and has already written the names of those who love him."

"You're absolutely right," said Dad with a smile.

HOW ABOUT YOU? Is your name registered in heaven? If not, talk to a trusted Christian friend or adult to find out what you need to do. *P.I.K.*

TO MEMORIZE: I saw the dead, both great and small, standing before God's throne. And the books were opened, including the Book of Life. And the dead were judged according to the things written in the books, according to what they had done. *Revelation 20:12*

THE DEAD LETTER OFFICE

WHEN THE DOORBELL rang, Maria came to the door. The mail carrier stood there, a letter in his hand. "Maria," he said, "did you address this letter? You didn't put down the zip code or the city and state. It's going to end up in the dead letter office."

"Oops!" exclaimed Maria. "I was going to ask Mother for Aunt Juliana's address, but I forgot. What's the dead letter office?"

"It's a department of the post office. Mail that can't be delivered goes there," explained Mr. Zachary. "Then clerks open it and look for return addresses inside. If there is one, the mail is returned to the sender."

"What if there isn't any return address?" asked Maria.

"Most of the letters are destroyed," said Mr. Zachary. "The contents of parcels are sold, and the money goes into the post office funds."

"Well, I don't want Aunt Juliana's letter to end up there," declared Maria.

At family devotions that evening Maria prayed: "Dear heavenly Father, thank you for a beautiful day and for my parents, and for . . ." She stopped. "I think my prayer is going to God's dead letter office," she said. Her parents looked at her in surprise. "I know he won't hear my prayers until I make something right first," added Maria. "Daddy, I took five dollars from your wallet. Please forgive me. I'll pay you back from my allowance."

"Of course I forgive you, Maria," said Dad. "But you must confess your sin to God, too."

Maria nodded her head. "I know," she said. "I'm going to do that right now."

FROM THE BIBLE:

Come and listen, all you who fear God,
and I will tell you what he did for me.
For I cried out to him for help,
praising him as I spoke.
If I had not confessed the sin in my heart,
my Lord would not have listened.
But God did listen!
He paid attention to my prayer.

Praise God, who did not ignore my prayer
and did not withdraw his unfailing love from me.

PSALM 66:16-20

Pray with a pure heart

HOW ABOUT YOU? Isn't prayer a wonderful privilege? But if there is unconfessed sin in your life, the Lord says he won't hear you. Make things right with others and with God. Then learn and experience the following verse. *M.R.P.*

TO MEMORIZE: But God did listen! He paid attention to my prayer. *Psalm 66:19*

15 August

VANESSA AND HER SHADOW

FROM THE BIBLE:

But you are not like that, for you are a chosen people. You are a kingdom of priests, God's holy nation, his very own possession. This is so you can show others the goodness of God, for he called you out of the darkness into his wonderful light.

"Once you were not a people;
  now you are the people of
    God.
Once you received none of God's
    mercy;
  now you have received his
    mercy."

Dear brothers and sisters, you are foreigners and aliens here. So I warn you to keep away from evil desires because they fight against your very souls. Be careful how you live among your unbelieving neighbors. Even if they accuse you of doing wrong, they will see your honorable behavior, and they will believe and give honor to God when he comes to judge the world.
1 PETER 2:9-12

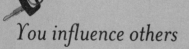

You influence others

"LOOK, MOTHER!" Mary Jo pointed to Vanessa in the backyard. Mother and Mary Jo laughed as they watched three-year-old Vanessa play with her shadow. The little girl ran as fast as she could, then turned around and saw her shadow coming along with her. Turning her back on her shadow, she took a big jump. She turned around again to find that her shadow had jumped, too.

At dinnertime Mother asked Mary Jo to set the table. "I'll help," piped up Vanessa—and she did, carefully copying the way Mary Jo placed the dishes and the silverware.

As they were eating, Mary Jo passed the lima beans to her brother, Jon. He passed them to Mother. "Help yourself first, Son," she said.

"Mary Jo doesn't have any," said Jon. As Mother passed the lima beans back to her, Mary Jo scowled but put a few on her plate.

After dinner Dad asked, "Who'd like to help me wash the car?"

Mary Jo spoke. "I will."

"I'll help, too," said Jon quickly.

"Me, too," added Vanessa.

Mary Jo laughed. "What is this—'copy Mary Jo' night?"

Mother smiled. "Remember Vanessa and the shadow?" she asked. "Whether she liked it or not, Vanessa had her shadow with her wherever she went. There was no way she could get away from it. The influence we have over others is like that. Whether we like it or not, what we do and say influences other people. It's important to influence them for good and not for bad."

HOW ABOUT YOU? What kind of influence do you have? As a Christian, it's important to be kind, honest, and faithful. Live in such a way that your life will cause others to want to know Jesus. *H.W.M.*

TO MEMORIZE: We are not our own masters when we live or when we die. . . . In life and in death, we belong to the Lord. *Romans 14:7-8*

"**MOM, WHY** do we have to go to church every Sunday?" Chad asked at breakfast. "Some of my friends don't go."

"Well, we do," his mother answered. "We go to be instructed from God's Word, so please get ready." When Chad was younger, he loved to go to church. But as he grew older, he didn't want to go.

That afternoon the subject came up again. "My friends are playing basketball tonight," said Chad. "May I go?"

"Chad, we're going to church," Dad answered.

"I don't see why we can't just read the Bible at home," Chad grumbled.

After supper the next day Chad covered a table with newspapers. "I'm going to work on my new model car. Just look at all those pieces!" he exclaimed. He began to work but soon asked, "Can you help me with this, Dad?"

Dad shrugged. "I don't think you need me," he said. "Just put the pieces together. It should turn out just fine."

"How would I know where the pieces go when I can't understand it?"

Dad walked over to the table. "Chad," he said, "trying to put this model together without my help is like trying to live your Christian life without help from God's people. Lately you've not wanted to go to church, yet our pastor and Sunday school teachers help us understand how God wants us to live."

"I hadn't thought about it that way," said Chad. "I guess you're right."

HOW ABOUT YOU? Do you think you don't need to go to church? It's great to read the Bible, and you should do that. But God has also provided godly men and women in your church and Sunday school who can help you understand his Word. Learn from them. *D.K.*

TO MEMORIZE: Teach me how to live, O Lord. Lead me along the path of honesty, for my enemies are waiting for me to fall. *Psalm 27:11*

MODEL BUILDING

FROM THE BIBLE:

You are my hiding place;
*   you protect me from trouble.*
You surround me with songs
*   of victory.*

The Lord says, "I will guide you
*   along the best pathway for*
*   your life.*
I will advise you and watch
*   over you.*
Do not be like a senseless horse
*   or mule*
*   that needs a bit and bridle to*
*   keep it under control."*

Many sorrows come to the
*   wicked,*
*   but unfailing love surrounds*
*   those who trust the Lord.*
So rejoice in the Lord and be
*   glad, all you who obey him!*
*   Shout for joy, all you whose*
*   hearts are pure!*

PSALM 32:7-11

Go to church

CITIZENSHIP

FROM THE BIBLE:

Don't forget that you Gentiles used to be outsiders by birth. You were called "the uncircumcised ones" by the Jews, who were proud of their circumcision, even though it affected only their bodies and not their hearts. In those days you were living apart from Christ. You were excluded from God's people, Israel, and you did not know the promises God had made to them. You lived in this world without God and without hope. But now you belong to Christ Jesus. Though you once were far away from God, now you have been brought near to him because of the blood of Christ.

For Christ himself has made peace between us Jews and you Gentiles by making us all one people. He has broken down the wall of hostility that used to separate us.

EPHESIANS 2:11-14

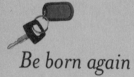

Be born again

CARLOS WAS GLAD to run an errand for Judge Patton. He liked to hear the retired judge's stories about his days in court. Today, after he and Judge Patton had talked a while, the judge asked, "Are you a Christian?"

"I think so," replied Carlos. "I try to be good."

"So you'd say you belong to God's kingdom because you're good?" asked the judge. "Let me tell you a story. I used to sit on the bench as a judge in southern California. One day a fine-looking man was brought before me. He had been living in our town for a number of years. But when he tried to buy some property, it was discovered that he was not a United States citizen. 'But Your Honor,' he said to me, 'I obey the laws. I pay my bills.' Now, Carlos, do you think I should have told him he had nothing more to do to become a citizen?"

Carlos shook his head. "A foreigner has to swear allegiance to the United States Constitution."

"And who makes the rules for citizenship—a foreigner or the United States government?" asked Judge Patton.

"The government, of course," said Carlos.

The judge nodded. "Well, Carlos," he said, "you expect God to make you a citizen in the kingdom of God based on *your* rules—by living a good life. But who has the right to set the rules for heavenly citizenship—you or God?"

"God does," said Carlos. "I guess it's time to apply for citizenship by God's rules."

HOW ABOUT YOU? Do you claim to be a citizen of God's kingdom? On what do you base your claim—doing good works or being a church member? Only those who are born again will enter heaven. *M.R.P.*

TO MEMORIZE: Jesus replied, "I assure you, unless you are born again, you can never see the Kingdom of God." *John 3:3*

"WHAT ARE YOU DOING, Dad?" asked Nathan as he dropped his bike on the lawn. His father was half-hidden under the raised car hood. "There's nothing wrong with the car, is there?"

"No, and I want it to stay that way," came Dad's muffled reply. "Ever hear the saying, 'An ounce of prevention is worth a pound of cure'?"

Nathan shook his head. "No. What does it mean?"

"It means it's better to keep a car from breaking down than to repair it." Dad slammed down the hood and picked up his tools. "Looks like we might be in for a thunderstorm."

Dad was right. There was a storm that evening! The wind howled, and rain poured down! As hailstones began pounding the house, Nathan had a sudden thought. "Oh, my bike!" he exclaimed. "I forgot to put it in the garage!"

"Again," added Dad. "Too late now."

Later, when the storm had stopped, Nathan put his bicycle in the garage and found several dents in the fenders. "Too bad," Dad said. "Preventing those dents would have been a lot easier than fixing them." Nathan hung his head.

At bedtime Mom and Dad called Nathan into the den for family devotions. "Why do we have to have devotions every evening?" Nathan grumbled.

"An ounce of prevention is worth a pound of cure," Dad quoted. "I maintain the car to keep it in good condition. You should do the same for your bicycle. But it's even more important to take care of the soul, the most valuable possession we have."

Nathan picked up his Bible and grinned at his dad. "Where shall we read?" he asked.

HOW ABOUT YOU? Do you practice spiritual maintenance every day? Prayer and reading the Bible will help you stay in tip-top spiritual condition. *B.J.W.*

TO MEMORIZE: Then I will always sing praises to your name as I fulfill my vows day after day. *Psalm 61:8*

AN OUNCE OF PREVENTION

FROM THE BIBLE:

O God, you are my God;
I earnestly search for you.
My soul thirsts for you;
my whole body longs for you
in this parched and weary land
where there is no water.
I have seen you in your sanctuary
and gazed upon your power and glory.
Your unfailing love is better to me than life itself;
how I praise you!
I will honor you as long as I live,
lifting up my hands to you in prayer.
You satisfy me more than the richest of foods.
I will praise you with songs of joy.

I lie awake thinking of you,
meditating on you through the night.
I think how much you have helped me;
I sing for joy in the shadow of your protecting wings.
I follow close behind you;
your strong right hand holds me securely.

PSALM 63:1-8

Care for your soul daily

19 August

A PERFECT SOLUTION

FROM THE BIBLE:

If you are wise and understand God's ways, live a life of steady goodness so that only good deeds will pour forth. And if you don't brag about the good you do, then you will be truly wise! But if you are bitterly jealous and there is selfish ambition in your hearts, don't brag about being wise. That is the worst kind of lie. For jealousy and selfishness are not God's kind of wisdom. Such things are earthly, unspiritual, and motivated by the Devil. For wherever there is jealousy and selfish ambition, there you will find disorder and every kind of evil.

But the wisdom that comes from heaven is first of all pure. It is also peace loving, gentle at all times, and willing to yield to others. It is full of mercy and good deeds. It shows no partiality and is always sincere. And those who are peacemakers will plant seeds of peace and reap a harvest of goodness.
JAMES 3:13-18

Don't fight

ONE LOOK at Daniel's face told Dad something was wrong. "How was school?" he asked.

"So-so." Daniel drew a deep, ragged breath, then blurted out, "If Jeff doesn't leave me alone on the bus, I'm going to have to fight him!"

"Oh?" Dad responded. "If you do, you'd better be prepared to take the consequences."

Daniel looked up. "Will you whip me?"

"No," Dad said, "but Jeff might. There must be a better solution. Let's pray about it."

The next day Daniel came home from school grinning from ear to ear. Before Dad could ask, he told him, "Jeff left me alone today."

"What did you do?" Dad asked.

Daniel chuckled. "I sat in the front seat of the bus," he said. "With the driver right there, Jeff didn't dare make trouble."

Daniel was surprised when Dad came over and gave him a hug a little later. "You've taught me a lesson today, Daniel. I've been having a little trouble with my temper lately," he confessed. "I haven't thought about having a fist fight with anybody, but there are a couple of people I've been tempted to tell off. But you've given me the perfect solution."

Daniel looked surprised. "What?"

"By getting just as close to Jesus as I can," Dad answered. "I need to move up to the 'front of the bus.'"

HOW ABOUT YOU? Are you tempted to use your fists to solve your problems? Think again. A fight would probably make matters worse. Get close to Jesus through reading his Word, praying, and keeping your thoughts on him. He can give you the solution for solving your problems peaceably. *B.J.W.*

TO MEMORIZE: Do your part to live in peace with everyone, as much as possible. *Romans 12:18*

DAVE EXCITEDLY helped Dad unpack the big box. The small old TV set had given out completely. Dave looked forward to watching his favorite team on a large screen. "I know how to hook up this baby," he told his father. "I helped Tony get his TV hooked up last Christmas." Dad smiled and let Dave work.

After connecting the VCR, he plugged the TV cord into the wall socket. He waited for the picture to come into view. When it did, it was blurred. "I know what's wrong," he said, adjusting a few buttons on the set. But still the picture was out of focus.

"Are you sure you've got it hooked up right?" his father asked, offering to check it out.

Dave pushed his father's hand away. "Sure," he said. "This set is practically the same as Tony's, and we got it together OK. There's got to be something wrong with this one."

"Read the instruction sheet," Dad suggested. "This set could be different from Tony's."

Dave picked up the instructions that had come with the set and began to read them. Then he went back to the set and fixed it.

Dave was embarrassed. "If all else fails," he said, "read the instructions."

"Better yet," said Dad, "read the instructions *first*. That principle is true in our Christian lives, too. The Bible is God's instruction book. It not only tells us how to receive Jesus as our Savior, it also tells us how to live the Christian life. But we won't know unless we read it."

HOW ABOUT YOU? Are you a Christian? Then the Bible, should be your guide, your instruction book. It explains what a Christian should do about sin. It commands every believer to love, to give, to witness, and many other things. God's book is very important. *R.I.J.*

TO MEMORIZE: You made me; you created me. Now give me the sense to follow your commands. *Psalm 119:73*

FOLLOW THE MANUAL

FROM THE BIBLE:

How can a young person stay pure?
  By obeying your word and following its rules.
I have tried my best to find you—
  don't let me wander from your commands.
I have hidden your word in my heart,
  that I might not sin against you.
Blessed are you, O Lord;
  teach me your principles.
I have recited aloud
  all the laws you have given us.
I have rejoiced in your decrees
  as much as in riches.
I will study your commandments
  and reflect on your ways.
I will delight in your principles
  and not forget your word.

Be good to your servant,
  that I may live and obey your word.
Open my eyes to see
  the wonderful truths in your law.

PSALM 119:9-18

Follow God's Book

21 August

OUT OF HARMONY

FROM THE BIBLE:

Is there any encouragement from belonging to Christ? Any comfort from his love? Any fellowship together in the Spirit? Are your hearts tender and sympathetic? Then make me truly happy by agreeing wholeheartedly with each other, loving one another, and working together with one heart and purpose.

Don't be selfish; don't live to make a good impression on others. Be humble, thinking of others as better than yourself. Don't think only about your own affairs, but be interested in others, too, and what they are doing.

Your attitude should be the same that Christ Jesus had. Though he was God, he did not demand and cling to his rights as God. He made himself nothing; he took the humble position of a slave and appeared in human form. And in human form he obediently humbled himself even further by dying a criminal's death on a cross.

PHILIPPIANS 2:1-8

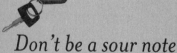

Don't be a sour note

MELANIE STOMPED down the hall and slammed the bedroom door. "Nothing I do is right anymore," she muttered angrily. "Everyone is mad at me."

From the living room came the sound of her mom playing the piano. Melanie grimaced. Something was wrong! Mom usually played so beautifully, but now the music was terrible.

Jumping up, Melanie ran into the living room. "That sounds awful," she blurted out. "What's the matter?"

"Oh?" said Mom. "Does this sound any better?" She ran her fingers over the keyboard.

"It sure does," Melanie answered.

"Sit down and let me show you something," invited Mom. She scooted over so Melanie could join her on the piano bench. "When the music sounded terrible, all I was doing was hitting one note wrong. Each time I hit it, it threw everything else out of harmony. Listen." She played several notes. "One wrong note in a chord causes a 'discord.' And one member of a family out of harmony with the other members causes discord in a home."

"Oh!" sputtered Melanie, jumping up and walking out of the room. She stopped when she saw her own angry face in the hall mirror. She knew *she* was the wrong note because her attitude had been sour lately.

"I think you need to call on the Lord Jesus and ask him to 'tune' your attitude," suggested Mom. "It would be nice for our family to be in harmony."

Melanie nodded and went to her room. This time she shut the door quietly behind her and knelt beside her bed.

HOW ABOUT YOU? Are you out of tune with everyone? Do you feel and sound off-key? Maybe you've been blaming others when you are the one who needs tuning. Don't be a "wrong note." Get in tune with God and your family. *B.J.W.*

TO MEMORIZE: He has given me a new song to sing, a hymn of praise to our God. *Psalm 40:3*

"IT'S SO DARK OUT!" said Kathy as she and her brother, Josh, stumbled along the path toward their campsite. They had been visiting some friends.

"Yeah," agreed Josh, "but we're almost—" His words were cut off as he caught his toe on a tree root and fell.

Kathy reached down to help him up. "Are you OK?"

"Yes," said Josh, brushing himself off, "but we'd better not go quite so fast." Kathy agreed, and the two of them moved slowly and carefully along until they reached the camp where their parents were waiting.

"We could hear you two coming," Mother greeted them. "Did someone fall?"

"Josh did," replied Kathy, "but he's not hurt. It was so dark we couldn't see."

"Why didn't you use your flashlight?" asked Dad.

"Flashlight?" Kathy and Josh looked at each other. "Oh, our flashlight!" They began to laugh.

"Real smart, Josh," teased Kathy. "You've got the flashlight, you know. You stuck it in your sweater pocket."

"I forgot I had it," admitted Josh.

"You two remind me of a lot of people," observed Dad. "They have a light for their path, but they either forget to use it, or they just don't bother."

"Like who?" Kathy wanted to know.

"Like all the Christians who don't read their Bibles," replied Dad, picking up his own. "God says his Word is a light to our path, but it doesn't do any good if we don't use it."

HOW ABOUT YOU? Do you read your Bible regularly? It contains many principles to help you in your daily life. It has a lot of practical advice. It offers comfort when you hurt. But unless you use it, it can't help you. *H.W.M.*

TO MEMORIZE: Your word is a lamp for my feet and a light for my path. *Psalm 119:105*

NEEDED: A LIGHT
(PART 1)

FROM THE BIBLE:

*Your word is a lamp for my feet
    and a light for my path.
I've promised it once, and I'll
        promise again:
    I will obey your wonderful
    laws.
I have suffered much, O Lord;
    restore my life again, just as
    you promised.
Lord, accept my grateful thanks
    and teach me your laws.
My life constantly hangs in the
    balance,
    but I will not stop obeying
    your law.
The wicked have set their traps
    for me along your path,
    but I will not turn from your
    commandments.
Your decrees are my treasure;
    they are truly my heart's
    delight.
I am determined to keep your
    principles,
    even forever, to the very end.*
PSALM 119:105-112

Use your Bible daily

23 August

NEEDED: A LIGHT
(PART 2)

FROM THE BIBLE:

*Your word is a lamp for my feet
and a light for my path.
I've promised it once, and I'll
promise again:
I will obey your wonderful
laws.
I have suffered much, O Lord;
restore my life again, just as
you promised.
Lord, accept my grateful thanks
and teach me your laws.
My life constantly hangs in the
balance,
but I will not stop obeying
your law.
The wicked have set their traps
for me along your path,
but I will not turn from your
commandments.
Your decrees are my treasure;
they are truly my heart's
delight.
I am determined to keep your
principles,
even forever, to the very end.*
PSALM 119:105-112

Apply God's Word to yourself

"WHY DON'T you sleep at our camp tonight?" Josh asked his friend Kendall. "My mom said it was OK with her."

"Can I, Mom?" Kendall looked over at his mother.

Kendall's mother laughed. "Take your sleeping bag and run along," she agreed.

Soon the boys were on their way. Josh snapped on his flashlight. "Last night I left this thing in my pocket all the way home. I'm not going to make the same mistake twice!" he said as he led the way. He turned back to flash the light on Kendall's path. He continued to leave the beam of light on the path behind him, making sure Kendall could see. "Last night I fell over a tree roo—" Down went Josh.

"Are you OK?" asked Kendall.

Josh got up and retrieved his flashlight. "Yeah," he mumbled. "Walk up here with me so we can both see where we're going."

When they arrived at Josh's campsite, his family was waiting. "We saw your light, and heard a crash," said Mother. "What happened?"

"Fell again, didn't you?" said Kathy with a smirk.

"Do you know who you remind me of tonight?" Dad asked.

Josh shook his head. "I was using my flashlight."

Dad nodded. "Yep, and you were pointing it on somebody else's path. You remind me of people who hear God's Word preached, and they think, *I hope so-and-so is listening. He really needs this.* Or maybe they read something from God's Word and apply it to somebody else's life. They fail to see that they need it themselves."

HOW ABOUT YOU? Did you notice that today's Scripture reading is the same as yesterday's? Read it again, and emphasize the words *I, my,* and *me.* Then when you read other passages in the Bible, such as "Be kind to each other," think of what you should do. *H.W.M.*

TO MEMORIZE: I am determined to keep your principles, even forever, to the very end. *Psalm 119:112*

THE TICKING WATCH

MARINA SCREAMED and sat up in bed. She began to cry. Her parents quickly came to her bedside, and her mother held her tightly. "Won't it ever stop?" asked Marina between sobs. "I had another nightmare about the accident when Aunt Karen died. I keep seeing the car wreck."

"Try to remember your aunt the way she used to be—lively, loving, and beautiful," Marina's father suggested.

"I try," said Marina, "but I can't seem to remember her that way."

"Honey, you know that Aunt Karen was a Christian," Mother reminded her, "so she's alive in heaven. Can you picture her there?"

Marina shook her head. "I can't see her that way either," she said.

"I want to show you something," said Father. He left the room, returning soon with a watch, which he placed in Marina's hand.

Marina shuddered. "Oh, take Aunt Karen's watch away," she begged. "It's all broken from the wreck—just like Aunt Karen."

Father took the watch. "Yes," he said, "like Aunt Karen. The case is scratched, and the crystal's broken. But let's look inside." After some prying, Marina's dad lifted the watch from the case. "Look, it's still running," he said. "Only the outside was ruined. And Aunt Karen is still living. Only the 'case' she lived in here—her body—is dead."

After a moment Marina looked up with a trembling smile. "Aunt Karen truly is still alive, isn't she?" she said.

"I'll get a new case for this watch, and you may have it as a reminder," said Father. "Remember, Aunt Karen will have a new body someday, too."

HOW ABOUT YOU? Has death taken away someone you love? If you and your loved one are Christians, you'll meet again at Christ's return, and you'll be together forever. *M.R.P.*

TO MEMORIZE: Yes, dear friends, we are already God's children, and we can't even imagine what we will be like when Christ returns. *1 John 3:2*

FROM THE BIBLE:

It is the same way for the resurrection of the dead. Our earthly bodies, which die and decay, will be different when they are resurrected, for they will never die. Our bodies now disappoint us, but when they are raised, they will be full of glory. They are weak now, but when they are raised, they will be full of power. They are natural human bodies now, but when they are raised, they will be spiritual bodies. For just as there are natural bodies, so also there are spiritual bodies.

The Scriptures tell us, "The first man, Adam, became a living person." But the last Adam—that is, Christ—is a life-giving Spirit. . . .

But let me tell you a wonderful secret God has revealed to us. Not all of us will die, but we will all be transformed.

1 CORINTHIANS 15:42-45, 51

The real person never dies

25 August

THE RAFT RESCUE

FROM THE BIBLE:

"For the Father loves the Son and tells him everything he is doing, and the Son will do far greater things than healing this man. You will be astonished at what he does. He will even raise from the dead anyone he wants to, just as the Father does. And the Father leaves all judgment to his Son, so that everyone will honor the Son, just as they honor the Father. But if you refuse to honor the Son, then you are certainly not honoring the Father who sent him.

"I assure you, those who listen to my message and believe in God who sent me have eternal life. They will never be condemned for their sins, but they have already passed from death into life."

JOHN 5:20-24

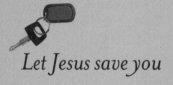

Let Jesus save you

"HELP! Save me!" Todd screamed as his home-made raft rushed toward the falls. Because the current was rough, he had tied the raft to a tree on the riverbank. However, the once-thick rope had become frayed. When he'd jumped onto the raft, the rope had snapped, sending the raft downstream.

Oh no! Todd thought. What now? I can't swim well enough to reach the shore. Two miles downstream the river plunges fifty feet over Drop-Off Point! The river ran right next to the road, so he waved his arms and yelled.

Todd's father was driving home from work when he looked out at the river. Upstream he could see the raft spinning around—and someone was on it! Quickly stopping the car, he kicked off his shoes and jumped into the river. Being a strong swimmer, he stroked toward the middle of the river and waited for the raft to reach him. How surprised he was to see his own son on it! He called out, "Todd, jump! I'll save you!"

Todd looked at the sturdy raft, then at his father in the swirling waters. He wasn't sure he wanted to leave the raft, but he knew it would mean death if he didn't! As he leaped into the surging water, his father caught him. Todd's father slowly made it back to the shore, with Todd in tow.

Back home, Dad said, "What I did for you today is sort of like what Jesus did for us. We couldn't save ourselves from our sins. Just as you had to trust me to save you when you jumped, so we need to be willing to trust the Lord."

HOW ABOUT YOU? Have you put your faith in Jesus Christ? If not, talk to a trusted Christian friend or adult to find out more. *C.V.M.*

TO MEMORIZE: For the wages of sin is death, but the free gift of God is eternal life through Christ Jesus our Lord. *Romans 6:23*

BLACKIE WAS a farm dog. When he was a little pup, he liked playing with his brothers and sisters. One by one, the puppies left for new homes, but Blackie stayed on the farm. He was the special pet of Jacob, the farmer's son.

Jacob taught Blackie to stay on their own land. "Stay, Blackie! Stay!" Jacob would often command, as he crossed the road to get the mail or to visit his neighbor.

Blackie liked to hunt for treasures—dog treasures. He would hunt for squirrels, chipmunks, and mice. One day he saw something moving in the tall grass across the road. The temptation was more than he could bear, and soon he crossed the road. What a treasure he found—a rabbit! He could hardly wait to get home with it. He bounded out of the tall grass, the rabbit in his mouth. Like a streak of lightning, he darted across the road—and he never saw the car coming! The driver blew his horn and hit the brakes. But Blackie, treasure in his mouth, was bumped by the car.

Hearing the commotion, Jacob rushed from the house. He gathered Blackie into his arms, and soon Dad was taking the dog to the veterinarian.

"He's hurt," the vet told them. "He could have lost his life, but I think he'll pull through all right."

HOW ABOUT YOU? Do you know that many young people have lost their lives running after "treasures" such as drugs, cigarettes, money, and even popularity? These things may look attractive now, but they are not worth what they may cost in the end. *P.R.*

TO MEMORIZE: No temptation has seized you except what is common to man. And God is faithful; he will not let you be tempted beyond what you can bear. But when you are tempted, he will also provide a way out so that you can stand up under it. *1 Corinthians 10:13* (NIV)

TREASURES

FROM THE BIBLE:

God blesses the people who patiently endure testing. Afterward they will receive the crown of life that God has promised to those who love him. And remember, no one who wants to do wrong should ever say, "God is tempting me." God is never tempted to do wrong, and he never tempts anyone else either. Temptation comes from the lure of our own evil desires. These evil desires lead to evil actions, and evil actions lead to death. So don't be misled, my dear brothers and sisters.
JAMES 1:12-16

Run from sin

27 August

OVERLOADED

FROM THE BIBLE:

And he called his twelve disciples together and sent them out two by two, with authority to cast out evil spirits. He told them to take nothing with them except a walking stick—no food, no traveler's bag, no money. He told them to wear sandals but not to take even an extra coat. "When you enter each village, be a guest in only one home," he said. "And if a village won't welcome you or listen to you, shake off its dust from your feet as you leave. It is a sign that you have abandoned that village to its fate."

So the disciples went out, telling all they met to turn from their sins. And they cast out many demons and healed many sick people, anointing them with olive oil. . . .

The apostles returned to Jesus from their ministry tour and told him all they had done and what they had taught. Then Jesus said, "Let's get away from the crowds for a while and rest." There were so many people coming and going that Jesus and his apostles didn't even have time to eat.

MARK 6:7-13, 30-31

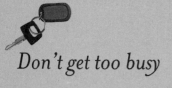

Don't get too busy

THE TAYLORS were on their way to a cottage they were renting near a lake. "I can hardly wait to get there," said Brianna. "It seems like years since we've been on a vacation."

"I know," sighed Mom. "We've been so busy getting your father's business started and redecorating the house. It's hard to find a time when we're all free to take a vacation. I'm glad we're getting a few days together before school starts."

When they arrived, Brianna and her brother, Justin, helped Dad unpack the car. "Phew! This place sure is musty," Justin said.

"It'll be all right once we've cleaned," replied Mom. "I'll plug in the coffeepot and put some water on the stove for hot chocolate." As soon as she did so, however, all the lights went off. "Oh, I've blown a fuse," she moaned.

"I'll check," said Dad, getting the flashlight and looking in the fuse box. "Looks to me like there are too many things on one small circuit," he said. "You'll have to turn off a few lights before you can make that coffee and use the stove." Mom hurried to do so and soon Dad was able to get the electricity back on.

Later, as they sat together with their hot drinks, Mom said thoughtfully, "Our family has been overloaded like that circuit. We've all been too busy to spend time together."

Dad nodded. "I think we should reevaluate our activities this week," he said. Then he picked up his Bible. "Let's have family devotions. That's one activity we should always take time for."

HOW ABOUT YOU? Have you been too busy lately? Make a list of things you do and put the really important ones first. Be sure to put daily devotions near the top, along with time spent with your family, proper rest, and meals. Don't get overloaded. *S.L.K.*

TO MEMORIZE: Then Jesus said, "Let's get away from the crowds for a while and rest." *Mark 6:31*

DRILL IT OUT

SAMUEL HATED going to the dentist. Even though it didn't hurt, he didn't like the loud buzzing of the drill. It was a relief when the buzzing stopped and Dr. Jiminez checked the tooth.

"Are you finished yet?" Samuel asked.

"Just a little more drilling, Sam," replied Dr. Jiminez. "I have to get all of the cavity cleaned out. Otherwise it will keep on decaying underneath the new filling. Then you could lose the whole tooth."

Finally Dr. Jiminez began to put in the new filling. "When I drill out a cavity, I can't leave any decayed material in the tooth because that would cause too many problems later on," said Dr. Jiminez. "It's that way in my life, too. If I leave any sins, they'll cause problems later on." Samuel just nodded.

"If I find myself telling even a little lie, I try to correct it," continued Dr. Jiminez. "I ask God to forgive me and help me to tell the truth."

Samuel thought about what Dr. Jiminez was saying. He thought about how he often said his homework or his chores were all done when that wasn't entirely true. He thought about how he no longer used bad language very often—but he did use it occasionally. Samuel realized he had to make some changes.

"How do you feel, Sam?" asked Dr. Jiminez as he helped him out of the chair.

Samuel looked at him soberly. "Great! I'm glad to be rid of that cavity," he answered. "But I've got a couple of sin 'cavities' I'm going to drill out, too, before they get too big."

HOW ABOUT YOU? Are there things in your life that you know aren't quite right? Maybe a little lying, a little cheating, or a little talking back to parents or teachers? Get rid of those things completely before they become harder to stop. *C.E.Y.*

TO MEMORIZE: But my choice is clear—I love your law. *Psalm 119:113*

FROM THE BIBLE:

Gehazi, Elisha's servant, said to himself, "My master should not have let this Aramean get away without accepting his gifts. As surely as the Lord lives, I will chase after him. . . .

"Is everything all right?" Naaman asked.

"Yes," Gehazi said, "but my master has sent me to tell you that two young prophets from the hill country of Ephraim have just arrived. He would like 75 pounds of silver and two sets of clothing to give to them."

"By all means, take 150 pounds of silver," Naaman insisted. He gave him two sets of clothing, tied up the money in two bags, and sent two of his servants to carry the gifts for Gehazi. . . .

When he went in to his master, Elisha asked him, ". . . Is this the time to receive money and clothing and olive groves and vineyards and sheep and oxen and servants? Because you have done this, you and your children and your children's children will suffer from Naaman's leprosy forever."

When Gehazi left the room, he was leprous; his skin was as white as snow.

2 KINGS 5:20-23, 25-27

Drill sin out

29 August

THE DONKEY'S TAIL

FROM THE BIBLE:

Follow God's example in every-
thing you do, because you are his
dear children. Live a life filled
with love for others, following
the example of Christ, who loved
you and gave himself as a sacri-
fice to take away your sins. And
God was pleased, because that
sacrifice was like sweet perfume
to him.

Let there be no sexual
immorality, impurity, or greed
among you. Such sins have no
place among God's people.
Obscene stories, foolish talk, and
coarse jokes—these are not for
you. Instead, let there be
thankfulness to God. You can be
sure that no immoral, impure, or
greedy person will inherit the
Kingdom of Christ and of God.
For a greedy person is really an
idolater who worships the things
of this world. Don't be fooled by
those who try to excuse these sins,
for the terrible anger of God
comes upon all those who disobey
him. Don't participate in the
things these people do. For though
your hearts were once full of
darkness, now you are full of light
from the Lord, and your behavior
should show it!
EPHESIANS 5:1-8

Get rid of spiritual
blindness

IT WAS the day of the church party, and Mrs. Gates, the teacher, tied a blindfold over Jeremy's eyes. His class had decided to play an old party game called "Pin the Tail on the Donkey." Against the wall was the picture of a donkey. Each child had a turn to be blindfolded and turned around a few times before attaching the tail.

"There you are," said Mrs. Gates, turning Jeremy around.

Jeremy took an uncertain step. This wasn't as easy as he expected. He walked forward, wobbling just a little. He reached out with his hand and—there! It was done. The other children laughed as he snatched off his blindfold. There stood the donkey with a tail growing right out of its nose!

When the game was over, Mrs. Gates called the group together before refreshments. "Think about the game we just played," she said. "It would be easy for any one of you to go right now and pin that tail in the right place. What made it hard during the game?"

"We were blindfolded," said one of the children.

"And dizzy from being turned around," added Jeremy.

"That's right," agreed Mrs. Gates. "As Christians, we're sometimes like that, too. We have spiritual blindfolds—things like laziness, selfishness, hate, or stubbornness. And worldly things such as TV and bad companions turn us the wrong way. Let's ask God to help get rid of our 'blindfolds' and stay facing in the right direction."

HOW ABOUT YOU? Are you wearing a spiritual blindfold? Are you turning away from pleasing the Lord because of your friends, things you read, or music you choose? Ask God to help you walk straight ahead—to live a life that is pleasing to him. *H.W.M.*

TO MEMORIZE: For though your hearts were once full of darkness, now you are full of light from the Lord, and your behavior should show it! *Ephesians 5:8*

CAMERON AND HIS FRIEND Drew burst into the living room. "Look, Dad. I've got a new model airplane."

"Nice!" approved Dad. "You must have quite a collection. You've brought home several models lately."

"Right! I've got a Tiger, and a Hornet, and a B-52—"

"Can I see them?" interrupted Drew.

Cameron hesitated. "Well, I haven't finished them yet. But I've got 'em all started."

Dad looked up, frowning. "In that case I think I'd better hold this one for you until the others are done. Leaving things unfinished is a waste of time and effort."

"Aw, Dad," protested Cameron, "it's just a model."

"Yes," agreed Dad, "but I'm afraid you're developing lifelong habits that will hurt you, Cameron. Remember the doghouse you started to build?"

"Don't remind me," groaned Cameron. "But don't worry. I'll finish it tomorrow."

Drew laughed. "My dad says that 'tomorrow never comes.'"

"He's right," agreed Dad. "God tells us we are to be faithful in the things we have to do, big or small. If you can't finish the things you start for your own pleasure, you probably won't finish the things you start for him either."

HOW ABOUT YOU? Do you lose interest in projects before you finish them? Have you ever promised the Lord you would be faithful in a certain area, such as praying or Bible reading, and then failed? God has the power to help you keep on working when the job may seem uninteresting or difficult. Ask him to give you his strength. *C.R.*

TO MEMORIZE: Unless you are faithful in small matters, you won't be faithful in large ones. If you cheat even a little, you won't be honest with greater responsibilities. *Luke 16:10*

A GOOD START, BUT . . .

FROM THE BIBLE:

"Unless you are faithful in small matters, you won't be faithful in large ones. If you cheat even a little, you won't be honest with greater responsibilities. And if you are untrustworthy about worldly wealth, who will trust you with the true riches of heaven? And if you are not faithful with other people's money, why should you be trusted with money of your own?

"No one can serve two masters. For you will hate one and love the other, or be devoted to one and despise the other. You cannot serve both God and money."

LUKE 16:10-13

Finish what you start

31 August

NO REJECTS

FROM THE BIBLE:

*Thank you for making me so
    wonderfully complex!
    Your workmanship is
    marvelous—and how well I
    know it.
You watched me as I was being
    formed in utter seclusion,
    as I was woven together in the
    dark of the womb.
You saw me before I was born.
    Every day of my life was
    recorded in your book.
Every moment was laid out
    before a single day had passed.*

*How precious are your thoughts
    about me, O God!
    They are innumerable!
I can't even count them;
    they outnumber the grains of
    sand!
And when I wake up in the
    morning,
    you are still with me!*
PSALM 139:14-18

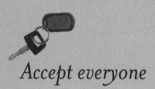

Accept everyone

"**MOTHER, YOU SHOULD** have seen the new kid at our youth group last night!" said Tom as he reached for a freshly baked chocolate chip cookie.

"What about him?" asked Mother as she pulled another batch from the oven.

"He's really weird!" exclaimed Tom.

"Oh?" Mother raised her eyebrows. "What's so different about him?"

"Well, for one thing, he dresses funny." Tom laughed as he remembered. "He had on these clothes that look twenty years old!"

"Maybe his family is short on money," suggested Mother.

Tom shrugged. "His clothes aren't all that's weird about him," he said. "He has a goofy-looking nose that—" He stopped short as he watched his mother sort through the cookies she had just baked. She inspected each one closely and then separated them onto different plates. "What are you doing?" he asked.

Mother picked up the fullest plate and walked toward the trash can. "Some of these didn't turn out quite right," she said. "I'll just dump them."

"Don't throw them away!" exclaimed Tom in disbelief.

"But they're not perfect, Tom," explained Mother. "I examined each one, and only a few have the right color and the exact number of chips I like in a cookie."

"They're still good though," protested Tom. "You have to expect them to be different. . . ." He hesitated and then added quietly, "Just like the new kid, huh?"

Mom nodded. "Just like the new kid," she agreed. "Just like all kids—and all men and women. God made them all different—he made them all special. He loves them all, and we should, too."

HOW ABOUT YOU? Do you have trouble liking people who dress or talk differently from you and your friends? Remember that God created them and loves them. Don't reject them. *D.A.B.*

TO MEMORIZE: Thank you for making me so wonderfully complex! Your workmanship is marvelous—and how well I know it. *Psalm 139:14*

1 September

JANA SIGHED as she sat down at the table one morning. "I wish I could do something important for the special services at church," she said. "Carlos and Jack are going to play a trumpet duet; and Melanie, Sherri, and Tara are singing a trio. Holly's playing the piano one evening, and Bonnie was asked to read her poem. Everybody's doing something but me."

"I thought you were helping in the nursery," said Mother.

"I always do that," said Jana, "but I'd like to do something really important."

Jana's older sister, Tracy, limped into the room. "How's the toe you hurt yesterday?" asked Mother.

"Much better," reported Tracy. "Before long, I'll be able to walk normally. I never realized before how important a little toe is!"

"Did you look at your little toes this morning, Jana?" Mother asked.

"Probably not," laughed Jana.

"Did you comb your hair?" asked Mother. "Did you look at your face?"

"Sure," said Jana. "What are you getting at, Mother?"

"Well," said Mother, "I'm just trying to point out that although we normally pay more attention to some parts of our body, like our hair and our face, every part is important. Even our little toes. Every member of the body of Christ—that is, every believer—is important, too. We tend to pay more attention to those who play instruments or sing or speak. But those who work in the nursery or sweep the church or pray as they sit quietly in their seats are just as important."

HOW ABOUT YOU? Do you feel unimportant? Some jobs seem more "glamorous" to us than others, but God won't reward you according to how glamorous your task is. He'll reward you according to how faithfully you perform the task he has given you to do. *H.W.M.*

TO MEMORIZE: Some of the parts that seem weakest and least important are really the most necessary. *1 Corinthians 12:22*

FROM THE BIBLE:

Yes, there are many parts, but only one body. The eye can never say to the hand, "I don't need you." The head can't say to the feet, "I don't need you."

In fact, some of the parts that seem weakest and least important are really the most necessary. And the parts we regard as less honorable are those we clothe with the greatest care. So we carefully protect from the eyes of others those parts that should not be seen, while other parts do not require this special care. So God has put the body together in such a way that extra honor and care are given to those parts that have less dignity. This makes for harmony among the members, so that all the members care for each other equally. If one part suffers, all the parts suffer with it, and if one part is honored, all the parts are glad.

Now all of you together are Christ's body, and each one of you is a separate and necessary part of it.

1 CORINTHIANS 12:20-27

You are important

2 September

NOT WORTH IT

FROM THE BIBLE:

Fear of the Lord lengthens one's life, but the years of the wicked are cut short.

The hopes of the godly result in happiness, but the expectations of the wicked are all in vain.

The Lord protects the upright but destroys the wicked.

The godly will never be disturbed, but the wicked will be removed from the land.

The godly person gives wise advice, but the tongue that deceives will be cut off.

The godly speak words that are helpful, but the wicked speak only what is corrupt.

PROVERBS 10:27-32

Don't smoke

DALE COUGHED violently, then rubbed the cigarette out. Ken, one of the other boys, noticed. "Anybody that wants to be in this club has to smoke," he stated.

"Well, I have to go now," said Dale. Leaving the clubhouse, he set off for his uncle's home. Uncle Vern was a doctor, and Dale had some questions for him. "Is it really true that smoking causes cancer?" Dale asked. "I mean, I know some old people who have smoked for years, and they've never gotten cancer."

Uncle Vern looked serious. "That's true," he agreed. "Not everyone's body reacts exactly the same. One person may not smoke much but may get cancer at an early age. Another person won't develop cancer for a long time even though he may smoke more. And another may not get cancer at all."

"So it's a big chance?" Dale asked.

"It's a chance *not* worth taking," said Uncle Vern. "There's a much stronger possibility of getting lung cancer if you smoke than if you don't. And smoking also causes heart damage and other problems."

"But not for certain?" Dale asked, anxious to justify smoking.

Uncle Vern frowned. "The problem is that no one knows how his body will react. God made our bodies to work most efficiently when we don't overtax or abuse them."

"Well, I guess smoking is out then," Dale concluded reluctantly.

Uncle Vern slapped him on the back. "I knew you were a smart guy!"

HOW ABOUT YOU? Are you a "smart guy or girl"? Smart enough not to smoke? God created your body. We honor him by taking care of the bodies he has given us. Decide right now not to smoke. That decision may result in a longer life for you. *C.E.Y.*

TO MEMORIZE: Fear of the Lord lengthens one's life. *Proverbs 10:27*

NO SNEAKING IN

"YES, I AM THE GATE. Those who come in through me will be saved." As Mr. Batos, Jerry's Sunday school teacher, read the words of Jesus, Jerry was puzzled. He wondered how Jesus could be a gate.

That night Jerry stayed at Tony's house so he'd be ready to leave on a camping trip early the next morning. After they had gone to bed, Jerry realized that he had forgotten his fishing gear. "Let's run to my house and get it," he said.

"Everybody will be sleeping," said Tony.

"We'll sneak in," said Jerry. "Come on."

Jerry tried the doors at his house, but they were all locked. He decided to pry the screen off his bedroom window and enter that way. The noise woke his parents, so his dad grabbed a bat and went to investigate. Jerry had one foot in the window when his dad yelled, "Stop, or I'll let you have it!"

Jerry froze. "Don't! It's me, Dad!" he said.

His father flicked on a light. "Jerry? Why are you sneaking in the window? Why didn't you come to the door?" he asked. "I would have let you in." Jerry gulped.

The next morning the boys told Mr. Batos about their adventure. "I didn't think it mattered how I got in," Jerry said, "but it did."

"That's a good example of why Jesus is called 'the gate.' It's only through him that we enter heaven. Some people think they can sneak into heaven by doing good works, attending church, or being baptized. But the only way to enter heaven is by the gate—by accepting Jesus as your Savior."

HOW ABOUT YOU? Are you trying to sneak into heaven? You can't do it. The only way to get into heaven is through Jesus Christ. *J.L.H.*

TO MEMORIZE: Yes, I am the gate. Those who come in through me will be saved. Wherever they go, they will find green pastures. *John 10:9*

FROM THE BIBLE:

"I assure you, anyone who sneaks over the wall of a sheepfold, rather than going through the gate, must surely be a thief and a robber! For a shepherd enters through the gate. The gatekeeper opens the gate for him, and the sheep hear his voice and come to him. He calls his own sheep by name and leads them out. After he has gathered his own flock, he walks ahead of them, and they follow him because they recognize his voice. They won't follow a stranger; they will run from him because they don't recognize his voice."

Those who heard Jesus use this illustration didn't understand what he meant, so he explained it to them. "I assure you, I am the gate for the sheep," he said. "All others who came before me were thieves and robbers. But the true sheep did not listen to them. Yes, I am the gate. Those who come in through me will be saved. Wherever they go, they will find green pastures. The thief's purpose is to steal and kill and destroy. My purpose is to give life in all its fullness."
JOHN 10:1-10

Enter heaven by the "gate"

4 September

PENCIL PROBLEMS
(PART 1)

FROM THE BIBLE:

I speak this way, using the illustration of slaves and masters, because it is easy to understand. Before, you let yourselves be slaves of impurity and lawlessness. Now you must choose to be slaves of righteousness so that you will become holy.

In those days, when you were slaves of sin, you weren't concerned with doing what was right. . . .

But there is another law at work within me that is at war with my mind. This law wins the fight and makes me a slave to the sin that is still within me. Oh, what a miserable person I am! Who will free me from this life that is dominated by sin?
ROMANS 6:19-20; 7:23-24

You belong to God

EAGERLY, Chad tore open the large envelope he had received in the mail. "Here's the pencil I ordered," he said. "See—it has my name on it." He pointed to his name, stamped in gold, on the side of the pencil. His little sister, Caryn, reached for the pencil, but Chad pulled it back. "You can't use it," he said. "This pencil cost me money, and nobody gets to use it but me."

"I can use it, too," insisted Caryn. She ran to ask her father. "Daddy, Chad has to share with me, doesn't he?" she asked. "Can I use the pencil, too?" But she was disappointed to see her father shake his head.

"It's Chad's pencil," said Dad. "He paid for it and his name is on it. He has the right to use that pencil any way he chooses."

"Hey, that's like my lesson last Sunday," said Chad. "My teacher says God has the right to use us to do his work because we belong to him."

Dad nodded. "Good point. This pencil can be a reminder of that. You bought and paid for it, so it's yours. God bought us. It cost the blood of Jesus to purchase our salvation. Now we are his. Your name is stamped on the pencil, marking it as your own. The Holy Spirit now lives within us, marking us as 'Christians.' We should always remember that our lives belong to God."

HOW ABOUT YOU? Do you belong to God? You do if you've accepted Jesus as your Savior. Yield yourself to him. Don't allow the world to "use" you. You are God's. Allow him to control you. Live to please him. *H.W.M.*

TO MEMORIZE: Don't you know that your body is the temple of the Holy Spirit, who lives in you and was given to you by God? You do not belong to yourself. *1 Corinthians 6:19*

5 September

"ARE YOU PREPARED for Bible club?" asked Chad's mother, "or should you learn your verse before you go out to play?"

Chad looked at the ball and mitt in his hand, then back at his mother. "Sometimes I get tired of having to go to Bible club and church," he grumbled. "I mean, I'm glad I'm a Christian, but I don't like having to study while the other kids play."

A few minutes later, Mother heard angry voices. "Give that to me, Caryn," demanded Chad. "It's mine." Mother heard sounds of a scuffle and hurried to investigate.

"Caryn's got my pencil," said Chad. His little sister stared at him defiantly.

"Give me the pencil," ordered Mother. Caryn reluctantly handed it over. Mother looked at Chad's name stamped on it. "Well, Son," she said, "suppose I break this in half and give you each a piece."

"No way!" Chad answered. "That would ruin it. I want my whole pencil."

"I can understand that," Mother agreed, handing it to him. "It's yours—the whole thing. I hope that seeing your name on it reminds you that you are God's. Not just half of you, but all of you."

Slowly Chad nodded. "So I shouldn't just go to church. I should become involved in Christian activities and in doing things for the Lord, right?" He grinned at his mother as he opened his book to study.

HOW ABOUT YOU? Are you a "Sunday Christian"? Do you want to do things *your* way the rest of the week? You belong entirely to God, and he wants you to love and serve him with your whole heart. Ask him to help you do that each day. *H.W.M.*

TO MEMORIZE: And now Israel, what does the Lord your God require of you? He requires you to fear him, to live according to his will, to love and worship him with all your heart and soul. *Deuteronomy 10:12*

PENCIL PROBLEMS
(PART 2)

FROM THE BIBLE:

One of the teachers of religious law . . . asked, "Of all the commandments, which is the most important?"

Jesus replied, "The most important commandment is this: 'Hear, O Israel! The Lord our God is the one and only Lord. And you must love the Lord your God with all your heart, all your soul, all your mind, and all your strength.' The second is equally important: 'Love your neighbor as yourself.' No other commandment is greater than these."

The teacher of religious law replied, "Well said, Teacher. You have spoken the truth by saying that there is only one God and no other. And I know it is important to love him with all my heart and all my understanding and all my strength, and to love my neighbors as myself. This is more important than to offer all of the burnt offerings and sacrifices required in the law."

Realizing this man's understanding, Jesus said to him, "You are not far from the Kingdom of God." And after that, no one dared to ask him any more questions.

MARK 12:28-34

Serve God all the time

6 September

A PUZZLING SITUATION
(PART 1)

FROM THE BIBLE:

Don't team up with those who are unbelievers. How can goodness be a partner with wickedness? How can light live with darkness? What harmony can there be between Christ and the Devil? How can a believer be a partner with an unbeliever? And what union can there be between God's temple and idols? For we are the temple of the living God. As God said:

"I will live in them
*   and walk among them.*
I will be their God,
*   and they will be my people.*
Therefore, come out from them
*   and separate yourselves from*
*   them, says the Lord.*
Don't touch their filthy things,
*   and I will welcome you."*

2 CORINTHIANS 6:14-17

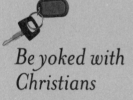

Be yoked with Christians

"CINDY!" exclaimed Josh. "You messed up our puzzle!"

"I help," insisted Cindy, stirring the pieces around.

Beth took a simple puzzle from a shelf and helped three-year-old Cindy get started on it. "You work this puzzle. Ours is too hard for you."

Josh and Beth enjoyed watching their puzzle picture develop. Then trouble started again. "Cindy, that piece belongs in your puzzle, not in this one!" protested Beth.

"Here, Cindy. Help me open the mail." Mother had just come in. While Cindy struggled with one envelope, Mother opened another. "Oh, dear," she sighed. "Your cousin, Paula, is getting married, and Dave, her fiancé, isn't a Christian."

"She thinks he'll attend church with her after they're married," remarked Beth.

"Well, I pray Dave will become a Christian," said Mother, "but they're starting out unwisely. God says Christians should not team up with unbelievers."

"Cindy!" yelled Josh. His little sister was messing with the puzzle again.

"You see," said Mother, "just as pieces from two different puzzles will never fit properly together, a believer and an unbeliever do not fit together. This is especially true for marriage. And it can affect the way we choose our friends."

"That's why you don't like me to get too chummy with Carl, right?" asked Josh.

Mother nodded. "You can be friends, but you also need Christian friends. And when you're old enough to marry, the mate you choose must be a Christian."

"Marry!" Josh made a face.

Mother laughed. "That time will come before you know it," she said.

HOW ABOUT YOU? Are some of your friends Christians? Are you determined that, when the time comes, you will choose a Christian mate? Don't disobey God on this important issue. *H.W.M.*

TO MEMORIZE: Don't team up with those who are unbelievers. How can goodness be a partner with wickedness? How can light live with darkness? *2 Corinthians 6:14*

BETH AND JOSH raced to put in the last few pieces of their puzzle. Finally, Beth picked up the very last one on the table. "You're hiding a piece," she accused Josh when she saw that one more piece was still missing from the puzzle. "You always think you have to put in the last piece."

"I don't have it," said Josh. "Maybe it's on the floor." He looked under the table, but nothing was there. The children began to search the rest of the room.

"What's going on?" asked Mother. They showed her the puzzle with the missing piece. "That's too bad," she said, "but I think you may as well forget it for now. It's almost time for dinner."

"Forget it?" objected Beth. "But we need it to finish the picture." They continued their search, and finally they found the missing piece.

"You certainly were persistent," observed Mother when she saw the finished puzzle. "Good for you!"

"Yeah," agreed Josh. "Hey, Mother, you always see neat little lessons in things that happen. Do you see one in this?"

Mother thought for a moment. "Actually, I do," she said. "I'm thinking of your friend Jim. He's like the missing puzzle piece. He's acting wild right now, so he really needs prayer. You need to be careful that he doesn't influence you to do wrong, but you can be persistent in praying for him and being his friend. Be as persistent as you were in finishing your puzzle."

HOW ABOUT YOU? Do you know a Christian who won't come to church? A Christian who does things you know are wrong? Sometimes it's necessary to avoid close friendship with such a person. But never stop praying for that person. Try to lead that person back to the Lord. *H.W.M.*

TO MEMORIZE: Take note of those who refuse to obey what we say in this letter. Stay away from them so they will be ashamed. *2 Thessalonians 3:14*

A PUZZLING SITUATION
(PART 2)

FROM THE BIBLE:

And now, dear brothers and sisters, we give you this command with the authority of our Lord Jesus Christ: Stay away from any Christian who lives in idleness and doesn't follow the tradition of hard work we gave you. For you know that you ought to follow our example. We were never lazy when we were with you. . . .

Take note of those who refuse to obey what we say in this letter. Stay away from them so they will be ashamed. Don't think of them as enemies, but speak to them as you would to a Christian who needs to be warned.

2 THESSALONIANS 3:6-7, 14-15

Pray for straying Christians

8 September

GOD COUNTS

FROM THE BIBLE:

"Not even a sparrow, worth only half a penny, can fall to the ground without your Father knowing it. And the very hairs on your head are all numbered."
MATTHEW 10:29-30

Don't steal

JASON AND SIMONE strolled past the booths at the crafts fair. "Look, Jason!" Simone squealed. "Isn't it beautiful?" She held up a doll with a china face.

"It's fine if you like dolls!" Jason shrugged. "Let's look at something else."

"Where'd Mom go?" Simone asked as she searched the crowd.

"I don't know," Jason answered, "but she'll find us. Don't worry."

The two continued down the midway of the fairgrounds. "Mmmm. Do you smell what I smell?" Jason asked.

"Smells like a bakery," Simone replied, "and there it is!"

Jason walked up to the booth where delicious baked goods were displayed. "Look at those doughnuts, Simone. I sure would like one."

"We spent all our money, remember?" Simone reminded her brother.

"So?" Jason smiled. "No one's around. The vendor must be taking a break. He won't miss one little doughnut."

"Don't take one, Jason! You know that would be stealing," warned Simone.

"Oh, Simone, no one will ever know," Jason sneered, looking carefully around. "I'm sure they didn't count every single doughnut. They'll never miss it."

"Maybe not," Simone admitted. "But perhaps God counted them."

Jason gulped and looked at Simone. After a few moments he replied, "You're right, Simone. God does count. The Bible says that even 'the hairs on our head are all numbered'!" Jason and Simone walked away from the booth empty-handed, but at peace.

HOW ABOUT YOU? Are you tempted to steal "little" things because you think that no one will ever know? Do you think it won't matter if you take things that belong to a brother or sister or even your parents? Remember, even little things matter to God. *B.D.*

TO MEMORIZE: The very hairs on your head are all numbered. *Matthew 10:30*

GRANDPARENTS' DAY

IT WAS Grandparents' Day at school. As usual, Raul's grandpa came for the program. Grandpa listened to the children read what they had written about why they liked their grandparents. Roberto liked his grandpa because he gave him nice gifts. Amanda liked her grandpa because he never scolded her. Raul's report was different. As he read it, he saw his grandpa smile.

After school Grandpa told Raul how pleased he was with what Raul wrote. "Well, you always do have time for me," said Raul. "You listen to me and take time to help me. And you're not afraid to say no to me or to scold me. I don't always like it, but I know you're right, so I'm glad you do it."

"I'm glad to hear you say that, Raul," Grandpa told him. "You know, the things you like about me are also some of the things I like about God."

"Really?"

Grandpa nodded. "God always listens when I pray and is there when I need him," he said. "He helps me say no to bad things. Then he helps me admit I'm wrong and apologize to people when I do wrong. He not only saved me, but he always does what is best for me."

"Yeah, God is like that, isn't he?" Raul said. "I'm even glad he doesn't always give us what we want. If he had, we wouldn't have moved to this town, and then I wouldn't have gotten to see so much of you."

HOW ABOUT YOU? Do you like people for what they give you or because you can get them to do what you want? You ought to love them for themselves, not for their gifts. This includes God, too. *A.G.L.*

TO MEMORIZE: Now you can have sincere love for each other as brothers and sisters because you were cleansed from your sins when you accepted the truth of the Good News. *1 Peter 1:22*

FROM THE BIBLE:

And have you entirely forgotten the encouraging words God spoke to you, his children? He said,

"My child, don't ignore it when the Lord disciplines you, and don't be discouraged when he corrects you.

For the Lord disciplines those he loves, and he punishes those he accepts as his children."

As you endure this divine discipline, remember that God is treating you as his own children. Whoever heard of a child who was never disciplined? If God doesn't discipline you as he does all of his children, it means that you are illegitimate and are not really his children after all. Since we respect our earthly fathers who disciplined us, should we not all the more cheerfully submit to the discipline of our heavenly Father and live forever? HEBREWS 12:5-9

Love people for themselves

10 September

CANTALOUPE EPISODE
(PART 1)

FROM THE BIBLE:

"Do not steal.
"Do not cheat one another.
"Do not lie.
"Do not use my name to swear a falsehood and so profane the name of your God. I am the Lord.
"Do not cheat or rob anyone.
"Always pay your hired workers promptly."
LEVITICUS 19:11-13

Don't steal

"LET'S GO," whispered Travis. "Mr. Brown just went into his house." He and his friend Philip crept up to the garden. Travis grabbed a big ripe cantaloupe, stuffed it under his shirt, and ran in a bent-over position to the path leading to the road. Philip was right behind him, also keeping low. When they reached the road, they ducked into some bushes near Travis's house. Philip handed his pocketknife to Travis, who cut through the juicy cantaloupe.

"We must have gotten the best melon out of Mr. Brown's garden," Travis said as he wiped his mouth with the back of his hand.

After dinner that evening, Travis's father got out some heavy gloves. "I have to go clear out a patch of poison ivy," he said. "Want to help, Travis?"

"Sure," Travis agreed.

They got shovels and put on the gloves. To Travis's surprise, Dad headed straight for the bushes where the boys had eaten the melon! "Look," said Dad, "someone's been eating cantaloupe in this patch of poison ivy!"

Just then Mr. Brown came up. "Someone stole my best cantaloupe this afternoon," he said. His eyes grew wide when he saw the rinds and seeds.

"I'm sorry to hear that," Travis's father replied.

"I was going to enter that big one in the fair. I'm sure it would have won a prize," exclaimed Mr. Brown.

Travis's heart was pounding as he began to help clear out the poison ivy. *I just meant to have some fun,* he thought. *But I guess taking that cantaloupe was really stealing.* Somehow he was sure the cantaloupe episode wasn't over yet.

HOW ABOUT YOU? Have you ever taken something that belonged to someone else to tease that person or to see if you could get away with it? It may seem like you're only having fun. But it's never fun for the person from whom you steal. *C.E.Y.*

TO MEMORIZE: "Do not steal." *Exodus 20:15*

CANTALOUPE EPISODE
(PART 2)

TRAVIS TOSSED and turned in bed. He just couldn't get to sleep. Oh, if only he hadn't taken Mr. Brown's prize cantaloupe! He knew now that taking the melon was not just "having a little fun." It was stealing. He wanted to talk with Dad about it. Even being grounded was better than feeling like this!

Travis got out of bed and knocked on his parents' bedroom door. "Dad, Mom, may I talk to you?" he asked. Soon he was telling them all about it.

"Son, I'm sorry you took Mr. Brown's melon," said Dad, "but I'm glad you've admitted it. Now you need to tell God you're sorry. And tomorrow you'll have to tell Mr. Brown you're sorry, too. Ask if you may help him in his garden to pay for the melon."

"I will, Dad," said Travis as the three prayed together. After Travis prayed, his parents gave him a hug. Travis squirmed. "Ouch," he said. "My skin feels like it's on fire. It really itches!"

They took a closer look. "It's poison ivy!" exclaimed Mom. She hurried away to get some soothing lotion.

"You see, Travis, sin can have two results," said Dad. "It hurts our conscience, making us feel far from God. We can remedy that by confessing our sin and receiving God's forgiveness. But sometimes sin hurts us in other ways, too. In this case, you'll have to suffer with poison ivy."

FROM THE BIBLE:

Don't be misled. Remember that you can't ignore God and get away with it. You will always reap what you sow! Those who live only to satisfy their own sinful desires will harvest the consequences of decay and death. But those who live to please the Spirit will harvest everlasting life from the Spirit. So don't get tired of doing what is good. Don't get discouraged and give up, for we will reap a harvest of blessing at the appropriate time. Whenever we have the opportunity, we should do good to everyone, especially to our Christian brothers and sisters.
GALATIANS 6:7-10

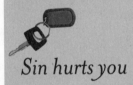

Sin hurts you

HOW ABOUT YOU? Are you suffering as a result of something you have done wrong? Sin must be confessed to God and to those you've wronged. But you may still have to experience a consequence as a result of your sin. If that's the case, accept it and learn from it. *C.E.Y.*

TO MEMORIZE: Don't be misled. Remember that you can't ignore God and get away with it. You will always reap what you sow! *Galatians 6:7*

12 September

THE FALSE HOOD

FROM THE BIBLE:

"Take care! Don't do your good deeds publicly, to be admired, because then you will lose the reward from your Father in heaven. When you give a gift to someone in need, don't shout about it as the hypocrites do—blowing trumpets in the synagogues and streets to call attention to their acts of charity! I assure you, they have received all the reward they will ever get. But when you give to someone, don't tell your left hand what your right hand is doing. Give your gifts in secret, and your Father, who knows all secrets, will reward you.

"And now about prayer. When you pray, don't be like the hypocrites who love to pray publicly on street corners and in the synagogues where everyone can see them. I assure you, that is all the reward they will ever get. But when you pray, go away by yourself, shut the door behind you, and pray to your Father secretly. Then your Father, who knows all secrets, will reward you."

MATTHEW 6:1-6

Be honest and obedient

"**DAD, WHAT'S** a falsehood?" asked Katie as she plunked herself in a chair.

"A falsehood?" Dad asked in surprise. "Well, a falsehood is a lie."

"That's what I thought," said Katie. "But why is it called a falsehood?"

"Hmmm," pondered Dad. "Well, one explanation I've heard is that it comes from something done hundreds of years ago. It was during a time when people wore hoods instead of hats, and they wore cloaks instead of coats."

"Like Little Red Riding Hood?" asked Katie.

"Sort of," answered Dad. "A person like a doctor or lawyer—or whatever profession—wore a certain type and color of hood."

"Then if you saw someone with a certain kind of hood, you would know what he was?" asked Katie.

"Yes, and that's where the falsehood comes in," Dad answered. "Some dishonest people would go to a town where they weren't known, wear a hood they hadn't earned, and set up a practice. They were living a lie. They were wearing a false hood."

Katie nodded. "I can see how the word came to mean a lie," she said. "I think it's a good word to use to describe people who pretend to be something they're not. Some kids are unkind at school but pretend to be Christians on Sunday. It's like they're hiding under a false hood."

"That's right!" answered Dad. "Be careful always to be honest before God and others."

"I will," Katie promised.

HOW ABOUT YOU? Are you pretending to be something you aren't? If you feel the need to pretend, ask yourself why. If you're honest and obedient as God wants you to be, you will not feel the need to hide under a "false hood." *A.I.L.*

TO MEMORIZE: You have rejected all who stray from your principles. They are only fooling themselves. *Psalm 119:118*

ONE SATURDAY MORNING, Molly was moping around the house. Mom noticed and said, "Why is my sweet girl so sad today?"

"Oh, Mom," Molly whimpered, "I'm no good at anything!"

"No good, huh?" her mother replied. "Well, I know one thing you're good at, and that's helping me to get lunch on the table." Molly smiled and seemed to forget her blue mood while they ate.

After lunch, much to the surprise of Molly and her mother, Dad sat down on the piano bench. He began to bang on the piano keys as he playfully sang in an off-key voice. Soon Molly and Mom were laughing hard. Molly put her hands over her ears as she shouted, "Daddy, please! Give our ears a break!"

As Dad stopped playing, Mom said, "Remember, Molly, you said you couldn't do anything very well. But it all depends on what you compare yourself to. Compared to Daddy, you do something very well—you play the piano."

Molly still wasn't convinced. "But I'm not good at sports like Daddy is, and I can't sing high notes like Cheryl does."

"Oh, Molly," admonished Mom, "don't compare yourself with others! You're much better at sports than I ever was! And Mrs. Pierce told me last week that you are one of the best altos in the junior choir."

"Molly, I know a Bible verse that you need to learn," said Dad. As Molly looked at 1 Peter 4:10, Dad pointed out that God wants his children to develop their own talents and not waste their time comparing themselves with their friends.

HOW ABOUT YOU? Do you want to be like someone you know, and are you constantly comparing yourself with that person? God wants you to just be you! *R.E.P.*

TO MEMORIZE: God has given gifts to each of you from his great variety of spiritual gifts. Manage them well so that God's generosity can flow through you. *1 Peter 4:10*

COMPARED WITH WHAT?

FROM THE BIBLE:

And so, dear Christian friends, I plead with you to give your bodies to God. Let them be a living and holy sacrifice—the kind he will accept. When you think of what he has done for you, is this too much to ask? Don't copy the behavior and customs of this world, but let God transform you into a new person by changing the way you think. Then you will know what God wants you to do, and you will know how good and pleasing and perfect his will really is.

As God's messenger, I give each of you this warning: Be honest in your estimate of yourselves. . . . Just as our bodies have many parts and each part has a special function, so it is with Christ's body. We are all parts of his one body, and each of us has different work to do. And since we are all one body in Christ, we belong to each other, and each of us needs all the others.

God has given each of us the ability to do certain things well.
ROMANS 12:1-6

Be yourself

14 September

PHONY JACKETS
(PART 1)

FROM THE BIBLE:

"No one can serve two masters. For you will hate one and love the other, or be devoted to one and despise the other. You cannot serve both God and money."

The Pharisees, who dearly loved their money, naturally scoffed at all this. Then he said to them, "You like to look good in public, but God knows your evil hearts. What this world honors is an abomination in the sight of God.

"Until John the Baptist began to preach, the laws of Moses and the messages of the prophets were your guides. But now the Good News of the Kingdom of God is preached, and eager multitudes are forcing their way in. But that doesn't mean that the law has lost its force in even the smallest point. It is stronger and more permanent than heaven and earth."

LUKE 16:13-17

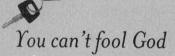

You can't fool God

"MOM, I GOT IT," announced Kathy after school one day.

"Got what?" asked her brother Ben. "Is it catching?"

"Silly!" Kathy held up a book. The picture on the jacket showed a girl in a long skirt cooking over an old-fashioned stove. "My teacher let me bring this home. It tells how to make 'vanity cakes' like they did years ago. Mom said she'd help me make some if I brought home the recipe." She turned to her mother. "Can we make them today?"

"Right after supper," Mom promised.

When they had finished the evening meal, Mom said Ben should do the dishes. Kathy ran to get the book she had brought home. She eagerly opened it. Then she closed the book and looked at the cover. Once more she opened it. "Mom," she wailed, "this cover is a phony! It says *Old Time Cooking,* but it's a book about antique cars!"

Mom came to investigate. "Somehow this book got the wrong jacket on it," she said. "I guess this proves the old saying, 'You can't tell a book by its cover.'"

"That jacket fooled Kathy," observed Dad, "until she looked inside. I'm reminded of people who put on a good cover. They go to church and do all sorts of good deeds. Their phony jackets fool lots of people who think such fine folks must be Christians. But they never fool God. He knows whether or not they've accepted Jesus."

HOW ABOUT YOU? Are you wearing a "jacket" that makes you appear to be something you're not? Others may think you're a Christian because you go to church, behave nicely, and talk about the Lord. But God is not fooled. He sees the real you. He knows if you've really been born again. *H.W.M.*

TO MEMORIZE: Then hear from heaven where you live, and forgive. Give your people whatever they deserve, for you alone know the human heart. *1 Kings 8:39*

PHONY JACKETS
(PART 2)

"GET OUT of my way," ordered Ben, as he gave his sister a shove.

"Who wants to watch this stupid program anyway?" retorted Kathy as she went to answer the phone.

"I'm going to sing with a few other kids two weeks from Sunday," Kathy reported when she returned. "We're singing 'Get That Frown Off Your Face.'"

"Big deal," said Ben. The phone rang again, and Ben jumped up to get it.

Soon he returned. "Guess what, Miss Smarty! I get to sing, too. Mrs. Snyder said she forgot she had two people to ask from this family."

Kathy turned to her mother, who had just come into the room. "Mom, Ben has my book—the one with the wrong jacket on it. Make him give it to me."

Mother sighed. "What song did you say you were singing?"

"It's one we just learned," replied Ben. "It goes, 'Get that frown off your face. Put a smile in its place. . . .'"

"It's a good song," said Mother. "I guess you'll be wearing jackets that day."

"Jackets?" Ben and Kathy were puzzled.

Mother nodded. "You know—like that book. Christians sometimes wear 'jackets,' too—jackets that say they're something they're not. In public, they act sweet, but in private they can't get along."

Kathy blushed. "That sounds like us," she admitted. "I'm sorry, Ben."

"I'm sorry, too," said Ben.

FROM THE BIBLE:

If you are wise and understand God's ways, live a life of steady goodness so that only good deeds will pour forth. And if you don't brag about the good you do, then you will be truly wise! But if you are bitterly jealous and there is selfish ambition in your hearts, don't brag about being wise. That is the worst kind of lie. For jealousy and selfishness are not God's kind of wisdom. Such things are earthly, unspiritual, and motivated by the Devil. For wherever there is jealousy and selfish ambition, there you will find disorder and every kind of evil.

But the wisdom that comes from heaven is first of all pure. It is also peace loving, gentle at all times, and willing to yield to others. It is full of mercy and good deeds. It shows no partiality and is always sincere. And those who are peacemakers will plant seeds of peace and reap a harvest of goodness.
JAMES 3:13-18

Don't be two-faced

HOW ABOUT YOU? Do you say "please" and "thank you" only when you're away from home? Do you talk nicely when you're at church and use bad language when you're at school? That's called "hypocrisy," or being "two-faced." Ask God to help you live a pure, honest life. *H.W.M.*

TO MEMORIZE: The wisdom that comes from heaven is first of all pure. It is also peace loving, gentle at all times, and willing to yield to others. It is full of mercy and good deeds. It shows no partiality and is always sincere. *James 3:17*

16 September

A DARK PLACE

Be God's Light

AS CAMMIE listened to the cheerful voices singing choruses at Bible club, she wished she could stay at Mrs. Steiner's house forever. She was glad she had come and heard about Jesus and that she had trusted him as her Savior.

Cammie lingered to help Mrs. Steiner straighten the family room. "Thank you, Cammie," said Mrs. Steiner. "Now, how about a dish of peaches before you go? Would you like to call your parents and make sure it's all right?"

"It'll be OK," Cammie answered. "Mom works late, and Dad will be passed out—I mean, sleeping on the couch."

"Well then, please get a jar of my home-canned peaches from the fruit cellar," Mrs. Steiner said. "I'll get out the dishes and milk." Cammie was limping when she returned from the basement.

"The light didn't go on," Cammie explained, "so I couldn't see very well. I ran into a ladder, but I'm fine."

"Oh, dear, the bulb must have burned out," Mrs. Steiner said. "I'm sorry. A light is needed in a dark place like the fruit cellar." She opened the jar and dished up the golden fruit. "How are things going at home?"

Cammie sighed and told how her mom worked late hours and her dad was an alcoholic.

"It must be hard for you, Cammie," sympathized Mrs. Steiner, "but Jesus needs you there in your home. Just like the fruit cellar really needed a light, you can be a light in your home to help your parents see the love of Christ."

HOW ABOUT YOU? Are you the only Christian in your home or in your classroom? It's difficult to stand alone. But it's in the dark that a light is needed the most. *J.L.H.*

TO MEMORIZE: You are to live clean, innocent lives as children of God in a dark world full of crooked and perverse people. Let your lives shine brightly before them. *Philippians 2:15*

GOOD FOR SOMETHING

"I DON'T LIKE spiders, do you?" Anna asked her friend.

"Ugh! No, I hate them!" Linda answered. "They're creepy."

A spider had stretched its web across a section of fence in Anna's backyard, and the girls had gone over to look at it. "The web sure is pretty, though," observed Anna as they leaned closer. Each silvery strand of the beautifully constructed web connected to make a lacy pattern. Dewdrops on the web sparkled in the morning sun.

"I wonder how the spider knows how to make a web like that," said Linda.

"Since God made everything, he must have made spiders so they'd know how to make their webs," answered Anna.

Just then an insect buzzed around their heads. When Anna swatted at it, the bug flew into the web. Quick as a wink, the spider dashed out from a corner of the web and wrapped silk around the insect until it was held fast.

"Wow! Did you see how fast that spider moved?" marveled Linda.

"Yeah, and it sure made quick work of that bug," replied Anna. "Good thing, or the bug might have bitten us. Looks like spiders are good for something after all. Some bugs eat our garden plants, and some carry diseases. Every bug that's caught by a spider is one that can't hurt us anymore."

"I never thought of that before," said Linda. "I guess God must have known we'd need spiders."

HOW ABOUT YOU? Have you ever thanked God for spiders? In their own quiet way, they are helping the earth every day. Stop and think how each creature fits into God's creation. It will help you appreciate the greatness of God. *C.E.Y.*

TO MEMORIZE: Since everything God created is good, we should not reject any of it. We may receive it gladly, with thankful hearts. *1 Timothy 4:4*

FROM THE BIBLE:

And God said, "Let the waters swarm with fish and other life. Let the skies be filled with birds of every kind." So God created great sea creatures and every sort of fish and every kind of bird. And God saw that it was good. Then God blessed them, saying, "Let the fish multiply and fill the oceans. Let the birds increase and fill the earth." This all happened on the fifth day.

And God said, "Let the earth bring forth every kind of animal—livestock, small animals, and wildlife." And so it was. God made all sorts of wild animals, livestock, and small animals, each able to reproduce more of its own kind. And God saw that it was good.

Then God said, "Let us make people in our image, to be like ourselves. They will be masters over all life—the fish in the sea, the birds in the sky, and all the livestock, wild animals, and small animals."

GENESIS 1:20-26

God made everything good

18 September

IN NEED OF A FRIEND

FROM THE BIBLE:

"I command you to love each other in the same way that I love you. And here is how to measure it—the greatest love is shown when people lay down their lives for their friends. You are my friends if you obey me. I no longer call you servants, because a master doesn't confide in his servants. Now you are my friends, since I have told you everything the Father told me. You didn't choose me. I chose you. I appointed you to go and produce fruit that will last, so that the Father will give you whatever you ask for, using my name. I command you to love each other."
JOHN 15:12-17

To have a friend, be one

STACIE CAME HOME in tears. "This is my third week at school, and I still don't have a friend," she wailed. "I wish we had never moved here!"

Mother ached for her. "I know you miss your old friends, honey," she said. "I've been praying about this."

"Everyone seems to stare at me," Stacie sobbed. "I'm so lonely."

The door flew open, and Tim blew in like a whirlwind. "Hey, Mom, is it all right if I go over to Paul's for a couple of hours? He needs help with his science project."

Mother nodded. "Just be home by five-thirty." The door slammed behind Tim. "Now, Stacie, dry your tears and take this casserole to Mrs. Carson next door. She just came home from the hospital today."

Stacie blew her nose loudly. "How do you know that?" she asked. "You seem to know everyone in this apartment building already. Why can't I make friends like you and Tim do?"

Mother took a deep breath. "Stacie, you've been looking for someone to be a friend to you, and you haven't found anyone. But Tim and I have found people everywhere who need a friend. Stop looking for a friend, and start trying to be one instead." Mother hugged Stacie gently.

An hour later Stacie came skipping into the apartment. "Guess what, Mom?" She was beaming. "I found someone who needs a friend. Her name is Tara, and she's Mrs. Carson's granddaughter. May I go over there after dinner?"

HOW ABOUT YOU? Are you lonely? Look around you. There are lonely people everywhere. The way to make friends is to be one. Try it. *B.J.W.*

TO MEMORIZE: I command you to love each other. *John 15:17*

TEARS TRICKLED down Katrina's cheeks as she repeated her request. "It wouldn't be a real date—just Jeff, Shana, Mark, and me."

Mother sighed deeply. "Katrina, I'm sorry. But twelve is too young."

"I'm too young for everything!" Katrina wailed.

Mother put her arm around Katrina's stiff shoulders. "Not too young to make your famous pecan fudge. You'll find the pecans on the table."

As Katrina cooked, she sniffed and slammed pans. The fudge was in the refrigerator, and Katrina was cleaning up the kitchen when Mother came in carrying another pail of pecans. "Remember when we planted our pecan tree, Katie?" she asked. "You were just a little girl. It took a long time, but it's finally producing!"

Katrina ignored her mother and opened the refrigerator to check on the fudge. "It isn't getting hard!" she whined.

Mother looked over her shoulder. "I'm afraid you didn't cook it long enough."

Later Mother helped Katrina pick pecans out of the shells for a second batch of fudge. "A lot of things in life take time—things like fudge and pecan trees and growing up," Mother said softly. "When we rush them, we often ruin them."

Katrina knew Mother was right. She gave Mother a tearful smile.

HOW ABOUT YOU? Are you fretting and stewing, wanting to do something your parents say you're not old enough to do? Ask the Lord to help you be patient. Whatever you're waiting for will be more enjoyable and valuable because of the wait. Meanwhile, use the experiences God is giving you right now to develop Christian virtues (including patience). *B.J.W.*

TO MEMORIZE: Therefore, since we are surrounded by such a huge crowd of witnesses to the life of faith, let us strip off every weight that slows us down, especially the sin that so easily hinders our progress. *Hebrews 12:1*

DON'T RUSH IT

FROM THE BIBLE:

Dear brothers and sisters, you must be patient as you wait for the Lord's return. Consider the farmers who eagerly look for the rains in the fall and in the spring. They patiently wait for the precious harvest to ripen. You, too, must be patient. And take courage, for the coming of the Lord is near.

Don't grumble about each other, my brothers and sisters, or God will judge you. For look! The great Judge is coming. He is standing at the door!

For examples of patience in suffering, dear brothers and sisters, look at the prophets who spoke in the name of the Lord. We give great honor to those who endure under suffering. Job is an example of a man who endured patiently. From his experience we see how the Lord's plan finally ended in good, for he is full of tenderness and mercy.

JAMES 5:7-11

Be patient

20 September

THE PITY PARTY

FROM THE BIBLE:

Praise the Lord, I tell myself,
and never forget the good
things he does for me.
He forgives all my sins
and heals all my diseases.
He ransoms me from death
and surrounds me with love
and tender mercies.
He fills my life with good things.
My youth is renewed like the
eagle's! . . .
The Lord is merciful and
gracious;
he is slow to get angry and full
of unfailing love.
He will not constantly accuse us,
nor remain angry forever.
He has not punished us for all
our sins,
nor does he deal with us as we
deserve.
For his unfailing love toward
those who fear him
is as great as the height of the
heavens above the earth.
He has removed our rebellious
acts
as far away from us as the
east is from the west.
The Lord is like a father to his
children,
tender and compassionate to
those who fear him.
PSALM 103:2-5, 8-13

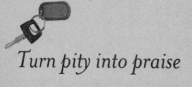

Turn pity into praise

JULIO WAS POUTING in the backseat of the car. When Mom asked why, his sister Maria laughed. "He's mad because Dad wouldn't let him buy that set of Indian arrowheads at the gift shop," she said.

"I don't see why I couldn't have it," Julio scowled. "It was only six dollars. I never get to buy anything."

Dad raised his eyebrows. "Sounds like you're having a pity party," he said. "That's what we call it when someone feels so sorry for himself that he doesn't even want to be cheered up."

"Well," Julio grumbled, "you've only let me buy one souvenir, and we've been on vacation four days. Besides, I always have to sit in the backseat."

"I've had to sit in the backseat, too," pouted Maria. "It's so hot, and you know I get carsick sometimes."

Dad and Mom exchanged glances. Mom's eyes twinkled. "Well, how about me?" she whined. "That mattress last night was so hard, I couldn't sleep, and the fried eggs I got for breakfast were cold and overdone. And I've got—"

"You think you've got it bad!" interrupted Dad. "I've spent a whole lot more on this trip than I planned because the rain kept us from camping out the last two nights. We had to stay in a motel."

The children stared. It seemed strange to hear their parents whining! Dad and Mom laughed at the expression on their faces. "Look at that magnificent view," Dad said, pulling into a scenic turnoff. "We were so busy with our pity party that we've been forgetting about the good things around us."

HOW ABOUT YOU? Do you sometimes complain and feel sorry for yourself? Having this attitude makes you blind to the blessings of God and to the needs of others. Be thankful instead. *S.L.K.*

TO MEMORIZE: Praise the Lord, I tell myself, and never forget the good things he does for me. *Psalm 103:2*

WATCH YOUR MOUTH

SARA WAS IN a terrible mood. She sat at the kitchen table, criticizing and complaining. "I just hate school! Mr. Martin is a jerk. Lisette and Emily are stuck-up." On and on she grumbled.

"Got anything to eat?" Jacob's entrance into the room interrupted his sister's monologue. As he took an apple from a bowl, he talked excitedly. "Brent and I are doing a science project on air waves. Mr. Nuevo says scientists believe that everything that's ever been said is still around in space."

"Aw," Sara scoffed, "I don't believe that."

Jacob pulled up a chair. "He read that on one of the first space flights, the radio picked up a program that had been aired twenty or thirty years before. Wouldn't it be great to develop a device that could pull voices out of the air? How would you like everyone to hear everything you've ever said?"

Sara shuddered at the idea of someone hearing a replay of her voice saying the things she had just said. "I wouldn't."

"I don't know the method God uses," said Mother, "but he keeps a record of everything we say. One day we'll give an account of every idle word we've spoken. Words, once they are spoken, never die."

"I didn't know that," said Sara. "Do you think you could invent a device that would stop me from saying things I shouldn't, Jacob?"

Jacob laughed, but Mother answered. "There already is such a device. It's called self-control. All you have to do is ask God to help you use it."

FROM THE BIBLE:

"You brood of snakes! How could evil men like you speak what is good and right? For whatever is in your heart determines what you say. A good person produces good words from a good heart, and an evil person produces evil words from an evil heart. And I tell you this, that you must give an account on judgment day of every idle word you speak. The words you say now reflect your fate then; either you will be justified by them or you will be condemned." MATTHEW 12:34-37

Don't speak thoughtlessly

HOW ABOUT YOU? Do you often say things you should not say? Then you need to pray, like David did, "Take control of what I say, O Lord, and keep my lips sealed." You need to ask the Lord to help you practice self-control. *B.J.W.*

TO MEMORIZE: Take control of what I say, O Lord, and keep my lips sealed. *Psalm 141:3*

22 September

UNARMED!

FROM THE BIBLE:

Put on all of God's armor so that you will be able to stand firm against all strategies and tricks of the Devil. For we are not fighting against people made of flesh and blood, but against the evil rulers and authorities of the unseen world, against those mighty powers of darkness who rule this world, and against wicked spirits in the heavenly realms.

Use every piece of God's armor to resist the enemy in the time of evil, so that after the battle you will still be standing firm. Stand your ground, putting on the sturdy belt of truth and the body armor of God's righteousness. For shoes, put on the peace that comes from the Good News, so that you will be fully prepared. In every battle you will need faith as your shield to stop the fiery arrows aimed at you by Satan. Put on salvation as your helmet, and take the sword of the Spirit, which is the word of God. Pray at all times and on every occasion in the power of the Holy Spirit. Stay alert and be persistent in your prayers for all Christians everywhere.

EPHESIANS 6:11-18

Carry your Bible

"OH NO!" Christopher exclaimed out loud, but not too loud. He didn't want Mom or Dad to hear. "I forgot my Bible again!" The Kerner family was on the way to church. They were too far from home to go back for the Bible. In class Mr. Lawrence told the boys to turn to Ephesians 6. Christopher quickly scooted his chair over to his friend's, hoping his teacher wouldn't notice the missing Bible.

Mr. Lawrence told a story. "Frederick was a soldier. He loved his country and believed in the laws of his government. When it was necessary to fight to protect those laws, he went to battle. One day Frederick came face-to-face with the enemy. But he cried out, 'I forgot my sword! I have nothing with which to fight!'" The boys laughed. It seemed funny for a soldier to forget his sword. Then Mr. Lawrence had one of the boys read Ephesians 6:17: "Put on salvation as your helmet, and take the sword of the Spirit, which is the word of God."

Even before Mr. Lawrence explained it, Christopher knew why he had told that story. As a Christian, Christopher was in a battle against Satan. The Word of God was what he needed to fight that battle! He needed the Bible to show him the difference between right and wrong. He needed the Bible in order to learn more about Jesus and the people who followed him. Now Christopher understood why it was important for him to remember his Bible.

HOW ABOUT YOU? Do you forget your Bible when you go to church? Do you take it other places? It is part of the armor you need. It's a good idea to have a pocket-size Bible or New Testament. You never know when you may need it! *L.M.W.*

TO MEMORIZE: Put on salvation as your helmet, and take the sword of the Spirit, which is the word of God. *Ephesians 6:17*

"**YUCK!**" Justin complained. "It smells terrible in here! What are you eating?"

"Just this hot dog," Ben answered with a shrug.

Justin looked at Ben's paper plate on the counter. "Onions! You're eating onions. That's what stinks!"

"What's a hot dog without onions?" Ben asked, smiling.

"It'll give you bad breath!" warned Justin.

"So?" laughed Ben. "If you don't like the smell, don't sit so close."

"Good idea!" Justin said, taking a hot dog and moving to the other side of the room. "I'm not spoiling my hot dog with any stinky onions!"

"Onions aren't bad, but your conversation about onions reminds me of what happens when we sin," observed Dad, who had been listening.

"Huh?" Ben mumbled with a full mouth.

Dad explained. "When a person feeds regularly on God's Word and obeys his commands, his life becomes 'sweet-smelling' to the Lord. But when a person refuses to follow God's commands, that person's life 'stinks' of sin."

"But onions taste good," Ben stated.

"Sometimes sin tastes good, too," Dad said, "at least for a while. The person who drinks or uses drugs probably feels important at the time, but often the end results are tragic. No matter how good sin looks, God hates it. To him, it stinks."

"Even worse than onions," agreed Ben. "I can still eat them, can't I?"

"Sure, as long as you brush your teeth," Justin suggested, smiling.

HOW ABOUT YOU? Consider your actions. How do you behave when your mom asks you to do something? Or when your younger brother breaks your things? Or when being honest is going to result in punishment? Or when someone tells a dirty joke? Is your behavior pleasing to God? *B.D.*

TO MEMORIZE: Follow God's example in everything you do, because you are his dear children. *Ephesians 5:1*

WORSE THAN ONIONS

FROM THE BIBLE:

Follow God's example in everything you do, because you are his dear children. Live a life filled with love for others, following the example of Christ, who loved you and gave himself as a sacrifice to take away your sins. And God was pleased, because that sacrifice was like sweet perfume to him.

Let there be no sexual immorality, impurity, or greed among you. Such sins have no place among God's people. Obscene stories, foolish talk, and coarse jokes—these are not for you. Instead, let there be thankfulness to God. You can be sure that no immoral, impure, or greedy person will inherit the Kingdom of Christ and of God. For a greedy person is really an idolater who worships the things of this world. Don't be fooled by those who try to excuse these sins, for the terrible anger of God comes upon all those who disobey him. Don't participate in the things these people do.

EPHESIANS 5:1-7

Choose to please God

24 September

HAPPY TO SERVE

FROM THE BIBLE:

Is there any encouragement from belonging to Christ? Any comfort from his love? Any fellowship together in the Spirit? Are your hearts tender and sympathetic? Then make me truly happy by agreeing wholeheartedly with each other, loving one another, and working together with one heart and purpose.

Don't be selfish; don't live to make a good impression on others. Be humble, thinking of others as better than yourself. Don't think only about your own affairs, but be interested in others, too, and what they are doing.

Your attitude should be the same that Christ Jesus had. Though he was God, he did not demand and cling to his rights as God. He made himself nothing; he took the humble position of a slave and appeared in human form. And in human form he obediently humbled himself even further by dying a criminal's death on a cross.

PHILIPPIANS 2:1-8

Service brings joy

TIM HAD a minibike, a generous allowance, and lots of toys. When he came home from school each day, Mother was there with a listening ear. Tim went to church regularly with his family. He was a member of the Boy Scouts and played baseball. Tim had everything a boy could want, but he wasn't happy.

When Grandmother came to spend a few weeks, she listened and watched. She saw Tim throw a fit because his friends wouldn't do as he ordered. She heard him demand a new baseball mitt because the old one had a little crack in it. She saw him get angry if anyone interrupted him while he was at his computer.

One day Grandmother asked, "Tim, would you take this magazine to Aunt May at the nursing home for me, please?" Tim did, and he came home whistling.

The next day Grandmother said, "Tim, would you please help me fix a birthday dinner for your mother?" Tim did and later went to bed smiling.

Then Grandmother had another idea. "The neighbors are going on vacation," she told Tim. "Why don't you offer to take care of their dog?" So Tim did.

At Grandmother's suggestion, Tim mowed the lawn for Mr. Nelson, who had broken his leg. He also washed the car for his dad.

Soon he moped and griped less and less—and smiled, laughed, and whistled more and more.

"What happened to Tim?" his parents wondered.

Grandmother smiled and said, "Doing things for others makes people happy."

HOW ABOUT YOU? Are you unhappy and wondering why? Maybe you need to start serving others. Giving yourself in service to others is one way to true happiness. *B.J.W.*

TO MEMORIZE: You have been called to live in freedom—not freedom to satisfy your sinful nature, but freedom to serve one another in love. *Galatians 5:13*

THE ANSWER

ERIN and her brother, Greg, had been praying that some of their friends would become Christians. Greg was overjoyed one Sunday when Chuck joined him at church. On the way home, Greg told his family that Chuck had accepted Jesus during Sunday school.

"That's great," Dad said with a smile.

"Wonderful!" added Mother. "Your prayers have been answered."

Erin spoke up. "I pray for Lynn. But God doesn't answer my prayers."

"Don't be discouraged," advised Dad. "Sometimes it takes a long time before a person is ready to accept Christ."

"Yeah," added Greg, "I invited Chuck to Sunday school a whole year ago."

"That's right," agreed Mother. She turned to Erin. "How often have you invited Lynn to go to church with you?"

"I haven't exactly invited her," stammered Erin. "But I let her know I go."

"Have you ever told her about Jesus?" asked Greg.

"Well, not exactly," admitted Erin. "I pray for her, though—a lot!"

"Hmmm," murmured Dad. "Remember the Bible story of Nehemiah and the people of Israel building a wall around Jerusalem? When they heard their enemies were coming, they prayed, and they prepared to fight. It's good that you pray for Lynn, but sometimes the Lord wants to use you to answer your own prayers."

HOW ABOUT YOU? Are you praying about something special—for someone's salvation, for money you need, or perhaps for help with your lessons? Prayer is very important, but don't just pray if there's something you could also do to help. Maybe the Lord wants you to talk to somebody, to mow a lawn, to be a friend, to study hard. Pray, and then with the Lord's help, do all you can to accomplish the task. *H.W.M.*

TO MEMORIZE: We prayed to our God and guarded the city day and night to protect ourselves. *Nehemiah 4:9*

FROM THE BIBLE:

At last the wall was completed to half its original height around the entire city, for the people had worked very hard. But when Sanballat and Tobiah and the Arabs, Ammonites, and Ashdodites heard that the work was going ahead and that the gaps in the wall were being repaired, they became furious. They all made plans to come and fight against Jerusalem and to bring about confusion there. But we prayed to our God and guarded the city day and night to protect ourselves.

Then the people of Judah began to complain that the workers were becoming tired. There was so much rubble to be moved that we could never get it done by ourselves. Meanwhile, our enemies were saying, "Before they know what's happening, we will swoop down on them and kill them and end their work."

The Jews who lived near the enemy came and told us again and again, "They will come from all directions and attack us!" So I placed armed guards behind the lowest parts of the wall in the exposed areas. I stationed the people to stand guard by families, armed with swords, spears, and bows.
NEHEMIAH 4:6-13

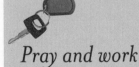

Pray and work

26 September

FORGOTTEN COMBINATION

FROM THE BIBLE:

But very early on Sunday morning the women came to the tomb, taking the spices they had prepared. They found that the stone covering the entrance had been rolled aside. So they went in, but they couldn't find the body of the Lord Jesus. They were puzzled, trying to think what could have happened to it. Suddenly, two men appeared to them, clothed in dazzling robes. The women were terrified and bowed low before them. Then the men asked, "Why are you looking in a tomb for someone who is alive? He isn't here! He has risen from the dead! Don't you remember what he told you back in Galilee, that the Son of Man must be betrayed into the hands of sinful men and be crucified, and that he would rise again the third day?"

Then they remembered that he had said this.

LUKE 24:1-8

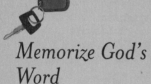

Memorize God's Word

"**OUR NEW LOCKERS** are great, but I can't get mine open." Amber frowned at the paper in her hand.

"Let me help you." Tonya took the paper, spun the dial, and the door opened.

"Thanks. I don't know what I did wrong," said Amber.

"You'd better memorize it," suggested Tonya.

"I don't need to. I'll just keep it here in my notebook." Amber dumped her books in her locker and closed the door.

The next morning Amber's family gathered around the table for breakfast. "What's the Bible verse for today?" Joey asked.

"I wish we didn't have to learn verses," Amber grumbled.

Mother ignored her. "It's Colossians 3:16: 'Let the words of Christ, in all their richness, live in your hearts and make you wise.'"

Joey grinned at Amber as he repeated the verse. He knew she hated memorizing. "Now it's your turn, Amber."

"I don't have time now. I'll learn it this evening." Amber changed the subject. "We have new combination lockers at school."

"What's your combination?" Dad asked.

"I don't remember, but I put it in my notebook." Amber reached for a piece of toast. "All I have to do is—" Her mouth dropped open. "All I have to do is look in my notebook. And my notebook is in my locker!" she wailed. "Oh, why didn't I memorize it like Tonya said? Maybe Tonya remembers it." She dashed for the phone. A few minutes later she returned. "Tonya remembered it. I've written it down, and I'll memorize it today. But right now I need to learn Colossians 3:16. It's not a good idea to postpone memorizing important things."

HOW ABOUT YOU? Do you complain about memorizing God's Word? It will unlock many doors in life for you. It's important to memorize it. *B.J.W.*

TO MEMORIZE: Let the words of Christ, in all their richness, live in your hearts and make you wise. *Colossians 3:16*

"IT LOOKS LIKE these tomatoes will be perfect for the fair next week," noted Mother as she examined Kara's vegetable garden. "You certainly have worked hard, honey."

"It was fun most of the time," said Kara. She moved the hose over to the carrots as she continued to think about the fair. "I wonder how Consuela is doing on the quilt she's making for the sewing exhibit."

"I'd like to see it sometime," said Mother, picking up the weeds she had pulled from the garden. "She's such a sweet girl. Has she enjoyed coming to church with us?"

"I think so," replied Kara, turning to her room with a look of concern. "I wish she'd become a Christian, though! I thought as soon as she heard about Jesus, she'd trust him as her Savior."

"The Bible says that when we tell someone about Jesus, it's like planting a seed," answered Mother. "Remember waiting for these vegetable seeds to grow?"

Kara nodded. "Some of them sprouted almost right away. Others didn't come up for several days."

"You didn't stop taking care of the seeds that didn't come up right away, did you?" asked Mother.

"No," answered Kara. "I don't think I'll ever understand exactly what goes on inside the ground to change small, dry seeds into radishes or cucumbers! But I knew that if I kept on watering the ground where we planted the seeds, eventually they would grow. Some just took longer than others."

"As we keep 'watering' the gospel 'seeds' by continuing to witness to our friends, God will make these 'seeds' grow, too," said Mother.

HOW ABOUT YOU? Have you been discouraged because someone you've been witnessing to hasn't trusted in Jesus as Savior and Lord yet? Don't give up! *D.L.R.*

TO MEMORIZE: My job was to plant the seeds in your hearts, and Apollos watered it, but it was God, not we, who made it grow. *1 Corinthians 3:6*

SEEDS FIRST

FROM THE BIBLE:

Jesus also said, "Here is another illustration of what the Kingdom of God is like: A farmer planted seeds in a field, and then he went on with his other activities. As the days went by, the seeds sprouted and grew without the farmer's help, because the earth produces crops on its own. First a leaf blade pushes through, then the heads of wheat are formed, and finally the grain ripens. And as soon as the grain is ready, the farmer comes and harvests it with a sickle." MARK 4:26-29

Keep witnessing

28 September

BUCKLE UP

FROM THE BIBLE:

The law of the Lord is perfect,
reviving the soul.
The decrees of the Lord are
trustworthy,
making wise the simple.
The commandments of the Lord
are right,
bringing joy to the heart.
The commands of the Lord are
clear,
giving insight to life.
Reverence for the Lord is pure,
lasting forever.
The laws of the Lord are true;
each one is fair.
They are more desirable than
gold,
even the finest gold.
They are sweeter than honey,
even honey dripping from the
comb.
They are a warning to those who
hear them;
there is great reward for those
who obey them.

PSALM 19:7-11

God's law
protects you

BRETT BURST through the kitchen door. "We have a stupid new rule at school. We have to stay in the lunchroom at least fifteen minutes!"

"What's so bad about that?" asked Mom.

"I could eat in five minutes and be out on the playground if it weren't for that rule."

"Exactly," said Mom, "and eating that fast isn't good for your digestion."

"Seems like I should be able to decide how long I need to eat," Brett argued.

"Come on," said Mom, changing the subject. "I have to pick up some shoes from the repair shop. You can ride along. Put Steven in the car seat for me, would you?"

As Brett put Steven in the baby seat, Steven fought him. "Steven doesn't want to be buckled up!" Brett told his mom. "Can't he just sit on my lap?"

"No, he must be buckled up," said Mom, buckling Steven into the seat. "It's the law here."

Later, another car ignored a yield sign and crashed into them. Although the cars were damaged, no one was hurt.

As the family had devotions that evening Dad said, "Good thing Steven was buckled up. You know, we've just been reading in Psalm 19 that there is reward in following God's commandments. I think we learned today that laws are for our good."

"Yes," agreed Mom. "That 'buckle up' law was made to protect lives, just like God gives us rules for our protection. Sometimes we feel God's laws strap us down, but they really keep us safe from harm."

HOW ABOUT YOU? Do you complain about the rules that God gives in his Word? Do you think they are too strict or tie you down? Remember God made you, and he knows what will keep you safe and happy. *J.L.H.*

TO MEMORIZE: But still, the law itself is holy and right and good. *Romans 7:12*

THE HOME RUN THAT WASN'T

DAVID SAT on the bench and waited for his turn at bat. His team was losing by a couple of runs, and it was the last inning. *I know*, David thought. *I'll pray that I get a home run.* So he whispered a prayer.

Finally it was David's turn. Confidently, he picked up his bat and walked to home plate. The pitcher threw the ball twice, and David missed—twice. Again, the pitcher threw the ball. This time David hit it, and it slowly rolled toward the third baseman. An easy out to end the game!

David walked over to meet his parents. How could he have missed? "I don't understand it," David said as they drove home. "I prayed that the Lord would give me a home run, but he didn't."

"Hmmm," Dad said. "The Gray boys were on the other team, and they're Christians, too. I wonder what they were praying!" David smiled. That was true. "Seriously, David," his father went on, "when we pray we need to be willing to accept the answer that God gives."

"But doesn't God care about the ball game?" David asked.

"Yes, God does care. He cares that you have a good attitude and that you do your best."

Next game, David decided he would ask the Lord to help him be a good sport whether he hit a home run or not.

HOW ABOUT YOU? Do you pray that you will hit a home run or that you will receive an *A* on a test (when you haven't even studied), or that you will get a new bike? You can ask God for anything, but you need to accept his answer. The Lord knows what is best for you. *L.M.W.*

TO MEMORIZE: We can be confident that he will listen to us whenever we ask him for anything in line with his will. *1 John 5:14*

FROM THE BIBLE:

And the Holy Spirit helps us in our distress. For we don't even know what we should pray for, nor how we should pray. But the Holy Spirit prays for us with groanings that cannot be expressed in words. And the Father who knows all hearts knows what the Spirit is saying, for the Spirit pleads for us believers in harmony with God's own will. And we know that God causes everything to work together for the good of those who love God and are called according to his purpose for them. For God knew his people in advance, and he chose them to become like his Son, so that his Son would be the firstborn, with many brothers and sisters. And having chosen them, he called them to come to him. And he gave them right standing with himself, and he promised them his glory.
ROMANS 8:26-30

Pray for God's will

30 September

CURE FOR LONELINESS

FROM THE BIBLE:

Love each other with genuine affection, and take delight in honoring each other. Never be lazy in your work, but serve the Lord enthusiastically.

Be glad for all God is planning for you. Be patient in trouble, and always be prayerful. When God's children are in need, be the one to help them out. And get into the habit of inviting guests home for dinner or, if they need lodging, for the night.

If people persecute you because you are a Christian, don't curse them; pray that God will bless them. When others are happy, be happy with them. If they are sad, share their sorrow. Live in harmony with each other. Don't try to act important, but enjoy the company of ordinary people. And don't think you know it all!

Never pay back evil for evil to anyone. Do things in such a way that everyone can see you are honorable. Do your part to live in peace with everyone, as much as possible.

ROMANS 12:10-18

Be friendly

"I'VE BEEN HERE a week, Mom, and I still don't know anyone," Paula complained. "The kids have their own friends. They don't need me."

"If you want to have friends, you must be friendly," Mom reminded her.

"Don't start preaching at me, Mom." Paula sobbed.

"Honey, I understand. I'm having that problem, too," Mom sighed. "We're the newcomers in town, and so we think others should make us welcome. But let's forget that. Let's go out of our way to be friendly," Mom suggested. "It will be fun. Every evening we can report our successes."

"Yeah—or our failures." Paula was doubtful, but she decided to give it a try.

The next evening Paula reported, "I loaned a pencil to Pat, the girl who sits next to me. She lives only a couple blocks away, and she's coming over tonight." Mom told how she had caught and returned the neighbor's runaway puppy. As a result, she had been invited for lunch on Saturday.

The next day Paula helped another girl with spelling. While she was doing that, a boy she had seen at church came over and asked a couple of questions. Paula's eyes sparkled as she told her mom about it later.

Mom had called the church and volunteered to "give a hand" wherever needed. She was invited to the Ladies' Bible Study the following evening.

After a week of going out of their way to be friendly, Mom and Paula were amazed at the results. "People here aren't like they were when we first came," Paula remarked. "They've changed." Then Paula realized who had really changed.

HOW ABOUT YOU? Do you think others are unfriendly? Maybe it's just that you are unapproachable. Smile and speak to others. Look for ways to help them. They need your friendship as much as you need theirs. *B.J.W.*

TO MEMORIZE: The heartfelt counsel of a friend is as sweet as perfume and incense. *Proverbs 27:9*

"THERE WAS a new girl in our class today," Lisa Maria announced at dinner. "I don't like her, though. She's a snob. She sits just like this." Lisa Maria turned her nose up, pushed her shoulders back, and sat very erect. "When Debi asked her if she wanted to jump rope with us, she said, 'No, thank you,' so prissy."

"Hmmm," murmured Mom as she passed the chicken. "Aren't you judging a little prematurely?"

Dad peered at the breaded chicken. "What is this?"

"A new recipe," said Mom.

"I don't want any," stated five-year-old Matteo. "I don't like it."

Lisa Maria laughed. "You've never tasted it," she said.

"I want you to try it," said Dad. "Take two bites, Matteo."

Matteo looked at his mom. "You heard your dad," she said. "Two bites." Matteo put a tiny bit on his spoon.

Matteo grimaced as he put the spoon to his mouth. He chewed and swallowed. "It *is* good!" he exclaimed.

Mom looked at Maria. "You are acting about the new girl just like Matteo did about the chicken. You need to give her a fair chance."

The next day Maria came in from school. "Guess what, Mom? I do like Latrice," she said. "She sits like she does because she wears a back brace. That's why she couldn't jump rope. She just didn't want to tell anybody."

Mom smiled. "I'm glad you gave her a fair chance," she said.

HOW ABOUT YOU? Are you afraid to try new things or meet new people? If you judge them on the basis of first impressions, you may miss some wonderful experiences. Determine now to give everyone you meet a fair chance to be your friend. *B.J.W.*

TO MEMORIZE: Stop judging others, and you will not be judged. Stop criticizing others, or it will all come back on you. If you forgive others, you will be forgiven. *Luke 6:37*

A FAIR CHANCE

FROM THE BIBLE:

"Stop judging others, and you will not be judged. For others will treat you as you treat them. Whatever measure you use in judging others, it will be used to measure how you are judged. And why worry about a speck in your friend's eye when you have a log in your own? How can you think of saying, 'Let me help you get rid of that speck in your eye,' when you can't see past the log in your own eye? Hypocrite! First get rid of the log from your own eye; then perhaps you will see well enough to deal with the speck in your friend's eye." MATTHEW 7:1-5

Give people a fair chance

2 October

THE COPYBOOK

FROM THE BIBLE:

For God is pleased with you when, for the sake of your conscience, you patiently endure unfair treatment. . . .
*   This suffering is all part of what God has called you to. Christ, who suffered for you, is your example. Follow in his steps. He never sinned, and he never deceived anyone. He did not retaliate when he was insulted. When he suffered, he did not threaten to get even. He left his case in the hands of God, who always judges fairly. He personally carried away our sins in his own body on the cross so we can be dead to sin and live for what is right. You have been healed by his wounds! Once you were wandering like lost sheep. But now you have turned to your Shepherd, the Guardian of your souls.*
1 PETER 2:19, 21-25

Copy Christ

AMANDA BOWED her head and closed her eyes to pray, just as she always did before eating lunch. When she opened her eyes, her lunch had disappeared. Every eye was on her, and the children were snickering.

"Who has my lunch?" asked Amanda. Everyone burst into laughter.

"Ask God where your lunch is, Miss Christian," said Brett.

Just then the teacher stood behind Amanda. "The person who has Amanda's lunch had better hand it over right now," she said. Brett pulled her lunch out from his lap under the table. Then the teacher dismissed him from the lunchroom. But for the rest of the day, all the children made fun of Amanda and called her "Miss Christian."

When Amanda arrived home, she told her mother about her lunch. "I was so embarrassed, Mom," she said. "I don't know how to act when the kids do that."

"Follow Jesus' example," advised Mom. "How did he act when he was made fun of?"

"Well, he didn't fight or talk back," replied Amanda.

Her mother nodded. "Do you remember the handwriting workbooks you used when you were learning to write? There were letters and words printed on them. They were your example. You copied them the best you could."

"And now Jesus is my example," said Amanda thoughtfully. "But I can't be perfect, as he is."

"No. But look at one of your old workbooks," Mom suggested. "Your writing is much more like the letters now than it was when you started. And as you follow Jesus' example, you'll become more and more like him."

HOW ABOUT YOU? Has anyone made fun of you for being a Christian? How did you react? Next time ask yourself, "How would Jesus act if he were in my place?" *M.R.P.*

TO MEMORIZE: This suffering is all part of what God has called you to. Christ, who suffered for you, is your example. Follow in his steps. *1 Peter 2:21*

BRAD HAD BEEN praying that his friend Ted would become a Christian. Now Ted had agreed to go with the church youth group to an amusement park, and Brad was delighted. Perhaps if Ted enjoyed himself, he'd come to church.

The group had a great time at the park. On the way home they discussed their favorite rides.

"I'd never go on that roller coaster," Jenny said.

"Why not?" Ted asked. "You don't know what you're missing."

"I'm missing a scary ride," said Jenny. "What if something would break, and the whole thing fell off the track?"

"Aw, ya gotta have more faith, Jenny," Ted teased. "The roller coaster is safe. Isn't that right, Mr. Benson?" He turned to the youth leader.

"It's safe but not foolproof," Mr. Benson said. "You know, it doesn't matter how much faith a person has; what matters is where that faith is placed."

"What do you mean?" Ted asked.

"Well, these rides are tested for safety, and people put their faith in them every day," Mr. Benson replied. "Yet occasionally one breaks down and someone gets hurt. No matter how much faith they had in the ride, it didn't help. They put their faith in the wrong thing that time."

"Yeah, I guess so," agreed Ted. "So there's nothing and nobody you can really trust, is there? Everything and everybody fails some time or other."

"All except Jesus," Mr. Benson added. "He will never fail you."

Ted looked doubtful, but he was listening. "Tell me more, Mr. Benson."

HOW ABOUT YOU? Where have you put your faith? In good works? In baptism? In church attendance? Only by placing your faith in Jesus Christ will you receive salvation. *J.L.H.*

TO MEMORIZE: We have believed in Christ Jesus, that we might be accepted by God because of our faith in Christ—and not because we have obeyed the law. For no one will ever be saved by obeying the law. *Galatians 2:16*

THE ROLLER COASTER

FROM THE BIBLE:

Abraham was, humanly speaking, the founder of our Jewish nation. What were his experiences concerning this question of being saved by faith? Was it because of his good deeds that God accepted him? If so, he would have had something to boast about. But from God's point of view Abraham had no basis at all for pride. For the Scriptures tell us, "Abraham believed God, so God declared him to be righteous."

When people work, their wages are not a gift. Workers earn what they receive. But people are declared righteous because of their faith, not because of their work.

King David spoke of this, describing the happiness of an undeserving sinner who is declared to be righteous:

"Oh, what joy for those whose disobedience is forgiven, whose sins are put out of sight."
ROMANS 4:1-7

Put faith in Christ

4 October

MATT GETS MAD

FROM THE BIBLE:

"Don't sin by letting anger gain control over you." Don't let the sun go down while you are still angry, for anger gives a mighty foothold to the Devil.

If you are a thief, stop stealing. Begin using your hands for honest work, and then give generously to others in need. Don't use foul or abusive language. Let everything you say be good and helpful, so that your words will be an encouragement to those who hear them.

And do not bring sorrow to God's Holy Spirit by the way you live. Remember, he is the one who has identified you as his own, guaranteeing that you will be saved on the day of redemption.

Get rid of all bitterness, rage, anger, harsh words, and slander, as well as all types of malicious behavior. Instead, be kind to each other, tenderhearted, forgiving one another, just as God through Christ has forgiven you.

EPHESIANS 4:26-32

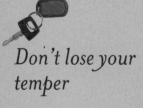

Don't lose your temper

BANG! went Matt's ankle against the dining room chair. *Crash!* went the chair as Matt kicked it over with his bare foot. "Ouch!" said Matt as he sat down to rub his sore ankle and toes.

"Dumb chair!" Matt shouted.

Just then Dad walked in. He set the chair up, then asked, "Who is it that you're mad at, Son?"

"I'm mad at the chair," replied Matt.

"I'm sorry you got hurt," Dad said. "But you're not really angry with the chair, are you? It's only a thing."

Matt pouted. "No, I guess not," he admitted. "But what's the big deal? Who cares if I yelled at the chair? It can't hear me."

"No, the chair can't, but God can," Dad replied. "Do you think he's pleased when you shout and kick the furniture whenever things don't go your way?" Matt hung his head. This was not the first time Dad had spoken to him about his anger. "You're responsible for your actions and for the words that come out of your mouth," continued Dad. "Displaying your temper won't make your anger go away. It only makes you, and everyone around you, more tense."

"Well, what should I do?" grumbled Matt.

"Deal with your anger God's way," Dad replied. "Pray that God will help you express it in a constructive way. Do what you can to solve the problem—like walking more slowly through the dining room."

"I'll try, Dad," said Matt. He turned toward the chair and smiled. "Sorry, chair. I'll think twice before I yell at you again."

HOW ABOUT YOU? Do you get angry when things don't turn out your way? Do you control your feelings of anger, or do you let them control you? Ask God to help you deal with your anger in appropriate ways. *S.L.K.*

TO MEMORIZE: It is better to be patient than powerful; it is better to have self-control than to conquer a city. *Proverbs 16:32*

"LOOK AT all the people!" exclaimed Andy.

"Yes," replied Dad. "This parade had better be good, or I'll wish I'd stayed home." He inched forward with the traffic. "A lot of cars are turning here," he added. "Maybe they know of a place to park." He made a right turn, following the car in front of him. But instead of finding a place to park, they found themselves on a ramp leading to a freeway. "Oh no," groaned Dad. "I never saw the sign for the interstate!" He scowled at the car ahead of him. "Thanks a lot, mister," he growled.

Mom laughed. "Oh, so it's his fault?"

"What about the car behind us?" asked Andy. "It followed, too. Is that your fault?"

"No," Dad said. "They should have watched where they were going."

"Sounds like someone else I know," Mom observed, looking at Andy.

Andy blushed. Just the night before he had excused his rowdy behavior at a hay ride by saying that everybody else was doing the same thing. He was only following the example of the older boys. At the same time he had insisted that he wasn't responsible for the way his little sister had copied his actions.

"At times we all tend to forget that God has given each of us a brain. He intends for us to use it instead of blindly following the crowd," said Dad. "On the other hand, he expects us to live in such a way that others may follow us."

HOW ABOUT YOU? God gave you a brain. Are you using it to think for yourself? Are you being a good example to others? Others are watching you. Lead them in the right way. *H.W.M.*

TO MEMORIZE: Don't let anyone think less of you because you are young. Be an example to all believers in what you teach, in the way you live, in your love, your faith, and your purity. *1 Timothy 4:12*

FOLLOWERS

FROM THE BIBLE:

And now, dear brothers and sisters, we give you this command with the authority of our Lord Jesus Christ: Stay away from any Christian who lives in idleness and doesn't follow the tradition of hard work we gave you. For you know that you ought to follow our example. We were never lazy when we were with you. We never accepted food from anyone without paying for it. We worked hard day and night so that we would not be a burden to any of you. It wasn't that we didn't have the right to ask you to feed us, but we wanted to give you an example to follow. . . .

Yet we hear that some of you are living idle lives, refusing to work and wasting time meddling in other people's business. In the name of the Lord Jesus Christ, we appeal to such people—no, we command them: Settle down and get to work. Earn your own living. And I say to the rest of you, dear brothers and sisters, never get tired of doing good.
2 THESSALONIANS 3:6-13

Follow Jesus, not the crowd

6 October

JOEY TAKES A STAND

FROM THE BIBLE:

*Some sat in darkness and
  deepest gloom,
  miserable prisoners in chains.
They rebelled against the words
  of God,
  scorning the counsel of the
  Most High.
That is why he broke them with
  hard labor;
  they fell, and no one helped
  them rise again.
"Lord, help!" they cried in their
  trouble,
  and he saved them from their
  distress.
He led them from the darkness
  and deepest gloom;
  he snapped their chains.
Let them praise the Lord for his
  great love
  and for all his wonderful
  deeds to them.
For he broke down their prison
  gates of bronze;
  he cut apart their bars of
  iron. . . .
"Lord, help!" they cried in their
  trouble,
  and he saved them from their
  distress.
He spoke, and they were
  healed . . .
Let them praise the Lord for his
  great love
  and for all his wonderful
  deeds to them.*
PSALM 107:10-16, 19-21

*Don't develop
bad habits*

"GUYS, LOOK what I found!" Joe picked up a short piece of chain from the sidewalk. "Bet you can't break it."

Bill and Adam examined it. "Bet you can't either," said Bill.

Another friend, Carl, didn't even look at the chain. "Come on, Joe, you're the smallest," he said. "Squeeze through this fence and get us some strawberries." Through the crack in the fence Joe could see Mr. Wilken's strawberry patch. "Go on," Carl urged.

Joe didn't want to go into Mr. Wilken's yard. But what would his friends think of him if he didn't go along with their plans? Would they make fun of him if he told them why he didn't want to do it? The chain he still held in his sweaty hand gave him an idea. Joe took a deep breath. "I'm a Christian," he said, "and I'm afraid of getting into bad habits—they're hard to break. We wouldn't be able to break the links in this chain no matter how hard we tried. And if we take stuff from people's gardens, we may get into the habit of stealing—a habit we might not be able to break."

"What's a few berries?" snorted Carl. "Come on, guys, let's leave this baby and see what old Mrs. Smith has in her garden."

Bill and Adam hesitated. Then Bill said, "We'll walk home with Joe." Joe smiled as they started off. He felt almost as big as the other boys.

HOW ABOUT YOU? Will you say no when someone suggests stealing, telling a lie, or making fun of another person? Ask God to help you "take a stand." Ask him to keep you from developing a sinful habit you may not be able to break. Maybe you already have a bad habit. God can give the strength you need to overcome it. *B.K.*

TO MEMORIZE: "Lord, help!" they cried in their trouble, and he saved them from their distress. *Psalm 107:13*

FROM THE TEXT:

*I prayed to the Lord, and he answered me,
freeing me from all my fears.
Those who look to him for help
will be radiant with joy;
no shadow of shame will
darken their faces.
I cried out to the Lord in my
suffering, and he heard me.
He set me free from all my
fears.
For the angel of the Lord guards
all who fear him,
and he rescues them.*

*Taste and see that the Lord is
good.
Oh, the joys of those who trust
in him!*

PSALM 34:4-8

Admit your need

EIGHT-YEAR-OLD HEIDI loved to crawl up on her great-grandpa Berger's lap and listen to stories about his days in Germany. Today he asked Heidi a question. "What did you learn in Sunday school, little one?"

"We're studying Matthew 5," Heidi answered. "We're learning some of the verses. My teacher calls them the Beatitudes."

"Oh, good!" he responded. "Have you learned any yet?"

"The first one is 'Blessed are the poor in spirit, for theirs is the kingdom of heaven.' But I didn't know you had to be poor to be a Christian," replied Heidi.

"You don't!" said Great-Grandpa. "You have to be poor *in spirit!* To be poor in spirit means you realize that you have a need! It reminds me of when I decided to leave Germany and come to America!

"In a sense, I had to be 'poor in spirit' to want to leave Germany. In other words, I had to see my own need. Now that step wasn't hard. Hitler had taken over the government, and it was plain to me that he was opposed to God and Christianity. Hitler's army was building up, and I knew if I didn't leave soon, I'd be forced to serve in it. Oh, I could have been proud and said, 'Hitler will never get me!' But that would have been foolish!"

"I get it," Heidi responded. "You had to see your need to get out of Germany so you could be free from Hitler."

"That's right," Great-Grandpa said with a smile. "And being poor in spirit means to see we need Jesus to free us from sin."

HOW ABOUT YOU? Do you realize that you need to be freed from sin? Do you see that you cannot free yourself? Because all are sinners, all need Jesus to take away that sin. *R.E.P.*

TO MEMORIZE: Blessed are the poor in spirit, for theirs is the kingdom of heaven. *Matthew 5:3* (NIV)

8 October

THE BEATITUDES (2)
THOSE WHO MOURN

FROM THE BIBLE:

"Hear me, Lord, and have mercy on me.
Help me, O Lord."

You have turned my mourning into joyful dancing.
You have taken away my clothes of mourning and clothed me with joy,
that I might sing praises to you and not be silent.
O Lord my God, I will give you thanks forever!

PSALM 30:10-12

Mourn over sin

"WHAT'S THE SECOND Beatitude, Heidi?" asked Great-Grandpa Berger.

"Blessed are those who mourn, for they will be comforted," said Heidi. "Does that mean it's good if somebody dies or something terrible happens to make us cry?"

Great-Grandpa smiled. "No," he replied. "I think the mourning referred to here means mourning over *sin*. To mourn is to have a deep concern to the point of action. Let's go back to our comparison of getting out of Germany, shall we? There were some people who saw the need to leave, but didn't try to get away. I did try. I ran from the Nazi soldiers in the night."

"That sounds scary," exclaimed Heidi.

"It was," he agreed. "You see, I cared so much that I would have done almost anything to get out of Germany. Sad to say, some people did not care enough about leaving."

Heidi was thinking deeply. "I know some kids who are like that about heaven! They know they need Jesus, but they don't seem to care enough to do anything about it. I guess they don't mourn—right?"

"That's right." The old man nodded. "And it could be that some of them just aren't ready to accept Jesus yet. However, if they don't mourn, they will never know the comfort salvation brings!" He paused a moment, then added, "There are also Christians who know of sin in their lives. They, too, need to mourn, or repent, and then they'll find the comfort of forgiveness that God has promised."

HOW ABOUT YOU? Do you mourn about the sin in your life? This means to care enough to want to change! Is your problem disobedience, pride, carelessness, or gossiping? Ask God to forgive you and to help you change. He will forgive and comfort you. *R.E.P.*

TO MEMORIZE: Blessed are those who mourn, for they will be comforted. *Matthew 5:4* (NIV)

"GREAT-GRANDPA, I learned another Beatitude," said Heidi. "It's 'Blessed are the meek, for they will inherit the earth.' Everyone at school calls one of the girls 'Meek Mindy' because she's a sissy! Why would Jesus give blessings to sissies?"

"Heidi," he replied, "*meek* doesn't mean 'weak.' A person can be strong and still be meek. I was meek when my ship from Germany landed in New York."

"I remember you told me you cried tears of joy when you saw the Statue of Liberty," Heidi said. "But that didn't mean you were meek! You were just happy to be in a free land!"

"Heidi, I really was meek." Great-Grandpa paused, then explained, "To be meek means you're willing to surrender your will to another and do what *he* wants. I was willing to do whatever was necessary to stay in this wonderful country! Later I gave up all allegiance to Germany and became a citizen here."

"Oh, I see. It's like you were switching your loyalty from Germany to America," said Heidi.

"That's right," said Great-Grandpa. "And when I became a Christian, I switched my loyalty to from Satan to Jesus. I surrendered my will to Jesus and promised to do what he wants. That is being meek."

"I love Jesus, too, but sometimes I still want my own way," Heidi confessed.

"Ah yes," said Great-Grandpa. "We all struggle with that. After I became an American citizen, I sometimes missed Germany. So I had to remind myself that I was an American. That's the way it is after we've given Jesus our loyalty. We must daily surrender to what he wants."

HOW ABOUT YOU? Do you love Jesus enough to give your loyalty to him and do whatever he wants you to do? That's one thing Jesus means by being meek! *R.E.P.*

TO MEMORIZE: Blessed are the meek, for they will inherit the earth. *Matthew 5:5* (NIV)

THE BEATITUDES (3)
THE MEEK

FROM THE BIBLE:

Give yourselves completely to God since you have been given new life. And use your whole body as a tool to do what is right for the glory of God. Sin is no longer your master, for you are no longer subject to the law, which enslaves you to sin. Instead, you are free by God's grace.

So since God's grace has set us free from the law, does this mean we can go on sinning? Of course not! Don't you realize that whatever you choose to obey becomes your master? You can choose sin, which leads to death, or you can choose to obey God and receive his approval. Thank God! Once you were slaves of sin, but now you have obeyed with all your heart the new teaching God has given you. Now you are free from sin, your old master, and you have become slaves to your new master, righteousness.

I speak this way, using the illustration of slaves and masters, because it is easy to understand. Before, you let yourselves be slaves of impurity and lawlessness. Now you must choose to be slaves of righteousness so that you will become holy.
ROMANS 6:13-19

Surrender your will

10 October

THOSE WHO HUNGER AND THIRST

FROM THE BIBLE:

They replied, "You must show us a miraculous sign if you want us to believe in you. What will you do for us? After all, our ancestors ate manna while they journeyed through the wilderness! As the Scriptures say, 'Moses gave them bread from heaven to eat.'"

Jesus said, "I assure you, Moses didn't give them bread from heaven. My Father did. And now he offers you the true bread from heaven. The true bread of God is the one who comes down from heaven and gives life to the world."

"Sir," they said, "give us that bread every day of our lives."

Jesus replied, "I am the bread of life. No one who comes to me will ever be hungry again. Those who believe in me will never thirst."

JOHN 6:30-35

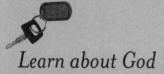

Learn about God

DISCUSSING THE BEATITUDES with her great-grandpa really helped Heidi understand them. One day she announced, "Guess what? My verse today is about hungering and thirsting after righteousness, and I think I understand it already. I think it means to want to know all about God. But can you tell me a story about it, anyway?"

"Let's see," said Great-Grandpa. "Well, after I got to this country and decided to become an American citizen, I wanted to learn all I could about America!"

"You had to learn to speak English, right?" asked Heidi.

"Yes, and that was hard! But I wasn't content just to learn the language. I wanted to learn all there was to know about the country, too," he explained. "As soon as I could speak well enough, I went to high school at night and studied American history. Some boys in the class made fun of the way I talked, but even that didn't discourage me. I was so hungry to learn about my new country."

"Great-Grandpa, have you ever been disappointed in America?" Heidi asked.

"Sometimes, but I still believe this country is the greatest in the world," he said. "The more I learn about it, the more I love it! It's like that with God, too. I have hungered and thirsted for his righteousness for many years. And the more I study about God and learn about him, the more I love him."

HOW ABOUT YOU? Do you hunger and thirst after righteousness? God wants you to know all you can about him. He has revealed himself in his Word. Study it; learn to know God better; to know him is to love him. He wants you to show his righteousness in your life. *R.E.P.*

TO MEMORIZE: Blessed are those who hunger and thirst for righteousness, for they will be filled. *Matthew 5:6* (NIV)

"BLESSED are the merciful, for they will be shown mercy," read Heidi as she studied a new verse. "Great-Grandpa, what is mercy?"

"Let's look in the dictionary," he suggested.

Heidi ran to get the dictionary, and together they found the word. "To show mercy means to forgive or to show compassion," said Heidi.

"Yes," said Great-Grandpa, "and God shows the most wonderful mercy of all. He's willing to forgive our sins instead of giving us the punishment we deserve. He wants us to follow his example and show mercy to others."

"Did anyone show you mercy when you came to America?" asked Heidi.

"Indeed, they did," said Great-Grandpa. "When I applied for work at the grocery store near our apartment, the man I talked with showed me a list of boys who were ahead of me in line for a job. As I turned to leave, the owner of the store came in. He must have seen the discouraged look on my face, for he stopped me and asked a lot of questions. The next day—"

"You got the job," interrupted Heidi.

"Right," said Great-Grandpa, "only it wasn't *the* job. It was a job the owner made up for me."

"Did you work there long?" Heidi asked.

"Quite a while," answered Great-Grandpa, "and the owner showed mercy more than once. I made many mistakes, but he never fired me."

HOW ABOUT YOU? Do you show mercy and forgiveness or do you try to get back at people who hurt you? If you see someone struggling with schoolwork or needing a friend to get a job done, do you show mercy and help? If you show mercy to others, God says you will also have mercy shown to you. *R.E.P.*

TO MEMORIZE: Blessed are the merciful, for they will be shown mercy. *Matthew 5:7* (NIV)

THE BEATITUDES (5)
THE MERCIFUL

FROM THE BIBLE:

"Give what you have to anyone who asks you for it; and when things are taken away from you, don't try to get them back. Do for others as you would like them to do for you.

"Do you think you deserve credit merely for loving those who love you? Even the sinners do that! And if you do good only to those who do good to you, is that so wonderful? Even sinners do that much! And if you lend money only to those who can repay you, what good is that? Even sinners will lend to their own kind for a full return.

"Love your enemies! Do good to them! Lend to them! And don't be concerned that they might not repay. Then your reward from heaven will be very great, and you will truly be acting as children of the Most High, for he is kind to the unthankful and to those who are wicked. You must be compassionate, just as your Father is compassionate."
LUKE 6:30-36

Show compassion

12 October

THE BEATITUDES (6)
THE PURE IN HEART

FROM THE BIBLE:

As they were walking along someone said to Jesus, "I will follow you no matter where you go."

But Jesus replied, "Foxes have dens to live in, and birds have nests, but I, the Son of Man, have no home of my own, not even a place to lay my head."

He said to another person, "Come, be my disciple."

The man agreed, but he said, "Lord, first let me return home and bury my father."

Jesus replied, "Let those who are spiritually dead care for their own dead. Your duty is to go and preach the coming of the Kingdom of God."

Another said, "Yes, Lord, I will follow you, but first let me say good-bye to my family."

But Jesus told him, "Anyone who puts a hand to the plow and then looks back is not fit for the Kingdom of God."

LUKE 9:57-62

Look to Jesus

"**GREAT-GRANDPA,** this Beatitude says the pure in heart will see God. What does it mean to be pure in heart?" asked Heidi.

Great-Grandpa looked thoughtful. "To be pure in heart means to have the love of God so fill us that there is no room for sin," he answered. "We must center our thoughts and actions on him, Heidi. We must not be double-minded."

"Double-minded?" Heidi asked, puzzled.

Great-Grandpa nodded. "Peter, a friend who came from Germany with me, was double-minded. All he ever seemed to talk about was our homeland. He never did learn to like America because he always compared it to Germany. The mountains here were not as pretty, the cities were not as clean—on and on he would go. Often I tried to tell him to get his eyes off Germany so he could see America, but he never did. He died a very bitter man. He wanted to be a citizen here, but he wanted to hold on to the old country, too."

"But you loved Germany, too, didn't you, Great-Grandpa?" the little girl asked. "How did you forget about Germany?"

"I chose to!" said her great-grandpa emphatically. "Although I did love Germany, I decided that America was my new home and I would not look back!"

"That reminds me of a chorus we sing in Sunday school," Heidi said, and she began to sing. "'I have decided to follow Jesus—no turning back, no turning back.'"

"That's exactly it, Heidi," agreed Great-Grandpa. "If you are single-minded, with your thoughts centered only on Jesus, you will be pure in heart."

HOW ABOUT YOU? How can you keep your life pure? By filling your mind and heart with good things. Be careful about what you watch, listen to, and read. *R.E.P.*

TO MEMORIZE: Blessed are the pure in heart, for they will see God. *Matthew 5:8* (NIV)

13 October

"GUESS WHAT?" said Heidi as she took her Bible from the shelf and went to sit beside Great-Grandpa. "Nancy and Rachel are friends, but they were mad at each other all day. For art class today we had to draw one of our favorite things, and they both drew rainbows. Nancy got mad—she said Rachel copied her. Then Rachel got mad—she said it was her idea in the first place." Heidi sighed as she opened her Bible to Matthew 5, ready to learn a new Beatitude.

"And what did you do?" asked Great-Grandpa.

"Nancy and Rachel both wanted to play with me at recess," answered Heidi. "I told them I would if they'd quit fighting. But they both stayed mad, so I played with Alyssa. Mom said it was OK to invite Nancy and Rachel to stay over-night on Saturday and go to church with us. We'll have fun, and maybe they'll like church and even learn to stop fighting."

"Good!" Great-Grandpa said, smiling. "Maybe they'll accept Jesus as their Savior as a re-sult of your invitation. Now, Heidi, let's get to work on that next Beatitude. I think you'll find it interesting because it applies to you."

Heidi looked at her open Bible. "Blessed are the peacemakers," she read slowly. A big smile lighted her face as she looked up at her great-grandpa. "Was I a peacemaker today?"

"I'd say so," he said. "You not only tried to bring peace between your friends, but you also did something to introduce them to Jesus."

HOW ABOUT YOU? When friends quarrel, do you listen to all the details and add a few comments of your own? Or do you try to bring peace between them? Helping people to get along is great. Also be sure to point your friends to Jesus, who gives peace that lasts. *R.E.P.*

TO MEMORIZE: Blessed are the peacemakers, for they will be called sons of God. *Matthew 5:9*

THE BEATITUDES (7)

THE PEACEMAKERS

FROM THE BIBLE:

For the Kingdom of God is not a matter of what we eat or drink, but of living a life of goodness and peace and joy in the Holy Spirit. If you serve Christ with this attitude, you will please God. And other people will approve of you, too. So then, let us aim for harmony in the church and try to build each other up.
ROMANS 14:17-19

Be a peacemaker

14 October

NUTCRACKER

FROM THE BIBLE:

He was despised and rejected—a man of sorrows, acquainted with bitterest grief. We turned our backs on him and looked the other way when he went by. He was despised, and we did not care.

Yet it was our weaknesses he carried; it was our sorrows that weighed him down. And we thought his troubles were a punishment from God for his own sins! But he was wounded and crushed for our sins. He was beaten that we might have peace. He was whipped, and we were healed! All of us have strayed away like sheep. We have left God's paths to follow our own. Yet the Lord laid on him the guilt and sins of us all.

He was oppressed and treated harshly, yet he never said a word. He was led as a lamb to the slaughter. And as a sheep is silent before the shearers, he did not open his mouth. From prison and trial they led him away to his death. But who among the people realized that he was dying for their sins—that he was suffering their punishment?
ISAIAH 53:3-8

Jesus took your punishment

"MOM, in Bible club today we learned that some people will miss heaven when they die." Mia was troubled as she reached for a pecan and placed it between the jaws of the nutcracker. "It scared me. What if I miss heaven?" She squeezed the ends of the nutcracker, but the nut slid out.

"You asked Jesus to be your Savior," Mom reminded her.

Mia nodded. "Yes, but I still worry about it sometimes," she confessed. She squeezed the nutcracker again, this time holding the pecan with her fingers. "Ouch!" she wailed as the nut again slipped away and the nutcracker closed on her finger. Tears filled Mia's eyes, and she put her finger to her mouth. "I'm keeping my fingers out of there," she declared.

"I'm not scared to put my finger in the nutcracker," boasted her brother Anthony. "Look!" He put his finger in the nutcracker, but before squeezing down on it, he placed a stick beside his finger. When he squeezed down, the stick held the jaws of the nutcracker open, preventing them from touching his finger. "See," he laughed. "It doesn't even hurt."

Mia made a face at her brother, but Mom said, "You've given us a good illustration, Anthony." She turned to Mia. "You see, honey, Anthony's finger deserves to be hurt since he's being so cocky, right? But the stick is taking the punishment his finger deserves. Jesus took all our punishment. So you don't need to worry about missing heaven."

HOW ABOUT YOU? If you have accepted Jesus as your Savior, you don't need to worry about missing heaven. If you haven't trusted in Jesus to forgive your sins and give you eternal life, talk to a trusted Christian friend or adult about how you can do that. *H.W.M.*

TO MEMORIZE: He was wounded and crushed for our sins. He was beaten that we might have peace. He was whipped, and we were healed! *Isaiah 53:5*

JEREMY WAS GOING on his first airplane ride, but he felt as dark and gloomy as the day around him. His parents were getting a divorce, and he was going to live with his grandparents for a while.

As they boarded the plane, Grandmother asked, "Scared?"

Inside, he said, *Yes, I'm scared! I'm scared of everything.* But he didn't say anything. As the plane sped down the runway, huge drops of rain splattered the windows. *Just like tears,* Jeremy thought. When the plane lifted from the earth, Jeremy felt his heart fly up into his throat.

Grandmother reached for his hand. "Don't be afraid, Jeremy. God will take care of us." Jeremy knew Grandmother was talking about more than the plane ride. He wanted to believe her, but he couldn't. "We'll go right through these dark clouds, Jeremy," she explained. "For a few minutes, we'll be in a thick fog. But just wait until we get above the clouds."

Suddenly they were in the clouds. The interior of the plane dimmed. Then, just as suddenly, a brilliant light came streaming through the windows. Jeremy squinted as he pressed his nose to the pane. "It's beautiful," he gasped.

Grandmother nodded. "Yes. Above the clouds, the sun is shining." Jeremy turn and look at his grandmother, who smiled gently. "Our family is going through a storm, Jeremy. Things look pretty dark. But God is in control. One day soon we'll break through the clouds, and life will be filled with beauty and happiness again."

HOW ABOUT YOU? Are you going through a storm in your life? Are you afraid of the future? Remember, even when you can't see the sun, it is shining. Even when you can't feel God, he is near. *B.J.W.*

TO MEMORIZE: See, God has come to save me. I will trust in him and not be afraid. The Lord God is my strength and my song; he has become my salvation. *Isaiah 12:2*

ABOVE THE CLOUDS

FROM THE BIBLE:

God is our refuge and strength, always ready to help in times of trouble.
So we will not fear, even if earthquakes come and the mountains crumble into the sea.
Let the oceans roar and foam. Let the mountains tremble as the waters surge!

A river brings joy to the city of our God, the sacred home of the Most High.
God himself lives in that city; it cannot be destroyed. God will protect it at the break of day. . . .

The Lord Almighty is here among us; the God of Israel is our fortress.

Come, see the glorious works of the Lord . . . He breaks the bow and snaps the spear in two; he burns the shields with fire.

"Be silent, and know that I am God! I will be honored by every nation. I will be honored throughout the world."
PSALM 46:1-5, 7-10

Don't fear— trust God

16 October

WHO'S RIGHT?

FROM THE BIBLE:

"I am praying not only for these disciples but also for all who will ever believe in me because of their testimony. My prayer for all of them is that they will be one, just as you and I are one, Father—that just as you are in me and I am in you, so they will be in us, and the world will believe you sent me.

"I have given them the glory you gave me, so that they may be one, as we are—I in them and you in me, all being perfected into one. Then the world will know that you sent me and will understand that you love them as much as you love me."
JOHN 17:20-23

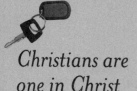

Christians are one in Christ

"DAD, WE DO things differently at our church than they do at Clint's church," Kenny said one day. "We had an argument about it. He said his church is right, and I said my church is right. Whose way is really right?"

Before Dad could attempt an answer, Kenny's little sister and brother came into the kitchen, carrying a keyboard. They set it on the table. "We want to play a song Daddy taught us," announced Cathy, and they proceeded to do so. At first, they carefully pressed the keys, and Kenny thought he recognized "Twinkle, Twinkle, Little Star." But then it became obvious that they were playing two different songs.

"That sounds awful," declared Kenny. "I think you need a new teacher."

"Wait a minute!" protested Dad. "The teacher's not the problem. They're not following my instructions."

When the children were gone, Dad grinned at Kenny. "That sure wasn't the way I intended their music to turn out," he said. "But what just happened reminds me of what happens to Christians. Can't you almost hear God saying, 'That wasn't what I intended,' as he watches us? Jesus intended for his followers to all 'play the same song.' He wanted all Christians to work together."

"But which song should we be playing? Whose way is right—Clint's church or our church?" Kenny asked again.

"God's way is right," Dad answered. "And any church that believes and teaches the Bible as the true Word of God is a good one."

HOW ABOUT YOU? Do you ever argue with people from other churches? If you attend churches that agree with the Bible, then quit arguing. Jesus wants for us to work together. *K.R.A.*

TO MEMORIZE: We are all one body, we have the same Spirit, and we have all been called to the same glorious future. There is only one Lord, one faith, one baptism, and there is only one God and Father. *Ephesians 4:4-6*

RYAN PLAYED the first page of his music. Then he thought about how the guys had snickered when his mother had called him to come in and practice. He wondered if any kids would make fun of him when he played in church Sunday. He sat at the piano staring at his music.

"Why did you quit?" Mom called.

"I don't want to play in church," Ryan said. "Piano is for girls."

"That isn't true," protested Mom, placing her hands on Ryan's shoulders. "God gave you an exceptional talent, and he wants you to use it."

"I can't," Ryan answered. Mom didn't insist that Ryan keep on practicing his special number, but she asked him to think and pray about it.

That night Ryan worked on a gift for his sister, Abby. It was a wristband like those many kids at school were wearing.

"Thank you," Abby said when she opened it on her birthday.

A few days later Ryan complained, "Abby, you never wear the wristband I made for you."

"Well, it's not really like the ones the other girls are wearing," Abby explained.

After Abby left the room, Mom looked at Ryan. "It hurts when you take special care with a gift for someone but that person doesn't use it," she observed. Ryan nodded sadly.

As Ryan considered his mother's words, someone knocked on the door. Ryan answered it. "Want to play ball?" invited Adam, who lived next door.

Ryan hesitated. "I'm going to practice piano first," he said.

HOW ABOUT YOU? Do you have a gift you aren't using? Maybe you're embarrassed to use it. Maybe you don't want to make the effort to develop it. God gave you gifts. He is pleased when you use them. *K.R.A.*

TO MEMORIZE: Once you were not a people; now you are the people of God. Once you received none of God's mercy; now you have received his mercy. *1 Peter 2:10*

UNUSED GIFTS

FROM THE BIBLE:

God has given each of us the ability to do certain things well. So if God has given you the ability to prophesy, speak out when you have faith that God is speaking through you. If your gift is that of serving others, serve them well. If you are a teacher, do a good job of teaching. If your gift is to encourage others, do it! If you have money, share it generously. If God has given you leadership ability, take the responsibility seriously. And if you have a gift for showing kindness to others, do it gladly.

Don't just pretend that you love others. Really love them. Hate what is wrong. Stand on the side of the good. Love each other with genuine affection, and take delight in honoring each other. Never be lazy in your work, but serve the Lord enthusiastically.

Be glad for all God is planning for you. Be patient in trouble, and always be prayerful.
ROMANS 12:6-12

Use your gifts

18 October

A PRICE TO PAY

FROM THE BIBLE:

Have mercy on me, O God,
  because of your unfailing love.
Because of your great
    compassion,
  blot out the stain of my sins.
Wash me clean from my guilt.
  Purify me from my sin.

For I recognize my shameful
    deeds—
  they haunt me day and night.
Against you, and you alone, have
    I sinned;
  I have done what is evil in
    your sight.
You will be proved right in what
    you say,
  and your judgment against me
    is just. . . .

Oh, give me back my joy again;
  you have broken me—
  now let me rejoice.

PSALM 51:1-4, 8

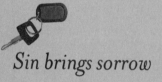

Sin brings sorrow

THIS IS SO BORING, Brenda thought as she trudged along behind her mother at the grocery store. "May I walk around while you wait in line for lunch meat?" she asked. Mother hesitated, but then agreed.

I'll see how many times I can circle up this aisle and down the next one before the woman at the deli calls the number on Mom's ticket, thought Brenda. "Oh no!" Brenda murmured as she finished her fourth round. "Mom's up next!" She increased her speed and raced around the bend. Her arm swung out, and *splat!* Two large jars of applesauce smashed to the floor.

Mother came quickly. She then led Brenda to the service desk. Brenda could hardly hold back tears as she told the assistant manager what happened. "Someone will clean up the mess right away," the woman assured her.

"And Brenda will pay for the jars," said Mother. As they walked to the checkout, Mother added, "I'll pay for the broken jars now, but you'll have to pay me back with your own money."

"But I don't have much money. And I'm sorry for what I did," whined Brenda.

Mother wrapped her arm around Brenda. "I know you're sorry, but the jars are still broken, and you still need to pay for them." She paused. "That's the way it is with sin," she added. "When we're sorry and confess our sin, God forgives us. But sin still has consequences."

HOW ABOUT YOU? Do you find yourself doing things you know you shouldn't do? When that happens, tell God what you've done and ask him to forgive you. But don't forget that even though you've been forgiven, there may still be a price to pay. *N.E.K.*

TO MEMORIZE: Keep me from deliberate sins! Don't let them control me. Then I will be free of guilt and innocent of great sin. *Psalm 19:13*

AS THE NELSON family drove to Granddad's farm, Dillon and his little sister argued about everything. Dad finally said, "If I hear one more word, you'll go straight to bed when we get there."

The first person Dillon saw at the farm was his cousin Paul. As the boys sat in the branches of the old oak tree a little later, Dillon said, "Granddad's birthday is almost as exciting as Christmas."

"Sure is," Paul agreed. "It's the only time, other than Christmas, when the entire family gets together."

Dillon nodded and said, "There's Uncle Ryan and Aunt Linda. But I don't see Uncle Joe and his family."

"They won't be here," said Paul. "Uncle Joe and his sister, Aunt Linda, are mad at each other."

"Time to sing 'Happy Birthday' and open the presents," called Dillon's mother. The boys scrambled to join the crowd on the big front porch.

After Granddad had opened the gifts and blown out all sixty-two candles, he stood up. Everyone was quiet. "Thank you for coming. And thank you for the nice gifts," he said. "But my birthday wish is that my children will love one another. Can a father be happy if his children love him but not each other?"

For several minutes no one spoke. Then Aunt Linda stood. "I'm going to call Joe and apologize. There's still time for him to come."

On the way home that night there was no fussing, and everyone agreed with Dillon when he said, "I'm glad Granddad's wish came true."

HOW ABOUT YOU? Do you love your parents? Then love your brothers and sisters. Do you love your Father in heaven? Then love his children—other Christians. *B.J.W.*

TO MEMORIZE: God himself has commanded that we must love not only him but our Christian brothers and sisters, too. *1 John 4:21*

A FATHER'S WISH

FROM THE BIBLE:

If someone says, "I love God," but hates a Christian brother or sister, that person is a liar; for if we don't love people we can see, how can we love God, whom we have not seen? And God himself has commanded that we must love not only him but our Christian brothers and sisters, too.
1 JOHN 4:20-21

Love one another

20 October

DANGER! CONTAGIOUS!

FROM THE BIBLE:

I only wish that those trouble-makers who want to mutilate you by circumcision would mutilate themselves.

For you have been called to live in freedom—not freedom to satisfy your sinful nature, but freedom to serve one another in love. For the whole law can be summed up in this one command: "Love your neighbor as yourself." But if instead of showing love among yourselves you are always biting and devouring one another, watch out! Beware of destroying one another.

So I advise you to live according to your new life in the Holy Spirit. Then you won't be doing what your sinful nature craves. GALATIANS 5:12-16

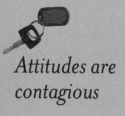

Attitudes are contagious

SERENA DROPPED her books on the end table. As she slumped down on the sofa with a sigh, Mother looked up. "What's wrong?"

"I had a terrible day," Serena whined. "Mrs. Carson doesn't like me. And Brenda got the solo part I wanted. And—"

"My, my!" Mother interrupted. "What is this, a pity party for Serena?"

Serena jumped up. "I knew you wouldn't understand. No one understands!"

Soon Mother heard angry words coming from her daughter's bedroom. The door opened, and Shandra came out, tears streaming down her cheeks. "Mother, make Serena leave me alone."

Mother frowned. "Girls," she began, but was interrupted by the telephone. A few minutes later she returned to the girls. "Amy is in the hospital."

"What's wrong?" Serena asked. "Can we go see her?" Amy was her cousin.

"No, but we must pray for her," answered Mother. "The doctor thinks she has meningitis. They have her in isolation because it's contagious. Only her parents are allowed in the room, and they must wear sterile masks and gowns." She looked at Serena as she continued. "Diseases are not the only things that are contagious. Attitudes are, too."

"Attitudes?" Serena asked.

"Yes, attitudes," Mother repeated. "When you came home, Serena, you had a bad attitude. It wasn't five minutes before that attitude had infected everyone in this family. If your attitude doesn't improve, I may have to put you in isolation—alone in your room for a while."

Serena looked down. She knew what Mother said was true. "I'll try to do better," she promised.

HOW ABOUT YOU? Do you have a bad attitude that has infected your family? Or does someone else in your family have a bad attitude? Counteract it with a smile or a kind word. Don't catch it, resist it. *B.J.W.*

TO MEMORIZE: Create in me a clean heart, O God. Renew a right spirit within me. *Psalm 51:10*

"HI, JAMAL." Ken nervously greeted his friend. He felt guilty whenever he saw Jamal. That's because Ken had accepted Jesus as Savior, but he'd never told Jamal. He wanted to—it was just that he was afraid Jamal would laugh.

"What did you get for your birthday yesterday?" Jamal asked.

Ken lifted his left hand and displayed a new baseball mitt. "How about this?"

Jamal smiled. "I could use one like that, too."

"My grandparents gave it to me," said Ken, "and this shirt is from my brother. My folks gave me a skateboard."

"Wow!" Jamal let out a long whistle. "I could use all those things."

"Well, you can't have 'em," laughed Ken. Suddenly he thought about the gift of eternal life he had received a month ago. That was a gift Jamal could have. He took a deep breath. "A month ago I got . . ." He stopped, afraid to finish. "I got a gift from God. I got my sins forgiven."

"Huh?" Jamal asked. "What on earth are you talking about?"

"I got the gift of eternal life, and if you want to, you can have that gift, too." Ken finished in a hurry. "I gotta go. 'Bye." He hurried down the street as Jamal stared after him. Ken was sure he hadn't done that very well. At the same time, he knew that at least it was a start. *I'm going to invite Jamal to church this week,* he decided. *I'll ask him tomorrow.*

HOW ABOUT YOU? Do you talk with your friends about anything and everything except the Lord? Are you afraid to witness to them? If you're a Christian, God has given you a wonderful gift, and they can have it, too. Tell them about it. *H.W.M.*

TO MEMORIZE: The Lord stood with me and gave me strength, that I might preach the Good News in all its fullness for all the Gentiles to hear. *2 Timothy 4:17*

GIFT TO SHARE

FROM THE BIBLE:

For the grace of God has been revealed, bringing salvation to all people. And we are instructed to turn from godless living and sinful pleasures. We should live in this evil world with self-control, right conduct, and devotion to God, while we look forward to that wonderful event when the glory of our great God and Savior, Jesus Christ, will be revealed. He gave his life to free us from every kind of sin, to cleanse us, and to make us his very own people, totally committed to doing what is right. You must teach these things and encourage your people to do them, correcting them when necessary. You have the authority to do this, so don't let anyone ignore you or disregard what you say.
TITUS 2:11-15

Witness for Jesus

22 October

CARELESS WORDS

We may know that these things make no difference, but we cannot just go ahead and do them to please ourselves. We must be considerate of the doubts and fears of those who think these things are wrong. We should please others. If we do what helps them, we will build them up in the Lord. For even Christ didn't please himself. As the Scriptures say, "Those who insult you are also insulting me." Such things were written in the Scriptures long ago to teach us. They give us hope and encouragement as we wait patiently for God's promises.

May God, who gives this patience and encouragement, help you live in complete harmony with each other—each with the attitude of Christ Jesus toward the other. Then all of you can join together with one voice, giving praise and glory to God, the Father of our Lord Jesus Christ.

So accept each other just as Christ has accepted you; then God will be glorified.

ROMANS 15:1-7

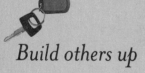

Build others up

THE STUDENTS at Lakeview Christian Academy looked at each other in disbelief. They had just learned that one of the students had attempted to commit suicide the night before!

"I didn't think that Christian kids ever got that depressed," was Susan's reaction. "Eric knows God loves him. What made him do a thing like that?"

"It's not that simple," responded Kevin. "You have lots of friends." Kevin looked down at his desk as he continued. "I remember when we'd make fun of Eric in gym class. I never thought he took it seriously."

"But he's so smart," emphasized Brad. "Didn't he know that we all wish we could be as smart as he is?"

"We don't always seem to recognize our good qualities," pointed out Mrs. Kelley. "Sometimes our weaknesses seem to get all of the attention." She picked up her Bible. "As Christians, we have the assurance of knowing that God loves us and accepts us just the way we are," she continued. "We also have the responsibility to love others the way God loves us. Listen to Ephesians 4:29: 'Don't use foul or abusive language. Let everything you say be good and helpful, so that your words will be an encouragement to those who hear them.'"

Kevin looked up soberly. "I sure can't say that all of the things I said to Eric were encouraging. I'd like another chance to really be his friend."

Mrs. Kelley smiled understandingly. "Let's pray you'll get that chance."

HOW ABOUT YOU? Are you careful about the things you say to others? Sometimes careless words may seem harmless or funny, yet they may hurt others. God wants your life to reflect his love to others. Show God's love through your kind words. *D.L.R.*

TO MEMORIZE: Do not use foul or abusive language. Let everything you say be good and helpful, so that your words will be an encouragement to those who hear them. *Ephesians 4:29*

HEART, NOT HAIR

CHRISTY WAS EXCITED about the birthday present Aunt Peggy had sent. It was a beauty gift certificate so Christy could have her hair cut and permed. It sounded like fun. But that was before Christy knew what the outcome would be!

"Mother, I can't go to school like this!" she wailed after getting the perm. "All the kids will laugh at me!"

"Why should they laugh at you?" teased Christy's brother Joe. "You do look a little like a poodle, but other than that, you look OK."

"Mother," Christy wailed again.

"That's enough, Joe," said Mother. "Christy feels bad enough without you kidding her. Actually, Christy, your hair looks nice. You just aren't used to it."

Christy looked in the mirror and scowled. She knew her mother would make her go to school tomorrow, and it was just too horrible to think about.

Mother looked at the grouchy expression on Christy's face. "Honey, remember that the Lord said it's not the outward appearance that counts, but what is on the inside. The fanciest hairstyle in the world isn't going to make up for a bad attitude and a grumpy look. On the other hand, if you'll be as kind and cheerful as you usually are, your hair will not be important."

Christy knew it was true. Her heart, not her hair, was what mattered. She would ask the Lord to help her give more attention to her inside appearance than to her outside appearance!

HOW ABOUT YOU? Do you care more about the latest hairstyles and fashions than you do about your inner beauty? Yes, it is important to be neat and clean and attractive, but God is more concerned about your heart than he is about your curly hair or new shirt! *L.M.W.*

TO MEMORIZE: People judge by outward appearance, but the Lord looks at a person's thoughts and intentions. *1 Samuel 16:7*

FROM THE BIBLE:

The Lord said to Samuel, ". . . Now fill your horn with olive oil and go to Bethlehem. Find a man named Jesse who lives there, for I have selected one of his sons to be my new king."

. . . I will show you which of his sons to anoint for me."

So Samuel did as the Lord instructed him. When he arrived at Bethlehem, the leaders of the town became afraid. "What's wrong?" they asked. "Do you come in peace?"

"Yes," Samuel replied. "I have come to sacrifice to the Lord. Purify yourselves and come with me to the sacrifice." Then Samuel performed the purification rite for Jesse and his sons and invited them, too.

When they arrived, Samuel took one look at Eliab and thought, "Surely this is the Lord's anointed!" But the Lord said to Samuel, "Don't judge by his appearance or height, for I have rejected him. The Lord doesn't make decisions the way you do! People judge by outward appearance, but the Lord looks at a person's thoughts and intentions."

1 SAMUEL 16:1, 3-7

Inside beauty counts

24 October

WHAT A MESS

FROM THE BIBLE:

*Show me the path where I
    should walk, O Lord;
    point out the right road for
    me to follow.
Lead me by your truth and
    teach me,
    for you are the God who
    saves me.
All day long I put my hope
    in you.*

*Remember, O Lord, your
    unfailing love and
    compassion,
    which you have shown from
    long ages past.
Forgive the rebellious sins of my
    youth;
    look instead through the eyes
    of your unfailing love,
    for you are merciful, O Lord.*

*The Lord is good and does what
    is right;
    he shows the proper path to
    those who go astray.
He leads the humble in what
    is right,
    teaching them his way.
The Lord leads with unfailing
    love and faithfulness
    all those who keep his
    covenant and obey his
    decrees.*

PSALM 25:4-10

*Follow God's
direction*

"I DON'T KNOW how I'm going to get everything done today," Mom said at the breakfast table. "I have several errands to run this morning, and somehow I'll have to find time to bake a birthday cake for Thomas."

"I can make Thomas's cake!" said Julie. "You've told me before that it's easy. Besides, Thomas is only two, and he'll eat anything!"

"Well, OK," agreed Mom hesitantly. "The mix and the frosting are in the cupboard. Be sure to read the directions." Julie started the cake soon after Mom left. She read the directions and was about to pour the mix into the bowl when the phone rang. It was her friend Stephanie.

After Julie hung up the phone, she went about making her cake, remembering what she had read earlier. At least, she thought she remembered. But when the cake was done, it didn't look quite right. When it cooled, she frosted it carefully, but it was no use. The cake was dry, and Thomas, who was known to eat many strange things, wouldn't touch it.

"What a mess!" Mom exclaimed. "Didn't you follow the directions?"

"I read them, but then Stephanie called, and I didn't look at them again," explained Julie. "I thought I was doing it the right way."

"That's the way many people live their lives," observed Dad. "They hear a sermon or read the Bible occasionally, and then they think they know all they need to know. But they forget what they heard. God gives directions, but some people ignore them, and their lives turn into big messes—just like that cake! Paying attention to directions is an important principle to learn."

HOW ABOUT YOU? Do you follow the directions the Lord gives in his Word? It's important to spend time each day in God's Word so you will know what those directions are. *L.M.W.*

TO MEMORIZE: Seek his will in all you do, and he will direct your paths. *Proverbs 3:6*

IN THE DITCH

WHEN RYAN'S MOTHER picked him up at school, he would not look at her. She had come for him because he and some other boys had been caught smoking, and he was too ashamed to say anything.

Rain pelted the windshield as they rode in silence. When they started up the hill toward their house, the car slipped and skidded. The street was being repaired, and it was a mess! "Be careful, Mom," Ryan exclaimed, "or we'll wind up in the di—"

At that exact moment the car skidded again and slid into a ditch! Mom shifted gears and rocked the car, but it was hopeless. "Nothing to do but walk home and call a tow truck," she said with a sigh. So they trudged up the muddy hill.

When Dad got home that evening, Ryan did his best to keep Dad's attention on the car. But the dreaded moment arrived when Dad asked what had happened at school. "I didn't want to smoke," Ryan said. "It's just that I couldn't let the other guys think I was a baby."

Dad frowned. "I thought you just told me you didn't like being on a slippery road," he said.

Ryan looked at him, puzzled. "What's that got to do with it?"

"Well," said Dad, "when you spend a lot of time with the wrong crowd, it's like being on a slippery road. And today you slid quite badly at school. You're a Christian, yet you've chosen friends who pressure you into doing things that you know are wrong. With the right kind of friends, life would be a lot smoother."

FROM THE BIBLE:

I am constantly aware of your unfailing love,
and I have lived according to your truth.

I do not spend time with liars or go along with hypocrites.
I hate the gatherings of those who do evil,
and I refuse to join in with the wicked. . . .

Don't let me suffer the fate of sinners.
Don't condemn me along with murderers.
Their hands are dirty with wicked schemes,
and they constantly take bribes.

But I am not like that; I do what is right.
So in your mercy, save me.
I have taken a stand,
and I will publicly praise the Lord.
PSALM 26:3-12

Choose the right friends

HOW ABOUT YOU? Are you associating with the wrong crowd? If so, you could be headed for a lot of trouble. Choose close friends who will be a help, not a hindrance, in living for Christ. *B.J.W.*

TO MEMORIZE: I hate the gatherings of those who do evil, and I refuse to join in with the wicked. *Psalm 26:5*

MACK, THE MONKEY

FROM THE BIBLE:

As the Scriptures say,

*"No one is good—
  not even one.
No one has real understanding;
  no one is seeking God.
All have turned away from God;
  all have gone wrong.
No one does good,
  not even one."* . . .

For no one can ever be made right in God's sight by doing what his law commands. For the more we know God's law, the clearer it becomes that we aren't obeying it.

But now God has shown us a different way of being right in his sight—not by obeying the law but by the way promised in the Scriptures long ago. We are made right in God's sight when we trust in Jesus Christ to take away our sins. And we all can be saved in this same way, no matter who we are or what we have done.

ROMANS 3:10-12, 20-22

You need Jesus

PATTI LISTENED eagerly as Mr. Dan began to talk. "I'm glad to be here," said Mr. Dan, "and now I'd like to ask my friend Mack to join me on the platform." For the first time, Patti noticed a brown hairy puppet hanging by its arms from the piano. "Come here, Mack," called Mr. Dan, but Mack didn't move. "Well, I guess Mack is going to be uncooperative," said Mr. Dan. "I think I know what I need to do. I need to snap my fingers, let go, and Mack will spring to life." When Mr. Dan did this, Mack just ended up in a pile on the floor. The children laughed.

Finally Mr. Dan looked at the boys and girls in the front row, where Patti was sitting. "What does Mack need?" he asked them.

Patti's hand shot into the air. "You have to put your hand inside and make him move," she said when Mr. Dan pointed to her.

"You are absolutely right," agreed Mr. Dan. "I could talk to Mack from now until it's time to go home, and he still wouldn't move. Without me, Mack can do nothing." He paused for a moment. "Did you know that the same is true of people? Jesus said to his disciples, 'Apart from me you can do nothing.' We can't get to heaven by ourselves. And we can't live the Christian life by ourselves."

Patti listened carefully to the rest of Mr. Dan's presentation. *I need to find out more about becoming a Christian,* she thought.

HOW ABOUT YOU? Do you know Jesus as your Savior? If not, talk to a trusted Christian friend or adult to find out more. *C.V.M.*

TO MEMORIZE: Yes, I am the vine; you are the branches. Those who remain in me, and I in them, will produce much fruit. For apart from me you can do nothing. *John 15:5*

THE RIGHT SOUNDS

AS JEFF TURNED the dial of his new radio, he counted the stations it could pick up. "Dad, how can I pick up so many stations?" Jeff asked. "I counted thirty."

"Sound waves from all those stations are right here in this room. "Your radio is a 'receiver,' so it picks out the various sound waves and makes it possible for you to hear them."

"The man who invented the radio must have been pretty smart," Jeff said.

"Yes," agreed Dad, "but you know, the one who made your ear to hear the sounds is even smarter."

"You mean God, don't you, Dad?" Jeff asked.

"That's right," said Dad. "Your ear can pick up the softest voice, but it can handle very loud noises as well. In a noisy room your ear can pick out a certain voice you want to hear while tuning out other noises. And since you have two ears, you can tell what direction a sound is coming from and also about how far away it is!"

"So the ear is like a radio," said Jeff. "They both receive sound waves."

Dad nodded. "And even as your radio can be tuned to receive all kinds of sounds from different stations, so your ears can receive all sorts of different sounds. Do you always treat your ears to the right kind of sounds?"

Jeff looked down, remembering jokes he had listened to with his friends.

"Jeff," continued Dad, "be careful not to drown out God's voice with the sounds of the world."

FROM THE BIBLE:

*How can a young person stay
    pure?
    By obeying your word and
    following its rules.
I have tried my best to find
    you—
    don't let me wander from your
    commands.
I have hidden your word in my
    heart,
    that I might not sin against
    you.
Blessed are you, O Lord;
    teach me your principles.
I have recited aloud
    all the laws you have given us.
I have rejoiced in your decrees
    as much as in riches.
I will study your commandments
    and reflect on your ways.
I will delight in your principles
    and not forget your word.*
PSALM 119:9-16

Listen to God

HOW ABOUT YOU? Are you using your ears to listen to the right kinds of things? Does the music you choose honor God? Do the jokes, stories, and programs you listen to please him? Thank Godfor your hearing, and promise him you'll use your ears to listen to good things! *C.V.M.*

TO MEMORIZE: Ears to hear and eyes to see—both are gifts from the Lord. *Proverbs 20:12*

28 October

IN THE DARK

FROM THE BIBLE:

"For God so loved the world that he gave his only Son, so that everyone who believes in him will not perish but have eternal life. God did not send his Son into the world to condemn it, but to save it.

"There is no judgment awaiting those who trust him. But those who do not trust him have already been judged for not believing in the only Son of God. Their judgment is based on this fact: The light from heaven came into the world, but they loved the darkness more than the light, for their actions were evil. They hate the light because they want to sin in the darkness. They stay away from the light for fear their sins will be exposed and they will be punished. But those who do what is right come to the light gladly, so everyone can see that they are doing what God wants."

JOHN 3:16-21

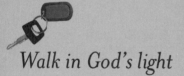

Walk in God's light

THE YOUTH GROUP arrived at church for a lock-in just before dark. They could see a storm brewing, so they quickly gathered in the fellowship hall for supper. Suddenly the storm struck! A power line was hit by lightning, and the church was enveloped in darkness.

"Just sit tight until the storm passes," Mr. Crane advised.

At first the children huddled where they were, but soon they got accustomed to the darkness. They ignored the leader's warning and started moving around. "Kelley, there's a mouse on your leg," Michael called.

"Quit teasing me," Kelley laughed. Just then Vanessa brushed a paper plate against Kelley's leg. Kelley screamed loudly and jumped back, bruising her knee on a table.

"Enough of that!" Mr. Crane said. "Sit down before someone gets hurt."

Reluctantly the group settled down. "This would be a good time for devotions," suggested Mr. Crane. "Think about how scared you were tonight when the lights first went out. But then you got used to the darkness. Soon you liked scaring each other, not thinking about the danger." Mr. Crane paused, then added, "As Christians, Christ is our light. If we walk in his light, we are safe, but if we wander off in the darkness of sin, there's danger. We may get used to the darkness and like it because it hides what we are doing. We don't realize the danger until we get hurt. Let's ask God to help us walk in his light."

HOW ABOUT YOU? If everything you did were brought into the light, how would you feel? Pleased or embarrassed? Christ is your light. Don't stumble in the darkness of sin when you can walk in the light. *J.L.H.*

TO MEMORIZE: If we are living in the light of God's presence, just as Christ is, then we have fellowship with each other, and the blood of Jesus, his Son, cleanses us from every sin. *1 John 1:7*

TIFFANY WAS EXCITED. It was Sunday morning, the day she and her two friends, Sara and Julia, were to sing in church. They had practiced their song several times the past two weeks. Now Tiffany stood at the church door waiting for her friends. She hoped this would be the first of many times that the three girls would sing. She had also prayed that her aunt, who was not a Christian, would come to church that day.

"Are you nervous?" Julia asked as she ran up the church steps. "I could hardly sleep last night."

"Kind of," Tiffany agreed, "but Mom prayed with me, and we asked the Lord to help all three of us to do our best."

Just then Sara's brother, Dave, walked by. "Where's Sara?" both girls asked.

"Oh, didn't you know?" Dave seemed surprised. "Our neighbors called last night, and Sara went to the new science museum with them."

Tiffany and Julia looked at each other! How could Sara do this? They hurried to find the pianist, who assured them that they should sing anyway.

Well, the girls did sing, and they did a good job. Even Tiffany's aunt said so. But Tiffany and Julia both knew that it would have sounded better if Sara had been there.

"This won't be the last time someone lets you down," Tiffany's mother told her. "Some people don't have a sense of responsibility. But God expects faithfulness from his children."

"I guess there are times when we all let other people down," Tiffany said. "But I'll remember this experience whenever I'm tempted to back out of something at the last minute."

HOW ABOUT YOU? Do you take your responsibilities seriously? Remember, faithfulness is important in being a witness for Christ. *L.M.W.*

TO MEMORIZE: Now, a person who is put in charge as a manager must be faithful. *1 Corinthians 4:2*

A TWO-MEMBER TRIO

FROM THE BIBLE:

"The Kingdom of Heaven can be illustrated by the story of a man going on a trip. He called together his servants and gave them money to invest for him while he was gone. He gave five bags of gold to one, two bags of gold to another, and one bag of gold to the last—dividing it in proportion to their abilities—and then left on his trip. The servant who received the five bags of gold began immediately to invest the money and soon doubled it. The servant with two bags of gold also went right to work and doubled the money. But the servant who received the one bag of gold dug a hole in the ground and hid the master's money for safekeeping.

"After a long time their master returned from his trip. . . .The servant to whom he had entrusted the five bags of gold said, 'Sir, . . . I have doubled the amount.' The master was full of praise. 'Well done, my good and faithful servant. You have been faithful in handling this small amount, so now I will give you many more responsibilities. Let's celebrate together!'"

MATTHEW 25:14-21

Take responsibility seriously

WHOSE SIDE?

FROM THE BIBLE:

Don't just pretend that you love others. Really love them. Hate what is wrong. Stand on the side of the good. Love each other with genuine affection, and take delight in honoring each other. Never be lazy in your work, but serve the Lord enthusiastically.

Be glad for all God is planning for you. Be patient in trouble, and always be prayerful. When God's children are in need, be the one to help them out. And get into the habit of inviting guests home for dinner or, if they need lodging, for the night.

If people persecute you because you are a Christian, don't curse them; pray that God will bless them. When others are happy, be happy with them. If they are sad, share their sorrow. Live in harmony with each other. Don't try to act important, but enjoy the company of ordinary people. And don't think you know it all!

Never pay back evil for evil to anyone. Do things in such a way that everyone can see you are honorable.

ROMANS 12:9-17

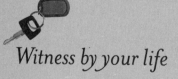

Witness by your life

"COME WITH ME Sunday. You'll hear more about Jesus." Dana's voice reached the kitchen, where her mother was working. Dana was talking on the phone with her new friend, Janice.

A little later Mother heard Dana and her brother talking as they played checkers. "Got caught peeking during a spelling test, didn't you?" asked Lee.

"Yeah," Dana admitted.

"Did you get a new kid in your class?" asked Lee.

Dana nodded. "Janice—she's a mess. Lives in that old place on Cherry Street." Dana looked up as her mother and her little sister, Nicole, came into the room.

"Which side are you on, Dana?" asked Nicole.

"The red," teased Dana as she moved a black checker.

"Are not," protested Nicole. "You moved a black one."

Dana laughed, but Mother didn't. "It's easy for Nicole to see which side you're really on," commented Mother. "I expect it's easy for Janice, too."

Dana stared at her mother. "What's that supposed to mean?"

"I heard your conversations with Janice and Lee," replied Mother. I was pleased that you were witnessing to Janice, but I doubt if she was impressed. Nicole didn't believe what you said when she saw the move you made just now. Janice won't believe your witness as she observes the wrong 'moves' you make at school."

"But I really am on God's side," Dana insisted. "I'm a Christian, and I want Janice to become one."

"Then she needs to see that Jesus makes a difference in your life," said Mother. "I'm afraid she couldn't tell that today."

HOW ABOUT YOU? When people see your actions, will they believe you're on the Lord's side? Actions speak louder than words. Let your actions say that you belong to Jesus. *H.W.M.*

TO MEMORIZE: Live in harmony with each other. Don't try to act important, but enjoy the company of ordinary people. And don't think you know it all! *Romans 12:16*

"WHERE ARE WE GOING, Dad?" asked Kevin.

"Wait and see," Dad said with a wink.

"'Madame Margarite, Spiritualist, Palm Reader,'" Sarah read as they drove past a sign on Main Street. "'Have Your Fortune Told Here.'"

"I'd like to know the future," Laura said. "Will Brad ask me to the party?"

"How much does it cost to have your fortune told, Dad?" Kevin asked.

"I don't know," Dad answered, "and I will never find out. God's Word warns against going to fortune-tellers."

"Why?" Sarah, Laura, and Kevin spoke in unison.

"It would be fun to know the future," Kevin argued.

"Suppose we had known last Christmas that Grandma Snider was going to have a stroke the next week. Would we have enjoyed Christmas?" Dad asked.

"No, I guess not," answered Laura.

"And fortune-tellers aren't always right. One young man was told that he would inherit a lot of money," Dad said. "He began buying expensive things on his credit cards. At the end of the year, instead of inheriting a lot of money, he was deeply in debt! People who base their life on false predictions are living dangerously," Dad warned.

Laura said, "I learned a psalm that said going to a fortune-teller is 'following the advice of the wicked.'"

The kids cheered as Dad drove into the parking lot of a new ice-cream shop. "The future is God's secret. He wants us to trust him, just as you trusted me today. God wisely hides sorrows from us, and he provides many surprises."

HOW ABOUT YOU? Do you worry about the future? Worry is a sin because it means you are not trusting God. When you are tempted to worry, remember that God loves you and he has everything under control. *B.J.W.*

TO MEMORIZE: Oh, the joys of those who do not follow the advice of the wicked, or stand around with sinners, or join in with scoffers. *Psalm 1:1*

WAIT AND SEE

FROM THE BIBLE:

"Look at the birds. They don't need to plant or harvest or put food in barns because your heavenly Father feeds them. And you are far more valuable to him than they are. Can all your worries add a single moment to your life? Of course not.

"And why worry about your clothes? Look at the lilies and how they grow. They don't work or make their clothing, yet Solomon in all his glory was not dressed as beautifully as they are. And if God cares so wonderfully for flowers that are here today and gone tomorrow, won't he more surely care for you? You have so little faith!

"So don't worry about having enough food or drink or clothing. Why be like the pagans who are so deeply concerned about these things? Your heavenly Father already knows all your needs, and he will give you all you need from day to day if you live for him and make the Kingdom of God your primary concern.

"So don't worry about tomorrow, for tomorrow will bring its own worries. Today's trouble is enough for today."
MATTHEW 6:26-34

Trust God for the future

1 November

THE TEN COMMANDMENTS (1)

WHAT'S IMPORTANT

FROM THE BIBLE:

Jesus replied, "'You must love the Lord your God with all your heart, all your soul, and all your mind.' This is the first and greatest commandment."
MATTHEW 22:37-38

Put God first

WHEN ANDY became a Christian, he was thrilled with his new faith! He spent a lot of time reading the Bible and praying. He especially prayed that his parents would become Christians. He also learned Scripture.

But all that was before Andy began his new hobby. Now all he could think about was BMX bike racing.

Andy's father was glad that Andy's new hobby took up so much time. "I was beginning to worry about you, Andy. You were taking this church stuff too seriously. But now that you're into BMX racing, you act normal."

Andy felt guilty. Was he allowing racing to get too important in his life?

On Sunday morning Andy awoke to thunder and pouring rain. Since Andy knew his BMX race would be canceled, he went to Sunday school.

The lesson was on the Ten Commandments. Andy had memorized them, so when Mr. Helms asked someone to give the first one, he raised his hand. "Do not worship any other gods besides me," he stated when the teacher called on him. Then Mr. Helms asked what that meant. "It means the people in Africa and places like that shouldn't worship idols," replied Andy.

"Yes," agreed Mr. Helms, "but it also means none of us should allow anything to become more important to us than God is!" Andy was thinking of his father's words and of how important BMX racing had become to him. Silently he asked God to forgive him. Then he asked God to help him be a good testimony to his parents.

HOW ABOUT YOU? Is there something in your life you have allowed to take first place over God? It could be a hobby or a TV show or another person. Even good things become wrong if you allow them to become "gods" in your life. Ask God to help you keep him in first place. *R.E.P.*

TO MEMORIZE: Do not worship any other gods besides me. *Exodus 20:3*

"**SUSAN, STOP** looking at yourself in the mirror!" exclaimed Mrs. Morgan.

"Oh, Mother, I just want to look my best. This new hairstyle makes me look years older, doesn't it?" Even as she said this, Susan was looking in the mirror again. Later Susan and her mother went shopping at the mall. Mother sighed when she noticed Susan constantly smiling at her reflection in the store windows.

After dinner Dad read the Ten Commandments. Then the family discussed what each one meant. "Thou shalt not make unto thee any graven image," Dad read from the King James Version. "What do you think 'graven images' are?" he asked.

"Idols," answered Susan promptly, "like people in other countries make to worship. And my Sunday school teacher said we should be careful, too, not to worship statues or pictures of Jesus. She said a lot of people worship the statue or picture instead of God himself."

The smile on Mother's face turned to a frown as she saw that, even while Susan was speaking, she was admiring her reflection in the kitchen window across the table from her. Just then eight-year-old Brent spoke up. "Well, I don't know what a graven image is, but I think some girls worship their own image!"

The whole family looked at Susan. She felt herself blushing as Mother said, "Technically, Susan's explanation of a graven image is more correct, but I think Brent does have a point."

"I guess I have been too impressed by my own looks lately," admitted Susan. "I'll try to do better."

HOW ABOUT YOU? Do you worship any "graven images"? Are you sometimes guilty of worshiping your own image? It's not wrong to want to look your best, but don't be guilty of "bowing down to" or "serving" yourself. Serve Christ. *R.E.P.*

TO MEMORIZE: Do not make idols of any kind, whether in the shape of birds or animals or fish. *Exodus 20:4*

THE TEN COMMANDMENTS (2)
NO GRAVEN IMAGES

FROM THE BIBLE:

"Do not make idols of any kind, whether in the shape of birds or animals or fish. You must never worship or bow down to them, for I, the Lord your God, am a jealous God who will not share your affection with any other god! I do not leave unpunished the sins of those who hate me, but I punish the children for the sins of their parents to the third and fourth generations. But I lavish my love on those who love me and obey my commands, even for a thousand generations."
EXODUS 20:4-6

Worship God only

3 November

THE TEN COMMANDMENTS (3)
NOT IN VAIN

FROM THE BIBLE:

"Do not misuse the name of the Lord your God. The Lord will not let you go unpunished if you misuse his name."

"You must faithfully keep all my commands by obeying them, for I am the Lord. Do not treat my holy name as common and ordinary. I must be treated as holy by the people of Israel. It is I, the Lord, who makes you holy."

EXODUS 20:7;
LEVITICUS 22:31-32

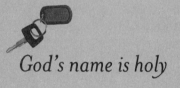

God's name is holy

DAVID WAS WATCHING his favorite TV program as Mom and Dad read the paper. The program was a comedy show.

David laughed when an embarrassing incident took place in the story, and the star of the show said, "Oh, my God!"

Hearing this, Dad looked up from his paper. "David, how can you laugh when people use God's name in vain like that?" he asked. "You claim to love God. Yet you seem to have forgotten that his name is holy."

"I know, Dad," David replied soberly. "I wish they didn't swear on TV so much, but what can I do about the swearing?"

"You can turn off the program," said Mom. "Then you could inform the TV station and those who sponsor the program that you don't like the bad language."

"Good suggestion," agreed Dad.

David thought about what his mother had said. He discussed it with his friends and his youth leader at church. Soon David was heading up a campaign for "Cleaner TV." Many of the kids decided to help. Through their local library they got the addresses of advertising sponsors, and they wrote letters objecting to the program's foul language. They said if the companies continued to sponsor such programs, they and their families would stop buying the products. They also contacted the station they were watching and let them know how they felt.

It was hard to tell sometimes if their "Cleaner TV" campaign was doing any good. But they knew they were doing what was right.

HOW ABOUT YOU? Have you heard people say, "Oh, my God!" or "Oh, my Lord!" so much that it doesn't even bother you anymore? When you're talking with friends and they use God's name in vain, do you ask them not to do that? Perhaps you could begin a campaign of your own to promote cleaner language on TV. *R.E.P.*

TO MEMORIZE: Do not misuse the name of the Lord your God. *Exodus 20:7*

"DADDY," asked Heidi, "why do we have church on Sunday? Carolyn's church meets on Saturday. She said that the Bible says that Saturday is the Sabbath."

"She's right about the Old Testament Sabbath being the same as our Saturday. But if she said our church is wrong to meet on Sunday, I can't agree with that. New Testament believers met on the *first* day of the week. This is mentioned in Acts 20:7 and 1 Corinthians 16:2," answered Dad.

"Why did they change?"

"Because Jesus arose from the grave on Sunday," Dad explained. "That's why we call it the Lord's Day, Heidi."

"Oh, well, I'll tell Carolyn," Heidi said as she skipped out of the room. But Heidi was a deep thinker, so in a few minutes she returned. "Daddy, do we still have to 'remember the Sabbath Day to keep it holy' like it says in the Ten Commandments?"

"Yes and no," chuckled Dad. "The people in the Old Testament lived under the Law. We don't, but we still believe that God wants us to set aside one day out of seven for him. So we remember the Resurrection on Sunday, and we try to keep that day holy for God."

"You know what?" Heidi asked solemnly. "Sherri and her family had a picnic at the beach last Sunday, and they went swimming! They weren't keeping the day holy, were they?"

"Whoa!" cautioned Dad. "There are things that I believe our family should keep for other days of the week, but let's be careful. We don't have a strict set of rules like they had for the Old Testament Sabbath. Romans 14 says we shouldn't judge others on these matters."

HOW ABOUT YOU? Do you set aside one day a week to worship and honor the Lord? If not, talk to your parents to see how you can do this. *R.E.P.*

TO MEMORIZE: Remember to observe the Sabbath day by keeping it holy. *Exodus 20:8*

---

4 November

THE TEN COMMANDMENTS (4)
KEEP IT HOLY

FROM THE BIBLE:

"Remember to observe the Sabbath day by keeping it holy. Six days a week are set apart for your daily duties and regular work, but the seventh day is a day of rest dedicated to the Lord your God. On that day no one in your household may do any kind of work. This includes you, your sons and daughters, your male and female servants, your livestock, and any foreigners living among you. For in six days the Lord made the heavens, the earth, the sea, and everything in them; then he rested on the seventh day. That is why the Lord blessed the Sabbath day and set it apart as holy."
EXODUS 20:8-11

Keep Sunday special

5 November

THE TEN COMMANDMENTS (5)
FATHER AND MOTHER

FROM THE BIBLE:

"Honor your father and mother. Then you will live a long, full life in the land the Lord your God will give you."

Children, obey your parents because you belong to the Lord, for this is the right thing to do. "Honor your father and mother." This is the first of the Ten Commandments that ends with a promise. And this is the promise: If you honor your father and mother, "you will live a long life, full of blessing."
EXODUS 20:12;
EPHESIANS 6:1-3

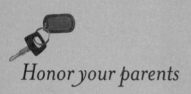

Honor your parents

BEFORE SUNDAY SCHOOL class began, all the sixth-grade boys gathered in a group outside. They didn't realize that a window was open near them, and their teacher was overhearing every remark they made.

Mark opened the conversation. "What did you guys do yesterday?"

"My old man made me help him paint our basement," Kyle grumbled.

"Well, my old lady had her parents over all day," said Terry. "They're both practically deaf. I spent the whole day saying things louder after they said, 'Huh?'"

Mark had a complaint, too. "Helen and George made me wash their car."

The others laughed. Then Kyle said, "Mark, how do you get away with calling your folks by their first names?"

Mark laughed. "Are you kidding? If I ever did that to their faces, old Baldhead would skin me alive. I have to call them "sir" and "ma'am" at home."

Just then a buzzer sounded and the boys filed into class. Mr. Beach asked, "How many of you know the Ten Commandments?" A few hands went up, and at Mr. Beach's nod, Mark recited them rapidly.

"Good," said Mr. Beach. "Now, how many of you realize you broke one of those commandments just a few minutes ago?" This time no hands went up, but there were many puzzled looks.

"Think about the Fifth Commandment," said Mr. Beach. "It says, 'Honor your father and your mother.' Then think about your conversation before class." After discussing it, Mr. Beach gave them a homework assignment for the next week. It was to put into practice the Fifth Commandment.

HOW ABOUT YOU? Do you honor your parents to their faces and make fun of them behind their backs? If so, you're breaking the Fifth Commandment. Ask God to forgive you and to help honor your parents!
R.E.P.

TO MEMORIZE: Honor your father and mother. Then you will live a long, full life in the land the Lord your God will give you. *Exodus 20:12*

JULIANNA WOKE UP in a terrible mood. She had an oral book report to do at school today, and she wasn't well prepared. Besides, it was pouring rain! Her hair would get all kinky and fuzzy from the moisture!

Julianna and her brother, José, both reached the bathroom door at the same time. "Ouch!" cried José as Julianna grabbed his arm. "Mom, Julianna pushed me against the wall!"

When Julianna emerged from the bathroom, Mother was waiting. "I'm ready to hear an explanation. What did José do to deserve this?" She showed Julianna the long scrape on the little boy's arm.

"He got in my way, that's what!" exclaimed Julianna. "My bus comes twenty minutes earlier than his. I've tried to tell the little creep that I should always be in the bathroom first, but he won't listen to me!"

"Julianna, I'm ashamed of the way you're acting," scolded Mother. "José hasn't done anything to you this morning. Now apologize, and get downstairs for breakfast!"

"I'm sorry," Julianna said with a scowl. Then, as she headed for the kitchen, she whispered, "But I hate you, you big baby!"

After breakfast the family had devotions. At Mother's request, Dad read Matthew 5:21-22 and 1 John 3:15. "Jesus is teaching the Ten Commandments," Dad said. "Here he explains that being angry with no cause, or hating someone is just as wrong in God's eyes as murder."

Julianna looked shocked as she glanced at José. She definitely didn't want to be a murderer! "I'm sorry," she whispered to him.

HOW ABOUT YOU? Do you ever get angry at people for no good reason? Christ said anyone guilty of these things is like someone who has broken the Sixth Commandment. "I hate you" are words you should never use. *R.E.P.*

TO MEMORIZE: Do not murder. *Exodus 20:13*

THE TEN COMMANDMENTS (6)
NO MURDER

FROM THE BIBLE:

"Do not murder."

"You have heard that the law of Moses says, 'Do not murder. If you commit murder, you are subject to judgment.' But I say, if you are angry with someone, you are subject to judgment! If you call someone an idiot, you are in danger of being brought before the high council. And if you curse someone, you are in danger of the fires of hell.

"So if you are standing before the altar in the Temple, offering a sacrifice to God, and you suddenly remember that someone has something against you, leave your sacrifice there beside the altar. Go and be reconciled to that person. Then come and offer your sacrifice to God."

EXODUS 20:13;
MATTHEW 5:21-24

Hatred kills

7 November

NO ADULTERY

FROM THE BIBLE:

"Do not commit adultery."

"You have heard that the law of Moses says, 'Do not commit adultery.' But I say, anyone who even looks at a woman with lust in his eye has already committed adultery with her in his heart. So if your eye—even if it is your good eye—causes you to lust, gouge it out and throw it away. It is better for you to lose one part of your body than for your whole body to be thrown into hell. And if your hand—even if it is your stronger hand—causes you to sin, cut it off and throw it away. It is better for you to lose one part of your body than for your whole body to be thrown into hell."

EXODUS 20:14;
MATTHEW 5:27-30

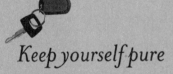

Keep yourself pure

ONE DAY Carl Stone and his friend Brad went to the beach with Carl's dad. Mr. Stone had gone back to the car for a magazine, so the boys thought they were alone. As he returned to the beach, Mr. Stone overheard this conversation.

"Hey, Carl, did you see that girl lying on the beach back there?" asked Brad.

"D'ya mean the one in the pink bikini?" replied Carl. "She sure has a tan!"

"Who cares about the tan? Get a look at the body! If she looks that good in a bikini, I wonder what she'd look like with nothing on!" Brad snickered.

"Shhh! Here comes Dad," answered Carl.

Mr. Stone was very concerned and prayed silently that God would show him how to teach the boys a special lesson. On the way home he began, "Boys, do you know the Ten Commandments?"

"Most of them!" answered Brad. Then he and Carl began to recite them.

When they got to the Seventh, Mr. Stone stopped them. "Do you know what that one means?" he asked.

"Our Sunday school teacher said adultery is referring to sexual sin," answered Carl. "He said it means we are supposed to have sex only with the person we're married to."

"That's right, Carl," replied his father. "But Jesus said in the New Testament that if a boy looks on a girl with lust in his heart, it's the same as having sex with her. To 'lust' means to want to do those things that we know are a privilege God reserves only for husbands and wives. It's important to ask God to help us keep our minds and bodies pure for him."

HOW ABOUT YOU? Do you ever wish you could have sexual contact with some boy or girl? Remember that God wants you to reserve your body for marriage. Ask God to keep your mind and body pure. *R.E.P.*

TO MEMORIZE: Do not commit adultery.
Exodus 20:14

MIKE WAS GLAD when he learned that his partners on the science project would be Ben and Dean. Everyone knew that Ben was the smartest boy in the class, and Dean was the best artist. *I won't have to do a thing!* Mike thought.

The three boys decided to build a model of a volcano. Ben would do the scientific part and figure out how to make it erupt. Dean would build the volcano. Mike, to his dismay, was to write a report. *Maybe Ben will do it for me*, he thought.

The evening before the science fair, Mike called Ben. "Help!" he cried. "I forgot to do the report!" Ben was angry but agreed to do it.

The next afternoon Miss Pope announced, "The best project this year is the volcano done by Ben, Mike, and Dean. You boys will receive an A."

Mike didn't feel as happy as he thought he would. He remembered that the Bible said a man has no right to eat unless he works, so that meant he had no right to receive rewards for which he had not worked.

The next day Mike explained to Miss Pope, "I feel like a thief—like I stole an A from you. I didn't do the work, so I don't deserve an A."

"Mike, I really respect you for confessing this to me," said Miss Pope. "I will have to give you an F on the project, but if I could grade you in honesty, it would be an A-plus!"

HOW ABOUT YOU? You don't have to steal things to be a thief. If you don't work when you are being paid to work, you're stealing time. If you take a grade you know you did not earn, you're stealing grades. Determine with God's help not to steal. *R.E.P.*

TO MEMORIZE: "Do not steal." *Exodus 20:15*

THE TEN COMMANDMENTS (8)
NO STEALING

FROM THE BIBLE:

"Do not steal."

If you are a thief, stop stealing. Begin using your hands for honest work, and then give generously to others in need.
EXODUS 20:15;
EPHESIANS 4:28

Don't be a thief

9 November

THE TEN COMMANDMENTS (9)
NO FALSE TESTIMONY

FROM THE BIBLE:

"Do not testify falsely against your neighbor."

An honest witness tells the truth; a false witness tells lies.

Some people make cutting remarks, but the words of the wise bring healing.

Truth stands the test of time; lies are soon exposed.

Deceit fills hearts that are plotting evil; joy fills hearts that are planning peace!

No real harm befalls the godly, but the wicked have their fill of trouble.

The Lord hates those who don't keep their word, but he delights in those who do.

EXODUS 20:16;
PROVERBS 12:17-22

Do not lie

THE THIRD-GRADE Sunday school class was studying the life of Moses. When they came to the story of the Ten Commandments, they talked about one or two each week. After each one was discussed, Jenny smiled and thought smugly, *I've never done that!*

Today's lesson began with the Ninth Commandment. "Who can tell me what this means?" asked Mrs. Bennetto.

Tina's hand shot up. "I was watching a new show on TV last night. It was called *Live Courtroom.* There were witnesses there. They were people who had to tell what they knew about the case. What they told is their testimony."

"Yes, that's right," said Mrs. Bennetto. "But what is a *false* testimony?"

Mary Lynn raised her hand. "A false testimony would be when one of those people in the court was lying."

Jenny smiled as she thought to herself, *I've never had to go to court and be a witness, so I'm OK on this commandment, too. I don't think I've ever broken any of the Ten Commandments!*

"Bearing false witness doesn't just mean in court," Mrs. Bennetto was saying. "Anytime we say anything that is not true, we are guilty of testifying falsely."

"Do you mean when we just fib a little?" asked Jenny incredulously. Mrs. Bennetto nodded. "Even if it's just a little white lie?" asked Jenny again.

"To God, a lie doesn't have a color," stated Mrs. Bennetto. "A lie is a lie." Even Jenny had to admit that she had told lies. She realized she needed God's forgiveness, too.

HOW ABOUT YOU? Have you ever thought you were perfect? Maybe you never have killed anyone or worshiped idols, but if you've ever told anything that is not true, you have lied. Lying is sin, and sin is offensive to God. So confess your sin, and let Jesus help you not to do it again. *R.E.P.*

TO MEMORIZE: Do not testify falsely against your neighbor. *Exodus 20:16*

JEROME'S BICYCLE was his favorite thing in all the world. It was a bright, shiny, silver color, and he rode it every day. He could even pop wheelies on it.

Then his neighbor, Tim, got a brand-new twenty-one-speed mountain bike. It was metallic blue, and it had a speedometer, padded handlebars, a comfortable gel seat, a rearview mirror, and a headlight. Jerome thought he had never seen anything so beautiful!

Mom and Dad began to notice that Jerome didn't ride his bike much any more. One day, Dad noticed Jerome staring at Tim who was riding his new mountain bike.

"I think I found out what's wrong with Jerome," Dad whispered to Mom. "He's jealous over Tim's bike. I hope this doesn't last too long."

At their time of family devotions that night, Dad read the Ten Commandments. Jerome wondered why, but he didn't have to wonder long. When Dad came to the last one, he read it this way: "Do not covet your neighbor's house. Do not covet your neighbor's wife, male or female servant, ox, mountain bike, or anything else your neighbor owns."

"It doesn't say that!" Jerome exclaimed.

"No, but maybe it should," Dad suggested. Then he prayed that the Lord would forgive each of them for wanting or coveting things belonging to someone else. He also asked God to make them content with what they had.

HOW ABOUT YOU? Have you ever wanted something that belonged to someone else—maybe a new bike, a video game, trading cards, or clothes? The Bible calls that coveting, and coveting is sin! We need to learn to be content with what we have. Ask God to help you. *R.E.P.*

TO MEMORIZE: Do not covet your neighbor's house. Do not covet your neighbor's wife, male or female servant, ox or donkey, or anything else your neighbor owns. *Exodus 20:17*

THE TEN COMMANDMENTS (10)

NO COVETING

FROM THE BIBLE:

"Do not covet your neighbor's house. Do not covet your neighbor's wife, male or female servant, ox or donkey, or anything else your neighbor owns."

Stay away from the love of money; be satisfied with what you have. For God has said, "I will never fail you. I will never forsake you."
EXODUS 20:17;
HEBREWS 13:5

Do not covet

11 November

NAIL HOLES

FROM THE BIBLE:

We all make many mistakes, but those who control their tongues can also control themselves in every other way. We can make a large horse turn around and go wherever we want by means of a small bit in its mouth. And a tiny rudder makes a huge ship turn wherever the pilot wants it to go, even though the winds are strong. So also, the tongue is a small thing, but what enormous damage it can do. A tiny spark can set a great forest on fire. And the tongue is a flame of fire. It is full of wickedness that can ruin your whole life. . . .

People can tame all kinds of animals and birds and reptiles and fish, but no one can tame the tongue. It is an uncontrollable evil, full of deadly poison. Sometimes it praises our Lord and Father, and sometimes it breaks out into curses against those who have been made in the image of God. And so blessing and cursing come pouring out of the same mouth. Surely, my brothers and sisters, this is not right!

JAMES 3:2-10

Think, then speak

BRAD STARTED toward the family room. "VAROOM!" sang out his little brother, Kevin, as he charged through the room, crashing into Brad.

"Watch where you're going, you moron," yelled Brad.

"You know that you are not to call people names," Dad said sternly.

Brad sighed. "I'll apologize." But just then the phone rang, and Brad picked it up. "Hello? Oh, hi, Jason. Yeah, I heard the rumor about Mrs. Simpson. Can you believe we have an alcoholic for a teacher? Did you notice how she stumbled over her words in class? Oh, Dad wants me for something. Talk to you later."

"You're going to call Jason back and apologize for that gossip I just heard," said Dad. "Did you know that Mrs. Simpson's husband is sick?" he asked. "She has to stay up nights caring for him. No wonder she's tired in class."

"Oh, I didn't know that. I'll call Jason after I apologize to Kevin."

"First come with me to my shop," said Dad. He picked up a hammer and some nails. "I want you to pound these nails about halfway into this board."

Brad obeyed with a puzzled look. "Now what?"

"Pull the nails out." Brad did so. "Brad, your words lately have been as sharp as these nails. They've been cutting and hurting. Saying you're sorry is fine. But look at this board. What do you see?"

"The nail holes," said Brad.

"Exactly," said Dad. "You can apologize and be forgiven, but you can never take back all the harm you've caused."

Brad picked up the board. "I get your point, Dad. I'll try to be more careful with my words."

HOW ABOUT YOU? Do you carelessly say things that hurt the feelings or reputations of others? An apology can bring forgiveness, but it can never erase all the harm. Ask the Lord to help you. *M.R.P.*

TO MEMORIZE: For I am determined not to sin in what I say. *Psalm 17:3*

GOOD FOR EVIL

"I CAN'T STAND Manuel!" exploded Brandon. "He's a big bag of hot air, saying he met the mayor, they got a new car, they're going to Bermuda, his dad's on the city council. Blah-blah-blah!"

"Not jealous, are you?" asked Mom.

"No!" snorted Brandon. "Just sick of his bragging. If he's not doing that, he's swearing. Mom, why does God let him have so many good things when he laughs at Christians and swears?"

"That's a good question," said Mom. "It used to bother me, too." She was interrupted as Misty stomped into the room.

"Old Mr. Matlock is so mean!" complained Misty. "He put barricades on the sidewalk in front of his house so Denise and I can't ride our bikes there. Denise said we ought to do something to get even with him."

"Oh no!" Mom shook her head. "Remember what we read from the Bible this morning? What did those verses tell you to do to Mr. Matlock?"

"Love him," mumbled Misty.

"That's not all," Mom reminded her. "What else?"

Brandon answered for Misty. "Pray for him and do good to him."

"Would you like to make some cookies, Misty?" asked Mom. "You could take a few to Mr. Matlock."

"You've got to be kidding!" Misty was shocked.

Mom shook her head. "No, I'm not. The best way to deal with enemies is to make them your friends." As she got out the cookbook, she turned to Brandon.

"God tells us to pray for our enemies and return good for evil," said Mom. "He's giving them an opportunity to change from enemies to friends."

FROM THE BIBLE:

"You have heard that the law of Moses says, 'Love your neighbor' and hate your enemy. But I say, love your enemies! Pray for those who persecute you! In that way, you will be acting as true children of your Father in heaven. For he gives his sunlight to both the evil and the good, and he sends rain on the just and on the unjust, too. If you love only those who love you, what good is that? Even corrupt tax collectors do that much. If you are kind only to your friends, how are you different from anyone else? Even pagans do that. But you are to be perfect, even as your Father in heaven is perfect."
MATTHEW 5:43-48

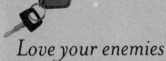

Love your enemies

HOW ABOUT YOU? Is there someone who is giving you a hard time? Try the formula Jesus used. Love your enemies and pray for those who persecute you. *B.J.W.*

TO MEMORIZE: If people persecute you because you are a Christian, don't curse them; pray that God will bless them. *Romans 12:14*

13 November

THE WRONG WAY

FROM THE BIBLE:

"This is what the Lord Almighty says: Consider how things are going for you! You have planted much but harvested little. You have food to eat, but not enough to fill you up. You have wine to drink, but not enough to satisfy your thirst. You have clothing to wear, but not enough to keep you warm. Your wages disappear as though you were putting them in pockets filled with holes!

"This is what the Lord Almighty says: Consider how things are going for you!"
HAGGAI 1:5-7

Jesus is the right way

"YOU SHOULD have seen Brianne today!" laughed Jim as the family began their dinner. His sister sent him a nasty look. "The girls wanted to play touch football with us guys, so we let them play with us today. Know what Brianne did? When she got the ball, she ran toward the wrong goal line! Almost made a touchdown, too—for the wrong team. What a riot!"

Brianne reluctantly joined in the laughter at her expense. "You're in good company," Dad consoled her. "It's happened before—to professionals! Way back in 1929, a fellow named Roy Riegels played for the California Golden Bears. One time when he got the ball, he lit out for the wrong goal with 'do-or-die' determination. One of his teammates finally managed to bring him down just a yard from the goal line. But his team still lost the game."

"Good thing it was only a game," observed Mother. "There's an important lesson for us, though. Some people are running long and hard in the game of life, and they don't realize they're running in the wrong direction."

"That's true," said Dad. "Many people are trying hard to live a good life. In fact, their 'good deeds' sometimes put Christians to shame. But in spite of those 'good deeds,' they're still sinners because they refuse to acknowledge Jesus as the only way to heaven. When all is said and done, they'll find that they went the wrong way. What a tragedy!"

"That's sad," declared Brianne. "Maybe I didn't know which way to run in the football game, but I'm sure glad I know the way to heaven."

HOW ABOUT YOU? Are you running the wrong way in life? You are if you're trying to get to heaven by any other way than through Jesus Christ. *H.W.M.*

TO MEMORIZE: There is a path before each person that seems right, but it ends in death. *Proverbs 14:12*

"I'M SICK OF being ordered around!" Brad griped as he put his bike away. "Someone's always tellin' me it's time to get up, time to catch the bus, time for the bell. Just once I'd like to do what I want to do when I want to do it."

Dad looked up from his tool bench. "Suppose there were no rules or schedules, Brad?"

"That would be great!" Brad exclaimed.

"I'm not so sure," Dad answered. "Just for fun, though, let's imagine we woke one morning and everyone could do anything they wanted. What would you do?"

"I'd spend the day at the zoo," Brad answered.

"How would you get there?"

"You would take me," Brad replied.

"Well, maybe. But remember, I don't have to do anything I don't want to do."

"Aw, you would want to go to the zoo," said Brad.

"OK," agreed Dad, "so we get in the car and start for the zoo. I'm not sure we'd get there. There are no rules, remember? No traffic laws. Everyone drives exactly like they want to—that is, until they run into someone."

Brad whistled. "Well, we couldn't do away with traffic laws. I guess maybe we do need rules for some things."

"Right!" agreed Dad. "When God created this world, he organized everything. The universe is run by laws and on a schedule. Even the sun has a schedule to keep." Dad looked at his watch. "According to my schedule, it's about time for lunch. How about a hamburger?"

HOW ABOUT YOU? Do you often complain about having to do things "on schedule"? Would you rather put things off? Working with family and friends in an organized way makes life much smoother. Make up your mind to get "on schedule." *B.J.W.*

TO MEMORIZE: Those who obey him will not be punished. Those who are wise will find a time and a way to do what is right. *Ecclesiastes 8:5*

FORGOTTEN SCHEDULES

FROM THE BIBLE:

There is a time for everything, a season for every activity under heaven.
A time to be born and a time to die.
A time to plant and a time to harvest.
A time to kill and a time to heal.
A time to tear down and a time to rebuild.
A time to cry and a time to laugh.
A time to grieve and a time to dance.
A time to scatter stones and a time to gather stones.
A time to embrace and a time to turn away.
A time to search and a time to lose.
A time to keep and a time to throw away.
A time to tear and a time to mend.
A time to be quiet and a time to speak up.
A time to love and a time to hate.
A time for war and a time for peace. . . .

God has made everything beautiful for its own time. He has planted eternity in the human heart, but even so, people cannot see the whole scope of God's work from beginning to end.
ECCLESIASTES 3:1-8, 11

Schedules aren't bad

15 November

ANIMAL CHARADES

FROM THE BIBLE:

After dark one evening, a Jewish religious leader named Nicodemus, a Pharisee, came to speak with Jesus. "Teacher," he said, "we all know that God has sent you to teach us. Your miraculous signs are proof enough that God is with you."

Jesus replied, "I assure you, unless you are born again, you can never see the Kingdom of God."

"What do you mean?" exclaimed Nicodemus. "How can an old man go back into his mother's womb and be born again?"

Jesus replied, "The truth is, no one can enter the Kingdom of God without being born of water and the Spirit. Humans can reproduce only human life, but the Holy Spirit gives new life from heaven. So don't be surprised at my statement that you must be born again. . . .

"For God so loved the world that he gave his only Son, so that everyone who believes in him will not perish but have eternal life."

JOHN 3:1-7, 16

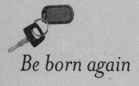

Be born again

AT THE SUNDAY SCHOOL class party, Lori listened eagerly as Miss Ellen explained the next game. "Tom will be 'It' first," said Miss Ellen. "He'll pretend to be an animal. The first one to guess that animal will be 'It' next."

Tom dropped to his hands and knees. Then he opened his mouth and barked. "You're a dog!" Pete shouted.

Now it was Pete's turn. He got down on his stomach and wriggled his way across the room. "Are you a worm?" someone asked. Pete shook his head. As he crawled, he rapidly stuck out his tongue several times. "A snake," squealed one of the girls, and it was her turn.

After several children had a turn, Miss Ellen was "It." She folded her hands and bowed her head. "You're a praying mantis," suggested Tom.

Miss Ellen shook her head. "I'll give you a clue," she said. "I'm a human, but what am I pretending to be?" She pretended to read her Bible. Next she sat down and appeared to be listening to someone. She made motions as though she were opening a book. She also opened and closed her mouth, but no sound came out. "She's singing," whispered someone, and Miss Ellen nodded. "She's in church," whispered someone else. Again Miss Ellen nodded.

Suddenly Lori knew the answer. "You're pretending to be a Christian!" she exclaimed.

"That's it," agreed Miss Ellen. "I want you to think about this: Pretending to be something doesn't make it so. You're not a Christian unless you are born into God's family."

HOW ABOUT YOU? Have you been born again? You may act like a Christian, but you're not one unless you've trusted Jesus and have been "born" into his family. Talk to a trusted Christian friend or adult to find out more. *H.W.M.*

TO MEMORIZE: Jesus replied, "The truth is, no one can enter the Kingdom of God without being born of water and the Spirit." *John 3:5*

"THIS IS RIDICULOUS!" exclaimed André. He tapped his pencil impatiently on the paper in front of him. "Whoever thought up this assignment for Sunday school certainly doesn't know Christa! I have to write down ten reasons why I like my sister, and I can't even think of one!"

"Thanks a lot!" Christa called from the living room. "See if I ever bake cookies for you again!"

"Oops! I forgot about them." André wrote it down.

"How about the time last year when you were sick, and Christa helped you with your homework?" suggested Mom.

"And how about the times I've played catch with you before a game?" Christa asked. "Or last week when I let you ride my bike because yours had a flat tire?"

André had forgotten all those things, too. He could see that Christa really was a nice sister. He felt guilty for all the times he had called her names or had been a nuisance to her. It was hard to admit, but André said, "I'm really kind of glad we had this assignment. It's made me appreciate my sister!"

"I can't believe I heard you say that," Christa laughed. "I think this calls for a celebration. How about if I, being the wonderful sister that I am, make some popcorn?"

"Sounds great to me!" André said. He wrote one more thing on his paper. "She makes delicious popcorn!"

HOW ABOUT YOU? Do you appreciate the brothers or sisters the Lord has given you? Do you get along with them, or do you often argue? Brother and sister conflicts are not new. They've been around since Cain and Abel! Brothers and sisters often overlook the good qualities in each other because they're so busy fighting. The Bible says that they are to help each other in times of trouble. *L.M.W.*

TO MEMORIZE: A friend is always loyal, and a brother is born to help in time of need. *Proverbs 17:17*

SISTER TROUBLE

FROM THE BIBLE:

How wonderful it is, how pleasant,
when brothers live together in harmony!
For harmony is as precious as the fragrant anointing oil
that was poured over Aaron's head,
that ran down his beard
and onto the border of his robe.
Harmony is as refreshing as the dew from Mount Hermon
that falls on the mountains of Zion.
And the Lord has pronounced his blessing,
even life forevermore.
PSALM 133:1-3

Appreciate brothers and sisters

17 November

NOT HUNGRY

FROM THE BIBLE:

"He knows where I am going. And when he has tested me like gold in a fire, he will pronounce me innocent.

"For I have stayed in God's paths; I have followed his ways and not turned aside. I have not departed from his commands but have treasured his word in my heart."

JOB 23:10-12

Watch your mental diet

WHEN BRIAN came in from school, Mother was gone, so he raided the refrigerator and cupboards. When Mother returned, he was just finishing an after-school snack of potato chips, soda pop, ice cream, and cookies.

Mother frowned. "Next time, don't eat junk food before supper," she said. As she started dinner, she added, "Mrs. Smith's grandson, Nicholas, will be going to Sunday school with us this week."

"I'm tired of Sunday school," said Brian as he took a comic book and settled down in front of the TV. The next thing he knew, Mother was calling him for dinner. At the table he wrinkled up his nose. "I don't want any."

"Mrs. Smith sent some cake for dessert," said Mother.

Brian grinned. "I might eat a little of that."

"Not until you eat some meat and vegetables," Dad ruled.

"But I'm not hungry," protested Brian.

"Because you filled up on junk food," Mother reminded him. As she passed the casserole to him, she added, "And that's exactly why you're not enjoying Sunday school."

Brian snorted. "I don't enjoy church because I eat potato chips? Aw, Mother!"

"You know what your mother means," said Dad. "Unless we keep after you, you feed your mind junk food—TV programs, comic books, and loud music."

Mother passed Brian the vegetables. "If you aren't careful, you're going to be sick—spiritually and physically," she added.

HOW ABOUT YOU? Are you filling your mind with junk food rather than wholesome spiritual food? Make up your mind to change your mental eating habits before you become spiritually sick. Read God's Word. Listen carefully to your Sunday school teacher and your pastor. Spend time with other Christians. *B.J.W.*

TO MEMORIZE: I have not departed from his commands but have treasured his word in my heart. *Job 23:12*

AS SOON AS Matt walked in the door, his mother knew something was wrong. He was quiet and thoughtful, not his usual happy self.

"How was school, Matt?" Mother asked.

Matt shrugged. "It was OK."

"You don't seem very happy," observed Mother.

Matt hesitated. "We had a discussion in social studies class. One of the kids started talking about nuclear war and how the whole world was going to end. Mr. Morgan, our teacher, agreed with him."

"What do you think, Matt?" asked Mother.

Matt gave his mother a little smile. "I think it's sort of scary. We talk about war at school. There are shows about it on TV." Matt paused. "Are you afraid?"

"Matt, this world is a messed-up place," answered Mother, "but when people tell frightening stories about war, I take time to thank the Lord that my future is in *his* hands. As Christians, we know that the Lord loves and cares for us. He is still in control. Only what he allows will happen."

"But our teacher says that if everyone would stop making nuclear weapons, the world would be peaceful and no one would fight," offered Matt.

"That sounds good, Matt," answered Mother, "but it's not what the Bible says. Nations want to be powerful and will do anything to gain that power. It's unrealistic to think that all nations will suddenly decide to stop fighting. There will always be war. Again, we must remember to put our trust in the Lord."

HOW ABOUT YOU? Are you frightened when you hear stories about war? As a Christian, you don't have to be afraid. Jesus says that your future is in his hands. Whatever that future holds, he will be with you and help you through it. *L.M.W.*

TO MEMORIZE: Don't be troubled. You trust God, now trust in me. *John 14:1*

WAR!

FROM THE BIBLE:

"When you hear of wars and insurrections, don't panic. Yes, these things must come, but the end won't follow immediately." Then he added, "Nations and kingdoms will proclaim war against each other. There will be great earthquakes, and there will be famines and epidemics in many lands, and there will be terrifying things and great miraculous signs in the heavens.

"But before all this occurs, there will be a time of great persecution. You will be dragged into synagogues and prisons, and you will be accused before kings and governors of being my followers. This will be your opportunity to tell them about me. So don't worry about how to answer the charges against you, for I will give you the right words and such wisdom that none of your opponents will be able to reply! Even those closest to you . . . will betray you. And . . . everyone will hate you because of your allegiance to me. But not a hair of your head will perish! By standing firm, you will win your souls."

LUKE 21:9-19

Don't fear— trust God

19 November

SPEND IT WISELY

FROM THE BIBLE:

*But the godly will flourish like
   palm trees
   and grow strong like the
   cedars of Lebanon.
For they are transplanted into
   the Lord's own house.
   They flourish in the courts of
   our God.
Even in old age they will still
   produce fruit;
   they will remain vital and
   green.
They will declare, "The Lord is
   just!
   He is my rock!
   There is nothing but goodness
   in him!"*

PSALM 92:12-15

Live wisely

LINDA AND HER MOTHER went to a nursing home one afternoon. First they saw Hattie Smith.

"It's about time someone came to visit!" snapped Mrs. Smith. Then she grumbled about the food, the nurses, and the rainy weather.

Linda felt sad as they walked down the hall, but when they got to Aunt Clara's room, everything changed. The thin old woman in the wheelchair greeted them with a smile on her rosy, wrinkled cheeks. "Praise the Lord! It's nice to see ya!" she said. "I've got so much joy bubblin' up in me today that I've been prayin' for someone to share it with. This here's Leona White. I've been talkin' to her about the Lord, and she asked him into her heart." Leona smiled.

After they left, Linda asked, "Mother, why are those ladies so different? They're both old, but Aunt Clara is happy and Mrs. Smith is grumpy."

"Let's think about it," Mother suggested. "Do you remember the shirt we bought for your father at the garage sale yesterday? We bought a skirt and blouse for you, too. We got all that for ten dollars."

"That's a lot for ten dollars!"

"Yes, we spent the money well," said Mother. Then she said, "I think Aunt Clara is happy because she has spent her life well and continues to do that, witnessing and praising the Lord. Perhaps Mrs. Smith looks back on her life with regret. Does that make sense?"

"I think so," Linda said. "I'm going to dedicate my life to God. Then, when I'm old, I'll be happy, too."

HOW ABOUT YOU? Are you afraid of growing old and dying? Don't be! Invest your life in serving God and others. He'll reward you in heaven. Whether your life on earth is long or short, spend it wisely! *S.L.K.*

TO MEMORIZE: Gray hair is a crown of glory; it is gained by living a godly life. *Proverbs 16:31*

"HELLO, RYAN," Grandpa Thompson said. "Is everything copasetic with my grandson today?"

"Copasetic? What does that mean, Grandpa?" Ryan asked, but he knew his grandpa wouldn't tell him. He'd make Ryan look it up in the dictionary.

Sure enough, Grandpa smiled and said, "That's what dictionaries are for!"

Ryan quickly looked up the word *copasetic* and read that it meant "very satisfying." He was just closing the dictionary when his older brother (who was in high school and liked to think he was very smart) walked in the door.

"Hi, Bruce," Ryan greeted him. "Everything copasetic?"

Bruce looked at Ryan strangely. "What are you talking about?" he asked.

Ryan looked at his grandpa and winked. "Look it up, Bruce. That's what dictionaries are for!"

While Bruce was flipping through the dictionary, Ryan went and sat down next to his grandpa on the couch. "You sure like using new words, don't you, Grandpa?"

Grandpa put his arm around Ryan. "Yes, I do. The way I look at it, the use of words is a gift from God. He gave man the ability to develop languages and to write words that express ideas and inventions. Communication is a vital part of life. Man can take that God-given ability and abuse it, or he can use it for good."

"Hmmm, I never thought about that before. I'm going to remember to thank the Lord for giving us the ability to use words," Ryan said.

HOW ABOUT YOU? Have you ever thought about the importance of words? Without words you could not communicate with others. Without words there would be no books, no conversations, or radio programs! Thank God for words. And remember, the most important words are those found in God's Word, the Bible. *L.M.W.*

TO MEMORIZE: A word aptly spoken is like apples of gold in settings of silver. *Proverbs 25:11* (NIV)

A "COPASETIC" DAY

FROM THE BIBLE:

Because the Teacher was wise, he taught the people everything he knew. He collected proverbs and classified them. Indeed, the Teacher taught the plain truth, and he did so in an interesting way.

A wise teacher's words spur students to action and emphasize important truths. The collected sayings of the wise are like guidance from a shepherd.

But, my child, be warned: There is no end of opinions ready to be expressed. Studying them can go on forever and become very exhausting!

Here is my final conclusion: Fear God and obey his commands, for this is the duty of every person.

ECCLESIASTES 12:9-13

Be thankful for words

21 November

TAKEN FOR GRANTED

FROM THE BIBLE:

Jesus soon saw a great crowd of people climbing the hill, looking for him. Turning to Philip, he asked, "Philip, where can we buy bread to feed all these people?" He was testing Philip, for he already knew what he was going to do.

Philip replied, "It would take a small fortune to feed them!"

Then Andrew, Simon Peter's brother, spoke up. "There's a young boy here with five barley loaves and two fish. But what good is that with this huge crowd?"

"Tell everyone to sit down," Jesus ordered. So all of them— the men alone numbered five thousand—sat down on the grassy slopes. Then Jesus took the loaves, gave thanks to God, and passed them out to the people. Afterward he did the same with the fish. And they all ate until they were full.

JOHN 6:5-11

Give thanks to God

ANTHONY BEGAN EATING his cereal. "You didn't pray," his sister said.

Anthony shrugged. "I'm in a hurry."

It was Anthony's turn to stack the breakfast dishes. Usually Mother thanked him for his help, but today she didn't say anything.

On the way to school, Anthony saw a younger child fall and drop several books. Anthony hurried to help him. The child grabbed the books and ran off without even looking at Anthony. *What an ungrateful kid!* thought Anthony.

At recess, Anthony offered to pass out papers. Up and down the rows he went, putting the papers on the desks. When he was finished, his teacher glanced up. "You can go now," she said absently. Didn't she even appreciate his help?

On his paper route, there was an old man crippled with arthritis. Since it was hard for him to bend over, Anthony always rang his doorbell and handed the paper to him. Today the man grumbled, "You're late!"

I don't mind the extra trouble of waiting for him to answer the door, Anthony thought. *But it sure would be nice to know he liked what I do for him.*

"Why the sad face, Anthony?" asked Mrs. Brown, a neighbor.

"Oh, nothing big. But it seems as though everyone takes me for granted," complained Anthony.

"I understand," said Mrs. Brown. "I'm sure God must feel that way often."

"Why would he feel that way?"

"Well, I appreciate all he does for me," said Mrs. Brown, "but so often I neglect to tell him."

Anthony nodded, but he was thoughtful as he walked home. The next morning he quietly thanked God for his food before he began to eat.

HOW ABOUT YOU? Do you get tired of thanking God for your food? How about all your other blessings? Maybe you appreciate them, but do you thank God for all he gives you? God enjoys your "thank you's." *C.E.Y.*

TO MEMORIZE: Now, our God, we give you thanks, and praise your glorious name. *1 Chronicles 29:13* (NIV)

GIFT OR GIVER

THE CARTER FAMILY was looking forward to a day at the petting zoo. "Oh, I can hardly wait!" exclaimed Tamara. As the family sat down for breakfast, Dad asked her to lead in prayer. "Dear Jesus," Tamara prayed, "bless this food. Give us good weather and a good time. Give us safety. Keep Jeremy from fussing. Amen." Dad looked thoughtful when she finished but said nothing.

After a quick breakfast, the family piled into the car for the trip. Soon they were enjoying the animals at the zoo. The children ran toward four ducks that were fighting over some food they had found on the ground. "The ducks are hungry," Tamara said. "I wish I had something to feed them."

Mom reached into the picnic basket. "You can give them some crackers."

Tamara crumbled the crackers as she walked toward the ducks. When they saw her coming, the ducks immediately surrounded her. "I think they like me," Tamara shouted. However, when the crackers were gone, the ducks were gone, too.

"Oh, Daddy, those ducks didn't like me!" Tamara exclaimed. "They just wanted my crackers!"

Dad nodded. "I'm afraid we act somewhat like those ducks," he said. He smiled at her puzzled look and went on to explain. "Our prayers often express more 'gimmie' than gratitude for what Jesus has already done for us."

"I guess you're right," Tamara said thoughtfully. "The next time I pray I'm going to thank the Lord for the things he's given me."

FROM THE BIBLE:

As Jesus continued on toward Jerusalem, he reached the border between Galilee and Samaria. As he entered a village there, ten lepers stood at a distance, crying out, "Jesus, Master, have mercy on us!"

He looked at them and said, "Go show yourselves to the priests." And as they went, their leprosy disappeared.

One of them, when he saw that he was healed, came back to Jesus, shouting, "Praise God, I'm healed!" He fell face down on the ground at Jesus' feet, thanking him for what he had done. This man was a Samaritan.

Jesus asked, "Didn't I heal ten men? Where are the other nine? Does only this foreigner return to give glory to God?" And Jesus said to the man, "Stand up and go. Your faith has made you well."

LUKE 17:11-19

Give thanks before asking

HOW ABOUT YOU? Have you ever prayed a prayer of thanksgiving without asking for anything? Have you ever simply said, "Lord, I love you"? He not only wants to hear your requests but also wants to hear your praise. *J.L.H.*

TO MEMORIZE: Devote yourselves to prayer with an alert mind and a thankful heart. *Colossians 4:2*

23 November

IT TAKES TWO

FROM THE BIBLE:

God decided to save us through our Lord Jesus Christ, not to pour out his anger on us. He died for us so that we can live with him forever, whether we are dead or alive at the time of his return. So encourage each other and build each other up, just as you are already doing.

Dear brothers and sisters, honor those who are your leaders in the Lord's work. They work hard among you and warn you against all that is wrong. Think highly of them and give them your wholehearted love because of their work. And remember to live peaceably with each other.

Brothers and sisters, we urge you to warn those who are lazy. Encourage those who are timid. Take tender care of those who are weak. Be patient with everyone.

See that no one pays back evil for evil, but always try to do good to each other and to everyone else.

1 THESSALONIANS 5:9-15

Don't quarrel

MOM SIGHED deeply as she heard raised voices coming from the basement. Soon Brad came bursting into the kitchen. "Mom, Tyler's being mean again! I wish he wouldn't come over if he's going to act like that."

"I know you boys haven't gotten along very well lately," said Mom, "but why can't you be the one to stop the quarreling that goes on between you?"

"Why me? Tyler's the one who always starts it," Brad said, defending himself.

"It takes two to quarrel," Mom pointed out. "If you refuse to fight, and if you ignore his teasing, there won't be any quarrel."

"If I don't stand up for my rights, he'll think I'm a sissy," protested Brad.

"Do you know what God thinks about all this?" asked Mom. "He says, 'Avoiding a fight is a mark of honor; only fools insist on quarreling.' Read it yourself in Proverbs chapter 20, verse 3. Anybody can quarrel, you know, but it takes a wise person to stop a quarrel. The same verse says that it's a fool who insists on quarreling."

"Tell that to Tyler!" demanded Brad.

"I'm not Tyler's mother. I'm yours, so I'm telling you," said Mom.

Brad took a deep breath. "All right, I'll try not to quarrel."

Several times in the next few days, Tyler tried to pick a quarrel. He rode Brad's bike without permission, he tossed pebbles at him, and he called him a sissy, but Brad just walked away. Finally Tyler could stand it no longer. "What's the matter with you?" he asked.

Brad grinned. "Read Proverbs 20:3," he advised.

HOW ABOUT YOU? Do you often quarrel with others? Remember what God says about someone who is quick to quarrel. Even if you think it's really the other person's fault, avoid arguing and fighting. *B.J.W.*

TO MEMORIZE: Avoiding a fight is a mark of honor; only fools insist on quarreling. *Proverbs 20:3*

STEPHANIE CLAPPED a hand over her mouth. As Mother took out the coffeepot, she looked at her daughter. "Don't use that word again," she said.

"I'm sorry, Mom," apologized Stephanie. "I didn't mean to say it, but I hear it so often at school." She watched Mother put a white paper into the coffeepot. "What's that for?"

"This filter," said Mother, "lets the water through but keeps the coffee grounds from going into the coffee. You need to be a 'filter,' too, filtering the things you hear and see. Allow only good things to settle down and stay with you. God will help you."

"I'll try, Mother," agreed Stephanie. She showed her mother a listing of the TV section of the paper. "Can I watch this program tonight?"

Mother read the description and shook her head. "This isn't the type of program you should see," she said.

"Oh, it'll be all right," teased Stephanie. "I'll 'filter' out all the bad stuff."

Mother shook her head. "Would it be OK to put garbage in the coffeepot and expect the filter to make it fit to drink?"

"Yuck," exclaimed Stephanie. "Deep down I know I shouldn't watch that program, but what you just said makes it more clear. We shouldn't dump 'garbage' into our minds on purpose. But when we can't help what we see and hear, that's when we should use our filters."

HOW ABOUT YOU? Do you find yourself automatically saying or doing things you know are wrong? The best policy is to avoid being where you will hear or see bad things. If that's impossible, ask the Lord to help you filter out the bad influences and to keep only the thoughts and ideas that are good. *H.W.M.*

TO MEMORIZE: Fix your thoughts on what is true and honorable and right. Think about things that are pure and lovely and admirable. Think about things that are excellent and worthy of praise. *Philippians 4:8*

CHRISTIAN FILTERS

FROM THE BIBLE:

And so, dear brothers and sisters, I plead with you to give your bodies to God. Let them be a living and holy sacrifice—the kind he will accept. When you think of what he has done for you, is this too much to ask? Don't copy the behavior and customs of this world, but let God transform you into a new person by changing the way you think. Then you will know what God wants you to do, and you will know how good and pleasing and perfect his will really is.

As God's messenger, I give each of you this warning: Be honest in your estimate of yourselves, measuring your value by how much faith God has given you.
ROMANS 12:1-3

Keep thoughts pure

25 November

THE BEST TEAM

FROM THE BIBLE:

The sin of this one man, Adam, caused death to rule over us, but all who receive God's wonderful, gracious gift of righteousness will live in triumph over sin and death through this one man, Jesus Christ.

Yes, Adam's one sin brought condemnation upon everyone, but Christ's one act of righteousness makes all people right in God's sight and gives them life. Because one person disobeyed God, many people became sinners. But because one other person obeyed God, many people will be made right in God's sight.

God's law was given so that all people could see how sinful they were. But as people sinned more and more, God's wonderful kindness became more abundant. So just as sin ruled over all people and brought them to death, now God's wonderful kindness rules instead, giving us right standing with God and resulting in eternal life through Jesus Christ our Lord.

ROMANS 5:17-21

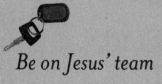

Be on Jesus' team

"OUR TEAM WON!" shouted Erica as she dashed into the house. "Look what I got!" She held out a first-prize ribbon. "We had an archery competition at school today, and my team won!"

"And you always say you're no good in archery," said Mom. "How many points did you make?"

"None, but it didn't matter because Cheryl was on our team," replied Erica. "She's the best archer in school, and she made enough points for all of us."

"So she really did the winning, but the whole team shared the victory, right?" asked Mom. "Well, I'm glad you had a good time today."

That evening Erica and her parents attended a special service at church. "I know just what the pastor meant tonight when he talked about Christians being righteous in God's sight," remarked Erica on the way home. "When we truly believe in Jesus as our Savior, his blood washes away all our sin. Then God sees his righteousness instead of our sin."

"That reminds me of your archery victory today," said Mom. "Just as you were on the winning team, we could say we're on Jesus' team."

"That's right," agreed Dad, "and just as Cheryl's points counted for all those on the team, the holiness of Jesus counts for everybody on his team. All Christians share in Jesus' victory over sin."

"And the prize we get is wonderful," Mom added. "Eternal life with Jesus!"

HOW ABOUT YOU? Are you on Jesus' team? There's no way you can "win points" on your own. Jesus has already won the victory, and he invites you to share in it. Will you accept him today? Then you'll be on the very best team! *H.W.M.*

TO MEMORIZE: How we thank God, who gives us victory over sin and death through Jesus Christ our Lord! *1 Corinthians 15:57*

MATT WAS QUIET as he and his father raked the lawn one Saturday. "Dad," he said finally as he leaned on his rake, "I sometimes wonder if I'm really a Christian. Lately I . . . well, sometimes I have bad thoughts that I know a Christian shouldn't have."

Dad was quiet for a moment. Then he led Matt to a cluster of small trees and moved back a branch to reveal a bird's nest. "I found this when I was pruning some branches," said Dad. "Do you notice anything strange about those eggs?"

"One is bigger than the others."

"That's because it wasn't laid by the bird that built this nest," explained Dad. "It was laid by a cowbird."

"A cowbird?" asked Matt. "Why would she do that?"

"So the other bird would think it was her own and care for the chick when it hatches," Dad replied. "The trouble is, the cowbird baby is usually bigger and stronger than the other baby birds and often takes their food or even pushes them out of the nest."

"What a mean trick!" exclaimed Matt. "Too bad the other bird can't tell that the big egg isn't her own. Then she could push it out before it hatches."

"That's right," Dad agreed. Then he added, "Satan is like that cowbird. He likes to put things into our minds that don't belong there. We need God's help to think and do the right things. We need to reject Satan's thoughts and push them out."

HOW ABOUT YOU? Do your thoughts sometimes make you feel like doing something you shouldn't? Don't dwell on these thoughts. Reject them. This is easier to do when you read the Bible regularly. Replace bad thoughts with good ones! *S.L.K.*

TO MEMORIZE: "In your anger do not sin": Do not let the sun go down while you are still angry, and do not give the devil a foothold. *Ephesians 4:26-27* (NIV)

BAD EGGS

FROM THE BIBLE:

Always be full of joy in the Lord. I say it again—rejoice! Let everyone see that you are considerate in all you do. Remember, the Lord is coming soon.

Don't worry about anything; instead, pray about everything. Tell God what you need, and thank him for all he has done. If you do this, you will experience God's peace, which is far more wonderful than the human mind can understand. His peace will guard your hearts and minds as you live in Christ Jesus.

And now, dear brothers and sisters, let me say one more thing as I close this letter. Fix your thoughts on what is true and honorable and right. Think about things that are pure and lovely and admirable. Think about things that are excellent and worthy of praise. Keep putting into practice all you learned from me and heard from me and saw me doing, and the God of peace will be with you.
PHILIPPIANS 4:4-9

Reject bad thoughts

27 November

WRONG IMPRESSION

FROM THE BIBLE:

God blesses the people who patiently endure testing. Afterward they will receive the crown of life that God has promised to those who love him. And remember, no one who wants to do wrong should ever say, "God is tempting me." God is never tempted to do wrong, and he never tempts anyone else either. Temptation comes from the lure of our own evil desires. These evil desires lead to evil actions, and evil actions lead to death. So don't be misled, my dear brothers and sisters.

JAMES 1:12-16

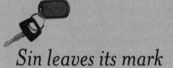

Sin leaves its mark

KENT AND HIS DAD went into the family room to watch a basketball game. "Hmmm, that's funny," said Dad. "The picture's never been this bad before." After examining the screen a few minutes, he took a small booklet from a drawer and looked through it. "I thought so!" he said a moment later. "You've been playing video games a lot lately, haven't you?" Kent nodded. "According to this, if a video game is played for too long on a TV, it may begin to leave permanent marks on the screen," said Dad. Then he looked at Kent seriously and added, "Speaking of pictures, there's something I've been meaning to talk to you about."

"What's that?" asked Kent.

"Your mother told me she found a calendar in your room," replied Dad. "She said it had pictures that did not honor the Lord. Did you throw it out?" Kent nodded. "Good," said Dad, "but did it leave any permanent marks on your mind?"

Kent looked startled. "What do you mean?"

"Well," said Dad, "the overuse of that video game left an 'impression' on the TV screen. The pictures you've been looking at might have left an impression on your mind."

Kent looked at the floor. "I do still think about the pictures," he admitted, "especially when I look at a girl."

Dad turned off the TV. "It's important to be careful about what you do and hear and see," he said. "Let's talk about some things you can do to erase the impression that was made."

HOW ABOUT YOU? Have you seen or heard something bad that made a lasting impression on you? Confess to God what has happened, admitting your fault. Spend time every day in Bible reading and prayer. Fill your life with books, friends, and programs that leave a good impression. *S.L.K.*

TO MEMORIZE: These evil desires lead to evil actions, and evil actions lead to death. *James 1:15*

A BIG MISTAKE

***I'D LIKE** to do that,* thought Melissa when Miss Baker asked for a volunteer to memorize Psalm 100 and recite it at the Thanksgiving program. *But if I made a mistake in front of all those people, I'd just die.* Some of the other girls in Melissa's Sunday school class expressed the same fear, and no one volunteered.

A little later Miss Baker told the Bible story of Peter walking on the water. She was such a good storyteller that Melissa could almost feel the water beneath her feet. The entire class seemed to relax when Peter and Jesus were finally in the boat with the other disciples and the sea was calm. "Who in this story made the biggest mistake?" asked Miss Baker.

"Peter," was Dawn's quick reply.

"Why do you think it was Peter?" Miss Baker asked.

"He was afraid," suggested Lucy.

"And he didn't trust Jesus," added Melissa.

Miss Baker shook her head. "Actually, Peter was the only one who *did* trust Jesus. He got out of the boat while the others sat and watched. The ones who made the biggest mistake were the eleven disciples who didn't have faith to do it. We're a lot like them. One of the worst mistakes we make is to allow fear to keep us from trying."

Melissa quickly raised her hand. "Miss Baker, I'll memorize Psalm 100 for the program," she volunteered.

Miss Baker smiled. "Thank you, Melissa."

HOW ABOUT YOU? Is there something you want to do for the Lord, but you're afraid to try? Remember Peter. He tried, and when he began to sink, Jesus was there to lift him up. Trying and failing isn't a mistake, but it's a big mistake to fail to try. *B.J.W.*

TO MEMORIZE: Do not gloat over me, my enemies! For though I fall, I will rise again. Though I sit in darkness, the Lord himself will be my light. *Micah 7:8*

FROM THE BIBLE:

Meanwhile, the disciples were in trouble far away from land, for a strong wind had risen, and they were fighting heavy waves.

About three o'clock in the morning Jesus came to them, walking on the water. When the disciples saw him, they screamed in terror, thinking he was a ghost. But Jesus spoke to them at once. "It's all right," he said. "I am here! Don't be afraid."

Then Peter called to him, "Lord, if it's really you, tell me to come to you by walking on water."

"All right, come," Jesus said.

So Peter went over the side of the boat and walked on the water toward Jesus. But when he looked around at the high waves, he was terrified and began to sink. "Save me, Lord!" he shouted.

Instantly Jesus reached out his hand and grabbed him. "You don't have much faith," Jesus said. "Why did you doubt me?" And when they climbed back into the boat, the wind stopped.

Then the disciples worshiped him. "You really are the Son of God!" they exclaimed.

MATTHEW 14:24-33

Dare to try

29 November

IMPORTANT WORK

FROM THE BIBLE:

Since God chose you to be the holy people whom he loves, you must clothe yourselves with tenderhearted mercy, kindness, humility, gentleness, and patience. You must make allowance for each other's faults and forgive the person who offends you. Remember, the Lord forgave you, so you must forgive others. And the most important piece of clothing you must wear is love. Love is what binds us all together in perfect harmony. And let the peace that comes from Christ rule in your hearts. For as members of one body you are all called to live in peace. And always be thankful.

Let the words of Christ, in all their richness, live in your hearts and make you wise. Use his words to teach and counsel each other. Sing psalms and hymns and spiritual songs to God with thankful hearts. And whatever you do or say, let it be as a representative of the Lord Jesus, all the while giving thanks through him to God the Father.
COLOSSIANS 3:12-17

Express thankfulness

"**MOM, MAY I GO** to the park and play ball?" Amahl asked.

"Are your thank-you notes finished?" asked Mom.

"I'll do that later," Amahl said. He picked up the baseball glove his grandparents had sent for his birthday. His three aunts had sent money, and he had spent some of it on a St. Louis Cardinals shirt.

"It's been a week since your birthday," Mom reminded him as he dashed out the door.

It was a perfect day for ball. Amahl's friends were waiting for him at the park. "Amahl! Play shortstop," Michael yelled. Amahl quickly got into position.

After playing about an hour, the boys were hot and tired. Amahl said, "Let's go to the drugstore. I'll buy you all a can of pop with the birthday money I still have left."

"Great!" they agreed.

At the store, each boy chose a can of pop from the case. As Amahl went to pay for the pop, a fire engine went racing down the street. "Let's go see the fire," called one of the boys, and they all ran out the door with their cans.

"Wait!" called Amahl, but no one paid attention to him. Amahl paid for the pop, and then he walked home and went straight to his room.

His mother found him there a little later. "You're home? And writing thank-you notes?" She was surprised.

Amahl explained how his friends had raced after the fire engine without waiting for him. "They didn't even thank me for the pop I bought them," he said. "It made me realize how important it is to say thank you."

HOW ABOUT YOU? Do you take time to let others know you appreciate what they've done for you? Thankfulness should be a characteristic of a Christian. Let your thankfulness be a testimony to others. *L.M.W.*

TO MEMORIZE: No matter what happens, always be thankful, for this is God's will for you who belong to Christ Jesus. *1 Thessalonians 5:18*

NEVER A MONKEY

"**MOM, HOW DO WE** know that we didn't just evolve?" Nathan asked one day. "My science teacher believes that people evolved from monkeys."

"Be careful not to believe everything you hear," Mother warned. "Satan likes to make the wrong seem right just to get us confused."

Nathan rested his chin in his hands. "Well, I know the Bible says God created everything. I've known that ever since I can remember. It's just that there are so many similarities between monkeys and humans."

"I can tell you have really been thinking," said Mother, handing Nathan a cookie and a glass of milk. "There are many people who are convinced that we evolved from other forms of life. Do you remember the time you took your hamster to school when it was going to have babies? Did anyone think they might come in one morning and find baby kittens in the cage?"

"Of course not!" Nathan looked puzzled. "Hamsters always have hamsters."

"Aren't there quite a few similarities, though, between hamsters and kittens?" Mother asked. "Do you think they might have evolved from each other?" Nathan was beginning to see that what his science teacher was teaching might not be so logical.

Mother continued. "I like to think of the similarities we see in nature as a reminder of God's orderly fashion of creating the world. The Bible says God created everything to reproduce 'more of its own kind.' In other words, monkeys will always be monkeys, and people will always be people. God created it that way."

HOW ABOUT YOU? Have you run into teachers at school who make evolution sound convincing? It's easy to get confused by the clever arguments of those who do not believe the truth of God's Word. The Bible tells us that nothing was ever made, except the things that God made. *D.L.R.*

TO MEMORIZE: He created everything there is. Nothing exists that he didn't make. *John 1:3*

FROM THE BIBLE:

God created great sea creatures and every sort of fish and every kind of bird. And God saw that it was good. Then God blessed them, saying, "Let the fish multiply and fill the oceans. Let the birds increase and fill the earth." This all happened on the fifth day.

And God said, "Let the earth bring forth every kind of animal. . . ." And so it was. God made all sorts of wild animals, livestock, and small animals, each able to reproduce more of its own kind. And God saw that it was good.

Then God said, "Let us make people in our image, to be like ourselves. They will be masters over all life. . . ."

So God created people in his own image; God patterned them after himself; male and female he created them.

Christ is the one through whom God created everything in heaven and earth. He made the things we can see and the things we can't see—kings, kingdoms, rulers, and authorities. Everything has been created through him and for him.

GENESIS 1:21-27;
COLOSSIANS 1:16

God created you

1 December

HOT COALS AND BARE FEET

FROM THE BIBLE:

When a crime is not punished, people feel it is safe to do wrong. But even though a person sins a hundred times and still lives a long time, I know that those who fear God will be better off. The wicked will never live long, good lives, for they do not fear God. Their days will never grow long like the evening shadows. . . .

Young man, it's wonderful to be young! Enjoy every minute of it. Do everything you want to do; take it all in. But remember that you must give an account to God for everything you do. . . .

Don't let the excitement of youth cause you to forget your Creator. Honor him in your youth before you grow old and no longer enjoy living.
ECCLESIASTES 8:11-13; 11:9; 12:1

Sin is always harmful

"**HI, MOM,**" said Tiffany as she came in the door.

"Hi," greeted Mom. "What did you do at Kay's?"

Tiffany hesitated. "Oh, nothing much."

Mom's brows creased. "You're hedging, Tiffany."

"Well . . . Kay wanted to watch a movie on TV that had a lot of violence and swearing," confessed Tiffany. "I didn't really want to, but I was her guest. But don't worry, Mom. I don't let things like that affect me."

"Fooling around with wrong things is like playing with fire," replied Mom. "I was just thinking of my cousin, Anna. I once went camping with Anna's family. Her father built a bonfire. When the flames died down, her father threw water over the coals. They turned gray, and the fire seemed to be gone.

"Anna and I played a game of tag. With her bare feet, Anna almost ran right over those coals because they looked as gray as the sand. She would have burned both her feet. In Proverbs it says, 'Can a man scoop fire into his lap and not be burned? Can he walk on hot coals and not blister his feet?' "

"Oh," said Tiffany, "that's what almost happened to Anna."

"Yes. But God isn't warning about real fire in this verse," Mom said. "He's talking about doing wrong things."

"Like watching bad TV and listening to rock music?" asked Tiffany. "I didn't think a little would hurt."

Mom nodded. "Yes. Like the gray coals that looked harmless, wrong things often seem innocent at first. But doing wrong always harms us."

HOW ABOUT YOU? Have you felt that a few worldly things wouldn't harm you? Treat every wrong thing as though it's a red-hot coal of fire. *M.R.P.*

TO MEMORIZE: Can a man scoop fire into his lap and not be burned? Can he walk on hot coals and not blister his feet? *Proverbs 6:27-28*

DANNY HARPER dragged his feet as he approached Mr. Grant, the man in the wheelchair. He was visiting the old man as a "Christian work assignment" for his youth group. "Uh, I'm Danny Harper from church," he managed to say.

Mr. Grant invited the boy to sit beside him. Then the old man began telling how he had helped start the church Danny now attended. "That was in the old days when I was a new Christian," said Mr. Grant. "I went door to door, inviting people to come to our new church. I had so much energy then! Oh, to be young again! That's when a person can really serve the Lord."

Danny laughed. He said, "And I've always thought that a kid like me can't do much for Jesus. I keep thinking that when I'm older, I'll really start working for the Lord."

Mr. Grant shook his finger in Danny's face. "Don't think that way," he said. "Young people can do much for the Lord. They're so fresh and excited about life! Already you've helped me realize that I ought to start serving God again like I used to. But I'll have to work pretty hard to keep up with a young whippersnapper like you!"

"Thanks, Mr. Grant!" said Danny. "You've helped me, too. Next time I won't be so afraid to visit someone just because he's got a few gray hairs!"

HOW ABOUT YOU? When was the last time you made friends with someone much older than yourself? You may feel that older people look down on you because of your youth. But actually you can do much for them by visiting and by helping with shopping or yard work. *S.L.K.*

TO MEMORIZE: Don't let anyone look down on you because you are young, but set an example for the believers in speech, in life, in love, in faith and in purity. *1 Timothy 4:12* (NIV)

A FEW GRAY HAIRS

FROM THE BIBLE:

But as for you, promote the kind of living that reflects right teaching. Teach the older men to exercise self-control, to be worthy of respect, and to live wisely. They must have strong faith and be filled with love and patience.

Similarly, teach the older women to live in a way that is appropriate for someone serving the Lord. They must not go around speaking evil of others and must not be heavy drinkers. Instead, they should teach others what is good. These older women must train the younger women to love their husbands and their children, to live wisely and be pure, to take care of their homes, to do good, and to be submissive to their husbands. Then they will not bring shame on the word of God.

In the same way, encourage the young men to live wisely in all they do. And you yourself must be an example to them by doing good deeds of every kind. Let everything you do reflect the integrity and seriousness of your teaching.

TITUS 2:1-7

Use the gift of youth

3 December

WORMS OF SIN

FROM THE BIBLE:

So we are lying if we say we have fellowship with God but go on living in spiritual darkness. We are not living in the truth. But if we are living in the light of God's presence, just as Christ is, then we have fellowship with each other, and the blood of Jesus, his Son, cleanses us from every sin.

If we say we have no sin, we are only fooling ourselves and refusing to accept the truth. But if we confess our sins to him, he is faithful and just to forgive us and to cleanse us from every wrong. If we claim we have not sinned, we are calling God a liar and showing that his word has no place in our hearts.

1 JOHN 1:6-10

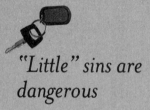

"Little" sins are dangerous

"BRRR!" SAID MONICA as she slammed the front door and kicked off her boots. "It's freezing out there, Mom! Isn't there a warmer cap I can wear?"

"There should be one in this closet. All the winter things are here," Mother replied, opening the closet door. She rummaged around and pulled out some wool hats, mittens, and scarves. She frowned when she saw that several contained large holes.

"Oh no!" groaned Mother. "Moths got into them."

"Moths?" asked Monica.

Mother nodded. "Actually, it's not adult moths that eat cloth but baby moths. They look like small worms."

Monica made a face. "Who would have thought such little things could cause all this damage!"

Mother glanced at her. "There's an important principle here," she said. "Sometimes we're tempted to think that the 'little' sinful things we do aren't so bad. We tell a 'little white lie' or cheat just 'a little.' We don't hit anybody or knock anyone over, but we're a 'little bit' mean to them. We keep back just 'a little' of the money we know we should give to God. We forget that in God's sight, sin is sin. And we forget that just as each moth lays many, many eggs, one 'little' sin leads to other sins." She paused, then added, "I know the idea of worms eating your mittens sounds gross to you. Remember that sin is gross too!"

HOW ABOUT YOU? Do you sometimes feel that "little" sins won't really hurt anything? Sin always brings consequences eventually. A "little" sin may make it easier for you to sin again in the future. It may encourage others to do wrong things. Or it may lead to hurt feelings and disappointment when others find out about it. Don't let sin "eat away" at your life. *S.L.K.*

TO MEMORIZE: If we say we have no sin, we are only fooling ourselves and refusing to accept the truth. *1 John 1:8*

"GOD SURE HAS ANSWERED a lot of prayers for us lately, hasn't he?" Luis said to his big sister, Maria.

"He sure has," Maria agreed. "He healed Grandma, gave Daddy a job, and even sent us some new friends!"

"I guess God will give us anything we want. All we have to do is ask him," five-year-old Luis reasoned. "What do you want, Maria?"

"I want a piano," Maria answered. "What do you want?"

"I want a new bicycle," exclaimed Luis. "Daddy said I'd have to wait until Christmas, but I want one now. Hey, let's ask God for what we want."

After Mother had tucked the children into bed that night, she returned to the living room, a frown on her face. "In their prayers tonight Maria asked God to send a piano right away, and Luis asked for a bike."

Dad grinned. "I guess they're taking their requests over our heads."

After a week of watching and waiting, Luis and Maria went to their mother. "I thought God always answered our prayers," Maria began.

"He does, Maria." Mother knew what was coming. "Did you ask for something you haven't received?"

Both children nodded. "We asked for a bicycle and a piano, but I guess God didn't hear us. Maybe we should pray louder," Luis said.

"I'm sure God heard you," replied Mother, "but I don't think you're hearing his answer. He's telling you the same thing Daddy and I told you. He's telling you to wait."

GOD'S ANSWER

FROM THE BIBLE:

We can be confident that he will listen to us whenever we ask him for anything in line with his will. And if we know he is listening when we make our requests, we can be sure that he will give us what we ask for.

What is causing the quarrels and fights among you? Isn't it the whole army of evil desires at war within you? You want what you don't have, so you scheme and kill to get it. You are jealous for what others have, and you can't possess it, so you fight and quarrel to take it away from them. And yet the reason you don't have what you want is that you don't ask God for it. And even when you do ask, you don't get it because your whole motive is wrong—you want only what will give you pleasure.

1 JOHN 5:14-15; JAMES 4:1-3

God answers prayer

HOW ABOUT YOU? Are you asking God for something your parents have said you cannot have or will have to wait for? When you pray, listen for God's answer. Sometimes he says yes. Sometimes he says no. And sometimes he says wait. God always answers your prayers. *B.J.W.*

TO MEMORIZE: If we know he is listening when we make our requests, we can be sure that he will give us what we ask for. *1 John 5:15*

5 December

SNOW DAY

FROM THE BIBLE:

And so, dear brothers and sisters, I plead with you to give your bodies to God. Let them be a living and holy sacrifice—the kind he will accept. When you think of what he has done for you, is this too much to ask? . . .

Just as our bodies have many parts and each part has a special function, so it is with Christ's body. We are all parts of his one body, and each of us has different work to do. And since we are all one body in Christ, we belong to each other, and each of us needs all the others.

God has given each of us the ability to do certain things well. So if God has given you the ability to prophesy, speak out when you have faith that God is speaking through you. . . .

Don't just pretend that you love others. Really love them. Hate what is wrong. Stand on the side of the good. Love each other with genuine affection, and take delight in honoring each other.

ROMANS 12:1, 4-6, 9-10

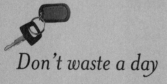

Don't waste a day

SALENA WEST was eating breakfast when the announcement came on the radio. "The following school closings have been reported due to the freezing temperatures and the icy condition of the roads: Springfield Public Schools, . . ."

That was all Salena had to hear to get upset! "Why today?" she groaned. "I planned to go home with Karen after school. Now I won't be able to visit her. Besides, what's there to do at home?"

Mother looked at Salena's scowling face. "That's not a very good attitude," her mother told her. "The Lord gave you this day." Salena knew that, but it didn't make her feel any better. Mother continued, "Since you can't think of anything you want to do today, why don't you dedicate the day to helping others?"

"How can I do that? I can't even go out of the house."

"You could bake cookies for Aunt Barb," suggested Mother.

"Well, I guess I could do that," said Salena with a smile.

"And you could write a letter to Christy Blaine," added Mother. "The two of you had a lot of fun when her family was home on furlough last year. Missionaries enjoy receiving mail from home. And you could write to your grandma, too."

Salena thought about her mother's ideas. Maybe it could be a fun day! It was a day God had given. She would dedicate it to showing his love to others.

HOW ABOUT YOU? What do you do when you have a free day? Do you waste it watching TV or fighting with your brother or sister? The next time you have a long day in front of you, see how many things you can do to show the Lord's love to others. Start making a list now, so you will be prepared. *L.M.W.*

TO MEMORIZE: Dear children, let us stop just saying we love each other; let us really show it by our actions. *1 John 3:18*

"WHAT'S ON your mind, John?" his mother asked. "You look so serious!"

"My Sunday school teacher said that God is a Trinity—he said God the Father, God the Son, and God the Holy Spirit are all one person. How could that be true? asked John"

"It seems impossible," agreed Mother, "but the Bible teaches—"

The telephone rang, interrupting her reply. "That was your father," she said after hanging up. "He wants me to get his suit from the clean—"

The phone rang again. "Hello? . . . Mom? . . . Sure, I'll take you to the doctor. See you at three. Good-bye."

John grinned at his mother. "Grandma wants you, too, doesn't she?"

Mother nodded. "Yes, and I also have to stop at Aunt Cindy's house. I promised to take the baby for her this afternoon."

"Wow! What do people think you are?" asked John. "Triplets?"

Mother laughed. "I don't mind. I'm Dad's wife, so he asks me to do things for him. I'm Mom's daughter, so she asks me to help her. And as Aunt Cindy's sister, she just asks me to be sisterly."

John thought a while. "A sister, a daughter, and a wife—yet you're only one person. Is that like God being more than one person?"

"Maybe a little, though there's nothing you can really compare with the Trinity," answered Mother. "There are some things we believe because the Bible says so, not because we understand them. That's faith."

HOW ABOUT YOU? Do you doubt what the Bible teaches because it "doesn't seem possible"? The Bible is the Word of God, and what it says is true. You think with a human mind, but God is far greater than our minds. *A.G.L.*

TO MEMORIZE: All Scripture is inspired by God and is useful to teach us what is true and to make us realize what is wrong in our lives. *2 Timothy 3:16*

NOT IMPOSSIBLE

FROM THE BIBLE:

"My thoughts are completely different from yours," says the Lord. "And my ways are far beyond anything you could imagine. For just as the heavens are higher than the earth, so are my ways higher than your ways and my thoughts higher than your thoughts.

"The rain and snow come down from the heavens and stay on the ground to water the earth. They cause the grain to grow, producing seed for the farmer and bread for the hungry. It is the same with my word. I send it out, and it always produces fruit. It will accomplish all I want it to, and it will prosper everywhere I send it."

ISAIAH 55:8-11

Believe all God says

7 December

THE WRONG FRIENDS

FROM THE BIBLE:

*Don't team up with those who
are unbelievers. How can
goodness be a partner with
wickedness? How can light live
with darkness? What harmony
can there be between Christ and
the Devil? How can a believer be
a partner with an unbeliever?
And what union can there be
between God's temple and idols?
For we are the temple of the
living God. As God said:*

*"I will live in them
 and walk among them.
I will be their God,
 and they will be my people.
Therefore, come out from them
 and separate yourselves from
  them, says the Lord.
Don't touch their filthy things,
 and I will welcome you."*

2 CORINTHIANS 6:14-17

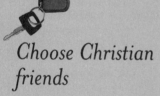

*Choose Christian
friends*

ALAN'S LITTLE SISTER reached up. "Hold my hand, Alan," she said.

"I don't need to hold your hand," he answered. "You're not a baby, Melinda!"

"But Mama holds my hand when—oh! I almost falled," Melinda exclaimed as she tripped over a crack in the sidewalk.

"If you'd look where you're going, you wouldn't trip!" Alan grabbed her hand. "Now hurry up!" Melinda chattered happily, but her big brother wasn't listening. He was still annoyed because Mother had insisted that he take Melinda to play in the park. He'd much rather be playing video games. But Mother didn't like him hanging around the arcade. And she didn't like the boys he hung around with either. Steve and Clay weren't so bad.

When Alan and Melinda returned home, they saw Mother in the yard. Melinda dashed ahead, tripped on the water hose, and fell. "She never looks where she's going," said Alan in disgust.

Mother helped Melinda stand up. "She's not the only one," she said. "You need to look where you're headed, too, Son. I just learned that Steve and Clay were caught shoplifting this afternoon. I'm glad you weren't with them. But if you keep hanging around those two, you are headed for a big fall."

Melinda reached up to her brother. "I'll hold your hand, Alan, so you won't fall."

Mother smiled at her. "I'm afraid you couldn't keep him from falling, but there's someone who can. Alan had better let God hold his hand."

HOW ABOUT YOU? Have you looked down the road you're traveling to see what is ahead of you? If you're following the wrong crowd, you're headed for a fall. Choose friends who will help you to do what is right. *B.J.W.*

TO MEMORIZE: "Quick!" he told the people, "Get away from the tents of these wicked men, and don't touch anything that belongs to them. If you do, you will be destroyed for their sins." *Numbers 16:26*

TOOTHPICKS OR TREASURE

"CARL!" CALLED Dad as he hung up the phone. Carl knew by the tone of Dad's voice that there was going to be trouble.

"That was your principal," said Dad. "He told me you were sent to his office today for goofing off in class and talking disrespectfully to your teacher."

Carl looked uncomfortable. "It wasn't my fault," he protested. "Jack started it. Besides, that class is boring!"

"Maybe it wouldn't be so boring if you studied your lessons more often," Dad replied sternly.

Carl shrugged. "Aw, Dad, if I studied all the time, I wouldn't have any fun!"

Dad was quiet for a moment. Then he said, "Come down to my workroom. I want to show you something."

After rummaging around in a box, Dad pulled out a small, thick piece of wood. "This belonged to Grandpa Williams," he said.

Carl looked at it curiously. "That can't be worth much," he said finally.

"Oh, but it is. It's solid cherry," said Dad. "Remember the hand-carved figure Mom has on the coffee table? Grandpa Williams used to carve those and sell them to collectors. They were made from the same kind of wood as this piece."

Carl whistled. "Wow! I guess that is valuable after all."

"On the other hand," said Dad, "if it were cut up into toothpicks, it wouldn't be worth much. The wood must be used properly. And the same thing is true of a life. Life is a gift from God. It's important to use it well. Don't be careless with it and waste it."

HOW ABOUT YOU? Do you think the most important thing in life is having fun? Are you careless in your schoolwork or lazy about prayer and Bible reading? Life passes quickly. Don't waste it. *S.L.K.*

TO MEMORIZE: Whatever your hand finds to do, do it with all your might. *Ecclesiastes 9:10* (NIV)

FROM THE BIBLE:

Seventy years are given to us!
Some may even reach eighty.
But even the best of these years are
filled with pain and trouble;
soon they disappear, and we
are gone. . . .

Teach us to make the most
of our time,
so that we may grow in
wisdom.

O Lord, come back to us!
How long will you delay?
Take pity on your servants!
Satisfy us in the morning with
your unfailing love,
so we may sing for joy to
the end of our lives.
Give us gladness in proportion to
our former misery!
Replace the evil years with
good.
Let us see your miracles again;
let our children see your glory
at work.
And may the Lord our God show
us his approval
and make our efforts
successful.
Yes, make our efforts
successful!
PSALM 90:10, 12-17

Use your life carefully

9 December

IT'S HEREDITARY

FROM THE BIBLE:

See how very much our heavenly Father loves us, for he allows us to be called his children, and we really are! But the people who belong to this world don't know God, so they don't understand that we are his children. Yes, dear friends, we are already God's children, and we can't even imagine what we will be like when Christ returns. But we do know that when he comes we will be like him, for we will see him as he really is. And all who believe this will keep themselves pure, just as Christ is pure.
1 JOHN 3:1-3

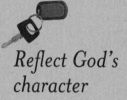

Reflect God's character

"OH, MOM! Why did I have to get freckles?" Becky complained as she studied her nose in the mirror.

"Be glad you don't have warts," consoled her younger brother, Jay. "Besides, what's wrong with freckles? Mom has freckles, and she's pretty."

"That's different," answered Becky. "She's a mother, and nobody cares if she has freckles."

"I'm not really surprised that you're getting freckles," Mom said. "After all, I've got them, and your grandma and great-grandma had freckles, too. They're one of the hereditary characteristics that I passed on to you."

"What does that mean, Mom?" Jay asked.

"It means that there's no hope for me," Becky moaned.

Mom smiled as she explained. "It means you have freckles because I have freckles. You and Becky have brown eyes because Daddy and I have brown eyes. We have brown eyes because our parents had brown eyes. What you are is a reflection of Daddy and me."

"I think I understand," Jay said. "We're a lot like you and Daddy because we were born into your family."

"Right," agreed Mom. "Becky may not appreciate all the characteristics she has inherited, but it's obvious that she's part of our family."

"Freckles and all!" Becky giggled.

"You know, kids," Mom mused, "as Christians, we're part of God's family, and that should be obvious, too."

HOW ABOUT YOU? Do you belong to God's family? Then you should reflect his character. There should be more friendliness, more helpfulness, more kind acts. In other words, you should be growing more like Jesus every day. *B.D.*

TO MEMORIZE: See how very much our heavenly Father loves us, for he allows us to be called his children, and we really are! *1 John 3:1*

JANA PLOPPED down on the couch. "I don't think Sara will ever become a Christian. I've witnessed to her lots of times, but it doesn't do any good. She just keeps on going to raunchy movies and watching those television shows you won't let me watch. I've told her what I think about all that, but she just laughs."

"She'll do those things until she has the Lord's power to overcome sin," Mother reasoned.

"But she doesn't want to overcome sin," Jana said as she shook her head. "She enjoys it."

Mother nodded. "That's natural. There are temporary pleasures in sin, but living for God is much bett—"

"Big Paw! Come back with that!" Brian's cry rang down the hall. "Mother! Big Paw has my marker!"

The dog ran under the dining room table. "Give it to me, Big Paw," ordered Mother. Big Paw growled softly.

Mother reached for the marker as she spoke. This time Big Paw growled louder.

Jana laughed. "You two are doing it all wrong!" She took a small piece of cold meat from the refrigerator. "Here, Big Paw! Want some meat?" Immediately the dog dropped the marker and snatched up the food.

As Mother picked up the marker, she grinned. "To get the marker, all we had to do was offer him something better."

Then Mother said to Jana, "Have you offered Sara something better than sin, Jana? You've told her all she shouldn't do, but have you told her all the good things she would get as a Christian?"

Jana looked surprised. "No, I guess not."

HOW ABOUT YOU? Do you witness by telling people all the things they are doing wrong and what they have to give up? Instead, tell them about the advantages of being a Christian. *B.J.W.*

TO MEMORIZE: The blessing of the Lord makes a person rich, and he adds no sorrow with it. *Proverbs 10:22*

A BETTER OFFER

FROM THE BIBLE:

Peter said to him, "We've given up everything to follow you. What will we get out of it?"

And Jesus replied, "I assure you that when I, the Son of Man, sit upon my glorious throne in the Kingdom, you who have been my followers will also sit on twelve thrones, judging the twelve tribes of Israel. And everyone who has given up houses or brothers or sisters or father or mother or children or property, for my sake, will receive a hundred times as much in return and will have eternal life. But many who seem to be important now will be the least important then, and those who are considered least here will be the greatest then.
MATTHEW 19:27-30

The Christian life is best

11 December

SONG OF THE WILD

FROM THE BIBLE:

Oh, the joys of those
  who do not follow the advice
    of the wicked,
  or stand around with sinners,
  or join in with scoffers.
But they delight in doing
    everything the Lord wants;
  day and night they think
    about his law.
They are like trees planted along
    the riverbank,
  bearing fruit each season
    without fail.
Their leaves never wither,
  and in all they do, they
    prosper.

But this is not true of the wicked.
  They are like worthless chaff,
    scattered by the wind.
They will be condemned at the
    time of judgment.
  Sinners will have no place
    among the godly.

For the Lord watches over the
    path of the godly,
  but the path of the wicked
    leads to destruction.
PSALM 1:1-6

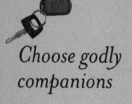

Choose godly companions

SALITA WAS SO excited she could hardly speak. "Look!" she yelled. "I caught a sparrow. Can I keep it, Mom? I found this old cage in the garage."

Salita's mother looked at the bird. "You can keep it a few days, but it's not a good idea to try to make pets of wild animals or birds."

"I know," Salita said. "I'll let it go soon. Do sparrows sing?"

Mother smiled. "Oh, they cheep and twitter, but they don't have the lovely call of a cardinal or a canary."

"Well, I'll put it next to Biddy's cage," Salita decided. "Biddy will teach the sparrow to sing."

A few minutes later, she asked if she could play at Angie's house.

Mother frowned. "What do you have planned?"

Salita shrugged. "She has lots of computer games and CDs . She has her own television, too. We'll find plenty to do."

"I'm sure that's true," said Mother, "but will it be the right kind of activity? Why don't you ask Angie to come over here more often?"

Salita answered, "She says our house is boring."

"You may go, but only for a short time," decided Mother. "Spending too much time with Angie may cause you to stop liking your own games and CDs."

A few days later, Salita decided to release the sparrow. "Instead of this bird learning to sing like a canary, Biddy is starting to chirp and tweet like the sparrow!" she told her mother. Then she added, "That's like Angie and me, isn't it?"

HOW ABOUT YOU? Do you think that by doing what non-Christian friends want you to do it will help them become Christians? Be very careful! Make sure your non-Christian friends aren't influencing you to do wrong. Make sure that your friends are helping you choose to do what's right. *C.R.*

TO MEMORIZE: The Lord watches over the path of the godly, but the path of the wicked leads to destruction. *Psalm 1:6*

"I'LL PICK YOU UP after school and take you to see your grandpa in the hospital," Mother told Andy and Lisa.

Andy tried to swallow the lump in his throat. "Is . . . is he going to die?"

Mother took a deep breath. "I don't know. I only know Grandpa is in God's hands. God will take care of him. Whatever is best for Grandpa is what we want, isn't it?"

Tears rolled down Andy's cheeks.

"Grandpa has been in a lot of pain lately," Mother reminded him. "And he hasn't been happy since Grandma died last spring. I think Grandpa wants to see Grandma and Jesus."

"But we need him," Andy protested, "and he doesn't want to leave us."

Lisa handed Andy two dollars. "Keep this money for me until after school, will you, Andy? I don't have any pockets, and I want to buy Grandpa a card before we go to the hospital."

Andy stuffed the dollars in his pocket. As they ran to catch the bus, Lisa said, "Take good care of my money, Andy."

The day crawled by for Andy. Every few minutes he reminded God, "Take good care of my grandpa, Lord."

After school the children climbed into Mother's car. "Is Grandpa any better?" asked Andy.

Mother shook her head. "No. He's about the same."

"Where are my two dollars, Andy?" Lisa asked as they went in to buy Grandpa's card. Andy pulled the money out of his pocket, and Lisa smiled. "Thanks for keeping my money for me."

As Lisa paid for her card, Mother turned to Andy. "Let's trust God to take care of Grandpa just as Lisa trusted you to take care of her money. Grandpa is in safekeeping."

HOW ABOUT YOU? Is someone you love sick? Trust God to take care of that person. *B.J.W.*

TO MEMORIZE: Let your favor shine on your servant. In your unfailing love, save me. *Psalm 31:16*

IN SAFEKEEPING

FROM THE BIBLE:

*O Lord, I have come to you for
   protection;
   don't let me be put to shame.
Rescue me, for you always do
   what is right.
Bend down and listen to me;
   rescue me quickly.
Be for me a great rock of safety,
   a fortress where my enemies
   cannot reach me.*

*You are my rock and my
   fortress.
   For the honor of your
   name, lead me out of
   this peril. . . .*

*But I am trusting you, O Lord,
   saying, "You are my God!"
My future is in your hands.
   Rescue me from those who
   hunt me down relentlessly.
Let your favor shine on your
   servant.
   In your unfailing love,
   save me.*
PSALM 31:1-3, 14-16

Trust God

13 December

NO PUNISHMENT

FROM THE BIBLE:

You may be saying, "What terrible people you have been talking about!" But you are just as bad, and you have no excuse! When you say they are wicked and should be punished, you are condemning yourself, for you do these very same things. And we know that God, in his justice, will punish anyone who does such things. Do you think that God will judge and condemn others for doing them and not judge you when you do them, too? Don't you realize how kind, tolerant, and patient God is with you? Or don't you care? Can't you see how kind he has been in giving you time to turn from your sin?

ROMANS 2:1-4

Love mercy

THE SOUND of breaking glass brought David running into the dining room. "Ooohhh, Melissa! Look what you've done!" he gasped. Melissa stared in horror at the shattered pieces of crystal on the floor. "You broke Mom's favorite vase!" David exclaimed. "It's the one Uncle Don bought her just before he died."

"I couldn't help it," said Melissa nervously.

"What's the matter?" The children both jumped at the sound of their mother's voice. Sorrow spread over her face as she realized what had happened.

Melissa burst into sobs. "I didn't mean to. I was just looking for a pencil, and it fell. Oh! I'm sorry."

Mom put her arm around Melissa. "There, there, honey. Don't cry so."

"Does she have to buy you another one?" asked David.

"No. Some things can't be replaced," said Mom sadly.

"Then are you going to ground her?" David wanted to know. Mom shook her head. "Spank her?" was David's next question. Again Mom shook her head. David was astonished. "Aren't you going to punish her at all?"

"No," Mom sighed. "Melissa has learned that she needs to be more careful."

David shrugged in disgust. "If I had broken it, I wouldn't have been able to sit down for a week!"

"That's not true!" Mom said. Then she wisely added, "Don't be jealous when mercy is shown to someone else. Mercy is something for which we should all be very grateful. Who knows? Tomorrow you may need it yourself."

HOW ABOUT YOU? Do you grumble when others are not punished as you think they should be? God tells you to "love mercy," even when it is given to others. If you are merciful, you will receive mercy. B.J.W.

TO MEMORIZE: The Lord has already told you what is good, and this is what he requires: to do what is right, to love mercy, and to walk humbly with your God. *Micah 6:8*

MEG WATCHED her big sister leave the house. "Why can't I go to the library with Tammy?" she asked. "I'll look at books while she studies."

"Meg," Mother said patiently, "It's almost your bedtime. You're eight years old. Tammy's in high school. When you're her age, you'll have a chance to go to the library at night, too."

"Tammy has a stereo in her room, and she goes to the mall, and . . ." Meg's words tumbled over each other.

Mother got up from the couch. "Bedtime," she said. "I'll go up with you."

At the stairway, Mother stopped. "Meg," she said, "when you were a baby, you went up these stairs on your hands and knees. Later, you held onto my hand so I could help you. Do you remember that?"

Meg laughed and shook her head. "No, but the little kids at church do that."

"Now you're much bigger," Mother continued, "and you walk up the stairs. Gradually you'll be able to do more and more things. Why, look at all you do now! You stayed overnight with your friend Lisa last week. You ride your bicycle to the street now. You couldn't do those things when you were two or even four, could you?" Slowly Meg shook her head. "God made us so we don't have to learn everything at once," Mother added. "We just have to take one step at a time."

HOW ABOUT YOU? Do you want to be grown-up right now? Do you think you should be allowed to do everything a big brother or sister is allowed to do? God has a time for everything. Take just one step at a time. *D.K.*

TO MEMORIZE: God has made everything beautiful for its own time. He has planted eternity in the human heart, but even so, people cannot see the whole scope of God's work from beginning to end. *Ecclesiastes 3:11*

JUST ONE STEP

FROM THE BIBLE:

There is a time for everything, a season for every activity under heaven.
A time to be born and a time to die.
A time to plant and a time to harvest.
A time to kill and a time to heal.
A time to tear down and a time to rebuild.
A time to cry and a time to laugh.
A time to grieve and a time to dance.
A time to scatter stones and a time to gather stones.
A time to embrace and a time to turn away.
A time to search and a time to lose.
A time to keep and a time to throw away.
A time to tear and a time to mend.
A time to be quiet and a time to speak up.
A time to love and a time to hate.
A time for war and a time for peace. . . .

God has made everything beautiful for its own time. He has planted eternity in the human heart, but even so, people cannot see the whole scope of God's work from beginning to end.
ECCLESIASTES 3:1-8, 11

Be content to be a kid

15 December

OUT OF TUNE

FROM THE BIBLE:

*Purify me from my sins, and I
     will be clean;
     wash me, and I will be whiter
     than snow.
Oh, give me back my joy again;
     you have broken me—
     now let me rejoice.
Don't keep looking at my sins.
     Remove the stain of my guilt.
Create in me a clean heart,
     O God.
     Renew a right spirit within
     me.
Do not banish me from your
     presence,
     and don't take your Holy
     Spirit from me.
Restore to me again the joy of
     your salvation,
     and make me willing to obey
     you.
Then I will teach your ways to
     sinners,
     and they will return to you.*
PSALM 51:7-13

Follow God's standards

"ARE YOU COMING to the Christmas concert at school this afternoon?" asked Katie as she finished her breakfast. "Melanie and I are playing a flute duet."

"I wouldn't miss it," Mother replied. As Katie stood up from the table, Mother gasped. "Where did you get that skirt?"

Katie shrugged. "Candy gave it to me. It was too small for her."

"Well, it's also too small for you!" declared Mother. "Please go up and change into something decent."

"Oh, Mother! You're so old-fashioned!" whined Katie. "All the girls wear skirts like this."

When Katie and Melanie began to play at the concert that afternoon, they realized at once that something was wrong. The notes they played just didn't sound right with the piano. Embarrassed, the girls began to make mistakes. They were glad when the song was over and they could sit down.

"It was so humiliating," groaned Katie that evening. "Melanie and I made sure our instruments were in tune with each other, but we didn't tune them with the piano."

"Katie, remember what we were talking about this morning?" asked Mother. "You seemed to feel that going along with fads was OK because 'everyone was doing it.' But you might be 'in tune' with the standards of the world and be 'out of tune' with God's standards."

HOW ABOUT YOU? Are your clothes in style? Do you listen to the same music and watch the same TV programs as everybody else? That's OK as long as you're meeting God's standards, too. Make sure you're "in tune" with him! *S.L.K.*

TO MEMORIZE: Don't copy the behavior and customs of this world, but let God transform you into a new person by changing the way you think. Then you will know what God wants you to do, and you will know how good and pleasing and perfect his will really is. *Romans 12:2*

"JEREMY, IT'S SOON time for bed," called Mom.

"Can I have five more minutes?" begged Jeremy. "I need help to understand a Bible verse." Jeremy was reading his Bible, but he was also trying to get out of going to bed.

Mom came into the room. "Tell me what you're reading, Jeremy."

"I'm reading John, chapter 3," he told his mother. "In verse 3 Jesus said, 'I *assure you.'* What does *assure* mean?"

"Remember what Dad told you to do when you don't know the meaning of a word in the Bible?" asked Mom.

"He said to look it up in different translations and in a dictionary."

"Why don't you do that now?" said Mom, smiling.

Taking two Bibles from a bookshelf and his dictionary out of his desk, Jerry opened one of the Bibles to John 3:3 and found the words "I tell you the *'truth.'"* In another translation he read, "'Verily, verily,' I say unto thee."

Jeremy looked up *assure* in his dictionary. "It means 'convince' or 'guarantee' according to Mr. Webster," Jeremy told his mother. "Did Jesus want to convince us or guarantee that what he said is true?"

"That's right. He wanted the people to believe what he was saying," Mom answered.

"I've read words I didn't understand before," Jeremy said. "But I never took the time to learn what they meant."

"Well, now that you know what *assure* means," said Mother, "you'll understand this: I assure you, it is time for you to go to bed!"

HOW ABOUT YOU? Do you sometimes have trouble understanding the words used in the Bible? It only takes a minute to look them up, and it will help you understand what God is saying to you. If you still don't understand, ask someone to help you. Learn about the Bible. *L.M.W.*

TO MEMORIZE: Jesus replied, "I assure you, unless you are born again, you can never see the Kingdom of God." *John 3:3*

THIS IS TRUE!

FROM THE BIBLE:

After dark one evening, a Jewish religious leader named Nicodemus, a Pharisee, came to speak with Jesus. "Teacher," he said, "we all know that God has sent you to teach us. Your miraculous signs are proof enough that God is with you."

Jesus replied, "I assure you, unless you are born again, you can never see the Kingdom of God."

"What do you mean?" exclaimed Nicodemus. "How can an old man go back into his mother's womb and be born again?"

Jesus replied, "The truth is, no one can enter the Kingdom of God without being born of water and the Spirit. . . .

"And as Moses lifted up the bronze snake on a pole in the wilderness, so I, the Son of Man, must be lifted up on a pole, so that everyone who believes in me will have eternal life.

"For God so loved the world that he gave his only Son, so that everyone who believes in him will not perish but have eternal life. God did not send his Son into the world to condemn it, but to save it.

JOHN 3:1-5, 14-17

Look up Bible words

17 December

ASK WHAT YOU CAN DO

FROM THE BIBLE:

*Let the whole earth sing to the
    Lord!
    Each day proclaim the good
    news that he saves.
Publish his glorious deeds among
    the nations.
    Tell everyone about the
    amazing things he does.
Great is the Lord! He is most
    worthy of praise!
    He is to be revered above all
    gods.
The gods of other nations are
    merely idols,
    but the Lord made the
    heavens!
Honor and majesty surround him;
    strength and beauty are in his
    dwelling.*

*O nations of the world,
    recognize the Lord,
    recognize that the Lord is
    glorious and strong.
Give to the Lord the glory he
    deserves!
    Bring your offering and come
    to worship him.
Worship the Lord in all his holy
    splendor.*
1 CHRONICLES 16:23-29

Be involved at church

CARLA WAS TIRED of her church. She told her mother, "I don't get anything out of the worship services. The music seems so dull, and I can't follow Pastor Reese's sermons. I wish I didn't always have to go!" Mother told Carla she would pray with her about it.

At school that week Carla was assigned to prepare an oral report on John F. Kennedy. She found some interesting facts about him. He was the youngest man ever elected president, and he was shot and killed while still in office.

When Carla finished her report, she asked her mom to listen as she practiced it. She ended with a quote from President Kennedy's inaugural address. "He is very famous for this line, 'Ask not what your country can do for you. Ask rather what you can do for your country.'"

Mom remained silent.

"Well, what do you think?" Carla asked.

"Oh, I'm sorry," said Mom. "It's good, dear, but that last line started me thinking. Remember what you told me about not being able to get anything out of the church services? Maybe we could apply President Kennedy's quote here. Ask not what your church can do for you, ask what you can do for your church."

"Hmmm, maybe so!" Carla responded. She thought a lot about it that week, and she decided to try it.

HOW ABOUT YOU? Do you just sit around expecting to receive blessings at church, or do you try to be a blessing to others? In church, as in other areas, you generally get out of it as much as you put into it. True worship involves giving glory to God, giving offerings to God, and giving ourselves to God. *R.E.P.*

TO MEMORIZE: Give to the Lord the glory he deserves! Bring your offering and come to worship him. Worship the Lord in all his holy splendor. *1 Chronicles 16:29*

BROOKE CAREFULLY DROPPED batter onto the cookie sheet, put it in the oven, and slumped into a nearby chair. "The last ones," she said. "As soon as they're baked and cooled, I'll pack them in a box for the school sale."

"You won't forget to clean up, will you?" asked Mother.

"I'll do it later," Brooke said, then added, "unless you'll do it."

Mother shook her head. "No, honey. I'm on my way to a meeting. Anyway, you promised to clean up the kitchen after you baked the cookies."

"I didn't know baking all these cookies would take so long," Brooke replied. "Can't I just help you clean up the kitchen at suppertime?" As she peeked into the oven she added, "I hate the cleanup part."

"Most of us do," Mother said, "but it has to be done."

Reluctantly Brooke dropped the messy bowls and spoons into the sink. "Can't I just soak them?" she persisted. "Everything is so sticky and . . ."

"Honey," said Mother, "there are many times that I wish I could leave the messy work for someone else to do. But that's not the way things work. I think it's especially important for Christians to be faithful in whatever we do. That means we must cheerfully do a complete job, including the less pleasant parts."

Brooke thought about her mother's words. It wouldn't be fair to leave the cleanup for Mother. With determination, Brooke began to clean up the work area.

HOW ABOUT YOU? Do you like to do all the fun things and leave the unpleasant jobs for someone else? When you do that, you're only doing half a job. Next time you face an unpleasant task, remember that the Lord expects faithfulness in even the small things. *R.I.J.*

TO MEMORIZE: Work hard and cheerfully at whatever you do, as though you were working for the Lord rather than for people. *Colossians 3:23*

ONLY HALF-DONE

FROM THE BIBLE:

"When a servant comes in from plowing or taking care of sheep, he doesn't just sit down and eat. He must first prepare his master's meal and serve him his supper before eating his own. And the servant is not even thanked, because he is merely doing what he is supposed to do. In the same way, when you obey me you should say, 'We are not worthy of praise. We are servants who have simply done our duty.'"

LUKE 17:7-10

"Half-done" is not done

Y IT AGAIN

.OM THE BIBLE:

Pray like this: Our Father in heaven, may your name be honored. May your Kingdom come soon. May your will be done here on earth, just as it is in heaven. Give us our food for today, and forgive us our sins, just as we have forgiven those who have sinned against us. And don't let us yield to temptation, but deliver us from the evil one.

"If you forgive those who sin against you, your heavenly Father will forgive you. But if you refuse to forgive others, your Father will not forgive your sins."

MATTHEW 6:9-15

Forgive sincerely

"WHO USED my markers?" asked Peter.

"Mom says you're supposed to share," Tina retorted.

"And you're *supposed* to put the caps on tight so they won't dry out," grumbled Peter.

"Sorry," Tina said lightly.

"Well, you don't sound sorry," Peter retorted as he jumped up. Puzzle pieces scattered all over.

"Peter!" screamed Melissa, who had been working on the puzzle.

"I didn't mean to," Peter whined.

When Mother told all three of them to pick up the scattered puzzle pieces, Tina objected. "I'm just reading," she said. "They made the mess."

"You can all help," said Mother firmly. "And since you don't seem to be able to talk nicely together, don't talk at all for a while. I'll play our favorite Christmas cassette tape, and I want you to work silently until the entire tape is finished."

Soon the words of Christmas carols were filling the air. As the children picked up the puzzle, they quietly sang along on "Silent Night" until the tape suddenly faltered and the words sounded garbled. Peter pulled out the cassette and tried to unravel the old worn tape. "Guess we heard that enough," he said.

"Yes," agreed Mother. "Like the words in our house."

"Huh? What do you mean?" asked Melissa.

"We say, 'I'm sorry,' 'I didn't mean to,' and 'It's not my fault,' but we don't mean what we say," explained Mother. "We sound like a worn-out cassette tape."

HOW ABOUT YOU? Are you sincere when you say, "I'm sorry," or do you just say the words because you know it's expected of you? The Lord's Prayer says, "Forgive us . . . as we forgive. . . ." Think about that. Then show by your actions that you truly forgive. *J.L.H.*

TO MEMORIZE: Peter came to him and asked, "Lord, how often should I forgive someone who sins against me? Seven times?" "No!" Jesus replied, "seventy times seven!" *Matthew 18:21-22*

CAMMIE CAME to the Village Bible Church shortly before Christmas. She had just moved to the area, and attending church was a new experience for her. She couldn't understand the lessons very well. But her teacher's love for her drew her back each week.

One Sunday Miss Weaver asked Cammie if she could get some evergreen branches for the class Christmas party. Miss Weaver said, "We just need a few small branches to decorate the tables."

Eager to please her teacher, Cammie agreed to get the branches. But some places that sold Christmas trees didn't have any branches at all, and others would give her branches only if she bought a tree.

Walking home from school one day, Cammie saw a pile of evergreen boughs at a Christmas tree lot. She had an idea. Instead of asking for free branches, she would buy some. *They shouldn't cost much*, she thought. Cammie ran home to get some money, but when she offered it to the owner for the boughs, he said, "They're not for sale." Disappointed, Cammie started to walk away. The man called her back quickly. "Young lady, they're free. Help yourself." Cammie eagerly took all she could carry.

Later, while decorating the tables, Cammie told Miss Weaver about her experiences. "That's a good illustration of salvation," Miss Weaver said. "Some people tell us we can buy our salvation by doing good deeds. But the Bible says salvation is a gift. We can't earn it or buy it. It's not for sale. We can only receive salvation by accepting Jesus as Savior."

"Now I understand it," Cammie said softly.

HOW ABOUT YOU? Are you trying to buy your salvation by being good, going to church, or getting baptized? It won't work! Salvation is a gift from God. *J.L.H.*

TO MEMORIZE: God saved you by his special favor when you believed. And you can't take credit for this; it is a gift from God. *Ephesians 2:8*

NOT FOR SALE

FROM THE BIBLE:

When the apostles back in Jerusalem heard that the people of Samaria had accepted God's message, they sent Peter and John there. As soon as they arrived, they prayed for these new Christians to receive the Holy Spirit. The Holy Spirit had not yet come upon any of them, for they had only been baptized in the name of the Lord Jesus. Then Peter and John laid their hands upon these believers, and they received the Holy Spirit.

When Simon saw that the Holy Spirit was given when the apostles placed their hands upon people's heads, he offered money to buy this power. "Let me have this power, too," he exclaimed, "so that when I lay my hands on people, they will receive the Holy Spirit!"

But Peter replied, "May your money perish with you for thinking God's gift can be bought! You can have no part in this, for your heart is not right before God. Turn from your wickedness and pray to the Lord. Perhaps he will forgive your evil thoughts, for I can see that you are full of bitterness and held captive by sin."
ACTS 8:14-23

Salvation is a gift

21 December

THE OLDER GENERATION
(PART 1)

FROM THE BIBLE:

*O God, you have taught me from
my earliest childhood,
and I have constantly told
others about the wonderful
things you do.
Now that I am old and gray,
do not abandon me, O God.
Let me proclaim your power to
this new generation,
your mighty miracles to all
who come after me.*

*Your righteousness, O God,
reaches to the highest
heavens.
You have done such wonderful
things.
Who can compare with you,
O God?
You have allowed me to suffer
much hardship,
but you will restore me to life
again
and lift me up from the depths
of the earth.
You will restore me to even
greater honor
and comfort me once again.*

*Then I will praise you with
music on the harp,
because you are faithful to
your promises, O God.
I will sing for you with a lyre,
O Holy One of Israel.*
PSALM 71:17-22

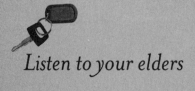

Listen to your elders

"WE'LL MEET HERE at the church Saturday after-noon and go together," Mrs. Kendall an-nounced. "Class dismissed."

As soon as the children were out the door, Mark groaned, "Who wants to go to the nursing home? What have I got in common with those old folks?"

Adam shrugged. "Not much! But we've got to go, or Mrs. Kendall will be disappointed."

Coming up behind them, Natalie added, "Mrs. Kendall is the best Sunday school teacher we have ever had. But visiting a nursing home is a dumb idea!"

Adam shrugged again. "Maybe we won't stay long."

The next Saturday afternoon, eight fifth-graders met at the church. "After we sing and read Scripture, go around and introduce your-selves," Mrs. Kendall instructed.

"What will we say to them?" Natalie asked.

Mrs. Kendall smiled. "You probably won't have to say much. Your main job will be listen-ing."

Two hours later the boys and girls again piled into Mrs. Kendall's van. "That Mr. Wilson is sharp. He used to be the mayor," Mark said. "He offered to help me with my paper on the history of our town."

"Did you know that Mr. Rowland was once the foreman of the Flying W Ranch?" asked Adam. "He told me how the Lord helped him in a blizzard."

"And Mrs. Baker is going to teach me how to crochet," Natalie said. "Next time we come, I need to bring . . ." Natalie paused, then continued, "We are coming again, aren't we, Mrs. Kendall?"

Mrs. Kendall smiled. "I'll leave that decision to you. Everyone who wants to come again say 'aye.'" A chorus of "ayes" filled the air.

HOW ABOUT YOU? Have you shunned older people because you didn't know how to talk to them? Many senior citizens need someone to listen to them. And you need to hear what they have to say. *B.J.W.*

TO MEMORIZE: Let each generation tell its children of your mighty acts. *Psalm 145:4*

MRS. KENDALL'S Sunday school class voted unanimously to visit the Greenwood Nursing Home on the fourth Saturday of every month. The next time they went, Natalie brought yarn and a crochet hook. Mark had a pencil and paper so he could take notes from Mr. Wilson on the history of Centerville. Adam had a picture book of the Old West to share with Mr. Rowland. The others carried fruit, cookies, and books.

After they sang and read Scripture, they visited with the friends they had made the month before. Then their teacher called for their attention. "The activity director, Mrs. Nelson, has asked us to sing for some who are unable to get out of bed," she said. Jay picked up his guitar. They went from room to room, singing.

As they prepared to leave later, Mrs. Nelson said, "Thank you so much. Some of these patients never have visitors."

As they piled into the van, Natalie spoke softly. "I learned more than how to chain stitch. I learned how important kindness is."

Mrs. Kendall nodded her agreement. "Compassion is a virtue all Christians should have."

"And I learned to be thankful for my health," Adam said. "Did you see that one man? He couldn't breathe without a special oxygen machine."

"And I learned how blessed I am to be your Sunday school teacher." Mrs. Kendall smiled as she started the van.

HOW ABOUT YOU? When you see elderly people whose minds are no longer sharp or people who are crippled or retarded, do you make fun of them? Or do you have a desire to help them? If you are truly Christlike, you'll be compassionate. That means you'll sympathize with them and want to help them. *B.J.W.*

TO MEMORIZE: All of you should be of one mind, full of sympathy toward each other, loving one another with tender hearts and humble minds.
1 Peter 3:8

THE OLDER GENERATION
(PART 2)

FROM THE BIBLE:

We know what real love is because Christ gave up his life for us. And so we also ought to give up our lives for our Christian brothers and sisters. But if anyone has enough money to live well and sees a brother or sister in need and refuses to help—how can God's love be in that person?

Dear children, let us stop just saying we love each other; let us really show it by our actions.
1 JOHN 3:16-18

Be compassionate

23 December

BRIAN'S PARTY

FROM THE BIBLE:

That night some shepherds were in the fields outside the village, guarding their flocks of sheep. Suddenly, an angel of the Lord appeared among them, and the radiance of the Lord's glory surrounded them. They were terribly frightened, but the angel reassured them. "Don't be afraid!" he said. "I bring you good news of great joy for everyone! The Savior—yes, the Messiah, the Lord—has been born tonight in Bethlehem, the city of David! And this is how you will recognize him: You will find a baby lying in a manger, wrapped snugly in strips of cloth!"

Suddenly, the angel was joined by a vast host of others— the armies of heaven—praising God:

"Glory to God in the highest heaven, and peace on earth to all whom God favors."

When the angels had returned to heaven, the shepherds said to each other, "Come on, let's go to Bethlehem! Let's see this wonderful thing that has happened, which the Lord has told us about."

LUKE 2:8-15

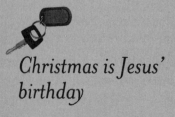

Christmas is Jesus' birthday

BRIAN SPOKE into the telephone. "We're still at the shopping mall, Mom," he said. "The car won't start. A serviceman from a garage across the street is working on it now. Dad says to tell you we'll be there as soon as we can, and the 'show must go on,' whatever that means."

Mom knew what Dad meant. He was talking about the surprise birthday party they had planned for Brian. Dad had taken Brian shopping to get him out of the house while his mother got things ready. The guests were in the living room now, so Mom knew that Dad was telling her to go ahead with the games and entertainment.

When Brian finally burst into the house, he was greeted with cries of "Surprise!" He was surprised indeed!

"About time you got here," teased one of the children. "We were about to give the gifts to somebody else."

"Uh-uh!" Brian's sister, Kelly, slipped her little hand into her big brother's. "They're Brian's. It's his birfday." Amid laughing and teasing, Brian opened the gifts from his friends.

When it was time to leave, some of the children said to Brian, "Glad you made it. Your birthday party just wasn't right without you."

After all his guests were gone, Brian sat down to eat a piece of his cake. "I wish I hadn't missed the games," he said, "but at least the car was fixed in time for me to see all the kids and open my presents!"

HOW ABOUT YOU? Did you know that Christmas is celebrated in honor of Jesus' birthday? Do you remember this as you attend various Christmas parties and events? Keep Christ in mind as you celebrate his birthday. *H.W.M.*

TO MEMORIZE: She gave birth to her firstborn, a son. She wrapped him in cloths and placed him in a manger, because there was no room for them in the inn. *Luke 2:7* (NIV)

THE MISSING TURKEY

JAMIE'S AUNT and uncle, who weren't Christians, were coming for Christmas dinner. Jamie and her parents had prayed that somehow, this Christmas, God would help them witness to Aunt Ellen and Uncle Joe. When they arrived, Uncle Joe held out presents. "Merry Christmas, Jamie! See what Santa Claus brought!"

"We almost didn't come," said Aunt Ellen. "Joe stayed late at the office party last night and came home even more drunk than usual." She winked at her husband, but Jamie felt sad. Was this what Christmas meant to her aunt and uncle?

At dinnertime the table was loaded with delicious food. After Dad gave thanks, Jamie took helpings of several different things. Now all she needed was a drumstick. She looked around the table. "Where's the turkey?" she asked.

Startled, Mother stared at the table. "The turkey!" she cried. She ran to the kitchen and returned shortly with a large platter of meat. "The main part of the meal, and I forgot all about it!"

Jamie giggled. "I guess we had so much other good stuff that we just didn't miss it at first," she said.

After dinner Uncle Joe stretched. "Now that was a good meal," he declared. "I'm glad someone remembered the turkey! It wouldn't have been the same without it."

Dad nodded. "This dinner without the turkey would have been like Christmas without Christ," he said. "Many people think they can enjoy Christmas without knowing Christ himself. It's true that they may have some good times, but they're missing the best part."

Uncle Joe and Aunt Ellen looked at each other, then settled back to listen as Dad began to read the Christmas story from the Bible.

HOW ABOUT YOU? Are you missing the "meat" of Christmas? Have you gotten so involved in the "fun" things to do that you've forgotten all about Jesus? S.L.K.

TO MEMORIZE: [Christ] existed before everything else began, and he holds all creation together. *Colossians 1:17*

FROM THE BIBLE:

In the beginning the Word already existed. He was with God, and he was God. He was in the beginning with God. He created everything there is. Nothing exists that he didn't make. Life itself was in him, and this life gives light to everyone. . . .

The one who is the true light, who gives light to everyone, was going to come into the world. . . .

So the Word became human and lived here on earth among us. He was full of unfailing love and faithfulness. And we have seen his glory, the glory of the only Son of the Father.

When the angels had returned to heaven, the shepherds said to each other, "Come on, let's go to Bethlehem! Let's see this wonderful thing that has happened, which the Lord has told us about."

They ran to the village and found Mary and Joseph. And there was the baby, lying in the manger. Then the shepherds told everyone what had happened and what the angel had said to them about this child.

JOHN 1:1-4, 9, 14; LUKE 2:15-17

Don't forget Christ

25 December

HERE I AM!

FROM THE BIBLE:

Jesus was born in the town of Bethlehem in Judea, during the reign of King Herod. About that time some wise men from eastern lands arrived in Jerusalem, asking, "Where is the newborn king of the Jews? We have seen his star as it arose, and we have come to worship him."

Herod . . . called a meeting of the leading priests and teachers of religious law. "Where did the prophets say the Messiah would be born?" he asked them.

"In Bethlehem," they said. . . .

Then Herod sent a private message to the wise men. . . . "Go to Bethlehem and search carefully for the child. And when you find him, come back and tell me so that I can go and worship him, too!"

After this interview the wise men went their way. Once again the star appeared to them . . . and stopped over the place where the child was. . . . They entered the house where the child and his mother, Mary, were, and they . . . worshiped him. Then they opened their treasure chests and gave him gifts of gold, frankincense, and myrrh.

MATTHEW 2:1-11

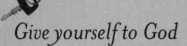

Give yourself to God

VERY EARLY on Christmas morning, Matt jumped out of bed and tapped lightly on his sister's door. Betsy took a huge decorated box from her closet and went down the stairs with Matt. "Are you sure this isn't a dumb idea?" whispered Matt as they went out to the front porch.

"Mom and Dad will love it," Betsy assured him. She lifted the cover off the box, and Matt stepped inside. Then Betsy handed him an assortment of signs. "I'm your errand boy," read one. "I'll clean Tim's room besides my own this month," read another. "I'll clean the garage," read a third. Matt put these, with several others, in a corner of the box. Betsy put the cover on the box and placed a large red bow on top.

"Matt heard a loud, persistent ring as Betsy rang the doorbell for him again and again. Then he heard the door close as Betsy disappeared inside the house.

Soon the door reopened, and Mark heard Dad's surprised voice. "Well! What have we here? Dorothy!" he called. "Come quickly! A present has arrived for us." In no time, Mom was there and opened the box with Dad.

"Merry Christmas!" called Matt. "I decided to give you myself this Christmas," he added, handing them the signs. "These are just some of the things I can do for you."

There were tears in Mom's eyes as she hugged him. Dad grinned and said, "You're the best present you could possibly give us!"

HOW ABOUT YOU? Did you think today about the fact that God gave his very best for you? What have you given him in return? What he wants most of all is the gift of yourself. Will you give that gift to him? *H.W.M.*

TO MEMORIZE: They first gave themselves to the Lord, and then to us by the will of God. *2 Corinthians 8:5* (NKJV)

26 December

A LITTLE SCRATCH

THE TIME IS 6:21 P.M.," announced Tim as he looked at his new digital watch.

"Well, thanks for keeping us informed," said his sister, Maddie, as she answered the phone. "For you, Tim," she said.

After he hung up, Mom asked, "Did I hear you tell Shawn you can't play tonight? I thought you and your friends were going to the gym for a while."

"Yeah, well, Shawn is such a klutz," said Tim, looking at his watch. "The time is now—"

"Don't change the subject," said Dad. "You lied to Shawn, didn't you?"

"Oh, Dad, it was such a little thing," protested Tim. "I mean it's no big deal—just a little lie." But Mom and Dad explained to Tim that God didn't see it that way. Although he refused to admit they were right, he agreed to call Shawn back and invite him to join him at the gym. "No answer," he said a few minutes later. "Well, at least I tried." He put on his jacket.

When Tim returned home, he wasn't quite so happy. "What's the problem?" asked Dad.

"I fell," replied Tim, holding out his arm. Across the face of the watch, Dad saw a small scratch.

"Oh, that's too bad," sympathized Dad. "But at least it's just a little scratch."

"Yeah," said Tim, "but it goes right across the numbers."

"A little scratch messes up a new watch," Mom said, "and a 'little' sin messes up one's testimony for the Lord."

Tim knew what she meant. "You're right," he admitted.

HOW ABOUT YOU? Have you told a "little" lie? Been a "little" unkind? Do you think a "little" sin doesn't matter? It does. Confess even the "small" sins and ask the Lord to help you overcome them. *H.W.M.*

TO MEMORIZE: The person who keeps all of the laws except one is as guilty as the person who has broken all of God's laws. *James 2:10*

FROM THE BIBLE:

So we are always confident, even though we know that as long as we live in these bodies we are not at home with the Lord. That is why we live by believing and not by seeing. Yes, we are fully confident, and we would rather be away from these bodies, for then we will be at home with the Lord.

2 CORINTHIANS 5:6-8

"Little" sins matter

27 December

A FRIEND OF SINNERS

FROM THE BIBLE:

That night Matthew invited Jesus and his disciples to be his dinner guests, along with his fellow tax collectors and many other notorious sinners. The Pharisees were indignant. "Why does your teacher eat with such scum?" they asked his disciples.

When he heard this, Jesus replied, "Healthy people don't need a doctor—sick people do." Then he added, "Now go and learn the meaning of this Scripture: 'I want you to be merciful; I don't want your sacrifices.' For I have come to call sinners, not those who think they are already good enough."

MATTHEW 9:10-13

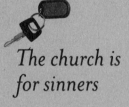

The church is for sinners

"YOU DIDN'T INVITE Joy Blackburn to go to Sunday school with us, did you?" Tiffany already knew the answer before Mother nodded. "Ooohhhh, Mother!" she wailed. "Joy talks loud and is so crude. She's everything you tell me not to be. I'm surprised you would want me to be friends with her." Tiffany picked up a knife and began to peel potatoes for dinner.

"I don't want you to be friends with her in the sense that you do what she does," said Mother, "but I want you to be kind to her."

"Ooohhhh!" Tiffany gasped. "I cut my hand!"

Mother grabbed a clean cloth and pressed it tightly against the cut. After examining it, she decided she had better take Tiffany to the emergency room. There a doctor stitched and bandaged Tiffany's hand. Soon they were ready to go home . "Oh, dear, we've made quite a mess," Mother exclaimed as she looked around the room.

"Don't worry about that," the nurse said kindly. "We just want your daughter's hand to heal."

That evening Tiffany showed her father the bandaged hand. "We got blood all over the emergency room, but they didn't even care," she told him. "They were just concerned about me."

Father smiled. "That's what hospitals are for—to take care of the sick and hurting."

"Something like church," mused Mother. "The church is a good place for hurting people who need Jesus. What if hospitals only allowed well people in?"

Tiffany sighed. "You're talking about Joy, I know. And you're right, Mother. I'm glad she's going to church with us."

HOW ABOUT YOU? Do you invite only nice or "cool" kids to go to church with you? This week look for kids with special needs, and invite them to church with you. *B.J.W.*

TO MEMORIZE: I have come to call sinners to turn from their sins, not to spend my time with those who think they are already good enough. *Luke 5:32*

THE FREE TICKETS

AS SHERANDA AND Kayla walked toward the gym, Sheranda asked, "Kayla, do you expect to be in heaven some day?"

"Oh, sure," replied Kayla. "I try to be good."

"But no one is good enough," said Sheranda.

"Well, I'm sure I stand a lot better chance of getting in than a murderer does," insisted Kayla, as they arrived at the gym. "Here we are. Got your money ready?"

"Money?" asked Sheranda. "My brother's on the team. I thought I could get in free."

"I doubt it," replied Kayla. "I brought a dollar."

At the ticket office, the girls found that they did need to pay, and tickets cost two dollars each. "Oh no! What are we going to do now?" moaned Kayla. "I really want to see this game!"

"Kayla, this is like what I told you about getting into heaven," said Sheranda. "You had a dollar, and I had nothing. Which one of us is getting into the gym?"

"Why, neither," answered Kayla. But before they could finish the discussion they turned to see Sheranda's father standing there.

"Oh, Daddy, I'm so glad to see you!" exclaimed Sheranda. "We don't have enough money to buy our tickets."

"I'll pay for them," answered her father.

The girls sat down in the bleachers just in time to see the teams take their places on the court. "You know, Kayla," said Sheranda, "we both got here because my father paid for the tickets. That's like what Jesus did for us. He paid the price to buy our 'tickets' for heaven."

HOW ABOUT YOU? Do you expect to get into heaven because you're better than others are? That's not the way it works. Be sure you're not so proud of your "dollar"—your own goodness—that you refuse Christ's "free ticket." *M.R.P.*

TO MEMORIZE: We are made right with God through faith and not by obeying the law. *Romans 3:28*

FROM THE BIBLE:

We are made right in God's sight when we trust in Jesus Christ to take away our sins. And we all can be saved in this same way, no matter who we are or what we have done.

For all have sinned; all fall short of God's glorious standard. Yet now God in his gracious kindness declares us not guilty. He has done this through Christ Jesus, who has freed us by taking away our sins. For God sent Jesus to take the punishment for our sins. . . . We are made right with God when we believe that Jesus shed his blood, sacrificing his life for us. God was being entirely fair and just when he did not punish those who sinned in former times. And he is entirely fair and just in this present time when he declares sinners to be right in his sight because they believe in Jesus.

Can we boast, then, that we have done anything to be accepted by God? No, because our acquittal is not based on our good deeds. It is based on our faith. So we are made right with God through faith and not by obeying the law.

ROMANS 3:22-28

Trust Jesus, not your "goodness"

29 December

A CITIZEN NOW

FROM THE BIBLE:

All these faithful ones died without receiving what God had promised them, but they saw it all from a distance and welcomed the promises of God. They agreed that they were no more than foreigners and nomads here on earth. And obviously people who talk like that are looking forward to a country they can call their own. If they had meant the country they came from, they would have found a way to go back. But they were looking for a better place, a heavenly homeland. That is why God is not ashamed to be called their God, for he has prepared a heavenly city for them.

HEBREWS 11:13-16

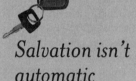

Salvation isn't automatic

TODD LOOKED OVER at his mother as she hung up the telephone. "I heard you tell Mrs. Lewis you'd be a witness. Did she have an accident?" he asked.

Mother smiled. "No, Mrs. Lewis wants to become an American citizen. I'm going to be a *character* witness for her."

"But she lives here," Todd said. "Isn't she an American citizen?"

"No," Mother replied. "Living in America doesn't automatically make her an American. She was born in another country and came here when she married. Now she has applied for citizenship."

When Mrs. Lewis was sworn in as a United States citizen, they all went out for ice cream to celebrate. "Why did you decide to become an American citizen?" Todd asked her.

"There was a lot I couldn't do before," Mrs. Lewis explained. "I couldn't vote, hold a public office, or do certain jobs. I'm glad to give up my citizenship in the old country and become a citizen here."

"That's what happens when we become Christians," Dad said. "We pledge our loyalty to Christ."

"That's right," Mother said. "No one is automatically a Christian because, in a sense, we're all born in a 'foreign country'—this world. To become a citizen of heaven, we must accept Jesus as Savior."

"And being a Christian gives us privileges," added Dad. "We receive forgiveness from sin and a home in heaven. God cares for our needs. Jesus prays for us, and the Holy Spirit guides us."

"I'm a citizen of the United States now," Mrs. Lewis said proudly. "But I'm a citizen of heaven, too. That's even better."

HOW ABOUT YOU? Where is your citizenship? Have you personally asked Jesus to forgive your sins and be your Savior? You must make that decision to become a citizen of heaven. *J.L.H.*

TO MEMORIZE: We are citizens of heaven, where the Lord Jesus Christ lives. And we are eagerly waiting for him to return as our Savior. *Philippians 3:20*

GREAT GAIN

WITH A TWINKLE in his eye, Brad sneaked up behind Dad's armchair and plugged in the tape recorder. He pushed a button, and a moment later Dad's voice came from the machine. "Whew! This heat is unbearable! I guarantee you I'll never complain about the cold again. I'd give a lot for the sight of snow."

Dad looked up from his newspaper, startled to hear his own voice. A moment before, he had said the cold was unbearable and he wished for a hot sun. "When did you record that?" he asked.

Brad laughed. "Last summer," he replied. "We hear the same thing every summer and every winter. I just wanted you to hear it yourself."

Dad laughed too. "How quickly we forget," he said.

Mother nodded as she listened from the dining room. "We often complain about what we don't have instead of giving thanks for what we do have," she said. "We're hard to please, aren't we?"

"Oh, I don't know," said Brad. "I like summer, and I like winter. I'm an easy fellow to get along with."

"Good!" said Mother. "Then I assume you're going to do the dishes for me without complaining? And you're going to remember with gratitude the good meal you just ate." Brad smiled and began to clear the table.

"And I'll shovel the driveway as I give thanks that I don't have to pull weeds today," declared Dad. He patted Brad's shoulder. "Thanks for the good lesson, Son."

HOW ABOUT YOU? Do you grumble about the rain or thank God that the grass is being watered? Do you murmur about someone who ignored you or thank the Lord for your friends? Do you long for a new shirt or give thanks for your new shoes? Be thankful for what you have. Don't always be wishing for something else. *H.W.M.*

TO MEMORIZE: True religion with contentment is great wealth. *1 Timothy 6:6*

FROM THE BIBLE:

True religion with contentment is great wealth. After all, we didn't bring anything with us when we came into the world, and we certainly cannot carry anything with us when we die. So if we have enough food and clothing, let us be content.

Praise the Lord, I tell myself;
with my whole heart, I will
praise his holy name.
Praise the Lord, I tell myself,
and never forget the good
things he does for me.
He forgives all my sins
and heals all my diseases.
He ransoms me from death
and surrounds me with love
and tender mercies.
He fills my life with good things.
My youth is renewed like the
eagle's!

1 TIMOTHY 6:6-8; PSALM 103:1-5

Be thankful always

31 December

RESOLUTIONS

FROM THE BIBLE:

O God, listen to my cry!
Hear my prayer!
From the ends of the earth,
I will cry to you for help,
for my heart is overwhelmed.
Lead me to the towering rock of
safety,
for you are my safe refuge,
a fortress where my enemies
cannot reach me.
Let me live forever in your
sanctuary,
safe beneath the shelter of
your wings!
For you have heard my vows,
O God.
You have given me an
inheritance reserved for
those who fear your name.

Add many years to the life
of the king!
May his years span the
generations!
May he reign under God's
protection forever.
Appoint your unfailing love
and faithfulness to watch
over him.

Then I will always sing praises
to your name
as I fulfill my vows day
after day.
PSALM 61:1-8

Succeed in God's strength

EVERY YEAR Jack cleaned out his desk on New Year's Eve. Usually he found lots of good stuff that he had forgotten about. His desktop was soon piled high with old school papers, the birthday card he had gotten from his sister, empty pop cans, and even a five dollar bill. Jack was reading a list of New Year's resolutions when he was interrupted by a knock on his bedroom door. "May I come in?" It was Dad.

"Sure, if you don't mind a mess," answered Jack. "I was just reading the resolutions I made last year and didn't keep. Here's one that says, 'Keep desk clean!'"

Dad grinned as he sat down on the bed. "What else did you write?"

"'Read Bible every day,'" read Jack. "I tried to do that, Dad, but I usually got busy or forgot about it. Maybe I'll skip making New Year's resolutions. That way I won't break them."

"When your mom and I were first married, we made a list of goals," Dad said. "But it wasn't until we turned that goal list into a prayer list that we saw progress."

"So you think I should pray about my New Year's resolutions?" Jack asked.

"You can either quit making resolutions or you can ask God to help you," said Dad.

"This year, I'll talk to the Lord about my goals," Jack said.

HOW ABOUT YOU? Have you decided over and over again to read your Bible every day, or to tell someone about the Lord? Have you been determined to get your homework done every night and then forgotten about it by the middle of the semester? Commit your plans to God. Ask him for the courage and strength to succeed. *D.L.R.*

TO MEMORIZE: Commit your work to the Lord, and then your plans will succeed. *Proverbs 16:3*

Holy Spirit
February 6; April 9; May 9; June 30

Honesty, lying
February 6; March 4, 11; May 22; July 29; August 28; September 12; November 9; December 26

Lord's Supper
March 5; May 28

Manners
March 5; August 8

Mercy
December 13

Movies
January 12

Moving
January 2; May 21; July 10; September 18, 30

Natural disasters
April 8

Occult
October 31

Older adults
March 20, 21, 22; April 19; September 9; November 19; December 2, 21, 22, 23

Parents, loving and respecting
March 15; May 11, 12, 13; June 16, 17, 18

Pastors
July 15

Patience
April 6, 8; September 19; October 5

Patriotism
May 28; July 3, 4

Peacemaking
October 13

Prayer
March 1; August 14; September 25, 29; December 4

Prejudice, judging, criticism
January 4; February 22, 26; March 23, 24; April 28; August 31; October 1

Pride
January 22; March 2, 13

Repentance
February 3

Rock music
January 21; March 3; April 10; July 1

Rules, discipline
March 12; April 3; June 17, 18; September 28; November 14

Sabbath, keeping the
January 3; November 4

Servant, being a
January 17, 19; April 27; May 15

Sexuality
November 7

Sickness
February 4; March 7; April 14; May 6; August 10, 11

Smoking
March 10; September 2

Spiritual growth
January 5, 9; April 23; May 17

Stealing
January 10, 18; June 30; September 8, 10, 11; October 6; November 8

Suicide
October 22

Swearing
February 9; April 18; July 13; November 3, 24

Teamwork
January 24

Teasing
July 14; October 22

Television viewing
April 5; June 21; December 1

Temptations, worldliness
January 12, 21; February 24; March 3; April 5,
10; May 18; June 21; July 1, 18, 21; August 9,
26; October 12, 27; November 1, 2, 7, 24;
December 1, 7, 10, 11, 15, 27

Ten Commandments
November 1, 2, 3, 4, 5, 6, 7, 8, 9, 10

Thankfulness
November 20, 21, 22, 29

Trinity, the
December 6

War
January 26; November 18

Witnessing
February 1; March 18; April 4; May 2; June 9, 10,
15, 23, 28, 29; July 7, 15, 16; August 7;
September 27; October 2, 21, 30

INDEX OF SCRIPTURE IN DAILY READINGS

James 5:7-11	*September 19*	1 John 3:1-3	*December 9*
		1 John 3:16-18	*December 22*
1 Peter 1:3-5	*May 8*	1 John 3:16-18, 23-24	*August 3*
1 Peter 2:9-12	*August 15*	1 John 4:7-12	*February 12*
1 Peter 2:19, 21-25	*October 2*	1 John 4:16-21	*July 11*
1 Peter 2:21-25	*July 29*	1 John 4:20-21	*October 19*
1 Peter 5:8-11	*June 19*	1 John 5:1, 9-13	*January 30*
		1 John 5:14-15	*December 4*
2 Peter 1:4, 19-21	*January 11*		
2 Peter 3:10-14	*January 20*	Jude 1:3-4, 12, 16-17	*January 8*
1 John 1:6-10	*December 3*	Revelation 21:3, 18, 21-23	*February 11*
		Revelation 21:22-27	*June 6*

John 12:49-50	*June 8*	1 Corinthians 12:14	*July 10*
John 13:34	*February 13*	1 Corinthians 12:22	*September 1*
John 14:1	*November 18*	1 Corinthians 12:27	*February 7*
John 14:3	*January 15*	1 Corinthians 13:1	*January 28*
John 15:5	*October 26*	1 Corinthians 15:33	*July 13*
John 15:17	*September 18*	1 Corinthians 15:43	*February 15*
John 16:13	*June 13*	1 Corinthians 15:57	*November 25*
John 20:29	*July 19*		
John 21:22	*March 30*	2 Corinthians 1:4	*May 6*
		2 Corinthians 1:5	*August 11*
Acts 16:31	*April 7*	2 Corinthians 3:18	*July 18*
Acts 22:15	*July 16*	2 Corinthians 5:8	*June 24*
Acts 24:16	*April 23*	2 Corinthians 5:17	*June 3*
Acts 26:28	*August 4*	2 Corinthians 6:2	*February 3*
		2 Corinthians 6:14	*September 6*
Romans 1:16	*June 29*	2 Corinthians 8:5	*December 25*
Romans 3:4	*July 30*	2 Corinthians 9:6	*July 20*
Romans 3:23	*February 16*	2 Corinthians 9:7	*January 19*
Romans 3:28	*December 28*	2 Corinthians 12:9	*March 21*
Romans 5:6	*February 28*	2 Corinthians 12:10	*April 9*
Romans 5:8	*February 14*		
Romans 6:6	*June 4*	Galatians 2:16	*October 3*
Romans 6:23	*August 25*	Galatians 2:20	*April 11*
Romans 7:12	*September 28*	Galatians 2:20	*August 2*
Romans 8:16	*May 9*	Galatians 5:13	*September 24*
Romans 8:18	*August 10*	Galatians 5:22-23	*April 25*
Romans 10:13	*March 23*	Galatians 6:7	*September 11*
Romans 12:2	*December 15*		
Romans 12:10	*February 22*	Ephesians 1:14	*February 6*
Romans 12:12	*February 4*	Ephesians 2:8	*December 20*
Romans 12:14	*November 12*	Ephesians 2:10	*February 18*
Romans 12:16	*October 30*	Ephesians 2:20	*February 10*
Romans 12:18	*August 19*	Ephesians 4:2	*April 6*
Romans 12:21	*July 26*	Ephesians 4:4-6	*October 16*
Romans 13:11	*May 14*	Ephesians 4:11-12	*July 15*
Romans 14:5	*May 24*	Ephesians 4:15	*May 17*
Romans 14:7-8	*August 15*	Ephesians 4:26-27	*November 26*
Romans 14:12	*January 10*	Ephesians 4:29	*October 22*
Romans 14:13	*May 25*	Ephesians 5:1	*February 21*
Romans 14:19	*July 17*	Ephesians 5:1	*September 23*
		Ephesians 5:8	*August 29*
1 Corinthians 3:6	*September 27*	Ephesians 5:15	*May 18*
1 Corinthians 4:2	*October 29*	Ephesians 5:19	*July 1*
1 Corinthians 6:19	*September 4*	Ephesians 6:1	*June 18*
1 Corinthians 6:20	*July 2*	Ephesians 6:2	*March 15*
1 Corinthians 8:9	*March 8*	Ephesians 6:11	*June 19*
1 Corinthians 10:10	*April 30*	Ephesians 6:17	*September 22*
1 Corinthians 10:13	*August 26*		
1 Corinthians 10:33	*August 8*	Philippians 1:3	*March 16*
1 Corinthians 11:24	*March 5*	Philippians 1:6	*July 27*
1 Corinthians 11:26	*May 28*	Philippians 2:15	*May 5*
1 Corinthians 12:12	*April 26*	Philippians 2:15	*September 16*

Philippians 3:9	*June 12*	Hebrews 13:8	*March 22*
Philippians 3:20	*July 4; December 29*		
Philippians 4:6-7	*January 26*	James 1:3	*April 14*
Philippians 4:8	*November 24*	James 1:15	*November 27*
Philippians 4:13	*February 8; March 17*	James 2:10	*December 26*
Philippians 4:19	*January 27*	James 2:17	*March 11*
		James 3:17	*September 15*
Colossians 1:17	*December 24*	James 4:7	*April 25*
Colossians 3:12	*April 4*	James 4:8	*January 17*
Colossians 3:13	*May 20*	James 4:15-16	*May 27*
Colossians 3:16	*September 26*	James 4:17	*May 19*
Colossians 3:17	*March 9*	James 5:8	*June 10*
Colossians 3:23	*March 31*		
Colossians 3:23	*December 18*	1 Peter 1:3	*May 8*
Colossians 3:24	*February 9*	1 Peter 1:22	*September 9*
Colossians 3:25	*January 12*	1 Peter 2:9	*July 21*
Colossians 4:2	*November 22*	1 Peter 2:10	*October 17*
		1 Peter 2:21	*July 29*
1 Thessalonians 5:11	*February 26*	1 Peter 2:21	*October 2*
1 Thessalonians 5:14	*February 20*	1 Peter 3:8	*February 23; December 22*
1 Thessalonians 5:17	*March 1*	1 Peter 3:15	*June 23*
1 Thessalonians 5:18	*November 29*	1 Peter 4:10	*September 13*
		1 Peter 5:7	*February 17*
2 Thessalonians 3:14	*September 7*	1 Peter 5:8	*May 4*
1 Timothy 4:4	*September 17*	2 Peter 3:11	*January 20*
1 Timothy 4:8	*January 1*	2 Peter 3:18	*January 5*
1 Timothy 4:12	*January 7*		
1 Timothy 4:12	*October 5*	1 John 1:7	*October 28*
1 Timothy 4:12	*December 2*	1 John 1:8	*December 3*
1 Timothy 6:6	*March 14*	1 John 1:9	*March 10*
1 Timothy 6:6	*December 30*	1 John 2:6	*April 16*
		1 John 2:17	*July 24*
2 Timothy 1:8	*March 18*	1 John 3:1	*December 9*
2 Timothy 1:12	*May 16*	1 John 3:2	*August 24*
2 Timothy 2:15	*March 25*	1 John 3:18	*August 3*
2 Timothy 2:19	*March 27*	1 John 3:18	*December 5*
2 Timothy 3:14	*February 27*	1 John 4:7	*February 12*
2 Timothy 3:16	*December 6*	1 John 4:10	*July 25*
2 Timothy 3:17	*May 10*	1 John 4:16	*July 11*
2 Timothy 4:5	*February 2*	1 John 4:19	*February 29*
2 Timothy 4:17	*October 21*	1 John 4:21	*October 19*
		1 John 5:12	*January 30*
Titus 3:14	*August 5*	1 John 5:14	*September 29*
		1 John 5:15	*December 4*
Hebrews 3:13	*July 23*	1 John 5:21	*March 3*
Hebrews 8:10	*August 9*		
Hebrews 9:27	*January 25*	2 John 1:8	*April 29*
Hebrews 10:24	*June 2*		
Hebrews 10:25	*March 28*	Jude 1:17	*January 8*
Hebrews 12:1	*May 29*	Revelation 3:20	*March 26*
Hebrews 12:1	*September 19*	Revelation 20:12	*August 13*
Hebrews 12:11	*July 14*